THE BEST OF HUGH KINGSMILL

THE BEST OF HUGH KINGSMILL

*Selections from his writings
edited and introduced by*

MICHAEL HOLROYD

LONDON
VICTOR GOLLANCZ LTD
1970

Printed in Great Britain by
The Camelot Press Ltd., London and Southampton

Contents

Introduction

BEHIND THE BIG names of twentieth-century literature there stands a shadow cabinet of writers waiting to take over once the Wind of Change has blown. My own vote goes to Hugh Kingsmill as leader of this opposition. Kingsmill, who died in 1949, is remembered by the reading public more as an ebullient personality, a man of abounding wit and vitality, than as a serious critic, novelist and biographer, so that, until recently, his books have been in danger of becoming forgotten altogether.

In a moving and unusual memoir comprising an exchange of letters, two of Kingsmill's closest friends, Malcolm Muggeridge and Hesketh Pearson, brilliantly succeeded in re-creating him as one of the most stimulating of companions. But they made little attempt to re-establish him as a clearly recognizable literary figure. To help achieve that is the purpose of this anthology—to introduce a sample of his writing to many to whom he has hitherto been little more than a name, and to acquaint them with some of those excellencies in his work that "should delight the reasonable reader".

*　　*　　*

Hugh Kingsmill Lunn, the second son of Sir Henry Lunn, was born at 46 Torrington Square, in London, on 21 November 1889. Not long after his birth the family moved to 5 Endsleigh Gardens on the northern boundary of Bloomsbury. But the happiest times of his childhood were spent in Switzerland, where the Lunns frequently went in connection with their travel business and the various religious organizations linked with it—the Church Travellers' Club and the Free Church Touring Guild.

At home, the Nonconformist-Evangelical atmosphere was less congenial to him. "We were an earnest and upright body of men in those parts," he afterwards acknowledged. Apart from his father, whose expanding business and religious industry were driving the rest of the family into the narrow upper regions of the house, there was his godfather, the Reverend Hugh Price Hughes, round the corner—a fiery Welsh orator whose ardour in promoting Social Purity was whipped by the Parnell case to a pitch of frenzy that makes W. T. Stead's utterances appear those of a veritable libertine. A little further down the road lived Sir Percy Bunting, editor of the *Contemporary Review*, a monthly journal dealing exclusively with the problem of social evil, in a manner that might not have seemed very real to the prostitutes wandering along the far side of the gardens. His sister, Mrs Sheldon Amos, was more realistic, and on one notable occasion at a railway station was moved to strike a Guards officer who had been found guilty of seduction, crying out as she delivered the blow: "You cad!" Besides such public-spirited friends as these, there also lived close at hand a Mr Algernon Coote, the founder and secretary of the National Vigilance Association, who saw to it that "girls coming from the provinces for employment in London should be met on arrival, steered through the multitudinous perils of the street, and penned in a fold where liberty of action was restricted to attending church on Sundays".

Fully conscious of their tremendous responsibilities to the community, when matters of especially grave importance arose, such as the purification of the Music Halls, or the Suppression of Nude Paintings, a number of this company would act in collaboration, calling on the Bishop of London to support them. And in national emergencies, under the zealous leadership of Sir Henry Lunn himself, the whole neighbourhood would rise up like a well-trained and formidable army of salvation.

This was the background in which Kingsmill's early years were spent, and against which much of his subsequent life and work was dedicated. "The trouble with reformers," he once wrote, "is that they seldom have any happiness in their natures, and so they can only see what is harmful in a pleasure, never what is beneficial."

From his parents, and especially perhaps from his mother, Kingsmill had inherited a vein of conventional religion. But he reacted strongly against his early Puritan environment, and at the age of twelve rejected orthodox Christianity, remarking that life would be far more pleasant if his mother made as many excuses for him as some clergymen did for God. Establishment religions had no place in his life, partly because such systems, he believed, "whatever the philosophy out of which they have grown, necessarily value truth less than victory over rival systems". Throughout his life he felt the weight of the millions who, by simplifying their emotional experiences, had narrowed themselves in Christ's name. His own inherited Puritanism was largely eclipsed by a deep strain of mysticism that, like all genuine mysticism, was in no way incompatible with humour or common sense. Something of his personal philosophy is summed up in the words of Polmont, the hero of his story *The End of the World*: "Personal salvation! That was the clue to life. Each man to perfect himself unobtrusively, without forcing on others a technique that was perhaps suitable only to himself. . . . Shakespeare says that the world itself is a dream, and we shall wake out of life into nothingness. But I say we shall wake into life. The world is real—houses and trees, men and women, motor buses and the moaning sea. But we have fallen asleep, and all these things, these simple and reasonable things, have been confused for us. But now the dream draws to its close, and we shall awake and smile at the perplexity and confusion that sleep has shed upon the world. Once more we shall see life as, even in this dream, I saw it a few minutes ago, the cab-horse and the stars, the chestnut trees and eternity, the great and the little, all parts of a self-explained and satisfying whole. My friends, be patient."

Kingsmill's stoical optimism was like a great river in flood which, stopped in its course by practical experience, rose and reached out over unknown territory. The normal sights of this world, of nature, he treated as symbols of some other life, and behind the ordinary events of everyday existence he saw the workings of an extraordinary power. He could never have conformed to any religion that is unsympathetic to the love of men and women, whether that love is purely sensual or, at the other extreme, the attempt to fuse two desires in a single happiness divined beyond this life. Love, he believed, while having its roots in earthly passion, could expand beyond this and exist without passion, while passion was meaningless and even unhappy without love.

In the summer of 1903, Kingsmill was awarded a scholarship to Harrow, going there as a day boy. He seems to have been almost wholly inept at the various sports that formed so large a part of public school life, and later on could only recall one pleasant memory there. This was his first collision, at the age of sixteen, with the opposite sex. He had met the lady, who was his senior by several years, by accident on a strip of waste land after dark while he was returning home after school. Since he had only fourpence on him at the time and felt that payment on such an occasion should be made on a more generous scale or not at all, no money changed hands.

From Harrow, at the age of eighteen, Kingsmill won an ex-hibition to New College, Oxford. To his dismay he found that he was expected to devote two years of his life "to a course of study grouped round Stubbs's investigations into the local government of our Anglo-Saxon ancestors". But he was proof against the obscure fascination of Stubbs, and with Oxford in general was greatly disappointed. As the most famous seat of culture in the world, it would hold, he thought, "the key to a poetic impassioned enjoyment of life". It did not take him long to discover his error—"about as long as it would take a man who went into a hen-house looking for birds of paradise".

It was while he was at Oxford that Kingsmill read Frank Harris's *The Man Shakespeare*. Harris's dissimilarity to all stereotyped Victorians, dons and Methodists alike was in itself ample re-commendation, and "his praise of sensuality", Kingsmill later wrote, "special pleading in one who has long since lost his illusions, sounded melodiously in the ear of youth, and I hastened to sit at the feet of a master whose message agreed so well with what I desired from life". His adventures with Harris, in particular as his assistant on *Hearth and Home*, "a blameless ladies' journal which did not long survive the ordeal of being edited by Harris", may be read in his extraordinarily witty and percipient biography of Harris.

His veneration for the master, much confused by these experiences, did not long survive, and by the outbreak of war had altogether vanished. In August 1914 he enlisted in a regiment of cyclists, and three months later he received a commission in the Royal Naval Volunteer Reserve (for service in the Royal Naval Division). He was an eccentric officer, and used to issue his orders for the day from his bed. These were taken by the sergeant-major, leaning through the window. On one occasion when he was supposed to inspect the guard but didn't like the idea of going through the mud, he sent for the guard and inspected them through the doorway, in slippers, with a newspaper under his arm. Such informalities somehow failed to prevent him from commanding a Company, as he recounts in his amusing war memoirs, *Behind Both Lines*.

"As acting Company commander, I was provided, against my will and better judgment, with a horse. Sterndale Bennet had returned to England for a few weeks, and our new C.O. was a cavalry colonel. My horse, fortunately a very phlegmatic animal, had this disadvantage, that when he resolved to be recalcitrant he was far too insensitive to bother about my hauling on his bit. There was a violent downpour at the first parade presided over by the new C.O. The rain drove slantingly into our eyes as we faced the colonel and after a moment's reflection my horse began to pivot slowly round. I struggled to keep him head on, but uselessly, and he ceased to rotate only when he and I were facing my company. The colonel did not refer to this obscene incident."

After some two years of parades such as this, and various mock attacks practised "with as close an approximation to the real thing as was consistent with the absence of an enemy and the presence of a general", Kingsmill reached the Western Front, where he was promptly captured, being led off behind the German lines quoting Heine.

The next fourteen months he spent at a prisoner-of-war camp at Karlsruhe, and it was here he wrote his first novel, *The Will to Love*. Another prisoner, Lance Sieveking, has given a description of him at work there. He used to write "in the Appel hut at Karlsruhe. There he sat, crouched over the rickety table working with happy concentration, slowly covering the sheet with his small neat handwriting while all about him a cheerful hubbub filled the air; four men just behind him playing ping-pong; two men wrestling; a man with a very loud unmusical voice singing ...

"More than once I saw Hughie look up with a pained expression during a lull in the din.

" 'Don't stop, old man!' he would shout to the pair at the piano, and then reproachfully to the resting ping-pong players: 'I say! You're not giving up, are you?' And then to me, or anyone standing near, in a semi-confidential tone: 'I find it helps me to concentrate, y'know, old man.' "

The Will to Love was the only one of his books to be published under the name of Hugh Lunn. For the rest of his career, he wrote as Hugh Kingsmill—his mother's maiden name. This was partly to differentiate himself from his elder brother, Sir Arnold Lunn, author of *The Harrovians*, and also his younger brother, Brian Lunn, who was to write an outstanding autobiography, *Switchback*. But it was also a sign of his growing estrangement with the Lunn family, and with his father in particular. For some years after the war, Kingsmill worked in his father's tourist agency but in 1927, when his first marriage (by which he had one daughter, Kathleen) broke down, he left the family business, and relations between him and his parents remained cool. "Friends," he bitterly remarked, "are God's apology for relations."

This was the turning-point in his career. He married again, a Miss Dorothy Vernon, by whom he had one son, Brooke, who became an Anglican priest, and two daughters, Edmée, now a nun in an Anglican Order, and Dorothy who married Willis Hall, the playwright. After this second marriage he devoted the rest of his life to writing. He produced a number of highly original biographies, many essays, some novels and a volume of parodies. He also compiled several anthologies, and was literary editor of

Punch and of the *New English Review*. He died at Brighton on
15 May 1949.

★   ★   ★

During his life only one of his books was very widely known—
the celebrated anthology *Invective and Abuse*. Of this, Kingsmill
ruefully commented: 'No author has much tenderness for his
most popular book, and his feeling that it is being favoured at the
expense of his real masterpieces is particularly strong when, as in
the present instance, it consists of extracts from other men's work".
Because of this "collection of insults", he figured in the public
mind as "a sort of literary Jack the Ripper, red-eyed and sabre-
toothed, scrabbling, year in, year out, among old folios for lost
jewels of vilification". Even at the end of his life Kingsmill would
encounter persons who said that of course they knew of his work
—"that thing of yours on abuse".

Rather more gratifying was the popularity of his parodies.
These days the art of parody has become a much-underrated
form of literary criticism. Kingsmill saw in parody potentially the
most perfect method of criticism, since it involved not an assertion
of the will but an exercise of the imagination. His own parodies,
of which three examples are given in this anthology, are less
malicious than, for example, those of Max Beerbohm. They are
penetrating rather than elaborate; that is to say they do not merely
exaggerate some pronounced verbal characteristics, but seek to
reveal, through the compression of caricature, the manner in
which an author's outlook becomes fused with his literary style.

The conflict of will versus imagination obsessed Kingsmill, who
made it the theme of several of his books. In his biography of
Matthew Arnold this conflict is presented quite simply. His aim
was to illustrate how the triumph of will over imagination led to
the collapse of a poet into a prophet. He interpreted Arnold's
occasional bursts of gaiety as little more than youthful indications
of half-hearted revolt against the pious and sober training of his
father; while his diluted Byronism was a mere gesture of filial
impiety directed against the man who could never bring himself

to read *Don Juan*. But the depression that took a deeper hold over him as the years advanced was produced, Kingsmill believed, by a disharmony arising from the unresolved struggle between his own naturally poetic temperament and the puritanical influence of his father's stronger personality.

Critics of Kingsmill's *Matthew Arnold* were particularly incensed by his assertion that Marguerite of the poems was a real person in Arnold's life. Five years later, in 1933, the publication of Arnold's letters made it impossible for anyone to deny her existence. Kingsmill maintained that Arnold sacrificed his love for her to ostensibly moral, though intrinsically worldly, considerations. His renunciation of her symbolized the victory of Dr Arnold's will over his own more sympathetic nature.

"The reward for renunciation," Kingsmill wrote, "is some good greater than the thing renounced. To renounce with no vision of such good, from fear or in automatic obedience to some formula, is to weaken the springs of life, and to diminish the soul's resistance to this world".

Kingsmill believed that the romantic fables and sentimental misconceptions that develop around a writer's reputation, and that masquerade as the truth, spring from the collective frustrations of people who come afterwards. By means of his criticism he sought to pare back the cuticle of lies, self-deceit and the habit and illusion that daily threaten to grow further over reality.

The four biographies that he published during the 1930's all illustrate this tendency. Each of them seeks to demolish some particular myth that had risen to a height of popularity where it was looked up to as being unchallengeable. The first of these, his life of Frank Harris, is a minor classic that has for ever shattered a never entirely secure legend. In place of a figure of vast creative power superior (as George Meredith asserted) to Balzac, and a spiritual equal (as Middleton Murry proclaimed) of Shakespeare himself, Kingsmill shows us a man of prodigious energy and a compendium of every form of charlatanism rampant in the complicated civilization of 1880 to 1914. A masterpiece of acute compression, of unsentimental yet sympathetic candour, the prose blends shrewdness, wit and humour in a way that discloses, yet at the same time seems to excuse, the weaknesses of human nature.

Kingsmill's next biography dealt with his favourite figure in English literary history, Samuel Johnson. His intention in this book was to qualify, by implication, the unstinted praise given by Macaulay and Carlyle to Boswell's *Johnson*. Certainly the penetrating character analysis he makes uncovers a deeper humanity than is readily discernible in Boswell's life. Boswell's insistence on Johnson's verbal ascendancy tended to promote the impression that he was the bigoted champion of social conventions and the established order, and to obscure his genuine individuality. Kingsmill supplanted the old John Bull conception with the portrait "of an essentially imaginative nature clogged by melancholia, a profound thinker limited by inborn and irrational fears, and an intensely loving and compassionate soul hampered in its expression by lifelong disabilities of mind and body".

An analytical rather than an impressionistic critic, Kingsmill liked to associate a literary work with the character of its author, with whom he partly identified himself. It was this relationship with his subject that accounts for the contrasting tone between his life of Samuel Johnson and his next biography, a life of Charles Dickens, which he called *The Sentimental Journey*. He found his own likeness to Johnson rather gratifying and extended to him a warm personal sympathy. But his points of similarity to Dickens irritated him so that he was at pains to distinguish himself from his subject and to stress his shortcomings.

Kingsmill's innate fairness of mind forbade him from expressing anything he felt to be of doubtful truth. He endeavoured to praise what he sincerely admired in Dickens—the humour of his minor characters and his wonderful descriptive powers—starting the paragraph with a few words of approbation, but then continuing with reservations which soon far exceed the opening eulogy. His own powers of imagination were free to expand only when the fate of his subject did not release in him pangs of personal envy. The hard struggle of Johnson brought out all his compassion. But Dickens's enormous early success exasperated him so much that his will was provoked to a pitch where, intermittently, it obliterated his sense of detachment.

Kingsmill's adversary in *The Sentimental Journey* was G. K. Chesterton, whose formulation of Dickens as a philanthropic and selfless social worker considerably vexed him. During his lifetime Dickens was considered vulgar, but after his death he became a great favourite with the refined and sophisticated classes of society, who felt that by reading him they were flirting with the newly-fashionable spirit of democracy. Chesterton, the spokesman for this modern attitude, saw Dickens as "a great-hearted lover of his kind, a laughing democrat blowing away all pretensions, social or intellectual, in the hurricane of his mirth". For Kingsmill, on the other hand, "his fascination lay in the immense gulf between his sentiments and his practice, in the fantastic, almost unbelievable extent to which he was not what Chesterton had painted him".

In 1938, four years after publishing *The Sentimental Journey*, Kingsmill brought out *D. H. Lawrence*, his last full-length biography. His purpose in this book was to dispel the fable that Lawrence himself had erected and which enthusiastic disciples were proclaiming to the world. In *Sons and Lovers* Lawrence had portrayed himself as the son of a good-for-nothing father and an earnest Congregationalist mother. Kingsmill felt that this version of the truth rested on only a flimsy foundation. He attempted to show that Lawrence's father loved his wife and children, while his mother was a savage egotist who despised her ineffectual, soft-hearted husband and focussed her thwarted ambitions on her youngest son.

The conflict between his parents was never resolved in Lawrence, and hindered the fruitful development of his genius. His marriage Kingsmill also saw as harmful to the poetic element in him, which he had come nearest to disentangling from his desire for a life of action during his youthful friendship with Jessie Chambers—Miriam in *Sons and Lovers*.

The theme that recurs in all these biographies is also present in several of Kingsmill's novels and critical essays, and illustrates the way in which remarkable men are simplified into myths by popular fancy acting through suggestible minds. The legends that enhaloed men as dissimilar as Cromwell and Casanova were, he maintained, bubbles blown up by unsatisfied desires for power and pleasure. Some of Kingsmill's literary essays were collected towards the end of his life in a brilliant volume entitled *The Progress of a Biographer*, which shows that his criticism was essentially classical in its approach. "He insisted," wrote Douglas Jerrold, "that a man's values must only be influenced by his good or ill fortune, his prejudices or his sentiments in so far as these influences had been formed by reason, illuminated by imagination and disciplined by an act of will directed to the search for truth."

For Kingsmill the pursuit of the imagination was love and truth; that of the will, lust and power. Through the imagination that yearned for union with another life, he believed we might apprehend a harmony that envelops though it does not penetrate our present existence. The will, with its passion to dominate and possess, destroyed this unity, leaving chaos and division.

★   ★   ★

Although a few percipient critics, including John Davenport and Edwin Muir, have testified eloquently to the individual nature of Kingsmill's talent, most have found themselves at a loss as to where to place him on the literary stage. Their task has been made no easier by Kingsmill's steadfast refusal to engage his own will in the cultural and political factions of the day. He did not inhabit Bloomsbury or visit Garsington; he did not belong to a Left or Right Book Club, or fight in the Spanish Civil War; he did not immure himself behind the fortifications of a university.

His three meetings with T. S. Eliot he likened to audiences given by the Pope to some obscure Nonconformist minister on a visit to Rome; and on the single occasion he met Wyndham Lewis, then in the trough of paranoia, he was suspected of poisoning the food and asked to leave. In the end he has been put down by some as a product of the Strachey school of biography, and by others as a Freudian critic. It is particularly ironic that this type of inept labelling against which he continuously fought so hard, should have become the chief cause of his own obscurity.

It is, of course, understandable that we should need guides to escort us through the vast and densely-grown jungle of the printed word. The sight of all those novels, plays, poems and biographies is tiring, and the prospect of plunging into them unaided, terrifying. To spare us this exertion, the English literature don has taken on the role of cicerone. What he recommends is read, and what is read must be published. But if we hold strictly to the well-worn routes laid out by him, we will miss much that is remarkable. Only in the last two years have the novels of Jean Rhys been exposed to view after a quarter of a century's neglect. It is ridiculous that the poems of Charlotte Mew and Martyn Skinner should still be quite unknown, the novels of William Gerhardie out of print for thirty years, the best works of John Stewart Collis unread, almost unobtainable. A growing discontent at the too rigid and over-simple system that dictates our reading and publishing habits is evident in the recent spate of literary reassessments in *The Times*, the *Times Literary Supplement*, *New Statesman* and elsewhere.

The Best of Hugh Kingsmill falls into this context. I have tried to make a unity of this volume and at the same time give a fair representation of Kingsmill's range and originality. Since it is impossible to detach sections from his novels and expect them to perform in isolation the same function as in their original settings, his fiction —much admired by so professional a novelist as Graham Greene —is under-represented. But Kingsmill, a versatile anthologist himself, is a good example of a writer whose reputation stands much to gain by being anthologized. His admirers seldom agree as to what is his finest book. Malcolm Muggeridge, I fancy, prefers his *Frank Harris*; Hesketh Pearson liked his *The Return of William Shakespeare*; and my own favourite is *The Progress of a Biographer*. In his recently published letters, George Orwell pronounced *The Sentimental Journey* to be the best biography of Dickens ever written—it has now been out of print for thirty years. He also reveals that he had made unsuccessful efforts to get *After Puritanism* reprinted—at least readers may see a part of it here.

Better even than *The Best of Hugh Kingsmill* would be the reprinting of these books. Far more might be achieved than justice to a single author. For twenty years the literary standards that he championed in the *New English Review* have been eclipsed by educationist critical systems whose control on taste and fashion has been paramount. Kingsmill himself belonged to no school of critics. He judged literature by its truthfulness, and by its power to reveal individual truths through humour, pathos, tenderness. No one had a sharper eye than he for detecting humbug. The truth he searched for was the truth we live, not speak. Were we to give currency to his uncompromising values, there might well be a revolution in our present tastes and literary attitudes.

Perhaps Kingsmill's isolated position during his career, his independent tone and lucid, beautifully balanced style are best conveyed in the final passage to his essay "The Genealogy of Hitler", a passage that may be read as an epitaph to his own life. "What is divine in man is elusive and impalpable," he wrote, "and he is easily tempted to embody it in a concrete form—a church, a country, a social system, a leader—so that he may realize it with less effort and serve it with more profit. Yet, as even Lincoln proved, the attempt to externalize the kingdom of heaven in a temporal shape must end in disaster. It cannot be created by charters and constitutions nor established by arms. Those who set out for it alone will reach it together, and those who seek it in company will perish by themselves."

MICHAEL HOLROYD

From

Samuel Johnson

(1933)

Johnson's Parents—School and Oxford— Marriage

I

"WHEN I SURVEY my past life," Johnson wrote in his old age, "I discover nothing but a barren waste of time, with some disorders of body and disturbances of the mind very near to madness."

His mental disturbances, which did not become acute before his twentieth year, were derived from his father. He had inherited a melancholy from his father, he once said, which had made him mad all his life, or at least not sober. His physical defects were accidental, not inherited, and are explained in his *Annals*, a fragment of an autobiography, the rest of which he burned shortly before his death. When he was a few weeks old he was put out to nurse. The son of his wet-nurse was short-sighted and scrofulous, and both these complaints soon developed in the baby Johnson. It is clear that he was infected by his nurse's milk. Johnson records that this was the opinion of his godfather, Dr Swinfen, and adds without comment that his mother thought his disease derived from her family. It was no doubt to lessen her remorse over her baby's condition that she attributed it to an hereditary taint and not to the nurse in whose charge she had placed him.

"In ten weeks," he says, "I was taken home, a poor diseased infant, almost blind."

The results of this infection afflicted Johnson throughout his life, his sight and hearing being permanently impaired, and the lower part of his face disfigured by scars. In society he was subject to what his stepdaughter, Lucy Porter, called "convulsive starts and odd gesticulations which tended to one's surprise and ridicule"; and though the cause of these has been disputed, it seems natural to suppose that they were due to the corrosion of his nervous system by the scrofula. These peculiarities of manner were so extraordinary that even those most familiar with him remained keenly conscious of them, while strangers could for some time see nothing else. A characteristic first impression is given by Thomas Campbell, an Irish clergyman, who met Johnson when Johnson was in his sixty-sixth year. "He has the aspect of an Idiot," Campbell wrote in his diary, "without the faintest ray of sense gleaming from any one feature—with the most awkward garb, and unpowdered grey wig, on one side only of his head—he is for ever dancing the devil's jig, and sometimes he makes the most driveling effort to whistle some thought in his absent paroxysms."

Of something more significant in Johnson's appearance than these peculiarities, we might have remained ignorant, had not Mrs Thrale once written a description of him which ends with these remarkable words: "His sight was near, and otherwise imperfect; yet his eyes were so wild, so piercing, and at times so fierce, that fear was, I believe, the first emotion in the hearts of all his beholders." This glimpse of the man who was concealed from most persons by external oddities is the more striking because it is at variance with Mrs Thrale's conscious view of Johnson as an unemotional philosopher, and records her spontaneous intuition of the lifelong struggle which he fought in defence of his mental and emotional balance. Of the odds against him in this struggle, the earliest to reveal itself, and perhaps the most complex in its after results, was his infantile infection, the outward signs of which provoked such derision among relatives and strangers alike.

The responsibility for the choice of the wet-nurse Johnson assigns to his father. His mother, whom he loved, he tries to exonerate from all suspicion of carelessness. She visited him every day, he says, and even left her fan or glove behind to have an excuse for returning again, but never discovered any signs of neglect. It is impossible to reconcile this apology with the fact that the nurse's son was diseased, and that within a few weeks the baby Johnson almost lost his sight, unless one assumes that Mrs

Johnson had a better heart than head. This inference is supported by Johnson's own account of her, for his love of her did not blind him to the narrowness of her intelligence and her petty outlook on life. In her *Anecdotes of Johnson*, Mrs Thrale, who drew more intimate confidences from him than any one else, narrates on his authority that his mother, as the daughter of a small country gentleman, used to make her husband, who was a bookseller, feel his social inferiority. She would worry him, too, with her anxieties over money, but as she knew nothing about business, her laments were equally vague and irritating. Had his mother been more literate, she would have been a better companion to her husband, Johnson says. Although he loved his mother and did not care for his father, his innate fairness of mind made him assign to his mother the greater share of the blame for the joyless married life of his parents. His own matrimonial experience may have strengthened his view that married happiness is more often impaired by the wife than by the husband, but his opinions on marriage seem to have been chiefly shaped by his early memories of his parents. When any matrimonial disputes were brought to his notice, Mrs Thrale records, Johnson always sided with the husband, whom, he would say, the woman had probably provoked so often that she would long since have forgotten how their dissensions first began. "Women," he said, "give great offence by a contemptuous spirit of non-compliance on petty occasions. The man calls his wife to walk with him in the shade, and she feels a strange desire just at that moment to sit in the sun; he offers to read her a play, or sing her a song, and she calls the children in to disturb them, or advises him to seize that opportunity of settling the family accounts. . . . Are the hours of pleasure so frequent in life, that when a man gets a couple of quiet ones to spend in familiar chat with his wife, they must be poisoned by petty mortifications?"

The reference to children in this passage is particularly applicable to Johnson's parents, who married late in life and had far more pleasure from their offspring than from each other. Michael Johnson was fifty-three, his wife forty, when their first child, Samuel, was born on September 18, 1709. The character of

Michael Johnson can be gathered from stray passages in his son's *Annals* and in Mrs Thrale's *Anecdotes*. Though lacking in business aptitude, and increasingly embarrassed for money as his life advanced, he must have had abilities above the average, for he rose to be a magistrate of Lichfield, the Staffordshire town where he worked at his trade of selling books. That he had much of his son's love of books for their own sakes is shown by a remarkable reference to him in a letter written from Trentham in 1716 by the chaplain to Lord Gower: "Johnson, the Litchfield Librarian, is now here; he propagates learning all over this diocese, and advanceth knowledge to its just height; all the clergy here are his pupils, and suck all they have from him."

This tribute to Michael Johnson's union of learning and piety would lead us to expect a close sympathy between him and his eldest son. Yet Johnson always spoke of his father with a coldness not far removed from aversion. He described him to Mrs Thrale as pious and worthy, but wrong-headed, positive, and melancholy; and added that it was only the long journeys on horseback which his father took in the course of business that preserved his sanity. The combination of positiveness and melancholia in the elder Johnson would not in themselves account for his son's lack of affection, exasperating though one's own faults or weaknesses are when reflected in a parent or a child. It was the petty scale on which Michael Johnson's positiveness asserted itself that disgusted his son. Like many men who are ineffectual in the outside world, Michael Johnson was consequential and self-assertive at home, laying a ban on tea as too expensive, and discouraging his wife from paying or receiving visits. Johnson narrates how once when his father came to fetch him and his younger brother from their aunt's house in Birmingham, he told the ostler that he had twelve miles home and two boys under his care. This offended Johnson. There seems small cause for offence in this episode. But Johnson had a hatred of pretentiousness which blinded him even as a grown man to its pathetic side. He was ten when this incident occurred, and if one pictures Michael assuming the air of a Caesar about to cross the Rubicon, the ostler grinning sardonically, and young Samuel writhing in the agony which children feel when their parents are making fools of themselves, one can understand the lasting impression this trivial scene made upon him.

Michael was proud of his son's intelligence, which showed itself at a very early age, but it was his own vanity, not a disinterested pleasure in his child's powers, which was gratified. Johnson soon learned to dislike his father's caresses, because he knew that he was being petted into a willingness to show off his cleverness before strangers, and used to run out of the house, when visitors arrived, and climb up a tree. "The great misery of late marriages," he once said, "is that the unhappy produce of them becomes the plaything of dotage: an old man's child leads much such a life, I think, as a little boy's dog, teized with awkward fondness, and forced to sit up and beg . . . to divert a company, who at last go away complaining of their disagreeable entertainment."

If he seems too harsh to his father, it should be remembered that the traces of his infantile malady must have been particularly marked in his childhood, so that the natural shyness of children before strangers would have been heightened in him almost to a panic. Later, when he learnt that his father was responsible for the choice of his nurse, his disgust at the insensitiveness which allowed him to parade his disfigured child before strangers would be intensified.

His dislike of his father turned all his early affection towards his mother, for whose favour he used to compete with his younger brother Nathanael. Nathanael, who died in his late twenties, once complained that Samuel scarcely treated him with common civility. Johnson's feeling that he was entitled on all occasions to preferential treatment, one of his most marked characteristics, was strengthened by his mother's spoiling of him, for she indulged him as far as her poverty allowed, partly no doubt to make up to him for his ill-health. This spoiling was so agreeable to him that, when he looked back on it in after-life, he quite forgot his usual severity as a moralist, and used to urge the importance of conciliating children by kindness, once saying that he would never have loved his mother so in later years, had she not given him coffee she could ill afford, to gratify his appetite when a boy.

A pathetic story which Boswell tells, in his life of Johnson, will satisfy rigid disciplinarians that Mrs Johnson over-indulged Samuel's moods as well as his appetites, and will illustrate for others how sensitive he was to his physical defects from his earliest years. One day when the servant who used to be sent to conduct him home from school had not come in time, he set out by himself, though he was then so near-sighted, that he was obliged to stoop down on his hands and knees to get over the gutter. His mistress, afraid that he might miss his way, or be run over by a cart, followed him. He happened to turn round and see her, and running at her in a rage, beat her as well as his strength would permit.

More than sixty years later, when Dr Percy, with as little intention of offending as this school-mistress, reminded Johnson that he was short-sighted, Johnson, after a preliminary insult which Dr Percy resented, fell upon him with the same fury he had shown against his teacher: "Hold, Sir! Don't talk of rudeness; remember, Sir, you told me (puffing hard with passion struggling for a vent) I was short-sighted. We have done with civility. We are to be as rude as we please." But the storm died down as quickly as it had arisen. "Percy: Upon my honour, Sir, I did not mean to be uncivil. Johnson: I cannot say so, Sir; for I *did* mean to be uncivil, thinking you had been uncivil."

Another proof of his mother's solicitude for him is her journey to London, when he was two and a half, to have him touched by Queen Anne, for the royal touch was in those days believed to be efficacious against his malady. The expense of the journey worried her greatly: she went to London in a coach, but, to save a few shillings, returned in a waggon, giving as her excuse his violent cough, which she feared might annoy their fellow-travellers in the coach. So their fellow-travellers in the waggon had to suffer instead. "We were troublesome to the passengers," Johnson says. "I was sick; one woman fondled me, the other was disgusted."

These scraps of memory were written down by Johnson in the sickness and solitude of his old age, to console him with the recollection of his poor mother's love and to charm him with the magic in which time clothes even the most trivial or wretched details of the past. On this journey to London, he records, his mother bought him a small silver cup and a spoon, and had them marked "Sam. I.," fearing that if they were marked "S.I.," her own initials, they might be taken from him after her death. She also bought him a speckled linen frock, which he always referred to as "my London frock." The spoon, he writes, was still in his possession, but his wife had sold the cup in the worst days of their poverty—"the cup was one of the last pieces which dear Tetty sold in our distress."

Thirty-eight pages are missing from the *Annals*, between his visit to London and his first days at school, to which the last surviving pages are devoted. The style here is easier, and if there was a progressive relaxation of his customary reserve in the hundreds of later pages which he destroyed, one can infer that he had revealed more of his life and emotions than he could bear the world to know. The complete manuscript may have been the greatest autobiography in our literature, and would certainly, written as it was from the inside by so sincere a man, have given a more truthful and complete picture of Johnson than we now possess.

The even balance which Johnson kept between his love for his mother and his clear sense of her limitations appears again in the last pages. He was once, he writes, very anxious about a piece of school work in which he had failed several times. His mother encouraged him, and he got on better. "When I told her of my good escape, 'We often,' said she, dear mother! 'come off best when we are most afraid.'" She was proud of his quick progress, he continues, and after illustrating her pride, by recalling some words of praise she one gave him, he concludes, "These little memorials soothe my mind." But he also narrates his mother's concern when, during a visit to his Birmingham aunt at the age of ten, he astonished his aunt by eating a vast portion of a boiled leg of mutton. His mother was greatly upset, and told him his greediness would never be forgotten.

The absence in Johnson of the sentiment of filial reverence will surprise those who think of him as a bigoted champion of all established conventions. But it was consistent both with his personal experience and with his general attitude to life. "Poor people's children," he said to Mrs Thrale, "never respect them: I did not respect my own mother, though I loved her; and one day, when in anger she called me a puppy, I asked her if she knew what they called a puppy's mother." So far from holding that parents are entitled to the gratitude of their children, he maintained that the only special obligation involved in the relationship of parents and children existed on the side of the parents. To have voluntarily become to any being, he wrote in *The Rambler*, the occasion of its existence produces an obligation to make that existence happy. As a corollary to this opinion, he maintained that parents had no rights, merely as parents, over their children. The parent's moral right could arise only from his kindness, and his civil right only from his money. One day when Mrs Thrale, referring to a passage in Xenophon, praised Cyrus for asking his father's permission to marry, Johnson burst out: "If Cyrus by his conquests had not purchased emancipation, he had conquered to little purpose indeed. Can you bear to see the folly of a fellow who has in his care the lives of thousands, when he begs his papa permission to be married, and confesses his inability to decide in a matter which concerns no man's happiness but his own?"

But the deepest reason for his small respect for parents lay in his preoccupation with the virtue of the individual. His observation of life had shown him that goodness is always rare, and that it is especially rare in the old. Men commonly grew wickeder as they grew older, he once said, and added that he was always on the young people's side when there was a dispute between them and the old ones, for a man had at least a chance of virtue till age had withered its very root.

This view he elaborated in *Rasselas*, in a passage which contrasts youth and age. "The old man pays regard to riches, and the youth reverences virtue. The old man deifies prudence: the youth commits himself to magnanimity and chance. The young man, who intends no ill, believes that none is intended, and therefore acts with openness and candour; but his father, having suffered the injuries of fraud, is impelled to suspect, and too often allured to practise it. . . ."

This attitude, however strange in a champion of the established order, was natural in a follower of Christ, who, when he was told that his mother and brethren desired to speak to him, pointed to his disciples and said, "Behold My mother and My brethren! For whosoever shall do the will of My Father which is in heaven, the same is My brother, and sister, and mother."

Even Johnson's penance at Uttoxeter, one of the most famous episodes in his life, was rather in expiation of his sin against God in indulging his pride than in expiation of his filial disobedience. He could not in general, he said, accuse himself of having been an undutiful son, but on one occasion he refused from pride to go with his father to Uttoxeter market. Many years later, desiring to atone for this fault, he went to Uttoxeter in very bad weather, and stood for a considerable time bareheaded in the rain, on the spot where his father's stall used to stand. "In contrition I stood, and I hope the penance was expiatory."

II

Young Johnson's disease was offset by two great advantages over his schoolfellows—his superiority in brains and in muscle. The extraordinary physical strength which he inherited from his father, and which was trained by a prize-fighting uncle, was useful to him not only as a boy, but contributed throughout his life to his ascendancy over other men. Even in the most civilised surroundings, the feeling that an argument could, if the other man chose, be terminated by his throwing one through the window tempers self-assertion; and in the eighteenth century brute force was more quickly resorted to than to-day. Johnson often used his strength in his early years in London, and the story of how he thrashed a bookseller, Tom Osborne, became a legend, about which Mrs Thrale one day begged him to give her the true particulars. "There is nothing to tell, dearest lady," Johnson answered complacently, "but that he was insolent and I beat him, and that he was a blockhead and told of it, which I should never have done; so the blows have been multiplying, and the wonder thickening for all these years. . . . I have beat many a fellow, but the rest had the wit to hold their tongues."

His strength was supported by unusual courage, which he

made a practice of testing when an occasion offered. Sir John Hawkins, in his life of Johnson, narrates that after not having swum for many years Johnson went into the river at Oxford, and swam away to a part of it that he had been told of as a dangerous place, and where a man had been drowned. More remarkable was his fight with four men who attacked him one night, and whom he kept at bay till the watch came up, and carried both him and them to the Round-house.

One would expect such a man to have been a prodigy even in his youth, and the little we know of Johnson as a boy bears out this expectation. The retort to his mother, already quoted, shows how intractable he was as a child. Nathanael's complaint that Samuel scarcely treated him with common civility suggests the excessively overbearing element in his character before it was modified by his latent goodness of heart; and Sir John Hawkins confirms the impression that he was spoilt and irritable with a picture of him in the house of a Lichfield neighbour. The children of the family, annoyed by his rudeness, used to call him the great boy. The father, once overhearing this, said: "You call him the great boy, but take my word for it, he will one day prove a great man." Beneath his physical strength and roughness, this prophecy shows, his moral and intellectual qualities were already discernible, and a few years later, when he was in his teens, they were already so developed as to give him, supported as they were by physical strength, a strange ascendancy over his schoolfellows. Edmund Hector, a friend of Johnson's at Lichfield Grammar School, used to call for him each morning with two other boys, one of whom took him on his back, while the other two supported him on each side. This ascendancy is the more remarkable because Johnson did not, like other youthful heroes, Clive, Napoleon, and du Guesclin, establish his authority by organising his school-fellows in mimic warfare or raids on property. Now, as later, his domination of others was due to nothing but his personal quali-ties. He did not even join with the other boys in their games, being prevented partly by his short sight and partly by his constitutional indolence, which was already remarkable. "A long, lank, lounging boy" is the description one of his contemporaries used to give of him in later life; and Edmund Hector told Boswell that Johnson's chief pleasure was sauntering in the fields with him, "during which he (Johnson) was more engaged in talking to himself than his companion." Even when there was a frost, he would not warm himself by sliding on the ice, but would request one of his schoolfellows to pull him along by a garter tied round his waist.

Though he once complained that Hunter, his headmaster at Lichfield, used to beat the boys unmercifully, Johnson favoured the rod as a stimulus to effort, and replied to some one who was expressing his pleasure that children were being less whipped than formerly—"What they gain at one end, they lose at the other." He approved the rod on moral grounds, too. It produced an effect which terminated in itself. A child was afraid of being whipped, and therefore learned his task, but by exciting emulation and comparisons of superiority the foundation of lasting mischief was laid. Yet his own achievements as a scholar were due more to his desire to excel than to the many thrashings he received from Hunter. Though too indolent to apply himself methodically to his work, he had fits of enormous energy during which he absorbed far more than the others, and the gratification his superiority gave him was not forgotten in later years. "They never," he told Boswell, "thought to raise me by comparing me to any one; they never said, Johnson is as good a scholar as such a one; but such a one is as good a scholar as Johnson; and this was said but of one, but of Lowe; and I do not think he was as good a scholar."

Intellectual development, so far as it can be distinguished from the other two, is less important than moral and imaginative development. Even as a small boy, Johnson was a moralist, and already divined and feared the temptations of life. Having, he narrates in the *Annals*, read in one of his classical authors that some man, when he hated another, made him rich, he went home and repeated this passage in the hearing of his mother, who, he says, could never conceive that riches could bring any evil. One would not be surprised to learn that it was on this occasion she was so unforeseeing as to call him a puppy.

The imaginative element in Johnson was very strong, and

B

would have made him a great poet, had he been able to harmonise it with the moral element, but the conflict between the two was never resolved. In *Rasselas*, thinking of those expectations of happiness and glory which outstrip what can be realised on earth, he speaks of "that hunger of imagination which preys incessantly upon life." Like Cervantes, he was much given to day-dreaming and the reading of romances. Even in later life, on a visit to Dr Percy, he spent most of his time reading an enormous Spanish romance in folio, and he would sometimes attribute to this passion the unsettled state of mind which had prevented him from taking up a profession. Here the moralist in Johnson is condemning the poet, but when Mrs Thrale defended *Goody Two Shoes, Tommy Prudent*, and the other moral tales for children which were coming into fashion in the last half of the eighteenth century, he rebuked her. "Babies do not want to hear about babies," he said; "they like to be told of giants and castles, and of somewhat which can stretch and stimulate their little minds."

It was largely this imaginative strain in Johnson which prevented him from being a scholar in the strict sense. He read voraciously as a boy, his chief period of study being between twelve and eighteen; but he read what his nature needed, and had none of the born scholar's capacity for patient progress along prescribed routes.

At fifteen Johnson left Lichfield for the Grammar School at Stourbridge, where he was on bad terms with the headmaster, Mr Wentworth. His approval of authority never, from his earliest years, included its application to himself. "Mr Wentworth," he told Boswell, "was a very able man, but an idle man, and to me very severe; but I cannot blame him much. I was then a big boy; he saw I did not reverence him; and that he should get no honour from me."

From Stourbridge he returned to his father's shop at Lichfield. Michael Johnson hoped to teach his son his own trade. But he was defeated by Samuel's inertia. Apart from his general unfitness for such a life, the romances which were his favourite reading must have disgusted him with the prospect of wasting himself in a shop. His vanity, at any rate in his youth, was humiliated by his low social position, and even in his old age he did not care to talk much of his family. One has little pleasure, he said, in reciting the anecdotes of beggary; and the same distaste is revealed in a letter to Mrs Thrale, in which he wrote: "Mr Cornelius Harrison was the only one of my relations who ever rose in fortune above penury, or in character above neglect."

The drudgery in the shop which Samuel declined fell on the shoulders of Nathanael, to whose laborious and unprivileged life and early death some of the sympathy expended on Samuel's youth might in fairness be diverted. Nathanael had, however, the the advantage over his brother of a cheerful nature. Johnson used to speak with pride of Nathanael's manly spirit, narrating how one day when the company were lamenting the badness of the roads, Nathanael inquired where they could be, for he travelled the country more than most people, and had never seen a bad road in his life.

As he would not be a bookseller, Samuel was sent to Oxford, entering Pembroke College at the end of October 1728, when he was nineteen years of age. Carlyle has drawn a melancholy but inaccurate picture of Johnson's humiliating situation as a servitor. Johnson was in fact a commoner, and used to join with the other commoners, Sir John Hawkins relates, in hunting the servitors: "and this they did, with the noise of pots and candlesticks, singing to the tune of Chevy Chase the words in the old ballad: 'To drive the deer with horn and hound.'"

But he was very poor, for he went to Oxford only on a promise of assistance from a school friend, and as this assistance was not forthcoming, and his father could no longer afford the small remittances which had been his sole support, he had to leave after he had been up less than fourteen months. The high spirits which impressed the servitors he hunted and the college tutors he defied were assumed to hide his resentment against life. "Ah, Sir, I was mad and violent," he said to Boswell. "It was bitterness which they mistook for frolick. I was miserably poor, and I thought to fight my way by my literature and my wit; so I disregarded all power and authority."

At Oxford, as at school, he resented discipline: tradition

relates that he was generally to be seen lounging at the college gate, with a circle of young students round him, whom he was amusing with his wit, and keeping from their work, if not inciting them to rebellion against the college discipline. Yet even at Oxford he was open to reason and sympathetic treatment, and confessed that the mild expostulations of Dr Adams, then a junior fellow, and later one of his greatest friends, made him ashamed of himself, though he was too proud to show it. He was, too, however little he benefited from Oxford, gratified to have been there. Shortly before his death, when he was on a visit to Dr Adams, he met Hannah More, and insisted on escorting her all over his old college. "He would let no one show it me but himself," she narrates. " 'This was my room; this Shenstone's.' Then, after pointing out all the rooms of the poets who had been of his college, 'In short,' said he, 'we were a nest of singing-birds. Here we walked, there we played at cricket,' "

It was during his Oxford period, when he was at home on vacation, that his latent melancholia first made itself strongly felt. So serious was the attack that his friend Edmund Hector was afraid that it might either impair his intellect or endanger his life. To counteract this attack, Johnson several times walked to Birmingham and back, but found so little relief that he decided to apply to his god-father, Dr Swinfen, and prepared an account of his condition in Latin. Impressed by the force and lucidity of this statement, Dr Swinfen showed it round Lichfield, as a proof of his godson's talents, much to Johnson's resentment, which could not have been much allayed by Dr Swinfen assuring him that his melancholia would probably end in madness.

From this time on, Johnson's life was conditioned by his fear of madness, against which he found, on the physical and mental side, remedies in constant occupation of the mind, a great deal of exercise, and restraint in eating and drinking; and on the spiritual side in prayer. As every handicap, if met with intelligence and resolution, produces counterbalancing benefits, Johnson's fear of insanity immensely strengthened his innate truthfulness and sense of reality, for the lies and illusions which make life more comfortable for ordinary men appeared to him as the first steps towards madness. But while his view of this world was made clearer through the danger which threatened him, the feeling of guilt, of being excluded from happiness, now and in any other state of being, which afflicts the emotionally diseased, warped his otherwise profound sense of an ultimate reality. In his most harmonious moments he believed that perfection existed beyond this world, and that the conditions of attaining it were proportioned to man's powers, concluding his poem, *The Vanity of Human Wishes*:

> "Pour forth thy fervours for a healthful mind,
>   Obedient passions, and a will resigned;
>   For love, which scarce collective man can fill,
>   For patience, sovereign o'er transmuted ill;
>   For faith, which, panting for a happier seat,
>   Counts death kind Nature's signal for retreat."

But he was often distracted with reasonless terrors, which embodied themselves in the avenging God of a theology he would have rejected as childish and savage, had he possessed perfect mental health.

"I am afraid I may be one of those who shall be damned," he said to Dr Adams, a few months before his death. "What do you mean by damned?" asked the gentle doctor. "Sent to hell, sir," Johnson answered loudly and passionately, "and punished everlastingly!" "You seem, Sir," Mrs Adams interposed, "to forget the merits of our Redeemer." "Madam," Johnson replied, "I do not forget the merits of my Redeemer; but my Redeemer has said that He will set some on His right hand and some on His left." The fears which had tormented him for more than fifty years, and which he was always struggling to repress, began to overcome him; he mastered them with a strong effort, and broke off the talk with, "I'll have no more on't."

III

Johnson did not take any decided steps towards making a living during the two and a half years between Oxford and his father's death, but lived at home, waiting for work to find him. A letter he wrote to a Mr Hickman, a few weeks before his father died, strikes almost a Micawber note:

> "As I am yet unemployed, I hope you will, if anything should offer, remember and recommend, Sir, your humble servant, SAM. JOHNSON."

Yet even during this period his ability was recognised in the highest society of Lichfield, partly through the exertions of Dr Swinfen, who was of a very old Staffordshire family; and he was made much of by a number of important residents, among them Captain Garrick, the father of the actor, and Gilbert Walmsley, Register of the Prerogative Court of Lichfield. How greatly he enjoyed this first experience of good society comes out in the tribute which he paid Gilbert Walmsley towards the close of his life. "I knew him very early; he was one of the first friends litera-ture procured me, and I hope that at least my gratitude made me worthy of his notice. He was of an advanced age, and I was only not a boy, yet he never received my notions with contempt. . . . At this man's table I enjoyed many cheerful and instructive hours, with companions, such as are not often found. . . ."

Michael Johnson died in the December of 1731. In the July of the following year, Johnson, having received only twenty pounds from his father's will, realised that some kind of exertion could no longer be avoided. His first attempt, as an usher in a school at Market Bosworth, in Leicestershire, lasted a very short time. He did not know, he wrote to Edmund Hector, whether it was more disagreeable for him to teach, or for the boys to learn. He was disgusted, too, by the insolence of the patron of the school, Sir Wolstan Dixey, at whose table he had to say grace; and, on receiving an invitation to Birmingham from Hector, threw up the job. Hector was lodging with Warren, the most flourishing bookseller in Birmingham. In those days booksellers were also publishers, and Warren found work for Johnson, printing some essays of his in a paper called *The Birmingham Journal*, and com-missioning him to translate *A Voyage to Abyssinia*, by Lobo, a

Portuguese Jesuit. The task was completed only through the persistence of Hector, who, having roused his friend with a picture of the misery in which the printer and his family were living owing to the slowness with which Johnson was supplying the copy, used to transcribe the translation as Johnson, lying in bed, read it out. The correction of the proof sheets also devolved upon Hector, to whom Johnson, perhaps remembering his friend's unselfish assiduity with some uneasiness, wrote more than twenty years later: "From that kind of melancholy indisposition which I had when we lived together at Birmingham, I have never been free, but have always had it operating against my health and my life with more or less violence."

The preface to this translation, written when Johnson was only twenty-four, is extraordinarily mature, both in style and thought, and foreshadows those conclusions about life on which his moral and his political philosophy were based. There was neither selfishness nor sentimentality in Johnson's conservatism, which derived from his conviction that this world is not an end in itself, but the testing-ground of a virtue which will be rewarded in another life. Utopia, he believed, never had existed on earth, nor ever would exist, and Utopianism was therefore a crime, because it diverted men with unrealisable hopes from the task of individual self-betterment.

The germ of this attitude is contained in his praise of Lobo's sober narrative:

"The Portuguese traveller . . . has amused his reader with no romantic absurdity, or incredible fictions . . . he meets with no basilisks that destroy with their eyes, his crocodiles devour their prey without tears, and his cataracts fall from the rocks without deafening the neighbouring inhabitants. The reader will find here no regions cursed with irremediable barrenness, or blessed with spontaneous fecundity; no perpetual gloom, or unceasing sunshine; nor are the nations here described either devoid of all sense of humanity, or consummate in all private or social virtues. Here are no Hottentots without religious polity or articulate language; no Chinese perfectly polite, and completely skilled in all sciences; he will discover, what will always be discovered by a diligent and impartial inquirer, that wherever human nature is to be found, there is a mixture of vice and virtue, a contest of passion and reason."

The subdued humour and balanced outlook shown in this passage were the reverse side of the passionate and romantic nature which delighted in the old tales of chivalry. But Johnson had no youthful period of love and adventure. His indolence and melancholia hampered his naturally enterprising character, and his strong attraction towards women, which troubled him all his life, was barred from any outlet before his marriage both by his physical disadvantages and by his religious principles. In his twenties he was lean and lank, and the immense structure of his bones was hideously striking to the eye, according to his step-daughter, Lucy Porter, to whom we are also obliged for the information that his convulsive starts and odd gesticulations excited surprise and ridicule. It was perhaps even more his extreme sensitiveness to contempt than his principles which kept him as strictly virtuous in his youth as Edmund Hector affirms him to have been, for he once told Thrale that he had never tried to please any one till he was over thirty, thinking the attempt would be useless.

At the house of Gilbert Walmsley, and elsewhere among the gentle folk of Lichfield, he met, and was attracted by, several young women. But though he put an unusual constraint on his roughness in their presence, he never trusted himself beyond ordinary courtesy. For one of these girls, Molly Aston, Gilbert Walmsley's sister-in-law, he felt the adoration which is inspired by the unattainable. The happiest year of his life, he told Mrs Thrale, was the one which had been sweetened by a single evening with Molly Aston. "That, indeed, was not happiness, it was rapture," he said. The evening alluded to, Mrs Thrale is careful to explain, was not passed *tête-à-tête* but in a select company.

Molly Aston had youth, beauty, and good birth. Mrs Porter, whom Johnson married when he was twenty-five, was twenty years his senior and the widow of a Birmingham tradesman. It might seem at first sight that in despair at the physical defects which prevented him from realising his youthful dreams of love he resigned himself to some one whose age would make her less fastidious, and who had, at any rate, the solid advantage of a small fortune. Against this simple explanation has to be set Johnson's equally simple statement that it was a love-match on both sides. The truth must lie between these extremes.

Anna Seward, "the Swan of Lichfield," whose admiration and dislike of Johnson were equally violent, mentions more than once that Johnson was in love with Lucy Porter, and only paid his addresses to her mother when Lucy, "disgusted by his ungainly form," rejected him. Anna's memory was sometimes enriched by imagination, and she was always ready to pass on as well-authenticated fact any Lichfield legend which gratified her mixed feelings about "the late stupendous but frail Dr Johnson," as she once called him. But if this story is true, some pique may at first have been behind Johnson's courtship of Mrs Porter, though as far as good talk was concerned, Mrs Porter must have attracted him more than Lucy. Her powers of retort seem on occasion to have been equal to those of Johnson himself, who used to recall with pleasure how, impatient at his constant complaints over the meals she served up, she once interrupted his grace with, "Nay, hold, Mr Johnson, and do not make a farce of thanking God for a dinner which in a few minutes you will protest not eatable." Even better, if it was ever made, was her reply to Johnson's confession of his disadvantages, when he proposed to her. Anna Seward is our authority for this story, which Boswell rejected on the ground that a very respectable lady of Lichfield, whom Anna had quoted in support of the story, disclaimed any recollection of it.

Johnson, Anna relates, was taken to task by his mother when he broke it to her that he wished to marry a widow almost twice his age. Mrs Johnson having pointed out that his prospective bride was old, and of extravagant habits, and that he himself was young, poor, and as yet incapable of earning a living, Johnson retorted: "Mother, I have not deceived Mrs Porter: I have told her the worst of me; that I am of mean extraction; that I have no money; and that I have had an uncle hanged. She replied that she valued no one more or less for his descent; that she had no more money than myself; and that, though she had not had a relation hanged, she had fifty who deserved hanging."

It was doubtless this intellectual sympathy which helped Johnson and Mrs Porter to overlook each other's disadvantages. Mrs Porter is reported to have said, soon after they met, that Johnson was the most sensible man she had ever seen. His first impressions of her are not recorded, but though he had perhaps to overcome a certain repugnance to her age, if not to her looks, he may, since he had suffered so much from his physical defects, have considered the unlikelihood that she would bear him children as an additional motive for marrying her. Once started, his courtship would not have been conducted in a despondent spirit. His physical desires were violent; when he was at table he ate with concentrated fierceness until his hunger was allayed, and though he could be abstemious he could not be temperate. Having abstained from sex through the most vigorous years of his life, his passion, as soon as it was encouraged, overwhelmed his taste, was never discriminating on the æsthetic side, and endowed his bride with beauties not visible to others, and with all the graces possessed by the heroines of his romances. As the one object of his passion, and the chief object of his tenderness, Mrs Johnson became and remained the centre of his life. More than twenty years after her death, he wrote in his diary, when he was travelling with the Thrales in France: "As I entered (the palace), my wife was in my mind: she would have been pleased. Having now nobody to please, I am little pleased." But that his idealisation of her did not obliterate his regret for Molly Aston may perhaps be inferred from a remark he once made about a friend's marriage: "He has done a very foolish thing, Sir; he has married a widow, when he might have had a maid."

The accounts of Mrs Porter's appearance are conflicting. That she was in her earlier years good-looking above the average is shown by the portrait of her that still exists, and Mrs Desmoulins, Dr Swinfen's daughter, said that she was still handsome at the time of her second marriage. Anna Seward's mother, on the other hand, who knew her when she married Johnson, said that she had a very red face and indifferent features, and that her manners had an unbecoming excess of girlish levity and disgusting affectation. David Garrick's description is even less flattering, but Garrick, who was a pupil in the school Johnson ran for a short period after his marriage, had many reasons for resentment against Johnson, and was further tempted to caricature by his powers of mimicry. He used to tell how he and the other boys at Johnson's school took it in turns to look through the keyhole while Johnson was indulging his tumultuous and awkward fondness for Tetty, as he used to call her; and Tetty herself Garrick described as very fat, with swollen, painted cheeks, fantastic in her dress and mincing in her behaviour.

Mrs Johnson's affectations were a symptom of the same suppressed romanticism which made her husband invest her with imaginary graces. There was, Hawkins says, something crazy in the behaviour of them both—profound respect on his side, and the airs of an antiquated beauty on hers.

They were married on July 9, 1735. On their wedding morning, when they rode together to church, Mrs Porter was capricious with her lover. "She had read the old romances," Johnson said, "and had got into her head the fantastical notion that a woman of spirit should use her lover like a dog. So, Sir, at first she told me that I rode too fast, and she could not keep up with me; and, when I rode a little slower, she passed me and complained that I lagged behind." Determined not to be made the slave of caprice, he says he pushed briskly on, and when he at last allowed her to overtake him, she was in tears. This was a favourite story of his, and when he told it to Mrs Thrale he murmured at the close in tender reminiscence: "Pretty dear creature!"

That Johnson did not wish to touch his wife's money, if any other way of making a living could be found, is shown by his application, a month after his marriage, for the headmastership of a school at Solihull. Gilbert Walmsley supported his application, which was rejected on two grounds. "All agree that he is an excellent caracter,"[1] wrote Mr Greswold, the intermediary between Gilbert Walmsley and the trustees of the school, "and on that account deserves much better than to be schoolmaster of

[1] Mr Greswold's spelling.

Solihull." But, Mr Greswold continued, Johnson had the reputation of being a very haughty and ill-natured gent, and his way of distorting his face might, it was feared, affect the lads. The "huffing" of the trustees by the late headmaster being still a sore point with them, they were anxious, said Mr Greswold, not to expose themselves to a second experience of the kind, and must therefore decline the application.

A few months later, Johnson opened a school with his wife's money. "At Edial, near Lichfield, in Staffordshire," the advertisement announced, "young gentlemen are boarded and taught the Latin and Greek languages, by Samuel Johnson." The pupils, who included Captain Garrick's two sons, David and George, numbered three in all. As Johnson had acquired his own knowledge in spurts, he was ill-qualified, in his own words, "to recall vagrant attention, to stimulate sluggish indifference, and to rectify absurd misapprehension." His appearance, too, was against him with the fathers and mothers of prospective pupils, and after struggling along for over a year without adding to his numbers, he decided to give up his school and try to find work in London as a writer. He was now in his twenty-eighth year.

It was on March 2, 1737, that he left Lichfield for town, accompanied by David Garrick, who had just turned twenty. They carried with them a letter from Gilbert Walmsley to the headmaster of a school at which David was to complete his education before taking up the law. "Davy Garrick," Gilbert Walmsley wrote, "is to be with you next week, and Mr Johnson to try his fate with a tragedy, and to see to get himself employed in some translation, either from the Latin or the French."

From

The Sentimental Journey
A LIFE OF CHARLES DICKENS

(1934)

The Son

In his brilliant but erratic book on Charles Dickens, Mr
G. K. Chesterton falls heavily on the 'purely artistic critic' who regards the popularity of Dickens with mistrust. 'The people like bad
literature,' Mr Chesterton makes this odious person say. 'If your
object is to show that Dickens was good literature, you should
rather apologize for his popularity, and try to explain it away. You
should seek to show that Dickens's work was good literature,
although it was popular. Yes, that is your task, to prove that
Dickens was admirable, although he was admired!'

As may be guessed from this quotation, the enormous popularity of Dickens is a cause of much irritability among
his critics, leading some to regard Dickens with distaste,
and leading others to overplay the part of the plain blunt man,
for whom the voice of the people is the voice of God. Our
judgment of other English writers is not confused in this way.
Millions of dumb admirers are not present to our consciousness
when we think about Fielding or Thackeray, or Scott or even
Shakespeare. The popularity of Dickens is unique and has interfered with a detached view of him both as a man and a writer.
To attain this detachment may be possible if his popularity is
treated not as an isolated phenomenon, to be assailed or exalted,
but as a by-product of his genius as a writer, his character as a
man, and the forcing-house effect on his temperament of the age
in which he grew to manhood.

Towards the close of his life, when he was at the height of his
fame, Dickens wrote a story called *George Silverman's Explanation*,
for which he received one thousand pounds, a price which no one
else had at that date received for so slight a piece of writing. As
literature, the story is silly to the point of imbecility, but as a clue

to the influences which shaped the life and work of Dickens it has a very high value. Dickens himself was obscurely aware of its significance, and wrote to his friend W. H. Wills: 'I feel as if I had read something (by somebody else), which I should never get out of my mind.'

The story is told, in the first person, in a slow dragging style, drenched in self-pity and self-abasement, and the figures in the story are both unreal and portentous, as in a dream.

George Silverman begins his narrative as follows:

'It happened in this wise—

'But, sitting with my pen in my hand looking at those words again, without descrying any hint in them of the words that should follow, it comes into my mind that they have an abrupt appearance. They may serve, however, if I let them remain, to suggest how very difficult I find it to explain my explanation. An uncouth phrase: and yet I do not see my way to a better.' His parents, George at last manages to tell his readers, were in a miserable condition of life, and his infant home was a cellar in Preston. Whenever he cried from cold or hunger, his mother, rolling her eyes round the cellar in a gaunt and hungry way, would scream at him that he was a worldly little devil. His father, with rounded shoulders, would sit quiet on a three-legged stool, looking at the empty grate, until his wife plucked the stool from him and bade him go bring some money home. After the death from starvation of his parents, George is taken charge of by a rascally dissenting lay preacher, who cheats him out of a fortune left him by his grandfather, and is blackmailed into handing over half the booty by another and equally rascally dissenting lay preacher. George meanwhile is sent to a farm, where he falls in love with a little girl, but he fears that he may contaminate her by the worldliness of which his mother had always accused him, so he shuns her, and will not join in the simple revelries of the farm people. 'Moody and broody,' the farmer calls him, and George writes: 'Ah! if they could have seen me . . . gliding out from behind the ghostly statue, listening to the music and the fall of dancing feet, and watching the lighted farmhouse windows from the quadrangle when all the ruin was dark; if they could have read my heart, as I crept to bed by the back way, comforting myself with the reflection, "They will take no harm from me,"—they would not have thought mine a morose or an unsocial nature.'

A scholarship at Cambridge, where he lives in friendless obscurity, enables George to study for the Church, and he is given a living by a Lady Fareway, a woman with 'a steady glare in her great round dark eyes.' This sinister woman has a daughter, Adelina, 'bright and beautiful and young, wise and fanciful and good.' George falls in love with Adelina, but divining that she is falling in love with him and feeling his utter unworthiness he diverts her affections to a Mr Granville, who though not wealthy is 'well-looking, clever, energetic, enthusiastic, bold; in the best sense of the term, a thorough young Anglo-Saxon.' Mr Granville is not a good match from the worldly standpoint, so George (whose hair gradually turns white under the strain of his self-abnegation) marries Mr Granville and Adelina secretly and then breaks the news to Lady Fareway. After a scene which ends with George feeling his way out of the room with his hands, Lady Fareway informs George's bishop that George had been bribed to perform the marriage ceremony. For years a cloud hangs over George, his name is tarnished, and his heart broken. The cloud lifts at last, he is presented with a living in a sequestered place, and there pens his explanation, sitting at an open window which looks on to a churchyard—'equal resting-place for sound hearts, wounded hearts, and broken hearts.'

Dickens's comment to Wills—'I feel as if I had read something (by somebody else)'—suggests that he wrote this story almost automatically; and it is in fact simply an allegory of his own life, written in an auto-intoxication of self-pity, his most constant and his strongest emotion.

George Silverman's savage mother is Mrs Dickens; the feckless father is Dickens-Micawber; the canting dissenters represent the long line of humbugs, from Stiggins through Chadband to Mr Honeythunder, whose vulgarity and claptrap disgusted what was best in Dickens by reminding him of what was worst; the child at the farm is David Copperfield's Little Em'ly; Adelina is the angelic girl, too pure for this world, whom Dickens loved in

Mary Hogarth and others; Mr Granville is a modified version of the captivating Steerforth; Lady Fareway is the witch who appears again and again in the novels, in Miss Murdstone, Mrs Clennam, Miss Havisham and other embodiments of a dread which all children feel and which Dickens, who never grew up emotionally, felt throughout his life; and the Church of England clergyman, George Silverman, is the ill-used, self-effacing, misunderstood, refined, cultured, altruistic and unworldly person whom Charles Dickens was capable, in certain moods, of mistaking for Charles Dickens.

If Dickens had possessed nothing more than he put into *George Silverman's Explanation*, he would long since have been forgotten, or remembered only as one of the minor voices of mid-Victorian emotionalism. But he possessed also a marvellous eye for the ludicrous and the grotesque. Had he been able to harmonize his comic genius and his emotions he would have been a writer of the first order. But the opposition between them was innate and irreconcilable, with the two-fold result that his emotions were unpurged by his humour, and his humour, except in occasional sudden flashes, was unenriched by his emotions. His restlessness, his over-emphasis both in life and literature, his extremes of sensibility and callousness, all sprang from this conflict, which never ceased and was never resolved.

Charles Dickens was born at Landport in Portsea, on the seventh of February, 1812, the second of seven children. His father, John Dickens, a clerk in the Navy pay office, was transferred to London when Charles was two, and a little later went to Chatham, where he remained till Charles was ten.

It is a delusion of to-day that mysterious things happen in childhood which entirely transform a child's nature, usually for the worse. Strong though first impressions are, the temperament which receives and uses them according to its instinctive needs is formed before birth. Dickens's self-absorption was innate, though it was clearly deepened by his early delicacy. He was, his biographer John Forster tells us, small and sickly as a child, and subject to violent spasms which prevented him from being a good cricketer, or a first-rate hand at marbles and prisoner's base. Had he felt these deficiencies keenly, he might have devoted his life to celebrating physical prowess, and so escaped the grave charge of being unable to portray an English gentleman. George Silverman, it is true, writes of his Varsity days: 'I can see others in the sunlight; I can see our boats' crews and our athletic young men on the glistening water, or speckled with the moving lights of sunlit leaves; but I myself am always in the shadow looking on. Not unsympathetically—God forbid!—but looking on alone.' This is no doubt Dickens's memory of himself as a small boy watching his schoolfellows at play, but even here it is his isolation, not his shortcomings as an athlete, which is emphasized. If we compare him with Scott, a man of powerful physique, hampered by lameness, Dickens's lack of interest in physical prowess becomes clear. It is usual to dismiss the youthful heroes of Dickens and Scott as lay figures, but unreal though they are they reflect the two men's different ideals of manhood. Scott's heroes are superb horsemen and swordsmen, always on the watch for any discourtesy which may afford a chance for a display of their readiness to engage in a hand to hand encounter. The young men in Dickens are chiefly remarkable for their charm of person, their innocence and their warm-heartedness. 'His figure,' Dickens writes of Nicholas Nickleby, 'was somewhat slight, but manly and wellformed; and, apart from the grace of youth and comeliness, there was an emanation from the warm young heart in his look and bearing.' Throughout the novel his attraction for women is noted, most explicitly in his effect on Fanny Squeers— 'I never,' she reflects on her first view of him, 'saw such legs in the whole course of my life.' But neither in Nicholas nor in any other of Dickens's heroes is there any desire to excel in physical strength and courage or even any recognition that such a desire exists. There are many thrashings in Dickens, there are many intimidations of the vile by the virtuous, but there are no fights. Squeers opposes no resistance to the beating administered by Nicholas. When Noah Claypole, who is twice the size of Oliver Twist, insults Oliver's dead mother, Oliver is supernaturally endowed with a strength which enables him to fell Noah with a single blow. Martin Chuzzlewit, affronted by Pecksniff, moves towards him, and Pecksniff providentially falls backwards over a chair, and does not attempt to rise until Martin, pointing at him with unutterable contempt and flinging his hat upon his head, leaves the room. Dickens's self-love was offended by the idea of one of his embodiments receiving as well as giving blows. The physical violence in his books is not an outlet for his love of the heroic, but for his grievances and resentments. It is always administered, it is never exchanged.

It was not only his self-love as an individual but also the social atmosphere of his early environment which made physical violence distasteful to him. The aristocrat takes punishment calmly because he knows that his turn to inflict it will arrive in due course. It is necessary, too, to his self-respect as a proof that luxury has not enervated him. The aristocrat welcomes danger and hardship in his sports, the poor man has too much of both in his daily life to suffer from the aristocrat's obsession with personal prowess. Rich and poor alike admire strength and courage, but the poor also admire knowledge and learning. The agony Dickens felt when his schooling was interrupted is an emotion almost outside the range of the upper classes. In the presence of danger, as he showed in a railway accident, Dickens was resourceful and self-controlled. But, within his limitations, it was a man's moral and mental faculties which he valued and cultivated, not his physical. Had he been born thirty years later, he might have felt differently, but the extension of the factory system to the wholesale manufacture of aristocrats at our public schools developed too late to influence Dickens. Born in 1842 he might have submerged England in stories of spindled-shanked scholarly boys dumbly worshipping curly-haired athletic boys. One cannot be too thankful he was born in 1812.

The suggestion that his outlook was that of a poor man would not have been approved by Dickens, for he was a true English child of the French Revolution. The effect of the French Revolution on the English social system illustrates the national genius for compromise. The French abolished gentlemen, the English multiplied gentlemen. The French aristocrat was beggared and exiled, the English aristocrat retained his money and his estates at the trivial cost of conceding the title of gentleman to the more aspiring members of the middle classes. In the second half of the nineteenth century, with the growth of the public schools, this concession became automatic. In Dickens's youth it was still capricious and spasmodic, but, with whatever internal misgivings, Dickens always regarded himself as a gentleman, and wrote unironically of Micawber, whom he drew from his father: 'There was a club in the prison, in which Mr Micawber, as a gentleman, was a great authority.'

During Dickens's childhood at Chatham, his father was fairly prosperous, and the house in which they lived, though next door to a Baptist meeting-house, had a charm for Dickens which coloured his description of David Copperfield's birthplace. In the opening chapters of *David Copperfield*, many passages are auto-biographical, having been transcribed direct from an account of his own childhood written by Dickens in his later thirties. Forster tells us, in his literal way, that Dickens's home had a plain-looking white-washed plaster front and a small garden at the back and at the front. David writes of 'the outside of our house, with the latticed bedroom-windows standing open to let in the sweet-smelling air, and the ragged old rooks' nests still dangling in the elm trees at the bottom of the front garden. Now I am in the garden at the back, ... where the fruit clusters on the trees, riper and richer than fruit has ever been since, in any other garden, and where my mother gathers some in a basket, while I stand by, bolting furtive gooseberries, and trying to look unmoved.'

There is a blend of poetry and humour in David's account of his early years which Dickens never attained elsewhere, a proof that his own childhood was relatively happy and free from self-pity. But he could not see even his distant childhood quite purely. After showing David's world as it appeared to David, the pigeon house on a pole without any pigeons in it, the kennel without any dog, a cock crowing fiercely at him from a post, a flock of geese waddling after him with outstretched necks, his mother reading the death of Lazarus to him and Peggotty in the doleful best parlour, Dickens suddenly uses David as a mouthpiece of his own feelings, turning the occasional self-pity of a child into its deepest emotion. 'There is nothing,' David says, 'half so green that I know anywhere, as the grass of that churchyard; nothing half so shady as its trees; nothing half so quiet as its tomb-stones.'

Being an imaginative child, Dickens was happiest when he was reading, and, as he tells us through David, often retreated to a little room upstairs and forgot reality in *Tom Jones* and *Roderick Random* and *The Vicar of Wakefield* and *Don Quixote* and *The Arabian Nights*. 'They kept alive my fancy,' he writes, 'and my hope of something beyond that place and time, . . . and did me no harm; for, whatever harm was in some of them, was not there for me; *I* knew nothing of it.'

He used to impersonate his favourite characters for days on end, though he never, he assures us, carried his impersonations beyond the limits proper to his childish innocence. 'I have been Tom Jones (a child's Tom Jones, a harmless creature) for a week together. I have sustained my own idea of Roderick Random for a month at a stretch, I verily believe . . . and for days and days I can remember to have gone about my region of our house, armed with the centre-piece out of an old set of boot-trees: the perfect realization of Captain Somebody, of the royal British navy, in danger of being beset by savages. . . .'

His natural bent as an actor and entertainer was brought out by these impersonations, and both at home and in the houses of friends he used to be stood on the table to tell stories and sing comic songs, to the delight of his charming but vain and consequential father. What was rich in Dickens, and also much of his vanity, came to him from his Prodigal Father, as he used to call him in later life; and they were further drawn together by the bond which connects a helpless father and a capable son, the son being flattered by the reversal of their natural parts, and the father being relieved, after the anxieties of an unprotected manhood, at finding one of his liabilities transformed into an asset. Even when Charles was very small, John Dickens may have felt in him an energy and practical sense which would give him what his father had enjoyed only in fancy—wealth and a good position in the world. Gadshill-place, the house Dickens bought when he was famous and where he lived till his death, stood on the highest point of the main road between Rochester and Gravesend, and John Dickens pointed it out one day to the tiny Charles and told him that if he worked hard enough he might live in it when he came to be a man.

The desire to live in a fine house must have been intense in Dickens even in his Chatham days for him to realize it in later life by purchasing this object of his childish admiration. Though not unhappy at Chatham, his precocious worldliness would have made him aware that neither his home nor his school was as grand as could be wished. At nine years he went to a school kept by a Mr William Giles, the minister of the Baptist meeting-house next door to Dickens's home. Forster, always a faithful if flat echo of Dickens's own feelings, describes Mr Giles in double negatives, with an effect of patronage: 'Nor does the influence of Mr Giles, such as it was, seem to have been other than favourable. Charles had himself a not ungrateful sense that this first of his masters, in his little cared for childhood, had pronounced him to be a boy of capacity.' The unvarying repulsiveness of the Dis-senters in the novels suggests that Dickens's gratitude, such as it was, fell far short of his feeling that he was entitled to something better than Mr Giles's little school.

His serious unhappiness began at the age of eleven, after John Dickens was recalled to London. John was by now the father of six children, and being incapable of the strict economy necessary to bring up so large a family on his small pay was finding himself increasingly harassed by creditors. In this situation he found some comfort in drawing up a 'deed' to which he used to refer with gloomy grandeur that deeply impressed the youthful Charles, though the deed was nothing more recondite than a theoretical composition with his creditors.

Their new home was in Bayham Street, Camden Town. A washerwoman lived next door, and a Bow Street officer over the way, and the house itself is described by Forster as a mean small tenement, with a wretched little backgarden abutting on a squalid court. There were no boys for Charles to play with, and no school for him to go to. His despair at being cut off from school was intensified by the election of his sister, Fanny, as a pupil at the Royal Academy of Music. 'What would I have given, if I had had anything to give,' he once said to Forster, 'to have been sent back to any other school, to have been taught something anywhere!' In spite of his indulgent affection for his father, whose admiration of Charles's comic songs covered nearly all his sins of omission, Dickens could never entirely forgive him for his indifference at this time to his son's education. 'He was proud of me, in his way,' Dickens told Forster, 'and had a great admiration of the comic singing. But, in the ease of his temperament, and the straitness of his means, he appears to have utterly lost at this time the idea of educating me at all, and to have utterly put from him the notion that I had any claim upon him, in that regard, whatever. So I degenerated into cleaning his boots of a morning and my own; and looking after my younger brothers and sisters (we were now six in all); and going on such poor errands as arose out of our poor way of living.'

As the months passed, and the 'deed' became less and less efficacious as a charm against creditors, Mrs Dickens resolved as a last desperate expedient to set up a school. The family moved to number four Gower Street North, a large brass plate was affixed to the door, bearing the words MRS DICKENS'S ESTABLISHMENT, circulars setting forth the merits of the establishment were printed, and Charles was sent out to distribute them. But no one came, no one even made any enquiries. The only visitors to number four were the butcher and the baker, and they were increasingly bitter. At last the resistance opposed to the enemy by the 'deed' collapsed, and following a brief period in a sponging-house John Dickens was taken to the debtor's prison, the Marshalsea, after a farewell speech to Charles in which he affirmed that the sun was set on him for ever.

During the next few weeks Charles transferred nearly everything at number four, including his volumes of Smollett and Fielding, to the pawnship, where more than once, arriving early in the morning, he found the pawn-broker in a turn-up bedstead, with a cut in his forehead or a black eye, evidence of his quarrelsomeness in his cups. With a shaking hand the pawnbroker would fumble in the pockets of his clothes, which were scattered on the floor, and at last produce the money, while his wife kept up a stream of reproaches.

At this juncture a distant cousin of Mrs Dickens, James Lamert, who had lived with the family at Chatham and later in Bayham Street, offered a job to Charles in a blacking warehouse, which belonged to his brother-in-law and in which he was himself the chief manager. Mrs Dickens's nearer relatives, including her brother, Thomas Barrow, had answered many of John Dickens's calls on their resources, and had made it clear that they would answer no more. In these circumstances Charles's parents decided to accept Lamert's offer to Charles.

In the autobiographical fragment which he incorporated with a few changes in *David Copperfield*, Dickens expressed the bitterness which throughout his life he felt with undiminishing intensity at what he looked upon as his parents' betrayal of him. 'It is wonderful to me,' he wrote, 'how I could have been so easily cast away at such an age. It is wonderful to me, that, even after my descent into the poor little drudge I had been since we came to London, no one had compassion enough on me—a child of singular abilities, quick, eager, delicate, and soon hurt, bodily or mentally—to suggest that something might have been spared, as certainly it might have been, to place me at any common school. Our friends, I take it, were tired out. No one made any sign. My father and mother were quite satisfied. They could hardly have been more so, if I had been twenty years of age, distinguished at a grammar school, and going to Cambridge.'

The damaging effect of self-pity on a man's sense of proportion and reality is well illustrated in this complaint. Absorbed in his own descent into a poor little drudge, Dickens forgets his mother's descent from a fairly comfortable life at Chatham to a house emptied of its furniture, a husband in a debtor's prison, and six children to feed with what she could extract from unpaid butchers, bakers and milkmen. As the friends of the family were tired of coming to the rescue, Mr and Mrs Dickens naturally welcomed a job for Charles at six shillings a week, under a good-natured relative; and Mrs Dickens, at any rate, probably hoped that Charles would rise quickly to a clerkship, and in due course become a manager.

Dickens gives a long account in his autobiographical fragment of his experience at the blacking warehouse. It was a crazy, tumbledown old house, abutting on the river at Hungerford stairs, and overrun with rats. 'Its wainscotted rooms,' he writes, 'and its rotten floors and staircase, and the old grey rats swarming down in the cellars, and the sound of their squeaking and scuffling coming up the stairs at all times, and the dirt and decay of the place, rise up vividly before me, as if I were there again.' At first his cousin James Lamert put him in the counting-house, apart from the other boys. His job was to cover the pots of paste-blacking with oil-paper and blue paper, and then tie them round with string. In this he was helped by one of the boys, Bob Fagin by name, who on Charles's first morning came up in a ragged apron and a paper cap and showed him the trick of using string and tying the knot. After a few days it was found impracticable for Charles to work upstairs, so he joined the other boys and worked side by side with Bob Fagin and Poll Green, whose father was a fireman at Drury Lane, and whose small sister did imps in the pantomime. Charles was treated with respect by Bob and Poll, and by the men in the warehouse, partly because he was the manager's cousin, but chiefly because of his innate faculty for imposing his own estimate of himself on his associates. Even at twelve he was self-contained and uncommunicative, and guarded his dignity with tireless vigilance. Realizing that he must do his work well if he wished to be treated with respect, he soon became at least as skilful as Bob and Poll.

'I worked,' he writes, 'from morning to night, with common men and boys, a shabby child.' But, he adds, though he was perfectly familiar with them, his conduct and manners were different enough from theirs to place a space between him and them, 'They (Bob and Poll), and the men, always spoke of me as "the young gentleman."' Fagin was especially impressed by the delicate haughty child, and served him with the love of a simple ignorant nature. One day when Charles had an attack of spasm,

Fagin filled empty blacking-bottles with hot water and applied them to his side for several hours, and would not let him go home alone. Another day he punched Poll's head, Poll having rebelled against Charles's gentlemanly airs.

Fagin's affection and the kindliness of the men did not stir any sense of fellowship in Dickens. 'No words,' he writes, 'can express the secret agony of my soul as I sunk into this companionship; compared these everyday associates with those of my happier childhood; and felt my early hopes of growing up a learned and distinguished man, crushed in my breast. The deep remembrance of the sense I had of being utterly neglected and hopeless; of the shame I felt in my position; of the misery it was to my young heart to believe that, day by day, what I had learned, and thought, and delighted in, and raised my fancy and emulation up by, was passing away from me, never to be brought back any more; cannot be written. My whole nature was so penetrated with the grief and humiliation of such considerations, that even now, famous and caressed and happy, I often forget in my dreams that I have a dear wife and children; even that I am a man; and wander desolately back to that time of my life.'

At twelve or thirteen boys lose much of their individual character, and first become keenly aware of their social advantages or the reverse. Dickens's intense suffering at this time was therefore understandable. What is astonishing is that in later years, at the height of a renown founded on his experience of poverty, he should still have been stuck fast in his adolescent self-pity and lack of detachment, should still have nursed his old rage and resentment, and felt no tenderness for the men and boys who had made the worst period of his life bearable to him. Wounded self-love has never shown a more perverse vindictiveness than when Dickens gave Fagin's name to a character who is not only the most repulsive in the long list of his villains, but whose special line of villainy, the corruption of the young, is an exact inversion of Bob Fagin's protective tenderness.

'I took the liberty,' Dickens writes, 'of using his (Fagin's) name, long afterwards, in *Oliver Twist*.' It is a liberty which Mr G. K. Chesterton, in a book devoted to praising Dickens's love of the poor, has not only abstained from criticizing, but has palliated by falsifying Dickens's own account of Fagin's unvarying kindness. 'A coarse and heavy lad,' Mr Chesterton calls Bob Fagin, 'who had often attacked Dickens on the not unreasonable ground of his being a "gentleman." '

During this period at the warehouse, the genius of Dickens, functioning in independence of his contempt for his associates and his despair at being cut off from school, was collecting much of the material of the Cockney fairyland which he created in his earlier novels, from Pickwick to David Copperfield. The rest of the family having joined John Dickens in the Marshalsea, Charles was boarded out with an old lady in Camden Town, and, after breakfasting off a penny cottage loaf and a penny-worth of milk, used to walk down Tottenham Court Road, where the stale pastry on the trays outside the confectioners often absorbed the money he was saving for his midday dinner. A slice of pudding had then to suffice him, followed at tea-time by bread and butter and half a pint of coffee at some coffee-house. One coffee-house in particular remained in his memory, because of its oval glass-plate, bearing the words COFFEE-ROOM, at which words, mysteriously inverted into MOOR-EEFFOC from where he sat, he used to stare in a dismal reverie. On Saturday nights, six shillings in his pocket, his spirits rose as he walked back along the Blackfriars Road, the smell of hat-making in his nostrils, and sometimes he would yield to the temptation of a show-van, and enter it with a motley crowd, and gape with them at the Fat Pig, the Wild Indian, and the Little Lady. At other times he explored the back streets of the Adelphi and the Adelphi arches, and visited a public-house, called the Fox-under-the-hill and approached by an underground passage. Above all the life of the Marshalsea fascinated him, and when he moved his lodging from Camden Town to the Borough, so as to be near his family, he used to join them at breakfast and again after work till nine o'clock, and get from his mother all she knew about the various inhabitants of the prison.

Towards the close of his stay John Dickens had been elected the chairman of a committee which regulated the internal order of the prison, and in this capacity he drew up a petition praying for a bounty in which the prisoners might drink His Majesty's birthday health. When the petition had been prepared, the officers of the committee assembled and stood by in grave dignity while the lesser inhabitants of the prison filed by the petition, affixing their signatures as they passed. Charles was watching the scene from a corner. 'Whatever was comical in this scene,' he writes, 'and whatever was pathetic, I sincerely believe I perceived in my corner ... quite as well as I should perceive it now. I made out my own little character and story for every man who put his name to the sheet of paper. ... Their different peculiarities of dress, of face, of gait, of manner, were written indelibly on my memory ... and I thought about it afterwards, over the pots of paste-blacking, often and often.'

John Dickens's stay in the Marshalsea lasted for a little over three months. A legacy of some hundreds from a relative set him free, and he moved with his family to a house in Somerstown. But Charles continued to go to the warehouse, in 'my poor white hat, little jacket, and corduroy trousers,' as he describes his dress during this time. One afternoon he was taken with the rest of the family to see his sister Fanny receive a prize at the Royal Academy of Music. 'I could not bear,' he writes, 'to think of myself— beyond the reach of all such honourable emulation and success. The tears ran down my face. I felt as if my heart was rent. I prayed when I went to bed that night, to be lifted out of the humiliation and neglect in which I was. I never had suffered so much before. There was no envy in this.' To add to his misery he now worked behind a window open to the street, in the Covent Garden premises to which the warehouse had been moved. The dexterity with which he and Fagin tied up the pots attracted the passers-by, and sometimes there would be quite a crowd in front of the window. One day John Dickens visited the warehouse, and Charles wondered how he could bear the sight of his son exposed in this fashion. Although he was now living with his family, he felt as isolated as ever, for he never heard a word of being taken away and sent to school. The only improvement in his condition was that his home provided him with his midday meal, which he carried to the warehouse in a small basin tied in a handkerchief.

The sympathy stirred by Dickens's narrative is weakened by the way in which he skims over any detail calculated to lessen the impression that his parents were indifferent to his sufferings. He wonders, for example, how his father could bear to see him in the window, yet it appears indirectly from his narrative that this incident led to a quarrel between James Lamert and John Dickens, and to Charles being removed from the warehouse. Counting the period at Hungerford stairs, Charles was not at the warehouse more than six months in all, though in his narrative he says he may have been there 'for a year, or much more, or less.' The period at Covent Garden, as far as one can infer, was about two months, and the quarrel between John Dickens and Lamert must therefore have followed shortly on John Dickens's visit to the Covent Garden premises.

'At last, one day,' Dickens writes, 'my father and the relative so often mentioned, quarrelled; quarrelled by letter. . . . It was about me. It may have had some backward reference, in part, for anything I know, to my employment at the window.' The letter enraged Lamert, and he told Charles he could not keep him any longer, but, though violent about John Dickens, Lamert was gentle to Charles himself. He seems indeed, like everyone else at the warehouse, to have always made things as easy as possible for the future creator of Oliver Twist, Smike and other helpless and savagely ill-used boys.

Mrs Dickens was extremely upset when Charles returned with the news that he had been discharged, and the next day she went to Lamert and persuaded him to withdraw the dismissal. But John Dickens would not agree to Charles being sent back. 'My father,' Dickens writes, 'said I should go back no more, and should go to school. I do not write resentfully or angrily; for I know how all these things have worked together to make me what I am; but I never afterwards forgot, I never shall forget, I never can forget, that my mother was warm for me going back.'

The affection with which Dickens portrayed Micawber and the contempt with which he pictured his mother as Mrs Nickleby sprang in the main from the way in which Mr and Mrs Dickens respectively behaved at this crisis. But Mrs Nickleby does not at all fit the part played on this occasion by Mrs Dickens, and Micawber fits John Dickens's part very loosely. One cannot imagine the imbecile Mrs Nickleby trying to adjust an important quarrel, and though one can imagine Micawber adorning a quarrel with large generalizations, the line taken by John Dickens both with Lamert and his wife is un-Micawberesque. Between Dickens's comic treatment of his parents in these two characters, and his serious treatment in the account of the break with Lamert, there is a discrepancy which needs to be adjusted. To get a coherent idea of John Dickens and his wife is important to our understanding of Dickens, and is also a belated act of justice to Mrs Dickens, who is known to the general reader only as an incongruous mixture of Mrs Nickleby and the harsh mother who tried to sacrifice her gifted son in the interests of a petty economy.

That Mrs Nickleby is a caricature of Mrs Dickens as she was after the troubles of her life had muddled her mind and disarranged without souring her natural sweetness may be inferred from the description of her given by Mary Weller, Charles's nurse at Chatham. She was, Mary Weller said, 'a dear good mother, and a fine woman, who spent a great deal of pains on teaching Charles before he went to school. Dickens himself told Forster that he learnt English and Latin from her, and Forster adds that Dickens's mother was in his mind when he wrote in *David Copperfield*, 'I faintly remember her teaching me the alphabet, and when I look upon the fat black letters in the primer, the puzzling novelty of their shapes, and the easy good nature of O and S always seem to present themselves before me as they used to do.'

Charles was Mrs Dickens's eldest son, and before the other babies arrived he was probably as happy with her as David Copperfield with his mother, before she re-married and bore a child to Mr Murdstone. Throughout his life Dickens had to be the centre of attention, and one may assume that the estrangement between David and his mother reflects the jealousy Charles felt when he was compelled to share Mrs Dickens's love with the younger children. But the affectionate strain in his nature made his egotism an obscure torment to him all his life. In the desire for death, which recurs again and again in his novels, there is self-dissatisfaction as well as self-pity. His settled resentments gave him many uncomfortable hours, and the remorse he felt for the bitterness he nourished against his mother is apparent in the passage describing David's return from school to find his mother nursing the new baby.

'I spoke to her, and she started and cried out. But seeing me she called me her dear Davy, her own boy! and coming half across the room to meet me, kneeled down upon the ground and kissed me, and laid my head down on her bosom near the little creature that was nestling there, and put its hand up to my lips.

'I wish I had died. I wish I had died then, with that feeling in my heart! I should have been more fit for Heaven than I have ever been since.'

The attention which Mrs. Dickens could give to Charles, already much diminished before the family left Chatham, dwindled still further in the struggle for bare necessities during the Bayham Street period. There is nothing to suggest that Mrs Dickens was qualified to deal with the situation in which her husband's vanity and incompetence had involved her. But a woman cannot be expected to support as well as bear and bring up a large family, and that Mrs Dickens was unequal to the feat only emphasizes her courage in attempting it. To her, submerged in problems she could not solve, Charles was a boy with a living to earn, not a gentleman's son entitled to a university education, and when he was offered a job by her cousin, she must have felt that he was very lucky to be started on a business career which would be made easy by family influence. His genius was completely hidden from her. A mother soon divines, and with some misgivings greatly values, practical genius in a son, but the relation between men of imaginative genius and their mothers is summed up in Hamlet's sardonic, 'O wonderful son, that can so astonish a mother!' If Dickens had understood this commonplace of human experience, much of his bitterness against his mother would have vanished, and he would have felt some gratitude for the kindnesses she was able to show him during this period. To satisfy his nightly curiosity about the debtors in the Marshalsea must have been an exhausting task, and even to send him to Covent Garden with his midday meal is a proof of her solicitude for him. It appears, too—a fact elicited by Forster when questioning Dickens about his narrative—that Mrs Dickens often visited him at the warehouse.

One may assume that Mrs Dickens did not regard what was left of her husband's legacy after the creditors had taken their share as a permanent bulwark against poverty, and her attempt to patch up the quarrel with Lamert therefore followed naturally from her anxiety to keep Charles in a job under a well-disposed relative. It remains to examine John Dickens's action on this occasion, and see how far it deserves the halo of disinterested concern for Charles's welfare with which it has been invested, in particular by Mr Chesterton, who contrasts it with what he calls Mrs Dickens's 'touch of strange harshness.'

In William Dorrit, the father of the Marshalsea, Dickens, some years after writing *David Copperfield*, showed the other side of the character he had made lovable in Micawber. The main traits of Dorrit are vanity, snobbishness, shamelessness in borrowing money, and an entire absence of gratitude to the persons from whom he borrows. When after twenty years in the Marshalsea he comes into a fortune, he shows the insolence of the professional sponger able at last to discard the affability by which he has hitherto lived. To Arthur Clennam, whose love for his daughter he has been discreetly exploiting, Dorrit says: 'I shall repay the—hum—the advances I have had from you, sir, with peculiar pleasure. I beg to be informed at your early convenience, what advances you have made my son.' Clennam suggests that a small loan, until Mr Dorrit's affairs are in order, may be convenient, and Dorrit replies: 'I accept with readiness, at the present moment, what I could not an hour ago have conscientiously taken. I am obliged to you for the temporary accommodation. . . . Be so kind, sir, as to add the amount to those former advances to which I have already referred. . . . A mere verbal statement of the gross amount is all I shall—ha—all I shall require.'

When the Marshal of the prison offers Dorrit the free use of two rooms in his house until his departure, Dorrit writes him a

c

cutting note, begging on behalf of himself and his family to repudiate the Marshal's offer, with all those thanks which its disinterested character and its perfect independence of all worldly considerations demanded. His attitude to his fellow-prisoners is more genial, but full of condescension, and when they assemble to see him off, he moves through them 'great, and sad, but not absorbed,' immersed in wonder how the poor creatures will get on without him.

In the light of these passages John Dickens's quarrel with James Lamert takes on a less disinterested aspect. Even in Micawber, who is always dunning or trying to dun Mrs Micawber's family, we see the resentment which John Dickens felt against his wife's relatives. 'Mrs Micawber's family,' Micawber tells David Copperfield, in reference to Mrs Micawber being yet again with child, 'have been so good as to express their dissatisfaction at this state of things. I have merely to observe that I am not aware it is any business of theirs, and that I repel that exhibition of feeling with scorn, and with defiance!'

With his wife's uncle, Thomas Barrow, John Dickens was, before he went to the Marshalsea, already on bad terms, and James Lamert, a more distant connection, was perhaps the only one of his wife's relatives with whom he was still friendly. The job Lamert offered Charles was, as Dickens tells us, accepted by his father without demur, and John Dickens's change of front and violent attack on Lamert, though some sympathy with Charles may be traced in it, must be chiefly attributed to the efflorescence of his gentlemanly feelings under the rays of his legacy. The letter he wrote Lamert was no doubt much in the strain of Dorrit's letter to the Marshal.

The creator of William Dorrit understood the nature of the quarrel between Lamert and John Dickens, but his gratitude at the result prevented him from analysing the causes leading to it. Apart from this feeling of gratitude, and apart also from the pleasure he derived from his father as the model of Micawber, Dickens was jealous on behalf of the general status of the head of the House of Dickens. His father's gentility was the one foible Dickens never made fun of, and when many years later John

Dickens was, through his son's influence, appointed manager of the reporting staff of the *Daily News*, Dickens resented the attitude of one of the owners in terms which could not have been bettered by William Dorrit: 'I must add, with great pain, that I have not always observed Mr Bradbury's treatment of my father (than whom there is not a more zealous, disinterested, or useful gentleman attached to the paper) to be very creditable to himself, or delicate towards me.'

The school to which Charles went after leaving the warehouse stood in the Hampstead Road, and was called Wellington House Academy. It served Dickens as the model for Salem House in *David Copperfield*, and its ignorant and brutal headmaster, a Welshman called Jones, reappeared in Creakle. But Dickens did not suffer at the headmaster's hands. He was a day boy, and Jones did not care to risk the resentment of a parent on receiving back a scourged and weeping child. A further reason for Dickens's immunity was his genius for being well-treated even in the most unpromising situations. His capacity for taking the lead was beginning to show itself, and even the most brutish masters respect a boy who is popular. Dickens got up theatricals, he issued a newspaper, written on scraps of copy-book paper and sold for marbles and pieces of slate pencil, and sometimes he led out small parties of boys who roamed the streets pretending to be beggars, and worrying old ladies for alms, which they doubtless pocketed, to maintain the illusion.

He was happy at the time, whatever his later opinion of the place, and full of renenewed confidence in life and in himself. 'My recollection of him,' an old schoolfellow told Forster, 'is that he was not very tall of his age, which was between thirteen and fourteen. He had a fresh rosy complexion, rather light brown hair, and good eyes, a wide forehead, but not very high. He walked very upright, almost more than upright, like leaning back a little. He had then rather a full lower lip. ... Dickens always struck me as being a sharp boy rather than a thoughtful one. He had nothing heavy or dreamy about him at that time. He was very particular with his clothes; ... and I never should have thought that he had been employed at humble work. He appeared always like a gentleman's son, rather aristocratic than otherwise.'

That Dickens did not remember Wellington House Academy with much pleasure is shown in an account he wrote of it, called 'Our School.' The comic bits are done with his usual gusto, but he concludes contemptuously: 'It (the world) had little reason to be proud of our school, and has done much better in that way, and will do far better yet.' He claims in this account to have been put into Vergil as soon as he arrived, and to have attained and held the eminent position of first boy, but one of his contemporaries wrote to Forster disputing these claims and stating that Dickens did not distinguish himself at work or win any prizes. There is certainly nothing in Dickens's writings to suggest that, whether or not he was put into Vergil, any perceptible amount of Vergil was put into him.

Dickens left school when he was nearly fifteen, and a few months later was taken into his office by an attorney of Gray's Inn, a Mr Edward Blackmore, who lodged with an aunt of Mrs Dickens. The hierarchy of lawyer's clerks is described in *Pickwick*: at the top the articled clerk who has paid a premium and will one day become an attorney; then the salaried clerk with thirty shillings a week—'a dirty caricature of the fashion which expired six months ago'; below the salaried clerk the middle-aged copying clerk, with a large family, always shabby and often drunk; and at the bottom the 'office lads in their first surtouts, who feel a befitting contempt for boys at day schools, club as they go home at night for saveloys and porter, and think there's nothing like "life." '

Dickens was one of the office lads with a salary of thirteen and sixpence a week, rising to fifteen shillings before he left, a year and a half later. On this sum he saw life under the guidance of a more experienced fellow-clerk, called Potter, with whom he used to visit taverns and play small parts at a neighbouring theatre. In one of the *Sketches by Boz* he has described his friendship with Potter, giving Potter's real name and disguising himself as Robert Smithers. 'As Mr Thomas Potter touchingly observed,' he writes, 'they were "thick-and-thin pals, and nothing but it." There was a spice of romance in Mr Smithers's disposition, a ray of poetry, a gleam of misery, a sort of consciousness of he didn't know what, coming across him he didn't precisely know why—which stood out in fine relief against the off-hand, dashing, amateur pickpocket sort of manner, which distinguished Mr Potter in an eminent degree.'

His mixed feelings about Potter and generally about his life at this time are obvious in this quotation. Potter is said to have been the original of Jingle, and doubtless he also contributed a good deal to Dick Swiveller and the other lawyer's clerks whom Dickens drew with such superb comic power. But one cannot infer from the fascination exercised over the reader by Swiveller, Jingle or Lowten that Dickens had any personal affection for the originals, such as one feels in Shakespeare for the originals of Falstaff and Dogberry and Master Silence, and even Bardolph and Aguecheek. Dickens's self-love interposed a barrier between himself and the outer world. A fellow-reporter describes him at twenty or so as exceedingly reserved, seldom speaking to anyone unless first addressed, and very observant. The world, as distinguished from his own private emotions, was a play to Dickens, and there was no mean for him between watching the play and taking a leading part in it. He could not mingle in the general life of men like Shakespeare, for whom the world of experience and the world of his own emotions explained and enriched one another.

The distaste Dickens felt for his fellow-clerks comes out in his account of Mr Lowten and his companions, on one of whose social evenings Mr Pickwick accidentally intruded. One of the company is described as 'a young gent with a whisker, a squint, and an open shirt collar (dirty).' Another, in a checked shirt and Mosaic studs, a cigar in his mouth, says to Mr Pickwick: ' "It's board and lodging to me, is smoke," ' and Mr Pickwick reflects that it would be a good thing if it were washing, too. Even Dick Swiveller, whom the development of the story converts into an attractive character, is pictured as very unprepossessing on his first introduction—'a figure of dirty smartness ... wiry hair, dull eyes, and sallow face . . . a strong savour of tobacco smoke, and a prevailing greasiness of appearance.'

Among these musty revellers Charles at sixteen was conspicuous for his neatness and smartness. A fellow-clerk describes him as carrying himself very upright, his head well up, as if he had been drilled by a military instructor. He was, the description continues, fashionably dressed, his complexion was a healthy pink, his eyes full of animation, and his mouth firmly set.

Dickens had no intention of drifting upwards to the position of a salaried clerk at thirty shillings a week. Having heard that many men who later distinguished themselves had begun life by reporting debates in Parliament, he left Mr Blackmore's office when he was sixteen, and set himself to learn shorthand. It is characteristic of him that he eventually became the best shorthand writer of the day. 'Whatever I have tried to do in life,' he says of himself, disguised as David Copperfield, 'I have tried with all my heart to do well. . . . Never to put one hand to anything on which I could throw my whole self, and never to affect depreciation of my work, whatever it was, I find now to have been my golden rules.'

Having mastered shorthand, he supported himself for two years as a reporter in Doctor's Commons. Some idea of the stage as an alternative to becoming a Parliamentary reporter must have occupied him at this time, for he visited the theatre nearly every night during these years, practised in his own room sometimes for five or six hours a day perfecting himself in entering and leaving a room and sitting down, and took lessons from a well-known actor.

That Dickens was fundamentally an actor, and ought to have gone on the stage, has sometimes been suggested. 'Dickens's essential faculty,' Carlyle said '. . . is that of a first-rate play-actor. Had he been born twenty of forty years earlier, we should most probably have had a second and greater Mathews, Incledon, or the like, and no writing Dickens.' Owing to his own uncertainty of aim, Carlyle was always suggesting that some man who had succeeded in one direction might have applied his power more satisfactorily in another direction. But before admitting that a man ought to have been something he wasn't, we must first be persuaded that he ought not to have been something he was. Carlyle does not attempt to convince us that Dickens lacked genius as a comic writer. Dickens had to find an outlet for his faculty of reproducing in words his impressions of the ludicrous and the grotesque, and it was this necessity which turned him into a writer instead of an actor. Further, although he was intensely theatrical, valuing his emotions as a means to moving others and afraid to diagnose them accurately and express them sincerely, his egotism was too extreme to be satisfied even by the stage. He was not prepared to be another man's mouthpiece, and as he knew of no theatre where he could both write the plays and take every part he abandoned his designs on the theatre. Later in life, when his comic vein was almost exhausted, and his fame made possible a one-man show, in which the actor was also the author, he illustrated the half truth in Carlyle's remark.

From

D. H. Lawrence

(1938)

Youth

DAVID HERBERT LAWRENCE was born at Eastwood, a Nottinghamshire mining-village, on September 11, 1885. He was the fourth child of John Arthur Lawrence, a coal miner who had worked at Brinsley Colliery since the age of seven.

In his autobiographical novel, *Sons and Lovers*, Lawrence drew his parents at full length as Walter and Gertrude Morel, and himself as Paul. Walter Morel, at the time of his marriage, was happy and unreflecting, a great dancer, friendly with every one, uninterested in books and ideas, but very clever with his hands, able to make or mend anything. Gertrude was serious and puritanical, fond of discussions about politics and religion, contemptuous of dancing, and subdued in her dress. For some months after their marriage they were very happy, but as the glow faded Mrs Morel began to be jarred by her husband, to whom she felt socially superior and who was unable to discuss anything serious, though respectfully attentive when she talked about matters beyond his understanding. Gradually she drew away from him, and he took to staying out late, and sometimes returned the worse for drink. After the birth of their first child the estrangement became complete, for Mrs Morel, as Lawrence unconsciously shows throughout, was the kind of woman who looks on her husband simply as an instrument for producing children and aggrandizing the family. Morel stayed out more frequently and to later hours, and when he came back his wife would flay him with her tongue, in a restrained sarcastic way which intimidated him.

By the time Paul was coming, Mrs Morel hated her husband, who still loved her and tried clumsily to make up for his drinking and extravagance by doing odd jobs during her pregnancy— 'He would bustle round in his slovenly fashion, poking out the ashes, rubbing the fireplace, sweeping the house before he went to work. Then, feeling very self-righteous, he went upstairs', where he would be greeted less gratefully than he had hoped. Gradually Mrs Morel and her children formed a solid front against him. The Morels moved from their old home to a house on the brow of a hill, and during their first winter there the disputes between husband and wife were unusually bitter—

> The children played in the street, on the brim of the wide, dark valley, until eight o'clock. Then they went to bed. Their mother sat sewing below. Having such a great space in front of the house gave the children a feeling of night, of vastness, and of terror. . . . Often Paul would wake up, after he had been asleep a long time, aware of thuds downstairs. Instantly he was wide awake. Then he heard the booming shouts of his father, come home nearly drunk, then the sharp replies of his mother, then the bang, bang, of his father's fist on the table. . . .

A silence would follow, and the children lay wondering what had happened, and could not go to sleep until they heard their father throw down his boots and tramp upstairs in his stockinged feet.

The children told their mother about everything that happened to them, but as soon as their father came in they stopped talking— 'Conversation was impossible between the father and any other member of the family. He was an outsider.' Of all the children Paul hated his father most. He was disgusted by the way in which his father ate, by his black hair slightly soiled with grey, his grimy face, and his weary sullen look. Only when he was at work on something, cobbling boots or mending the kettle or his pit-bottle, was Morel momentarily in favour with his children. What they enjoyed most was when he made fuses, setting a heap of gun-powder in the middle of the table, and a little pile of black grains upon the white-scrubbed board, and making and trimming the straws while the children filled and plugged them. 'Paul loved to see the black grains trickle down a crack in his palm into the mouth of the straw, peppering jollily downwards till the straw was full.'

In spite of Lawrence's hatred of his father, Morel's love for his children breaks through in several scenes. When Paul had bronchitis, Morel came into the bedroom, and asked 'Are ter asleep, my darlin'?' Paul replied irritably. It got on his nerves having his father standing undecidedly on the hearthrug, and he sent him out two or three times to fetch his mother, who was busy ironing below. At last Morel, after having stood looking at his son for some time, said softly—'Good night, my darlin' ', and Paul turned round in his relief at being alone. The eldest son, William, dies in London, and Paul takes the news to his father at the pit-head.

'Is it thee, Paul?' Morel exclaims. 'Is 'e worse?'

'You've got to go to London.'

' 'E's niver gone, child?'

'Yes.'

Morel walks on a few strides, then leans against a truck-side, his hand over his eyes—'Paul stood looking round, waiting. On the weighing-machine a truck trundled slowly. Paul saw everything, except his father leaning against the truck as if he were tired.'

Morel's habits grew worse as the years passed; and as he was more and more thrust out from the family circle, Paul drew closer to his mother, the death of her eldest son still further intensifying the feeling between them. Once, when he was dangerously ill in his late teens, and his mother was sleeping with him, he felt that he was dying and called to her. She lifted him in her arms, crying in a small voice, 'Oh, my son—my son!'

'That brought him to. He realized her. His whole will rose up and arrested him. He put his head on her breast, and took ease of her for love.'

Paul became friends with a neighbouring girl, called Miriam, and there were bitter scenes between mother and son. One evening she burst out against him, and when he said that she wasn't interested in Herbert Spencer and the other authors he and Miriam discussed, she cried—'How do you know I don't care? Do you ever try?' Her agony grew, and he suddenly could not bear it any longer. He stooped to kiss her, and she threw her arms round his neck, hid her face in his shoulder, and whimpered—

'I've never—you know, Paul—I've never had a husband—not really.' Paul stroked his mother's hair, and kissed her throat, and his mother responded with a long fervent kiss. As he was gently stroking her face, Morel came in, walking unevenly, and said bitterly, 'At your mischief again?'

His mother, Paul realized, wanted him to climb into the middle classes, and one of her objections to Miriam was that she was not a lady. Paul tried to persuade his mother that he liked 'common people' best. From the middle classes, he said, one got ideas, but from the common people life itself, warmth. Why, then, Mrs Morel asked him, didn't he go and talk with his father's pals? They, Paul replied, were rather different. 'Not at all. They're the common people. After all, whom do you mix with now—among the common people? Those that exchange ideas, like the middle classes. The rest don't interest you.'

Mrs Morel fell ill, and after a period of uncertainty it was discovered she had cancer. She did not want her husband near her, and when he was with her he was awkward and humble, and looked at her as if he wanted to run away. She resisted death, and when the parson said that she would have her parents and sisters and dead son in the Other Land, she retorted that she had done without them for a long time, and could go on doing without them—'It is the living I want, not the dead.' She would lie, thinking of the past, her mouth in a hard line, and sometimes she talked to Paul about her husband, whom she hated and would not forgive. As she was dying, Paul put his arms round her, whispering, 'My love, my love, oh, my love!' and after her death he went to look at her—

She lay like a girl asleep and dreaming of her love. . . . He looked again at the eyebrows, at the small winsome nose a bit on one side. She was young again. Only the hair as it arched so beautifully from her temples was mixed with silver. . . . She would wake up. She would lift her eyelids. He bent and kissed her passionately. But there was coldness against his mouth. He bit his lip with horror. Looking at her, he felt he could never, never let her go.

The book ends with Paul struggling against his desire to follow his mother into the darkness—

> Beyond the town the country, little smouldering spots for more towns—the sea—the night—on and on! And he had no place in it! Whatever spot he stood on, there he stood alone. From his breast, from his mouth, sprang the endless space, and it was there behind him, everywhere. The people hurrying along the streets offered no obstruction to the void in which he found himself. They were small shadows whose footsteps and voices could be heard, but in each of them the same night, the same silence. . . . His soul could not leave her, wherever she was. Now she was gone abroad into the night, and he was with her still. They were together still. But yet there was his body, his chest, that leaned against the stile. They seemed something. Where was he?—one tiny upright speck of flesh, less than an ear of wheat lost in the field. He could not bear it. . . . 'Mother!' he whispered—'Mother!' . . . But no, he would not give in. Turning sharply, he walked towards the city's gold phosphorescence. His fists were shut, his mouth set fast. He would not take that direction, to the darkness, to follow her. He walked towards the faintly humming, glowing town, quickly.

Lawrence's intense bias in favour of his mother, and his hatred of his father, were not strong enough to obliterate his sense of reality where the first and strongest impressions of his life were concerned. The reader receives a different impression from *Sons and Lovers* from that which Lawrence wished to convey. Mrs Morel, dying of cancer, does not emerge as her husband's victim, but as a person who has been devoured by her own maternal possessiveness and social ambitions. Her husband had attracted her physically, but as soon as that attraction is exhausted she makes him pay for her disappointed aspirations, social and intellectual, by turning him into the pariah of the home circle. With her sons she is equally ruthless, trying to centre their emotions on herself by her ceaseless self-pity, and struggling to monopolize their love at the expense not only of their father but also of the girls by whom they are attracted. Morel, jovial and loving, lacks his wife's force, tenacity and quick-wittedness, and is to that extent her inferior. He needs to be supported by affection, and as he receives nothing but contempt he loses his self-respect and, outlawed by his wife and children, retaliates by exaggerating the coarse habits which offend their gentility. The tragedy of Gertrude and Walter Morel is that all the will is on one side and all the heart on the other.

In the reminiscences of Lawrence by his sister, Mrs Ada Clarke, we get the same impression of Lawrence's parents as in *Sons and Lovers*; but although Mrs Clarke sides with her mother, whom she idolized for her lady-like behaviour and admired for her resourcefulness in keeping the home together on less than two pounds a week, she concedes that if the children had tried to interest themselves in the things for which their father cared, they would have been spared many unhappy and sordid scenes. Mrs Clarke gives a photograph of the family, taken when Lawrence was a small boy. Mrs Lawrence is in the centre, forcing a pained smile, and Lawrence is standing between her and her husband, who though in his best suit and on his best behaviour looks with his curling beard and friendly eyes as genial as the inauspicious circumstances will permit.

The photographs of Lawrence as a small boy, of which Aldous Huxley[1] gives one, and Middleton Murry[2] another, showing him with limp sausagey ringlets fresh from the curling-tongs, are of a spoilt fretful child, who excites more sympathy than dislike because of the wretched look in his eyes. If his mother's hatred of her husband had made her indifferent to Lawrence, he would at least have been free from her, but the effect of her hatred was to make her determined not to share him with her husband or any one else. She wished to keep him to herself, not to give him to the world, and so he was not fully born into life. There was an un-fledged look about him, the Miriam[3] of *Sons and Lovers* says, something incomplete. This grip of his mother's upon him, which he attributed to tenderness not to egotism, is reproduced by

[1] *The Letters of D. H. Lawrence.*   [2] *Son of Woman.*
[3] *D. H. Lawrence: A Personal Record by E. T.*

Lawrence in a scene at the beginning of *Sons and Lovers*. One afternoon, shortly after Paul was born, Mrs Morel went out with him, and seating herself looked down at the baby—

> She noticed the peculiar knitting of the baby's brows, and the peculiar heaviness of its eyes, as if it were trying to understand something that was pain. . . . She had not wanted this child to come, and there it lay in her arms and pulled at her heart. She felt as if the navel string that had connected its frail little body with hers had not been broken. She held it close to her face and breast. With all her force, with all her soul, she would make up to it for having brought it into the world unloved. She would love it all the more now it was here; carry it in her love.

The conflict set up in a child who is conceived and born in disharmony was peculiarly rending in Lawrence, because while his will repudiated his father absolutely, and attached itself fiercely to his mother, it was from his father that he inherited what was glowing and tender in his nature. The Dark Unconscious, the Dark God, the dark otherness, which he preached, was the prenatal state from which he had never fully emerged, and into which he longed to be absorbed again. With this craving the love of life inherited from his father fought a ceaseless battle, driving him all over the world in search of something to which he could attach himself, until at last he abandoned the fight and died. It is this search which is prefigured at the close of *Sons and Lovers*, when he turns from the darkness, and walks quickly towards the distant glowing town, impelled rather by revulsion from what lay behind than by any hope of what lay before.

The division in Lawrence's character appears in the first incident which he describes in the childhood of himself as Paul Morel. One day Paul accidentally broke Arabella, his sister Annie's doll, and was as miserable about it as she, but when they had both recovered he proposed that they should make a sacrifice of the doll. Though horrified, Annie gave her consent, and he drenched Arabella in paraffin—

So long as the stupid big doll burned he rejoiced in silence. At the end he poked among the embers with a stick, fished out the arms and legs, all blackened, and smashed them under the stones. 'That's the sacrifice of Missis Arabella,' he said. 'An' I'm glad there's nothing left of her.' Which disturbed Annie inwardly. . . . He seemed to hate the doll so intensely, because he had broken it.

In a somewhat later incident, Paul and his mother are worrying because Morel is late back, and again Paul's sympathy turns to rage, and he almost hates his mother for suffering because his father did not come home from work.

These quick changes of feeling went with a frail physique and unsubstantial frame. He had been a pale quiet baby, who sometimes had long crying fits, and as he grew older he was only happy under the wing of his mother or sister—'Paul was towed round at the heels of Annie, sharing her game. . . . He was quiet and not noticeable. But his sister adored him.' On fine winter evenings, after the colliers had gone home and the street was deserted, he used to go out with Annie and his little brother Arthur, to play with two or three friends, Annie sometimes sending them on ahead—

The children looked anxiously down the road at the one lamp-post, which stood at the end of the field path. If the little, luminous space were deserted, the two boys felt genuine desolation. They stood with their hands in their pockets under the lamp, turning their backs on the night, quite miserable, watching the dark houses. Suddenly a pinafore under a short coat was seen, and a long-legged girl came flying up. 'Where's Billy Pillins an' your Annie an' Eddie Dakin?'—'I don't know.' But it did not matter much—there were three now. They set up a game round the lamp-post, till the others rushed up. Then the play went fast and furious.

When he was fourteen, Paul went to work in Nottingham, in a factory which manufactured surgical appliances. His mother accompanied him to his first interview with his future employer, whom Paul at once hates. Afterwards his mother tells him he mustn't mind people so much—'They're not being disagreeable to *you*—it's their way. You always think people are meaning things for you. But they don't.' Paul kept himself apart from the men workers at the factory, who seemed to him common and dull, but the girls all took to him, often gathering in a little circle while he sat on a bench and held forth, 'so serious, yet so bright and jolly, and always so delicate in his way with them'.

A little later Paul and Miriam became friends, and it is with the story of their relationship that the second part of *Sons and Lovers* is chiefly concerned. Miriam has given her own account of this relationship in *D. H. Lawrence: A Personal Record*, a wonderful picture of Lawrence as a boy and young man, vivid in its details, and magnanimous and profound in its spirit.

It was on a day in early summer, Miriam narrates, that Lawrence first came to Hagg's Farm, where she lived with her parents and brothers. His mother was with him, and after Mrs Lawrence had greeted Miriam's mother, they sat down to an early tea before the rest of the family returned. Miriam had to go into the kitchen to boil eggs, and was surprised when the tall, fair boy followed her, and stood silently looking about him in a curious, intent way. After tea they all went out, and the two mothers moved away together, Mrs Lawrence talking with a tinge of patronage in her voice. Lawrence was silent with Miriam, they walked into a field, and Lawrence stood there quite still, as if fascinated by the view of the Annesley Hills and High Park wood, with the reservoir gleaming below. Miriam, who knew that he had been at the High School and had studied French and German, suddenly felt conscious of her own deficiencies, and to bring him down from his heights asked him abruptly how old he was—
'Fifteen.'
'I thought so. I'm fourteen. . . . You go to school?'
'Yes, to the High.'
A pause.
'I don't care for the name Bertie. It's a girlish name. Do they call you Bertie at school?'

'No, of course not. They call me Lawrence.'

'That's nicer, I think. I'd rather call you Lawrence.'

'Do call me Lawrence,' he replied quickly, 'I'd like it better.'

They returned to the farm, and Miriam, to show her indifference, put on her hat and cloak to visit a friend on the opposite side of the wood. Meeting her at the door, Lawrence exclaimed, 'Are you going out?' She told him where she was going, and he asked excitedly, 'How do you get there? Which way do you go?' and when she said through the wood, he echoed her eagerly, and nodded towards it.

After this visit Lawrence came out to the farm nearly every week, but he was slow at making friends with Miriam and her brothers, and found more in common with her father, who used to talk with him almost as though he were grown up. When the summer ended, Lawrence left school and went to work in Nottingham. His brother Ernest died in the late autumn, and a few weeks later he himself was dangerously ill. 'I don't know,' Miriam's mother said, 'whatever Mrs Lawrence will do if that son's taken from her. She told me when she was here with him that however much she loved Ernest it was nothing to what she felt for the one she brought with her.'

One day in early spring when Lawrence was convalescent, Miriam's father drove him out to the farm on the milk-float. He was pale and thin, but delighted to be with them again. From this time on he was almost one of the family, and once in later years said that in these days he was only happy when he was at the farm or on his way to it, and that his mother had told him he might as well pack his things and stay there for good.

Lawrence was extraordinarily kind and willing to help with whatever task was afoot. He was most considerate to mother, with her big, unruly family, so hard to manage, each of us at a different stage of development. . . . Several times when he came in and found her with more to do than she could get through he fetched water for the boiler, tidied up the hearth, and made a fire in the parlour. . . . I well remember a basket of tiny pickling onions that stood on the stone slab outside the back door, waiting to be peeled. They suddenly disappeared, and mother said that Bert had peeled them; he just sat down and did them without a word to any one. . . . It was the same at harvest-time. Lawrence would spend whole days working with my father and brothers in the fields at Greasely. These fields lay four miles away, and we used to pack a big basket of provisions to last all day, so that hay harvest had a picnic flavour. . . . I heard father say to mother: 'Work goes like fun when Bert's there, it's no trouble at all to keep them going.' . . . One could not help being affected by his vitality and charm. Mother made a remark that set me speculating. She said: 'I should like to be next to Bert in heaven.'

Miriam was discontented and rebellious at this time. She was the family drudge, and was humiliated by her lack of education. There were frequent quarrels with her brothers, who tried to order her about. She felt an Ishmael, with no one to understand and sympathize with her—

I did not know that Lawrence was aware of my state of mind, but one day he suddenly took an end of chalk from his pocket and wrote on the stable door: 'Nil desperandum.' 'What does it mean?' I asked, although I knew. 'Never despair,' he replied, with an enigmatic smile, and ran away.

Eventually Miriam was sent back to school, and became a pupil-teacher. She was happier now, and her friendship with Lawrence became more intimate. They often walked in the neighbouring wood, where there was hardly a flower or even weed whose name and qualities Lawrence did not know. At first Miriam was sceptical of his knowledge, and asked him how he could always be so certain. He knew, he answered. 'But *how* do you know? You may be wrong.'—'I know *because* I know. How dare you ask me how I know?' One day she took him to see a colony of tall foxgloves she had come across. They stood there like Red Indian braves, she said, but he ignored this fancy, and looked at the foxgloves with his usual intent glance.

He did not like growing up, and was most reluctant to begin shaving, to which he had to be forced by severe criticism. Lawrence, Miriam says, found the present so good he wanted it to last.

There were parties at one house or another during the holidays, and always thrilling charades at our house, with Lawrence directing things, and father joining in the play like one of us. Then towards midnight, to escort our friends through the Warren and over the dim field path, singing, with the stars flashing above the silent woods, and the pale light over the water, was perhaps the most wonderful bit of all. We seemed to be living in a world within a world, created out of the energy of the imagination.

Lawrence did not return to the warehouse in Nottingham after his illness; from seventeen till twenty-three he was training to be a teacher, and spent the last two years of this period at Nottingham University. It was from seventeen to twenty that he and Miriam were happiest together. They read all the same books, beginning with Louisa Alcott's *Little Women*, Rider Haggard and Anthony Hope, and passing on to Dickens, in whose David Copperfield Lawrence felt a great likeness to himself, Tennyson, George Eliot, Browning and Balzac. Lawrence was now beginning to realize that he was out of the ordinary, and he and Miriam used to discuss his future. 'Every great man.' he said to her, 'is founded in some woman. Why shouldn't *you* be the woman I am founded in?' He told her about Blake, how he made pictures and wrote poems that were interdependent, and did the painting and engraving himself, producing the book entirely by his own hands, and how his wife was a poor girl whom he taught to read and also to print and engrave, and what a marvellous helpmate she was to him—'For a little time we lived with Blake and his wife.' A man with special gifts, he said, must share them with others, and perhaps he might have a big house, with gardens and terraces, like the ones in the Park, and they could all live there together. 'Wouldn't it be fine . . . mother and all the people we like together? Wouldn't it be fine?' Miriam doubted whether a number of people all living in the same house would agree, and Lawrence was vexed. 'It *would* be all right, I'm sure it would. People aren't really bad, not when you get to know them.'

On Friday evenings she used to visit his home for French lessons, and when the door closed behind Mrs Lawrence, going marketing, they had a magical sense of being alone together, and often put the lesson aside to talk of other things. Once they discussed the differences in their characters, and Lawrence said Miriam was high and very deep, whereas he was very broad and comparatively shallow—'Your impulse,' he said, 'is to go higher and higher, towards perfection, and mine is to go forward, on and on, for æons and æons.'—'What is an æon?'—'Time past all reckoning. Beyond for ever and for ever,' he replied with shining eyes.

The turning-point in their relations came when Lawrence was twenty. On Easter Sunday Miriam went with him to his home after chapel. His mother and eldest sister, Emily, were in the house, and Miriam felt as always their hostility to her. Emily, who was married, asked Lawrence petulantly when he was coming to see her, and Lawrence, with a quick smile at Miriam, replied, 'Jamais', adding, when Emily asked what he meant, 'Oh, I'll come some time.' Lawrence left with Miriam, and as they parted leant towards her and said, 'I shall come up to-morrow—early.'

Miriam expected him about midday, but it was late in the afternoon before he arrived, and he avoided her glance. After tea they read French together for a short time, then he closed the book, and in a strained voice began to discuss their friendship— 'Is it keeping even. . . . Is it getting out of balance, do you think?' Miriam said she did not know what he meant. 'I was afraid,' he went on, with difficulty, 'that the balance might be going down on your side. You might, I thought, I don't know, you might be getting to care too much for me.' Miriam in deep dismay asked why he was saying this, and he replied that his mother and Emily had been talking about them the previous evening, and agreed they ought either to be engaged or not go about together. 'Ah I, always thought your mother didn't like me,' Miriam said, but Lawrence denied this eagerly—'It's for your sake she spoke. She says . . . I may be preventing you from getting some one else.' He paused, and went on with an effort—'She says I ought to know how I feel. I've looked into my heart and I cannot feel that I love you as a husband should his wife. Perhaps I shall, in time. If ever I find I do, I'll tell you. What about you? If you think you love me, tell me, and we'll be engaged. What do you think?'

'I was conscious of a fierce pain, of the body as well as the spirit,' Miriam says. 'As clearly as if in actuality I saw the golden apple of life that had been lying at my finger-tips recede irretrievably.

She could not speak for some time, but when she had collected herself she said that they must not meet again. Lawrence protested vehemently—'We can't give it all up. There's the question of writing, we want to talk about that. And there's the French. . . .' They could go on reading in the house, he said, where the others could see them. They could still go to chapel together—that was important; and the youngsters could accompany them on their walks. Miriam, who perceived that he had come up with this plan of chaperonage all worked out, did not answer, and after a pause Lawrence asked her if she would tell her mother. It had nothing to do with her mother, Miriam said, and added, 'I manage my own affairs.'

In all that he had said one sentence alone had significance for me—the words . . . 'I have looked into my heart and I cannot find that I love you as a husband should love his wife.' . . . I was too ignorant and unacquainted with life to understand that Lawrence used the word 'love' in a restricted and special sense. I understood the word only in its total application. . . . My instinct was to break off completely.

Lawrence would not give her up, and the routine of their friendship was soon re-established, but the old naturalness was gone. He became very critical of her, and was irritated if she stooped to touch a flower, or took her little brother in her arms and hugged him—'Why must you *touch* in order to enjoy? What you need to cultivate is detachment.' She felt that he was trying to turn her into an abstraction, so that their friendship might continue without emotional eddies, but she realized that he was even more tormented than herself, for she was consoled by her love for him, and was not racked by a divided nature.

The deepest cause of Lawrence's exasperation can be inferred at various points of Miriam's narrative. Now that he was passing out of adolescence into early manhood he wanted to be reassured about his physical attractiveness and to be relieved from his growing fear that he did not feel as normally about women as the other young men he knew. When she touched a flower or hugged her little brother, it seemed a reflection on himself, with whom she appeared content to share only intellectual pleasures. In his resentment he put the blame for the nature of their relationship entirely on her. She was too introspective and intense, he said; she was unlikeable owing to her intense self-absorption, she had no sense of humour, and, above all, she was absolutely lacking in sexual attraction. It was useless to try to divert him from this dismembering of herself, which exhausted her and made her intensely wretched—'I would often wake with a start just before dawn when the air was filled with the unearthly twitterings of the birds, and, realizing instantly the blight that had settled on my life, feel like a castaway on some inhuman shore.'

On her twenty-first birthday Lawrence wrote her a long letter in which he said that it was not the kissable and embraceable part of her that attracted him, although it was so fine with the silken toss of hair curling over her ears. She was a nun to him, and he gave her what he would give a holy nun, but she must let him marry a woman he could kiss and embrace and make the mother of his children. Love, he explained, when they discussed this letter, was divided into physical love and spiritual love. His love for her was spiritual, but for marriage physical love was the prime necessity. 'Most men marry in the animal way—at least nearly all men of intellect do,' he said, and told her that he had found a girl who would satisfy his physical needs, which he implied were strong. 'Quant a moi,' he wrote about this time in the French diary Miriam kept, 'je suis grand animal', and when she was puzzled by this claim he insisted—'Yes, yes, I *am*.'

It was in Schopenhauer's essay on sex he had found the view that men of intellect marry from a purely sensual impulse. As his doubts about his sexual nature increased, he was driven increasingly towards materialism as a refuge from the sense of his own fragility, and swallowed Huxley and Haeckel with an avidity which Miriam saw to be out of accord with his real sympathies.

There were still times when they were happy together. Lawrence brought her his first experiments in writing, and she would tell him whether his characters were developing naturally, and if their talk was lifelike. Sometimes his love for her would flash out with the old spontaneity. She used to spend her annual holiday with the Lawrences on the Lincolnshire coast. One morning it was windy, and she tied her hat on with a broad silk scarf—

> Lawrence was looking at me with shining eyes. 'Does it suit me?' I asked, laughing. He turned to his mother. 'Look at her, mother. She says, does it suit her?' His mother gave me a bitter glance, and turned away, and the light died out of Lawrence's face.

That evening he and Miriam walked by the sea, and as the moon rose Lawrence broke into wild reproaches, upbraiding her bitterly, and then blaming himself still more passionately. Two summers later, when they were again by the sea, he had a still wilder outburst, skipping from boulder to boulder in a frenzy which almost made her doubt if he were human—'I was really frightened then —not physically, but deep in my soul. He created an atmosphere not of death, which after all is part of mortality, but of an utter negation of life, as though he had become dehumanized.'

In the autumn of 1908, when he was twenty-three, Lawrence left Eastwood for Croydon, where he had been given a post at the Davidson Road School. His mother resented him going away— 'And where,' she exclaimed fiercely to Miriam, 'would he have been without me to call him up in the morning, and have his porridge and everything ready for him? He'd never have got off to College every day if I hadn't seen to things.' Lawrence went out

to the farm to say good-bye, and after supper Miriam accompanied him to the beginning of the field path along which he used to
come to the farm—' "La dernière fois," he said, inclining his head
towards the farm and the wood. I burst into tears, and he put his
arms round me. He kissed me and stroked my cheek, murmuring,
"I'm so sorry, so sorry, so sorry." '

On his second day in Croydon Lawrence wrote Miriam a letter
which was 'like a howl of terror'. How could he live away from
them all?—he dreaded morning and the school with the anguish of
a sick girl—he would grow into something black and ugly, cut off
from them all, like some loathsome bird. In a postscript he told her
not to say anything of this to his mother, to whom he had written
that everything was all right, and that he was getting on well.
After a week or two his letters became calmer, he began to
explore London, and wrote to Miriam about the lights that flowered when darkness came. He liked the family he was living with,
a Lancashire man and his wife, with two children, one a baby a
few months old, whom he sometimes sang to sleep. 'I was glad
when I knew there was a baby,' Mrs Lawrence said to Miriam.
'It will keep him pure.'

Lawrence was now writing poems, which he sent to Miriam,
and in the June of 1909 she selected some of them, and with
Lawrence's permission sent them to the editor of the *English
Review*, Ford Madox Hueffer, saying that the author was a young
man who had been writing for a number of years, and would be
grateful for any recognition. Hueffer replied with an invitation to
Lawrence to come and see him, and in September Lawrence called
on him, and found him 'fairish, fat, about forty, and the kindest
man on earth'.

A little later Miriam went up to London to see Lawrence, who
wanted to discuss his literary projects with her, and to show her a
girl he was thinking of marrying. Miriam knew of her already, for
in an earlier letter Lawrence had written—'It is snowing; and I
ought to be out on Wimbledon Common with a girl, a teacher
here . . . I have almost made up my mind to marry her. I think I
shall. I am almost sure I shall.' Miriam stayed the night with the
family where Lawrence was living, and she and Lawrence sat in

the parlour after the others had gone to bed. She was tired, having left home at six in the morning, and it was now one, but he pressed her to remain a little longer. She consented, and he began by asking her in a very earnest tone what she expected from life, what she hoped for. She didn't hope for anything much, she replied, bending her head, while her tears fell into her lap, but she would get along somehow. He looked hard at her, and went on to say what a terrible strain he found the new life, the excitement, and the meeting with such different people. He needed to be married, it was so difficult to bear the stress of life alone. 'You know,' he said softly, 'I could so easily peg out.'—'Well,' Miriam replied, 'you have only to make a choice.' He reflected on this for a time, and then said that he had no money, and wouldn't be able to marry for ever so long—'I think I shall ask some girl if she will give me . . . that . . . without marriage. Do you think any girl would?'—''I don't know,' Miriam answered. 'The kind of girl who would I think you wouldn't like.'—'Would you think it wrong?'—'No, I wouldn't think it wrong. But all the girls I know would.'—'But *you* wouldn't?' he insisted, and she replied, 'Not *wrong*. But it would be very difficult.' After a pause he said he thought he would ask the girl of whom he had told her, and there was another silence, which she broke at last by saying that it was two o'clock, and she was really tired now. 'It's two o'clock,' he repeated, 'it's two o'clock. *Must* you go to bed?' She said she must, and rose. 'Very well. I'll let you go. You shall go.'

The next morning Lawrence introduced her to his friend, a girl with auburn hair, who talked to Lawrence rather like an elder sister, to which Lawrence responded with an air of bravado, covering a lack of self-confidence. The girl greeted Miriam warmly, pinning a spray of red berries in her coat, and left them after Lawrence had fixed a date for their next meeting. Lawrence and Miriam went up to town, where they lunched with Violet Hunt and Hueffer, and Hueffer walked with them part of the way to King's Cross. He was kind and sympathetic, and Miriam was touched by the interest he showed in them both, but when he left them Lawrence exclaimed, 'Isn't he fat, and doesn't he walk slow! He says he walks about London two hours every day to keep his fat down. But he won't keep much down if he always walks at that pace.'

Shortly after Miriam's return from London, Lawrence sent her a short peom, 'Aware', in which he compared her to the moon rising out of a mist—

. . . . and I in amaze
See in the sky before me, a woman I did not know
I loved, but there she goes, and her beauty hurts my heart;
I follow her down the night, begging her not to depart.

When he came home at Christmas he told her that he had given up the idea of marrying the girl at Croydon, and that everything was over between them. He loved Miriam, he had been mistaken all these years about his feelings, and now realized that he must have loved her all along without knowing it. They must be engaged, but must keep it secret for the present. In spite of her desire to believe in this declaration and in the poem, Miriam felt in both the forced note always present in his attempts to resolve his internal conflict. She consented to the engagement, however, and for a short time Lawrence, who was revising *The White Peacock*, his first novel, was more tranquil than he had been for some years. He had occasionally in the past been remorseful over taking up so much of Miriam's time, but now he felt that she would fulfil her destiny in marriage with him, and said to her one day during the Easter holidays that he was doubtful if she would ever be a writer—'You have a *wonderful* sympathy, and that's perhaps your gift. I think God intended you to make a *good* wife—and not much more. Do you mind?' Miriam replied that she was well content, but a week or two later he wrote from Croydon to tell her about a school-teacher with whom he had begun an affair, and who was to be the heroine of his second novel. He dashed off this novel, *The Trespasser*, between the Whit-suntide and midsummer of 1910, and wrote to Miriam that she must not attempt to hold him—'I need Helen (the heroine of the novel), but I must *always* return to you, only you must always leave me free.'

They discussed the situation when he came home in August—

I could not move from my old standpoint of all or nothing, even when Lawrence said, 'Then I am afraid it must be nothing.' We agreed not even to correspond. Within a week there came an importunate note from him; '*Do* read Barrie's *Sentimental Tommy* and *Tommy and Grizel*. I've just had them out of the library here. They'll help you to understand how it is with me. I'm in exactly the same predicament.'

His mother fell ill before the end of the holidays, and he came from Croydon on alternate week-ends to see her. Miriam and he met occasionally, but she could not pierce the absorption of his misery; he seemed completely shut off in his grief. On the day before his mother's funeral, he sent for her, and they went for a walk. It was a grey December day, they hardly spoke and at last remained standing in silence by a railway track leading down to the pits.

'You know,' Lawrence said suddenly, speaking with great difficulty, 'I've always loved my mother.'

'I know you have,' Miriam replied.

'I don't mean that,' he returned quickly. 'I've *loved* her, like a lover. That's why I could never love you.'

During the year which followed his mother's death, Lawrence and Miriam met only three or four times. He was lost and miserable, without any direction in life—

I am not strong like you [he wrote to Miriam]. You can fight your battle and have done with it, but I *have* to run away, or I couldn't bear things. I have to fight a bit, and then run away, and then fight a bit more. So I really do go on fighting, only it has to be at intervals. . . . At times I am afflicted by a perversity amounting to minor insanity. But the best man in me belongs to you. One me is yours, a fine, strong one . . . I have great faith still that things will come right in the end.

His mother's hold on him seemed to Miriam to have been strengthened by her death, and in the hope that if he could be made to see how it had worked against his happiness he might shake it off, she sent him an account of the day, five years earlier, when he told her he did not love her as a husand should love his wife. In an agonized reply, he wrote, 'They tore you from me, the love of my life. . . . It was the slaughter of the fœtus in the womb', but her effort had no other effect, and he continued his friendship with Helen of *The Trespasser*, and a lackadaisical engagement to a woman who lived near his home. Some months later, he met Miriam and they had a long talk. His engagement was over, he said, and he asked her whether, if they married, she would expect him to stay at home. Home, she said, was the place one works in, but he replied that he didn't want a home, he wanted to be free, and would probably go abroad, down the Rhine, and then farther afield. 'I saw his utter loneliness,' Miriam writes, 'his separation, as it seemed, from everything else in life; and, as always, I was overcome with pity. I slipped my hand into his that was hanging limp.'

It was this meeting that Lawrence commemorated in 'After Many Days'—

> Long have I waited, never once confessed,
> Even to myself, how bitter the separation:
> Now, being come again, how make the best
>   Reparation?
> If I could cast this clothing off from me,
> If I could lift my naked soul to you,
> Or if only you would repulse me. . . .
>
> But that you hold me still so kindly cold
> Aloof, my flaming heart will not allow;
> Yea, but I loathe you that you should withhold
>   Your greeting now.

Lawrence was now rewriting *Sons and Lovers*. In its first form it had been stilted and unreal, and Miriam, partly for the sake of the book and partly in the hope of freeing him from his obsession with his mother, advised him to write it again, and keep it true to life. As he revised it, he sent her the manuscript, and they met fairly often, for he was on sick leave from Croydon after a severe illness, and was doubtful if he would go back. The simple vivid earlier pages delighted her, but

> the break came in the treatment of Miriam. . . . I had not doubted that he would work the problem out with integrity. But he burked the real issue. . . . His mother had to be supreme, and for the sake of that supremacy every disloyalty was permissible.

Lawrence asked for her comments, but she would not give them, they ceased to meet, and he sent her the manuscript by post, as he wrote it.

The years of happiness, when they were both in their teens, are slurred over in *Sons and Lovers*, and Lawrence's love for the farm which was so long the centre of his life comes out only in two or three passages, in one of which he writes—

> The farm had originally been a labourer's cottage. And the farmhouse was old and battered. But Paul loved it—loved the sack-bag that formed the hearthrug, and the funny little corner under the stairs, and the small window deep in the corner, through which, bending a little, he could see the plum-trees in the backgarden and the lovely round hills beyond.

Miriam, when she first appears, is shy with Paul. She looks after the pigs, and this makes her ashamed, for she is a great reader, living in a dream of herself as a heroine of romance, and is afraid that Paul, 'who looked something like a Walter Scott hero', might see her simply as a swine-girl, and not divine the princess beneath. Like Paul, who shrank from the common men at the warehouse, Miriam 'quivered in anguish from the vulgarity of the other choir-girls'. Paul attracts her—

> On the whole, she scorned the male sex. But here was a new specimen, quick, light, graceful, who could be gentle and who

could be sad, and who was clever, and who knew a lot. . . .
Yet she tried hard to scorn him, because he would not see in
her the princess but only the swine-girl. And he scarcely
observed her.

Lawrence passes quickly to that stage in their intimacy when he
became savagely critical of her—'Her intensity . . . irritated the
youth into a frenzy. . . . He was used to his mother's reserve. And
on such occasions he was thankful in his heart and soul that he had
his mother, so sane and wholesome.' All Miriam's life, he says,
was in her eyes. Her body was not flexible and living, the life
which shone in her eyes did not flow into her limbs and body.
Very occasionally the bitterness with which he pursues her
throughout the book vanishes, and he reveals the feeling which
drew them together over so many years. He tells how in chapel
on Sunday evening he used to wait for her to appear—

He was anxious for fear she would not come: it was so far,
and there were so many rainy Sundays. Then, often very late
indeed, she came in, with her long stride, her head bowed. . . .
Her face, as she sat opposite, was always in shadow. But it gave
him a very keen feeling, as if all his soul stirred within him, to
see her there. It was not the same glow, happiness, and pride,
that he felt in having his mother in charge: something more
wonderful, less human, and tinged to intensity by a pain, as if
there were something he could not get to.

The same feeling used to overpower him when he was taking her
home at night, and they stood and watched the constellations, and
especially Orion, gazing at him in these 'strange surcharged hours,
until they seemed themselves to live in every one of his stars'. On
his way home, after leaving her, he would have a violent revulsion
against her—

Why did his mother sit at home and suffer? He knew she
suffered badly. . . . And why did he hate Miriam, and feel so
cruel towards her, at the thought of his mother. If Miriam
caused his mother suffering, then he hated her—and he easily

D

hated her. Why did she make him feel as if he were uncertain of himself, insecure, an indefinite thing, as if he had not sufficient sheathing to prevent the night and the space breaking into him? How he hated her! And then, what a rush of tenderness and humility!

She made him feel so spiritual, he once complained, 'and I don't want to feel spiritual!' The 'blanched and chaste fashion' in which their friendship progressed hurt his vanity. He wanted her to recognize the male in him, he simmered while they 'read Balzac, and did composition, and felt highly cultured', and frequently broke into rages, in one of which he threw his pencil in her face, exasperated by its eager, silent, almost blind look. She made him feel insubstantial, obscurely contemptuous of himself, and so his hostility to her deepened, and sometimes when he visited her there was 'a cold correctness' in the way he put his bicycle in its place which made her heart sink—'She knew him well by now, and could tell from that keen-looking, aloof young body of his what was happening inside him.' On these occasions he turned to Miriam's mother to have his pride salved. She 'did him the great kindness of treating him almost with reverence'. He would be gentle and humble with her, and 'could have wept with gratitude that she was deferential to him'. If the mother was not about there was Miriam's eldest brother, with whom for a time he was very friendly.

In the last part of *Sons and Lovers* Lawrence invented freely in order to soothe the vanity which Miriam had wounded. He had been too afraid of his mother to marry Miriam, and of Miriam to ask her to be his mistress. Their talk at Croydon shows that he desired this in his fitful undetermined way, and in one of his poems he writes—

> I wonder if only
> You had taken me then, how different
> Life would have been? Should I have spent
> Myself in anger, and you have bent
> Your head through being lonely?

What he could not obtain in reality, he imagined in *Sons and Lovers*. From a brief affair with Miriam, Paul passes to another woman, Clara Dawes, who has a strong form that seems to slumber with power. Paul loves her for 'being so luxuriously heavy, yet so quick. Himself was light; she went with a beautiful rush'. This affair also fades out, and the book closes with a final parting from Miriam, because she cannot 'take him and relieve him of the responsibility of himself'.

The shock of *Sons and Lovers*, Miriam says, gave the death-blow to their friendship—'I had a strange feeling of separation from the body. The daily life was sheer illusion. The only reality was the betrayal of *Sons and Lovers*.' What hurt her most was that he had left out altogether the years of devotion to the development of his genius, 'a devotion that had been pure joy'.

What else but the devotion to a common end had held us together against his mother's repeated assaults? . . . The one gleam of light was the realization that Lawrence had overstated his case; that some day his epic of maternal love and filial devotion would be viewed from another angle, that of his own final despair.

After Miriam had finished the manuscript, Lawrence tried to find out what she thought of it, and it was finally arranged that he should meet her at the house of her married sister. Miriam and he went for a short walk. It was a day in March, and Lawrence kept a sharp lookout for violets in the hedgerows. He said there must be some about because his sister had seen youths coming home from the pit with bunches of violets and celandines in their hands.

At the mention of violets and celandines I had hard work to keep the tears back. . . . Until then his manner had been bleak and forbidding, but now he softened a little and said almost wistfully, 'I thought perhaps you would have something to say about the writing.' I felt as if I was sinking in deep water. But...

the time for speaking had gone by, and I merely replied, 'I've put some notes in with the manuscript', and he replied quietly, as though he was suddenly out of breath, 'Oh, all right. I thought you might like to say something. That's all.'

They returned, and at tea Lawrence's manner was much easier, but after Miriam had gone, he said to her sister, 'She's wild with me, isn't she? She's angry about something', and he would not accept the sister's denial, insisting, 'She is, she's angry. Hasn't she told you about it?'

Some weeks later, on the last Sunday in April, 1912, Miriam and Lawrence met for the last time, at her sister's cottage, where Lawrence was spending the week-end. Miriam's father was with her, and after tea Lawrence drove part of the way with them, but there was little talk, and Miriam noticed that he winced at her father's casual tone, so different from the warmth of old days. Lawrence, who had met his future wife, Mrs Frieda Weekley, some weeks earlier, and was now about to leave England with her, mentioned that he was going to Germany in a few days.

On the level above Watnall Hill he got out of the trap to return by the footpath over the fields. We shook hands and said good-bye like casual acquaintances, and father hoped he would manage to keep in better health. . . . Before we disappeared round a bend in the road I turned and saw him still standing where he had alighted, looking after us. I waved my hand and he raised his hat with the familiar gesture. I never saw him again.

Lawrence returned to the cottage. He was subdued during the midday meal, but in the afternoon, as he and Miriam's brother-in-law were lying out in the field on rugs, he suddenly exclaimed, 'Bill, I like a *gushing* woman.'

In the spring of the following year, Lawrence sent Miriam his first book of poems through the publisher. She replied, and a little later received a bulky parcel containing the proof-sheets of *Sons and Lovers*, and a letter in which Lawrence said—

This last year hasn't been all roses for me. I've had my ups and downs with Frieda. But we mean to marry as soon as the divorce is through. . . . Frieda and I discuss you endlessly. We should like you to come out to us some time, if you would care to. . . .

After Miriam had read the letter, she looked at the proofs to see if he had softened or cut out any of the worst passages, but he had changed nothing. After long hesitation and with some misgiving, Miriam decided to return the proofs and the letter—'I thought it was just possible that he would write and say he hadn't meant to be so stupid. But he never wrote to me again, and I never really wished him to, nor did I ever write to him.'

During the ten years with Miriam, Lawrence was fighting to integrate his nature, so that he might be able to develop the genius which he felt he possessed. But his mother's will, imposed on him before he was born, proved too strong for the imaginative and spiritual element to which Miriam appealed, as it had previously proved too strong for the tenderness he inherited from his father. The spell which his mother exercised over him was not the physical one he pretended to Miriam when he said he had loved his mother like a lover. That was an attempt to lay his doubts about his claim to be 'grand animal'. His subjection to his mother was less melodramatic and far deeper. He needed her to protect him against the fear which overwhelmed him when he rose above the will into the imagination. She had wrapped him round in her will, and Miriam took the wrappings off, and so his need of Miriam was always followed by a recoil of fear—'Why did she make him feel uncertain of himself, insecure, an indefinite thing, as if he had not sufficient sheathing to prevent the night and the space breaking into him?' Miriam describes the same recoil—

There were moments, too, in our desperate struggle, when we seemed to touch another sphere of existence, and it flashed upon me that never here in this life, but somewhere beyond the human bourne lay the unity we were striving for. He perhaps felt something similar, because he once exclaimed, 'You push me beyond the very bounds of human consciousness.'

Unable to develop normally, he needed a woman who could give him at least a momentary sense of being her lover, while really restoring to him some of the security he had felt when he rested without consciousness in his mother's womb.

From

Frank Harris

(1932)

Wales or Galway?

IN THE THREE or four years before the first world war, Dan Rider's bookshop, off St. Martin's Lane, used to be a meeting-place for a number of writers, painters, and journalists: Joseph Simpson, Lovat Fraser, Middleton Murry, Haldane Macfall, Holbrook Jackson, and others. One afternoon, in the middle of June 1912, about half a dozen of us were in Dan's inner room, waiting for Frank Harris, who had just returned from Nice. Middleton Murry had brought Katherine Mansfield with him to introduce her to Harris, whose books she had been reading with Murry during the spring. Although only in the early twenties, Murry had already founded a literary and artistic monthly, *Rhythm*, and was publishing an article on Harris in the July number. Harris had, I think, already seen this article in proof; or at any rate knew its general contents.

'To re-create this soul,' Murry wrote of Harris's work on Shakespeare, 'was one of the highest tasks that a great artist could undertake. To achieve where Coleridge and Goethe failed needed a man on a spiritual equality with William Shakespeare, perhaps without the supreme poetic gift, yet for intellect and power of divination his spiritual equal. . . . Who is the man who has done this thing? This man is Frank Harris, acknowledged by all the great men of letters of his time to be greater than they; accepted by artists as their superior, unknown to the vast British public, greater than his contemporaries because he is a master of life.'

Elsewhere in this article, Murry placed Harris's short stories, *Montes the Matador*, *Sonia*, and *The Miracle of the Stigmata* 'among the supreme creations of art.'

Our talk, as we waited for Harris, was desultory, like the talk on the battlements of Elsinore before the arrival of Hamlet's full-throated father. A stir in the outer room of the shop, a movement of the air such as precedes an avalanche, and Frank Harris was with us. In his hand he brandished the June number of *Rhythm*. 'Good God, Murry!' he roared. 'What have you done here?'

'What is it, Frank? What have I . . .?' Murry rose to his feet, very pale.

'Listen to this!' Harris laid the paper on the table and turned the leaves over with rapid, scornful jerks. 'Listen, all of you! "James Stephens is the greatest poet of our day. With this book he has stepped at once into the company of those whom we consider the greatest poets the world has ever known. Henceforward,"— listen to this, the lot of you!—"henceforward James Stephens stands with Sappho, Catullus, Shakespeare . . ." Pah!'

'But, Frankie . . .'

'You wrote this, eh?'

'Yes . . . but . . .'

Harris placed his finger on a passage, quoted by Murry as better than Milton, in which God tells how he——

'threw down the sky
And stamped upon it, buffeted a star
With my great fist, and flung the sun afar.'

'God's great fist!' Harris roared. 'And you call this better than Milton! You, Murry, put this drivel above *Paradise Lost*!'

Most of those present knew that the next number of *Rhythm* contained Murry's comparison of Harris and Shakespeare. His terrible situation moved our pity, we were conscious of Katherine Mansfield's sharp brown eyes staring at Harris, but none of us ventured to intervene except Kenneth Hare, who could be heard through the thunder of Harris's scorn supporting Murry's faltering plea for this and that quotation.

On the table lay the contents bill of the July number of *Rhythm*, headed by the article on Harris: 'Who is the Man?' Harris picked it up and read out the first three items:

'Who is the Man?'
'Drawing.'
'The Shirt.'

'The Shirt!' he repeated, and threw the bill down with a laugh. 'Drawing of a man in a shirt, eh? By God, Murry, this paper of yours is going to make a stir,' and he was beginning to improvise in Rabelaisian vein on the man in the shirt when Murry burst into tears and ran out of the shop.

'Good God!' Harris stared round in amazement.

'Oh, he'll kill himself!' Katherine Mansfield cried, and rushed after Murry.

'What the . . .?' Harris gasped.

'That's Katherine Mansfield,' I said.

'Katherine Mansfield!' He struck his brow with his hand. 'Katherine Mansfield!' He turned to Harold Weston: 'I thought she was a girl of yours.'

Weston shook his head modestly.

'Why didn't any of you tell me?'

There was a long silence, and my next memory is of Harris and myself outside the shop.

'Go and bring them back, Lunn,'[1] he was saying. 'Tell them I am infinitely sorry. I would not have had this happen for worlds.' His hand went to his waistcoat pocket. 'Take a taxi both ways.' He pressed two coins into my hand—pennies, but the moment was too tense for trivial adjustments. 'Both ways, Lunn,' he repeated, and went back into Dan's.

Katherine Mansfield and Murry were sitting opposite one another on either side of the fireplace in their Gray's Inn Road flat. They had been crying, but were now composed.

'Harris is awfully sorry,' I said. 'It was just his . . . you know. He wants you to come back. He sent me in a taxi.'

They shook their heads. 'He's wonderful, wonderful!' Murry sighed. 'But . . . No, not just yet. Not to-day.'

'Not to-day,' Katherine Mansfield echoed.

'He'll be awfully worried if you don't. He was frightfully

[1] Hugh Kingsmill Lunn

upset. It was just his ... he didn't mean it. You know how carried away he gets. I've never seen him so upset....'

They rose, and we returned to Dan's. Harris and Katherine Mansfield were introduced, Weston, in the general exhaustion, produced one of his plays and read it out, and afterwards Harris took Katherine Mansfield, Murry and me to the Café Royal, where I left them in friendly but relatively subdued talk.

'Who is the Man?' duly appeared in the next number of *Rhythm*. Harris, Murry wrote at the end of the article, was 'a man whose word of praise can change the whole of life for me for months, and a word of condemnation make me cry till I think my heart would break. Even if *Rhythm* achieves nothing else that is ultimately permanent, it shall be rescued from oblivion by this alone, that it told the truth about Frank Harris.'

Frank Harris was fifty-seven at this time. His two books on Shakespeare and his anarchist novel, *The Bomb*, had not long been published; his *Oscar Wilde* was in manuscript; he was writing short stories and portraits of his contemporaries in the *English Review*, and a number of young enthusiasts were beginning to collect round him. Everything was in his favour, except himself; and the exception, as always, ruined his chances. In Murry, whose enthusiasm did not long survive the incident just recorded, Harris lost the most valuable of his youthful disciples, and the others were alienated in turn. Within two years of Murry's welcome of him as Shakespeare's spiritual peer, Harris was in exile in France as an undischarged bankrupt. The advance of the German armies drove him from Paris, and at sixty he found himself in New York again, with little more sense of direction or knowledge of what would happen to him next than when he first landed there, a fourteen-year-old runaway from an English school.

Harris was born on the 14th of February 1855, according to his autobiography, which was written in his old age, and a year later, according to his statement in *Who's Who*. Precision on this point, as on all other points where Harris is our sole authority, is impossible, for in writing about himself he touched nothing which he did not adorn. His autobiography, though valuable as a self-revelation, is far more unreliable about facts even than his earlier books and talk. It was written between ten and fifteen years after I knew him, and contains several incidents which he had told me in a more convincing form. I have preferred any authority to it, but have been compelled to use it from time to time for his earlier years.

Harris himself, in the second volume of the autobiography, confides to the reader that often a story told him by someone would lie dormant for years, and then suddenly re-emerge as his own experience; and he would tell it as if he had been present, and fill it with dramatic effects far beyond the original narration.

Whether he was born in 1855 or 1856 is unimportant. Miss Kate Stephens, who knew him in his youth, suggests that he may have been born as early as 1852. I have therefore chosen 1855 as a compromise. More important is the doubt about his birthplace. He gives Galway in his autobiography, and says that he passed his first twelve years in Ireland. But when he entered the University of Kansas in 1874, he registered himself as James F. Harris, Tenby, Wales. Yet Tenby is mentioned only once in his autobiography; he visited his father and sister there in his early twenties, he tells us. The mystery of his birthplace connects itself with the mystery of his race. Sometimes he spoke of himself as an Irishman, sometimes as a Welsh-Celt, and frequently, while expressing his admiration for the Jews, denied that he was one himself. If he was, as seems probable from various indications, of mixed Welsh and Jewish blood, his desire to pass for a pure Celt would make him anxious to conceal his birthplace, and choose another, as far removed from Tenby as was possible within the confines of the United Kingdom.

Whatever the truth about his race and place of birth, there can be no question that he was sensitive about his social position. Shortly before the war he wrote an autobiographical novel, *Great Days*, the scene of which is laid in England and France in the age of Napoleon. The hero, Jack, the son of an innkeeper and smuggler, is ashamed when he has to accompany his father to chapel, instead of to the church where the gentry go; and his shame is intensified when his father puts on a skullcap during the service. In his autobiography Harris is less candid. He speaks of his father as in the Navy, a lieutenant in command of a revenue cutter or gunboat, and assigns the affair of the skullcap to an old Methodist he once stayed with in Belfast. The old man used to force him to go to chapel, and would put on a skullcap during the service, to the shame and loathing of young Harris. It seems probable that he has here transformed his middle-aged Jewish father, covering his head in a synagogue, into a Methodist acquaintance old enough to justify the use of a skullcap in a chapel.

Whether a Jew or a Welshman, the elder Harris was a remarkable man. His son often spoke of him and always with admiration for his force and courage, modified by a vivid memory of the fear his temper had inspired. 'I did not get to know and like him,' Harris once said, 'until I came back from America, and could meet him as an equal. He was a Puritan of the Puritans, was indeed rigorously faithful to my mother, but I told him women, and lots of 'em, were a necessity to me. He simply nodded. A great man!'

Only on one occasion, during my acquaintance with him, did Harris speak of his father as an officer of the Royal Navy. 'A fellow,' he growled, 'once addressed me on an envelope as "Mr Frank Harris." I told him my father was a naval captain, and that I was therefore entitled to the "esquire." '

Harris's mother, the daughter of a Baptist minister, according to the Tobin-Gertz *Life*,[1] died when he was three. He always spoke of her as an infinitely gentle and lovable woman, nor did the fact that she died in his infancy prevent him from attaching great importance to the perfect relations which had existed between them. They appeared to him typical of the close bond which he supposed to exist between a mother and a son of genius. In his novel, *The Bomb*, the anarchist hero, Lingg, adores his mother. In *Great Days* the republican idealist, de Vinzel, says to Jack: 'Whatever I am, or whatever I may become, I owe to

[1] *Frank Harris*, by A. I. Tobin and Elmer Gertz. An American study based on a great deal of research, and full of interesting stories.

my mother,' adding a little later that, in spite of his mother's care and teaching, he began at sixteen to think for himself, and soon came to doubt everything his mother had taught him. Even in Shakespeare, who makes Hamlet exclaim: 'O wonderful son, that can so astonish a mother!' Harris divines a son who loved his mother, the confidante of his dreams and ambitions in boyhood. No man in the world, Harris insists, owed more to his mother than Shakespeare, who, according to Harris, was thinking of her when Coriolanus calls Volumnia 'The most noble mother of the world.' With Jesus, Harris is embarrassed by the estrangement between mother and son suggested in the Gospel narrative, but, in compensation, he makes Jesus say, in *The Miracle of the Stigmata*: 'Oh, Judith, if I had to live my life over again, I don't think I should act in the same way. I must have hurt my mother, and it seems to me now that the higher love ought to include the lower and not exclude it.'

The most convincing touch in Harris's account of his early years is when he says that, unlike Rousseau, he certainly loved no one as a boy. A story he gives of himself at the age of four supports this claim. Having surprised his nurse in bed with a man, he threatened to tell unless she gave him sugar on his bread and butter. Yet, he adds, he had then no inkling of modern journalism. A little later his interest in sex began to stir. Sent to a girls' boarding-school and put, because of his proficiency in arithmetic, in a class with the older girls, he dropped his pencil one day so as to have a pretence for examining their legs. Having discovered a pair worthy of attention, he reached between them to retrieve his pencil. The girl shrieked and drew back her legs, closing them over his hand. 'What are you doing there?' she cried. 'Getting my pencil,' he replied humbly. 'It rolled.'

But nothing in his early life, he writes, was comparable in joy to the emotion with which, at the age of eleven, he listened to the fourteen-year-old son of the local vicar, as he described in detail an affair he had just entered upon with the nurse of his younger sisters.

From Ireland, or Wales, he was sent to the grammar-school

of Ruabon, on the Welsh border. In his autobiography he speaks of going to an English public school, and in later life, while wearing an old Etonian tie, would sometimes refer to his school-days at Rugby.

On what foundation of actual fact Harris has erected the super-structure of his youthful triumphs, even the most indulgent reader of his autobiography will pause to wonder. At the age of thirteen he was already in the school cricket eleven; he had learnt *Paradise Lost* by heart in a week; as Shylock he had anticipated the particular piece of business so much applauded fifteen years later in Henry Irving's rendering of that part; he had made love to a girl of his own age in church, and had come within measurable distance of overpowering a French governess in a rustic summer-house; he had rejected the supernatural element in religion, but hoped to profit by the example of Christ's life; he had awakened to the beauty of nature, and at all times of day and night, he tells us, caught glimpses that ravished him with delight and turned his being into a hymn of praise and beauty; and he had thrashed the school bully, a boy of seventeen or eighteen, the captain of the cricket eleven.

The probability of this last exploit can be gauged by a story he told me. To revenge himself on a certain master he soaped the two top steps of the staircase outside his dormitory, and the master slipped and fell to the bottom. This incident is also told in his autobiography, but he omits the sequel. After watching his enemy's discomfiture he fled in sudden panic, and rushed into the maids' bedroom, where he sought shelter with the cook. 'I was very small for my age,' he said, 'and the cook just laughed and took me in her arms. I liked the sensation, I don't know why, and the next night I ran in again in seeming terror, and got into bed with one of the housemaids, who was younger and prettier than the cook. But I was foolish and forgot my cue, which was to play the infant, and the others, headed by the cook, banded themselves against me, and put me out of the room.'

A boy of thirteen who was very small for his age could not, however tough, have stood up to the captain of the cricket eleven in an open fight and beaten him. But an incident which he told me, and which he records in his autobiography, is within the bounds of likelihood. Made desperate by the bullying of this boy, he threw a cricket ball at him, at the opening of a match against another school. The boy dodged, escaping the full force of the blow. But every one stood amazed: only people who know the strength of English conventions, Harris says, could appreciate the situation.

The feeling that he was a pariah, an outcast from the community, is strong here. It is a feeling which, in some degree, all remarkable natures have in youth, and never altogether lose. But with Harris it was dominant throughout life, and became more intense as he grew older. The chief sympton of this internal discomfort was his vanity, which he himself, speaking of his childhood, calls inordinate. As a man, and obviously as a boy, too, he at once felt himself estranged from his companions if they were remiss in placating his vanity. Such morbid sensibility was not, as he thought, a proof of self-confidence, but of self-mistrust and self-contempt.

The social standing of his parents, his small stature, and possibly his racial origin, were less the causes of his uneasiness than the points at which his uneasiness made itself felt. He was born uneasy; the elements of his nature were ill-mixed and his life was the expression of this inherent disharmony. The intense hatred he felt against his English school coincided with his emergence at thirteen into self-consciousness, and was in essence a transformation of his internal conflict into a conflict with his surroundings. The conflict ended in defeat, and his flight to America was an evasion, not a triumph. Certainly it was an evasion which few boys of fourteen would have the courage to achieve; but in this retreat, as in all the later ones which it prefigured, Harris used his resourcefulness to escape from difficulties instead of overcoming them.

One other reminiscence of his schooldays is important as revealing how anxious he always was to insist both on his æsthetic sensibility and on his intimacy with what he calls 'the better class of English.' One day when he was thirteen, he was invited (by what concurrence of circumstances he does not disclose) to lunch at Wynnstay. After lunch Lady Watkin Wynn took him into the garden, and they walked between rows four or five yards deep of every sort of flower. For the first time he saw the glory of their colouring, and the exquisite fragility of their blossoms: his senses were ravished and his eyes filled with tears.

The means by which, after he had decided to run away to America, he obtained the fifteen pounds for his passage-money are recorded in his autobiography. As they include an impromptu speech which he delivered in the presence of the head master, a Cambridge examining professor, and the whole school, followed by an interview with the head master, who is represented as the eager victim of Harris's powers of bluff, it would be a pity to spoil the episode by condensing the original narrative.

The night before he left Liverpool he visited a theatre for the first time, an act, he says, requiring more courage than to run away to America, for his father had always spoken of the theatre as the open door to Hell. The play was called *Two Roses*, and the heroine, lovely and affectionate and true, enraptured him. He told me that she impressed him so deeply that for her sake he remained chaste for three years. This, according to his autobiography, was an overstatement, for as soon as he was on board he began to make love to a girl called Jessie, the daughter of the chief engineer, and failed to conquer her completely only because of her own obduracy and a sister's vigilance. But that he remembered the heroine of *Two Roses* all his life reveals the poetic and romantic strain in his mixed nature. One may accept as authentic the picture of a rugged imp, with large ears and cocked nose, gazing with fond eyes at the heroine of a mid-Victorian sentimental comedy.

The morning after his arrival in New York, he tells us, he asked a bootblack if he might assist him. The bootblack consented, and Harris was soon shining two pairs to his employer's one. Better pay, as a workman in the caissons of Brooklyn Bridge, drew him for a time from his bootblacking. In spite of his youth, and the danger and strain of the work, he soon proved himself more efficient than the others. 'You're the best in the shift,' the foreman told him; 'the best I've ever seen, a great little pony.' To have more leisure for his courtship of Jessie, he returned to the bootblack, who was glad to get him back on the basis of a fifty-fifty partnership. But his relations with Jessie did not follow the line he had marked out for them. Jessie wished him to marry her. 'I was horrified; married at my age; no, sir!' It seemed absurd to him. He saw she was pretty and bright, but she knew nothing, had never read anything. He couldn't marry her. The idea made him snort. But he agreed for the moment, on the understanding that he must first get regular work.

The regular work came to him in the shape of a position as night-clerk in a Chicago hotel, the Fremont House. A Mr Kendrick, to whom Harris had inadvertently quoted Virgil while blacking his boots, insisted that he was meant for higher things, and offered him this position at Fremont House, which he managed on behalf of the proprietor, a Mr Cotton, his uncle. So Harris left New York and Jessie. He was rather pleased to leave her without even a word, he writes, for he was mortified by her refusal to be seduced.

As a night-clerk he astonished the visitors to Fremont House. 'You have a dandy night-clerk,' they told Mr Kendrick. 'Spares no pains ... pleasant manners ... knows everything ... some clerk, yes, sir!'

But the way up, he writes, was barred by two superiors, the book-keeper, Curtis, and the steward, Payne. In a couple of months he had picked up book-keeping from Curtis. Curtis, who was unhappily married, was glad to drown his unhappiness in drink, whenever he could get away from his work, and Harris was soon doing Curtis's job as well as his own. The shield which, out of loyalty, he interposed between the negligent book-keeper and the proprietor of the hotel attracted the proprietor's curiosity. Curtis was dismissed, and Harris stepped into his job. Payne soon followed Curtis. During a dinner to which Harris invited him, Payne confided in his host that he received a commission from the butcher who supplied the hotel with meat. As soon as he had all the facts clear, Harris asked the nephew (Mr Kendrick) to dine with him, and laid the situation before him. He had, he says, only one loyalty, to his employers and the good of the ship.

Kendrick, to his astonishment, was at first annoyed, and wanted to know why Harris couldn't stick to his own job and leave the others alone. After all, what was there in a commission?

Harris told him. Kendrick was amazed to learn how much Payne's arrangement was costing the hotel, and Harris stepped into Payne's job.

The way up was now barred only by Mr Kendrick and Mr Cotton, which may explain why Harris left the Fremont House rather abruptly. His own explanation is that three Western cattlemen had come to the hotel, that one of them had taught him to ride ('Reece told me I shaped better at riding than anyone he had ever seen'), and that, filled with sheer boyish adventure lust, he threw up his job and rode away with his new friends.

One might have expected that, at any rate, Harris's record of his life among the cowboys of the early 'seventies would escape a pedantic examination of dates and facts. But when he brought out *On the Trail* in 1930, reminiscences probably based on an unpublished youthful novel, an ex-cowboy septuagenarian rose up out of the past, reached for his pen, and in the columns of a Western daily shot Harris's story to bits. Still, it would be carrying scepticism too far to infer that Harris never fought Red Indians or lifted cattle across the Mexican border. Here, as elsewhere, his autobiography bears a certain, if much distorted relation to reality, and is, at its most unreliable, of value as revealing what Harris wished to believe about himself. He remembers his æsthetic sensibility, for instance, even while depicting himself as the associate of fighting, drinking and womanising desperadoes, and gives us a glimpse of himself returning to the midday camp with a new wildflower in his hand whose name he wished to learn. He kept up his reading, too, carrying Mill's *Political Economy* in his saddle-bag, and Carlyle's *Heroes and Hero-Worship*. So, at least, he tells us in the first volume of the autobiography; though in the fourth, in language borrowed from Wordsworth and Shakespeare, he attributes any originality of thought he may possess to the fact that when a cowboy on the trail fifty years ago he had no books, and by the camp fire at night had to answer the obstinate questionings of sense and outward things without any help from the choice and master spirits of his time.

With his fellow-cowboys Harris was, he tells us, Sir Oracle on all deep subjects. One may accept this as roughly true, for it was always Harris's practice to assume in any environment a character unfamiliar to those with whom he was for the moment associating. Cowboys wondered at him as a Socrates, and literary London gaped at him as a cowboy.

His lust for adventure was sated in two years. He was filled, he says, with an infinite disgust for a merely physical life. His vanity, his perpetual desire to excel, had, one may infer, been baffled, and once more he set out to find some region or way of life in which he would be undisputed master. Tough and wiry though he was, he had some physical handicaps which, together with a certain prudence concealed under his show of recklessness, prevented him from reaching heroic proportions as a gunman. He suffered from astigmatism, too, and even glasses, he discovered later, could not clear his blurred sight. It was the second or third disappointment of his life, he says, the others being the conviction of his personal ugliness and the fact that he would always be too short and small to be a great fighter or athlete.

From

The Poisoned Crown
(1944)

The Genealogy of Hitler

I

MOST OF THE avoidable suffering in life springs from our attempts to escape the unavoidable suffering inherent in the fragmentary nature of our present existence. We expect immortal satisfactions from mortal conditions, and lasting and perfect happiness in the midst of universal change. To encourage this expectation, to persuade mankind that the ideal is realisable in this world, after a few preliminary changes in external conditions, is the distinguishing mark of all charlatans, whether in thought or action. In the middle of the eighteenth century Johnson wrote: "We will not endeavour to fix the destiny of kingdoms: it is our business to consider what beings like us may perform." A little later Rousseau wrote: "Man is born free, and is everywhere in chains." Johnson's sober truth kindled no one, Rousseau's seductive lie founded the secular religion which in various forms has dominated Europe since Rousseau's death.

Although tinged with a vague deism, Rousseau's religion of the natural man treated this life as essentially a complete and self-contained experience, a view which tends to stimulate both self-glorification and Utopianism. The *Confessions* of Rousseau opened with the claim that he was a unique individual. Frustrated and embittered, he could mitigate the unsatisfactoriness of his appearance on the stage of life only by pitting his singularity against the featureless mediocrity of the indifferent world. At the same time, partly out of a desire to blame circumstances for his wretchedness, and partly out of that feeling of solidarity with the general life which even the most obdurate egotist feels until he is required to translate it into action, Rousseau looked forward to an earthly paradise in which a liberated humanity would attain the felicity denied to those born, like him, into the night of privilege, tyranny and greed; for Utopianism is the transference to society of the individual's disappointed expectation of personal happiness.

Rousseau's gospel found its first practical expression in the French Revolution, which followed the usual course of Utopianism in action—wild rejoicing among the masses at the destruction of old abuses and the ruin of their oppressors, the improvisation of a new order, the necessity in the general confusion for ruthless methods of imposing it, the increasingly rapid elimination of those Utopians in whom humanity was stronger than practical sense, the welcome threat of foreign intervention and ensuing diversion of revolutionary passion, now a menace to the Utopians at the top, into patriotic fervour, and finally a military dictatorship and a series of crusades against reactionary neighbours. Out of this welter emerged a figure well suited to be the god of the new religion and the new century. Napoleon's first appeal to men's imaginations was as a liberator, and even after he mounted a higher throne than any he had overturned, he was still to millions the man of the people who had avenged their agelong sufferings and humiliations. This view of him, blurred during his later years of power, blossomed again as soon as he was dead. In 1814 the poet laureate, Robert Southey, called him "Remorseless, godless, full of frauds and lies, and black with murders and with treacheries"; and the *Times* lamented that no description could more than faintly portray the foul and ghastly features of the grim idol worshipped by the French. A few years later, when the news of his death reached England, the *Times*, after regretting that he had not used his extraordinary gifts to better purpose, noted mildly that he was steady and faithful in his friendships, and not vindictive even when he could have been so with impunity. Since this could be written in 1821, it is not surprising that as the century advanced his exile became a martyrdom, and that before the close of the century Prometheus on his rock and even Christ in Gethsemane were being invoked to measure the extremity of Napoleon's dereliction on St Helena. Mixed with this view of him as a supremely tragic figure, the baffled liberator of mankind, was adoration of him as the Man of Destiny, the incarnation of willpower, ruthless and irresistible. The two aspects complemented each other, and together formed a god.

Byron soon joined Napoleon in the new pantheon. The uprush

of energy in the second half of the eighteenth century had poured itself into poetry as well as action, and for a short period, poised between the age of reason and the age of romance, the mist which veils reality thinned in a few imaginations. Mozart and Beethoven, Blake and Goethe and Wordsworth, wrote as representatives of mankind, not as unique specimens of it; their work was inspired not by their own singularity but by the whole of which they felt themselves to be parts. It meant little to most people, and the stirring of men's minds and imaginations by the Revolution and Napoleon had to be satisfied on a different level.

Like Napoleon, Byron possessed the twofold appeal of a liberator and an embodiment of the untrammelled will. His politics were of the usual revolutionary kind. He expected nothing from the world as it was, and everything from the world as it was shortly to be—"Give me a republic. The king times are fast finishing; there will be blood shed like water and tears like mist, but the peoples will conquer in the end." In the opinion of the public his death at Missolonghi proved the sincerity of his love for freedom; and his disinterestedness being thus established, it was possible to surrender without qualms to the spell of his egotism. In his essay on Byron Macaulay wondered why egotism, so distasteful in personal intercourse, should be so attractive in poetry. The explanation (to borrow one of Macaulay's formulas) is a very simple one. The reader identifies himself with the poet; and the readers of Byron, even when not in mere fact of noble birth and young and beautiful, fatal to all they loved, lonely wanderers over high mountains and misunderstood roamers on far-off strands, quickly became all these things in fancy. In the vacuum created by Napoleon's downfall Byron's image of himself enchanted all Europe, and the star-crossed lover took his place beside the star-crossed conqueror as the second of the two divinities presiding over the new age.

II

In his preface to *Ruy Blas*, which appeared in 1838, Victor Hugo wrote that the hero of the play was not Ruy Blas, but the people "without a present, but looking to the future; humble in station, yet aspiring high, and with the premonition of genius." Hugo, in the direct line of descent from Rousseau through Napoleon and Byron, was both a unique personality and a Utopian, but, as this quotation suggests, he was aware that romantic individualism, symbolised by Ruy Blas, was on the wane, and that Utopianism was becoming the more important element in a great man's make-up. The age of progress had set in, applied science was multiplying the comforts of life, and the masses, temporarily suppressed after Waterloo, were beginning to stir again.

The rich, too, were looking to the future, but with a premonition of trouble, not of genius. Increasingly aware of the poor ever since the Revolution, they were trying to reassure themselves by crediting the man in the street with exactly those virtues which he had patently failed to exhibit during the Terror. As employees infer a fine nature in the head of a firm on evidence which would not raise the office boy in their esteem, so from 1789 onwards the well-to-do began to detect high qualities in what they now called "the sovereign people." "Poor but honest," a realistic phrase previously in common use, was seldom heard after the Revolution, and the possessing classes inclined instead to the fallacy that because saints are usually poor men, therefore poor men are usually saints.

A less sweeping and majestic witness to the emergence of the people than Hugo, but a more perceptive one, was Heine. A German Jew, whose later years were spent in France, he had a wider range of experience than Hugo, and reflected the changing spirit of the age more completely perhaps than any other writer in the second quarter of the century. The heroes of his youth were Byron and Napoleon, Byron with his broken heart and unbroken will, and Napoleon who had abolished the Ghettos of Germany and scourged the hated Prussians, but had perished at last, as all great spirits perish, in vain conflict with the insensate hostility of the world. For Heine himself at this time the hostility of the world was expressed in the indifference to his love of a beautiful cousin, and the indifference to his poverty of her father, a rich Hamburg banker. A luckless Atlas bearing on his shoulders the whole world's woe was how he saw himself when he was feeling like Napoleon, and a poet whose songs and sorrows were on every German tongue when he was feeling like Byron. The charm of the Romantic age, as well as its closely interwoven foolishness, suffused these early verses, with their nostalgia for far-off lands and ages, their nightingales echoing the poet's pain, their moonlit waters and fairy-haunted woods, and at the end of every vista death, the goal of all desire because its only cure. But the poet lived on, and, like Byron in *Don Juan*, began to correct false sentiment with cynicism, using a jarring last line to let daylight into the moonshine. As his humour and his emotions became more harmonised he dropped this trick, which, however, expressed his permanent feeling of the antithesis between truth and beauty. Beauty was the romantic illusion he and his age had outgrown, truth the repulsive reality they could no longer evade; and by truth he meant the nature of things as they are experienced in the ordinary course of life. He was willing to believe that life could be beautiful in other lands, or had been beautiful in other ages, or even in his own youth when Byron and Napoleon were still on earth. But now the mob was in the ascendant, the drab era of the sovereign people was beginning. As a poet, and therefore by romantic convention an aristocrat, the prospect disgusted him. As a Utopian, a "soldier in the liberation war of humanity," as he called himself, he welcomed it. For a year or two in the eighteen-forties he was a close friend of Karl Marx, whose political philosophy he condensed into a few stanzas of a satirical poem called "Deutschland." The people, that great booby (he wrote), had been fooled long enough by the old hymn of renunciation, the lullaby of heaven, with its promise of a world up there to recompense them for all their suffering below. He had a new, a better, hymn to sing. Let them build the kingdom of heaven here on earth. There was bread, and cakes, enough for every man. Leave heaven to the angels and the sparrows.

With this prevision of the Bolshevist millennium went the craving for violence which is induced by a glut of material well being, whether in fancy or in fact. In a famous passage he warned

France to beware of the hammer of Thor which Germany, breaking through its crust of Christianity, would bring crashing down on the cathedrals of Christendom; but though he loved France and civilised life there was a note of exultation in the warning. Give me bloody and colossal crimes (he cried in one of his poems), but not this smug virtue of solvent traders; and in another poem he hailed Germany as a child whom its nurse, the sun, was suckling not with milk but wild flames, and on whose forehead a diamond-studded crown would presently be sparkling.

III

While Heine was looking backwards with regret and forwards with a mixture of repulsion and excitement, Balzac was carving an epic out of the new age of money and machines. He was not a Utopian. With his vast appetite for the concrete, the present was feast enough for him. But he was intensely romantic. His ambition, he said, was to achieve with his pen what Napoleon had achieved with his sword. He wanted to pass the whole of life through his imagination, and stamp his picture of it on every mind. It was the hallucination of a man whose enormous natural vitality had been stimulated throughout a childhood and youth passed in Napoleon's world, and galvanised into delirium by the conquest of matter which in the second quarter of the century seemed to all Europe to prelude a millennium of earthly felicity. In England this illusion was still strongly tinged by Christianity. "Commerce, till lately comparatively inert," an Oxford graduate wrote in 1854, "is springing and running and flying with a more rapid motion of every limb, no longer dependent on the slowness of road-travel or the fitfulness of breezes, but self-propelled by the living and roaring leviathan within her bosom. . . . We have celebrated the festival of material civilisation in the great Exhibition of the nations' industry, and called all the ends of the earth to unite with us in patient and laborious progress. It was a noticeable fact, that in a bay of that Exhibition was a stand of books open to all readers; they were spread outside to attract the gaze of those who should pass by. It was the Book, the Word of God, the revelation of Christianity, published in more than a hundred languages of the nations of the earth. That fact is not a solitary or an isolated one; for coeval with the advance of commerce and of practical science there has taken place a mighty advance of Christianity." This was not how Balzac felt about the conquest of matter. Though a Catholic and Royalist, he was neither of those things out of a tenderness for religion or the past, but because in a country subject to revolutions a conservative theory of society seemed to him a necessary safeguard against the disruption and dispersal of the individual will which was symbolised for him in Napoleon. Though his books pulsate with energy and teem with life, there are really only two men in them: the man who is like Napoleon and the man who isn't. The first may be a country solicitor, a money-lender, or a gossip-writer on the Parisian press, but Balzac blows him out into a daemonic creature, grappling with society in a life-and-death struggle. The other man is a cross between a village idiot and Balzac's idea of Christ, which it is not easy to distinguish from the ordinary idea of a village idiot. There are also only two women: the one a ruthless, triumphant courtesan, the other a victimised Madonna.

The belief that goodness is due to an absence of will, not to a presence of spirit, expanded with the growing materialism of the age. Balzac, who died in 1850, could drop a tear over the hapless plight of virtue, but a few years later the philosophy deduced from Darwin's *Origin of Species* dignified egotism as the universal law of life. Confined within the material universe, spirit dismissed as an illusion, and matter elevated into the ultimate reality, the European mind turned to science as the sole repository of truth. The vastness of the universe, which so tormented Tennyson and which he was the first poet to feel and express, became a part of the general consciousness. Space and time, now absolute realities, stretched behind and before into sickening distances, and a feeling of his inexpressible insignificance descended upon man. This did not last long. His insignificance bred a sense of irresponsibility, his sense of irresponsibility a sense of power, and the net result of realising that he measured about six feet from end to end, as compared with the x billion miles of the universe, was greatly to increase his self-conceit. Rid of God, he felt himself superior to anything that remained, or at least to anything within view. This, however, was a collective feeling rather than an individual one, a huddling together of the herd in the presence of a mechanistic universe.

The descent of man from a spiritual being to a self-dependent personality, and from a self-dependent personality to a unit of the collective consciousness, was quickening fast—a change which sounds catastrophic, but which in practice was immensely modified by the fact that the mass of mankind is always swaying about between the highest and lowest conceptions of its nature, with flashes of divinity in an age of atheism and flashes of devilry in an age of religion. Nevertheless, the change portended great disasters, which in the twenty to thirty years following the *Origin of Species* were foreshadowed by Dostoevsky and Nietzsche.

IV

The fundamental impulse in Dostoevsky's work was to dramatise the conflict in his nature between will-worship and spiritual freedom. When he wrote *Crime and Punishment*, will-worship was embodied for him in Napoleon and spiritual freedom in Christ; the hero of the book murdering an old woman in order to demonstrate his Napoleonic self-sufficiency, and repenting later under the influence of a prostitute who reads the Gospel of St John to him. In his last novel, *The Brothers Karamazov*, the conflict is less simply presented. There is a young priest, Alyosha, who is supposed to embody the spirit of universal love, but in spite of much effort by Dostoevsky he plays a minor and vapid part in the book. The true field of Dostoevsky's genius was not the heights of the human spirit but the depths of the human consciousness. He was most at home in the underworld, the literal one of St Petersburg, the metaphorical one of his own nature, and the most directly self-revealing of his stories, because the freest from false sentiment, is *Letters from the Underworld*, the confession of a small government official, shabby, insignificant and savagely resentful, whose longing for happiness and love is twisted into a devilish satisfaction in undeceiving and humiliating a prostitute who thinks she has found in him a refuge from the cruelty of life.

It was out of this inferno of perverted impulses, shot at intervals with gleams of spiritual insight, that the gospel of Dostoevsky rose into the upper air of the late nineteenth century, a strange exhalation which in the thickening twilight was mistaken for an apparition from heaven. Although what the Oxford graduate of 1854 had described as the triumph of patient and laborious progress was still in full spate, it inspired now less exultation than fear. In the more advanced countries of Europe the desire of the rich to think highly of the poor, to which Victor Hugo and Dickens had so freely ministered, was being more and more thwarted by the increasing demand of the poor for greater power and better conditions. No wonder, then, that in the closing decades of the century and the years before the war of 1914, western Europeans of the cultured classes turned with relief from labour organising itself for battle to Dostoevsky's vision of brotherly love among the uncomplaining Russian poor. It was among university professors and first-class civil servants, popular novelists of the better sort and the lettered members of great banking and commercial families, that Dostoevsky's most ardent admirers were to be found. "The love which is in Dostoevsky's work," one of these admirers wrote, "is so great, so bountiful, so over-flowing that it is impossible to find a parallel to it, either in ancient or in modern literature. Supposing the Gospel of St John were to be annihilated and lost to us for ever, although nothing could replace it, Dostoevsky's work would go nearer to replacing it than any other books written by any other man." What these enthusiasts divined in Dostoevsky was, on an enormously larger scale, their own guilt and fear and desire to placate an unknown and growing power. They, no more than Dickens or Victor Hugo or Dostoevsky, were attracted by the idea of self-chosen poverty. It was poverty as the great mass of mankind knows it that they wanted to be glorified as a privileged experience and a purifying destiny—a view of poverty which makes affluence seem almost a deprivation.

E

With the desire to idealise the masses is usually associated a desire to manage and use them, and it was this desire, stimulated by the growing collectivism of the age, which in Dostoevsky's last years blurred his earlier antithesis between Napoleon and Christ, producing a mixture of the two in which will-worship masqueraded as universal love. By this time Dostoevsky had become a fanatical nationalist, who was urging that Constantinople should be incorporated in the Russian Empire, beyond which relatively modest aim he saw the gradual absorption of the whole world by Russia. In a speech in honour of Pushkin, which he delivered just before his death and which aroused great popular enthusiasm, he said: "What is the strength of the Russian national spirit other than an aspiration towards a universal spirit which shall embrace the whole world and the whole of mankind? . . . To be a real Russian must signify simply this: to strive to bring about a solution and an end to European conflicts; to show to Europe a way to escape from its anguish in the Russian soul, which is universal and all-embracing; to instil into her a brotherly love for all men, and in the end perhaps to utter the great and final word of universal harmony, the fraternal and lasting concord of all people according to the gospel of Christ."

This totalitarian fantasy was his refuge from the panorama of malice, lust and despair which he displayed with all the intensity of his genius in *The Brothers Karamazov*. The clue to what in this last phase of his development he really felt about the masses is to be found not in his Pushkin speech but in the Legend of the Grand Inquisitor which he inserted in *The Brothers Karamazov*. In this legend Christ returns to earth in the sixteenth century, and is brought before the Grand Inquisitor in Seville. The Grand Inquisitor in a lengthy apologia presents himself as an enlightened sage, full of pity for the multitude, whom he directs and rules in their own interest, knowing them to be too weak for the burden of spiritual freedom imposed upon them by Christ. One would not, of course, expect a Calvin, a Torquemada or a Robespierre to present himself as a warped and savage soul which hates and seeks to destroy the happiness of others. But his true motives and impulses would be revealed incidentally as he talked.

Dostoevsky's Grand Inquisitor is throughout unintermittently high-minded and disinterested, and even when he tells Christ that he must be killed, so that men may be saved from a gospel too hard for them, his majestic serenity remains unflawed by any gleam of satisfaction. Christ's response is to lean forward and kiss the Inquisitor on the lips; the Inquisitor shudders, and Christ passes out into the night, leaving the Inquisitor to roast his fellow-creatures in peace.

Like Dostoevsky's Christ, the Christs who round about this time made occasional appearances in the fiction of western Europe no longer contend against evil. Now and then a look of pain reveals their distress at wrong-doing, but their real business is to suggest that if the worst came to the worst, and there really should be another life, there would be loving-kindness enough and to spare for every one at the Day of Judgment.

v

The advisability of identifying oneself with some communal faith or activity was by the closing decades of the century clear to every one who wished to bring himself to the notice of the public. After 1870 even Wagner, the most flamboyant of romantic individualists, aligned his music with the aspirations of the new Germany. Ten years later, Dostoevsky became a Russian idol overnight with his speech on Pushkin, and in the next fifty years or so all the world-wide reputations, both in literature and in action, were made by men who drew attention to themselves by denouncing the individual and exalting the community—Shaw, Kipling and Wells, Lenin, Mussolini and Hitler.

Nietzsche reached maturity just as this landslide of self-effacing self-advancement was beginning to gather momentum, but he did not slide along with the rest. There was nothing of the opportunist in him, no point of contact with ordinary men. Of clerical stock on both sides, even in his childhood he was remote from life, earnest, scrupulous and thoughtful, with a budding didacticism which led the other children to call him "the little pastor." Living entirely in his mind, he could have jogged through the world comfortably enough as a professor, but for his genius. There was an enormous power in him which could find nothing to feed on. His passions came to him in the form of ideas, he passed from one idea to another instead of from one experience to another, and for want of the balance between experience and thought which keeps genius sane collapsed at last under the unrelieved pressure of his thoughts on his emotions.

Looking at the world as a starving child looks through a window at people eating in a restaurant, he refused to blunt the pangs of his unsatisfied appetite with any hope of another life, or belief in a supernatural order. Matter was for him the only reality, the struggle and suffering of life were justified by the courage they evoked to endure them, only great individuals had any value, and the greatness of the individual was measured by the exaltation inspired in him by his tragic destiny. The philosophy which he based on this attitude and which he preached in his third and final stage was an extreme individualism, equally opposed to Christianty and to all forms of collectivism, democratic or nationalistic. Christianity he held to be a trick by which the herd had disarmed the aristocrat. Its humanitarianism was based not on love but on cowardice, it turned noble savages into sick monks, and hated and feared all that was strong and happy. Democracy, the modern secularised form of Christianity, levelled all superiorities. Slavery was essential to culture, and the enormous majority ought to be ruthlessly subjected to life's struggle, so that a select minority might expand without restraint. War he of course approved— "Man shall be trained for war, and woman for the recreation of the warrior." Yet he disliked Prussian nationalism only less than democratic pacifism, denouncing "this bovine nationalism" and warning Germany to free itself from "this fatal Prussia with its repugnance to culture." That the effective conduct of a war pre-supposes a strong collective emotion, and that nationalism is the form which a strong collective emotion necessarily takes when one country is fighting or preparing to fight another, clashed with his picture of glorious individuals hurling themselves into self-engendered frays. Reaching far out into the future, he found there a Utopia of his own, a world which had passed beyond the collectivism without tears of other founders of Utopia: "There, where the State ceaseth—pray look thither, my brethren! Do ye not see it, the rainbow and the bridges of the Superman?" In this paradise of happy warriors, transfigured Caesar Borgias, resounding with "the final, cheerfullest, exuberantly maddest and merriest Yea to life," there would be a supreme wisdom of soul and body, a perfect harmonisation of joy and strength—"light feet, wit, fire, grave grand logic, stellar dancing, wanton intellectuality."

This vision brought him no readers, one by one his friends were estranged by his growing conviction that he was destined to be the second and final saviour of mankind, and in his despair he turned back from his distant dream to the Europe of the later 'eighties, congested with prosperity and sick of progress. What could save it, he asked himself, and found the answer in the prospect of huge socialistic crises which would throw up the barbarians of the twentieth century to refresh and renovate an outworn world. "Would not the democratic movement itself," he wrote, "find a sort of goal, salvation, and justification, if someone appeared who availed himself of it, so that at last, besides its new and sublime product, slavery (for this would be the end of European democracy), that higher species of ruling and Caesarian spirits might also be produced, which would stand upon it, hold to it, and elevate themselves through it?"

Not long after this greeting to the collective frenzies he had tried to escape from in the dream of a Superman, at the beginning of 1889, a few months before the birth of Hitler, Nietzsche became insane.

VI

In the year of Hitler's birth and Nietzsche's mental collapse, James Payn wrote to Conan Doyle, who had just brought out a story of the Monmouth Rebellion: "How can you, how can you, waste your time and wits writing historical novels?" The solid domestic themes which had made Anthony Trollope the most representative novelist of the 'sixties and 'seventies were still, in the opinion of a novelist well acquainted with popular taste, the most likely to please the public. Nevertheless, the first rumbling of the eruption against peace and prosperity and all the values summed up in the Victorian aphorism that the true knight of the modern world was the knight of commerce could already be heard. Kipling's Indian stories were coming out, Stevenson had written *Treasure Island* and *Kidnapped*, Stanley Weyman's *A Gentleman of France*, ostensibly the history of a soldier of fortune in sixteenth-century France and really the daydream of a gentleman in late Victorian England, was soon to appear and sell in thousands, and Conan Doyle was about to become the medium through which the ordinary Englishman of the eighteen-nineties expressed most fully and variously his nostalgia for excitement and adventure. In his Shelock Holmes stories Doyle peopled London with bizarre criminals, dotting a few over the countryside to suggest the horrors beneath its peaceful surface; and in other stories he ranged from diabolical pirates of the Spanish Main to murderous reanimated mummies. In his mediaeval romances he unrolled a landscape full of chivalrous knights and valiant bowmen, with here and there a flagellating hermit or white-livered clerk in holy orders. In *Rodney Stone* he pictured the bucks and bare-fist fighters of the Regency, and in his Napoleonic tales he resurrected the gigantic figure of Napoleon for, as he put it, "you who live so gently and peacefully now."

There was nothing of the revolutionary in Conan Doyle, a solid English individualist, or in Kipling, who early in his career attached himself to the ruling classes. In H. G. Wells, on the other hand, the element of violence was closely connected with his revolutionary sympathies. He was both generous and resentful by nature, but his early years of poverty deepened his resentment at the expense of his generosity. Overlooking the treatment saints and poets have received from churches and universities, he identified religion with the Church of England and culture with Oxford and Cambridge, and fell into a habit of disparaging the great men of the past as though they were merely dummies set up by snobs and pedants to intimidate the unlettered. His enthusiasm for science, a study disdained by the upper classes in

his youth, was therefore not entirely impersonal, and his material-
istic creed not the spontaneous exuberant materialism of the
first half of the century, but a mixed product of a desire for power
and of a dogged resistance to the spiritual element in his nature.

The hero of all his books, which fall into three categories,
novels, scientific romances and Utopias, is the Little Man. In
his early novels, based on his own youth, the Little Man is drawn
with great humour, tenderness and warmth in his aspiration
towards the happiness which life seems to hold for leisured and
prosperous people. But Hoopdriver, Mr Lewisham and Kipps
are not allowed to develop the confused poetry in their natures.
Forced by his creed and by his own development to look for the
kingdom of heaven anywhere except within the individual,
Wells had either to give them money and position or leave them
unblessed and unspoiled by prosperity. In his tenderness for them
and deep obscure regret for what they still possessed and he had
lost, he left them where they were, reserving for novels based,
somewhat loosely, on his later years the transmogrification of the
Little Man into a powerful figure in politics and big business. In
his scientific romances, Wells transformed the Little Man into a
magician, a being, that is, who concentrates on the mastery of
natural forces and rejects spiritual development. Thus endowed,
the Little Man ranges to the furthest limits of past and future
time, flies to the moon, discovers the secret of invisibility, and
turns himself into a giant. Some reality still adheres to him in
these transformations. His powers do not bring him much
happiness, and from time to time he misuses them in outbursts of
rage and destructiveness. In the Utopian fantasies, put forward
by Wells as valuable contributions to political thought, the Little
Man, leaving all reality behind him, takes wholesale vengeance
on the insolent past, abolishing all nations, wiping out all religions,
and erecting on the ruins a social order founded on applied
science and enlightened sexual relations.

The Little Man as pictured by Wells in his best days passed
away in 1914. Surfeited with the material triumphs of the previous hundred years, Europe was ready for an explosion, and the
first effect of the war was a sense of overwhelming relief, to which

the *Daily Mail* gave eloquent expression early in August 1914:
"We of this generation are destined to see hours glorious beyond
hope and imagination; we are already entering upon them. We
have passed from the twilight of sloth and indulgence into the
clear day of action and self-sacrifice." There was the same exaltation in Germany, where Thomas Mann spoke of the hearts of
poets standing in flame, "for now it is war! . . . Nothing better,
more beautiful, happier could befall them in the whole world."
For the time being each of the warring nations was unified within
itself, the external enemy became a symbol of the evil in life,
the Little Man laid aside his resentments, and the rich man his
pleasures and security.

Under the strain of the war revolution broke out in Russia, a
worm-eaten autocracy ripe to yield to a new order in which the
nineteenth-century illusions of progress and prosperity and the
magical benefits of applied science could find fresh soil to blossom
in. In the highly industrialised nations of western Europe, which
Karl Marx had considered sufficiently well organised to be transferred at the right moment from bourgeois-capitalist control to
the control of the proletariat, the chief effect of the infinite suffering of the war was a deep disillusionment with all the hopes
engendered by the previous century. Materialism, once a solid
daylight faith, now took strange shapes, lapsing into the dark
night of the unconscious, the world of dreams and atavistic
impulses, in which blind guides, pillars of cloud by night, led
their stumbling followers in circles.

The Little Man of this new world was Charlie Chaplin, whose
inconsequential moods and actions, and alternations of hope and
dejection, mirrored the general disintegration. His fame in the
nineteen-twenties was universal. No one in his own lifetime had
ever been known to so many millions, who in every land saw
themselves in the forlorn little man in his battered bowler and
huge shapeless boots, his trim officer's moustache an emblem of
his social aspirations, his final disappearance beyond the twilit
skyline the confession of his defeat. Wearying at last of the pathos
of failure, Chaplin in 1925 produced "The Gold Rush," in which
the Little Man triumphed both in love and in the pursuit of

wealth. The film was revived in 1942, and as one watched the Little Man struggling in a world of husky toughs, one remembered how in the intervening years another down-and-out, with the same kind of moustache and a not much more impressive appearance, had overturned the whole planet, toughs and all. This parallel in mind, one followed the Little Man's search for gold in Alaska with a different kind of interest. The fantastically unsuitable get-up in which he braved the snowy wastes now seemed part of his technique. When, as he tottered along the edge of a precipice, a bear sniffed at him and turned away, one was relieved rather for the bear than for the Little Man. The gale that blew him back into Black Larsen's cabin, after Black Larsen had ejected him, seemed to come from a million lungs, and one was not surprised when Black Larsen later on ran into an Alaskan equivalent of the Night of the Long Knives. The huge bulk of the Little Man's partner seemed appropriate, and the happy ending inevitable—both of them multi-millionaires, the Little Man in fashionable clothes strutting up and down his suite on an ocean liner, and the beauty he has adored mute and blissful beside him.

What the Little Man of "The Gold Rush" desired was money and women, what Hitler desired was power, these desires forming together the sum of what most men want from the world. Hitler, who was born in the same week of April 1889 as Chaplin, was his complement not his antithesis, the Napoleon of the mass-consciousness as Chaplin was its Byron, and therefore cast for the more ungrateful part, since it has fallen to him to demonstrate, on the widest possible scale, that the obverse of self-pity is not pity for others, but hatred, and that no one has less sympathy with the poor than the down-and-out who has managed to become an up-and-in.

After a century and a half of emptying the divine out of life, the epoch which opened with the uniqueness and Utopianism of Rousseau has collapsed in the self-deification and New Order of Hitler. Many remedies for a shattered world are now being offered to mankind, but they are all collective remedies, and collective remedies do not heal the ills produced by collective action. The purpose of this book is not to suggest the true remedy, except indirectly, but to illustrate in four famous examples the barren results of action and the destructive effect of power. Naturally, it is not disputed that benefits of a secondary order may flow from the achievements of able rulers; it was clearly to the advantage of England in the second half of the sixteenth century to be governed by Queen Elizabeth and not by Queen Anne. But, on a much deeper level of reality, it was not to the advantage either of Elizabeth or of those who served her that she should set herself up as a semi-divine figure, a Virgin Queen exalted high above common humanity. What is divine in man is elusive and impalpable, and he is easily tempted to embody it in a concrete form—a church, a country, a social system, a leader—so that he may realise it with less effort and serve it with more profit. Yet, as even Lincoln proved, the attempt to externalise the kingdom of heaven in a temporal shape must end in disaster. It cannot be created by charters and constitutions nor established by arms. Those who set out for it alone will reach it together, and those who seek it in company will perish by themselves.

From

*The Return of
William Shakespeare*
(1929)

The Return of William Shakespeare *tells how Shakespeare was restored to life in the nineteen-twenties, and of the duel in which two newspaper proprietors, anxious to exploit him, engage. In this framework is set the central portion of the book, "Shakespeare at Marley Farm", which is Shakespeare's account of himself, communicated in a colloquy with a student of his works, Cecil Wilkinson, who has taken him into the country to get him away from the imbroglio in London.*

Shakespeare at Marley Farm

CHAPTER ONE

IT WAS THE twenty-first of June. In the orchard, Shakespeare, in a basket chair, smoked his pipe. Cecil, fingering a cigarette, faced him on a stool.

"I love these still evenings of early summer," Shakespeare said, "when the air is warm, but not yet heavy. Life seems to hang poised between expectation and satiety, April and August. Content, the exile, returns for a moment to the heart."

"A mood, master, which is, is it not, often expressed in your —or, since you wish it—in Shakespeare's writings?"

"As, for example?"

"The moonlight scene in *The Merchant of Venice*, so exquisitely free from the turbid emotionalism which most poets would have thought relevant to the situation."

"The runaway lovers, you mean, Lorenzo and Jessica?"

Cecil nodded, and murmured:

> Here will we sit, and let the sounds of music
> Creep in our ears: soft stillness and the night
> Become the touches of sweet harmony.

"Lines almost exactly echoed," said Shakespeare, "in *Much Ado*:

> How still the evening is,
> As hush'd on purpose to grace harmony!

But, so far as I remember, you will hardly find this mood expressed before 1597—the year, I think, of *The Merchant*, and certainly not after 1598, when *Much Ado* was written."

"*Twelfth Night*, master?

That strain again, it had a dying fall. . . ."

"No. The speaker is too present to us there. In his very early works—*Venus and Adonis*, for example—where 'cedar-tops and hills seem burnish'd gold,' all is beauty, nothing man. As the world of his youthful imagination faded, and his unhappiness grew, beauty and humanity drew nearer, and are perfectly balanced against each other for a long moment in those lines you quoted. This exact balance does not occur again.

> O, it came o'er my ear like the sweet sound
> That breathes upon a bank of violets,
> Stealing and giving odour,

is more lovely than Lorenzo's 'How sweet the moonlight sleeps upon this bank,' but the equipoise is gone."

"Yes, I see, I see. Perfectly said!"

"The more I read him, the more sure I become that 1598 and 1599 are the dividing years of his life." Cecil flicked the ash from his cigarette, and moved uneasily.

"His unhappiness was coming to a head; humiliation in love and friendship, discontent with his own success—a mere player's triumph—and a growing disgust, half envy, half contempt, for the Court and the aristocracy."

"But surely, master, these considerations . . . irrelevant . . . mere surmise . . ." This protest, hardly above a murmur, died away. It was, after all, impossible and impertinent openly to oppose Shakespeare's speculations about himself, even though it was the present humour of the Shakespeare in front of Cecil to regard the Elizabethan Shakespeare as a different person. Yet if he could be diverted from these personal excavations, led back to the æsthetic level——

"Already, in *As You Like It*, the flute and song which the Italian nights of *The Merchant* and *Much Ado* graced with their stillness . . ."

"Ah, master, and I can offer you nothing but Mrs Oldfield's piano! But I interrupt . . ."

Shakespeare moved testily. "I have no desire to hear Mrs Oldfield on the flute. Her piano-playing suffices. Since there is no flute-player on the farm, I must enjoy your orchard without music. Even I do not desire the piano to be brought out here."

"It is a riddle to me, master, how you can listen to it, or to her. She must fatigue you dreadfully. I understand that to-day she spent almost an hour talking while she cleared your lunch. If a word from me . . ."

"No, no. You mustn't say anything. Promise me that!"

"Of course not, if you forbid it."

"The critics," said Shakespeare, diverted to a new train of thought, "have much to say about Shakespeare's universal sympathy. To and fro they send him, easing from the hearts of common men and women their dearest secrets. Attentive, gently smiling. Pooh!"

"I understand your meaning. Sentimental exaggeration. Precisely."

"Precisely! Why 'precisely'? And what are you smiling at?"

"Well, actually, master, at the recollection of Mrs Oldfield's lament to me yesterday."

"Lament?"

"She said you had passed her without a look, and had later spoken sharply to her—I think about the non-arrival of your tobacco. It seems she had already rung up twice about it."

"If I cannot even——! And after the hours I have heard her on her neuralgia, and on the endless labour of keeping everything about the house nice and clean, early morning till late at night, year in, year out. And to-day, did I not listen to-day, for the third time, to the story of her wanton prime, thirty years ago, in London? Those evenings at St James's Hall, when the spell of the Reverend Hugh Price Hughes and the Reverend Mark Guy Pearse was upon her. Who better than I knows that the black beard and burning eyes of Hughes tempered her ecstasy with dread, while to the honeyed words of the smooth-shaven Pearse she yielded herself in unperturbed surrender?

"Am I to watch her every mood, greet her lovingly each time we encounter, be for ever the bucket into which the pumps the brackish flow of her memories and lamentations? A moment of abstraction, is that to be noted against me? A curt word, must I bleed for that?"

"Please, please!" These sudden outbursts about nothing in particular, though Cecil was getting used to them, still frightened him. They were clearly connected with some disturbance in Shakespeare's former life, and were for that reason alarming, since it was impossible to forecast to what lengths his re-awakened emotions might carry him.

"The poor creature!" Shakespeare said presently. "The kindest, dearest old thing. Why I should burst forth like that . . ." He stroked his beard, looking a little shame-faced. "However!" Drawing a long breath, he expelled it through pursed lips, and made a dismissive gesture with his hand—a royal gesture, as of some great man brushing a trivial, importunate thought away. "He has," Wilkinson noted in his record on this occasion, "little tricks of manner, every now and then, oddly at variance with his usual naturalness. I shrink from the profanity, but in another person I should qualify these tricks with the epithet 'theatrical.' Odd and disconcerting thought! Shakespeare was an actor. One is apt to forget that fact. And, tradition tells us, he played kingly parts for preference."

"There's a vein of malice in you, Cecil," Shakespeare observed, after a short pause. "Yes, most certainly a vein of malice."

Cecil laughed weakly.

"But I will return kindness for evil, and, knowing your tiger appetite for flesh and blood, will unfold to you the man whom you have laboured so long to divine behind his writings. And, as I unfold him, it will appear how wide or confined, how variable or constant, his sympathy was. That interruption of yours has shaken into a pattern a thousand scattered ideas. I am indeed obliged to you."

"Hoist with my own petard," Cecil murmured.

Shakespeare, appeased, leant forward and patted Cecil's knee. "I shall try to make it as little painful as possible, though why you —but I'm digressing again."

Shakespeare settled himself in his basket chair, crossed his legs, and began:

"The first conscious thoughts which Shakespeare had about the world, so far as we can guess at them from his writings and the events of his life, concerned themselves with the glorious men and women of the nobility. He was in his twelfth year when the festivities, given by the Earl of Leicester in honour of Queen Elizabeth, were held at Kenilworth. The mermaid on a dolphin's back in *A Midsummer Night's Dream* may, his biographers suggest, be a memory of what he had himself seen on the ornamental lake as he prowled about the Kenilworth grounds, watching from a distance the inventions designed to amuse the Queen, and worshipping the superbly-dressed men and women, or, more likely, choosing one man or woman to receive the full force of his adoration. An awkward, skulking imp, as I see him, just at the age when boys are speechless in the society of older persons, where they sit sullen or grinning foolishly at one another, but among themselves noisy as monkeys or parrots; silence and din alike masking the discomfort of their growing desire for the happiness of life, from which the just distaste they inspire in the mature seems to debar them."

"A little overcharged," Cecil murmured.

"One is always overcharged when one speaks generally. But it is so that I see Shakespeare at twelve, though I do not positively affirm he was at Kenilworth during the festivities. Were it not for the entire respectability of the incident, which avouches its truth, I might doubt Sir Sidney Lee's picture of Shakespeare and his father walking the fifteen miles between Stratford and Kenilworth. Ten miles as the crow flies, says Joseph Quincy Adams, who outstrips even Sir Sidney in his anxiety to see young William at these festivities. Perhaps young William got there horsed on the back of a Stratford crow.

"But whether at Kenilworth or Stratford, the magnificence of life sank deep into his mind during these years. Outward show, the devout religion of the eye, is the chief difference between those days and this sober-suited age. Your London traffic, your tubes and rolling stairways, and the wide streets and high buildings of the richer quarters, would not amaze an Elizabethan for more than a few hours:

> Thy pyramids built up with newer might
> To me are nothing novel, nothing strange:
> They are but dressings of a former sight.

More lasting would be his astonishment at the uniformity of dress. In Elizabeth's time, a man's wealth and rank, or poverty and low occupation, clothed him wherever he went, so that the young received the gradations of the world as their first and deepest impression. All inferiorities are felt most keenly when life is still fresh, one's own powers unknown, and those of others rated more highly than they deserve. So you must see the youthful Shakespeare not only roaming in the meadows round Stratford, or in the Forest of Arden listening to the lark that tirra-lirra chants, to the wren, and to the throstle, but also brooding—in a meadow, if you like—on the misfortune that had made him the son of a glover and tanner instead of a nobleman's heir.

"The worst of it was, he reflected often, if only his father had been more careful with his money, his application for a coat-of-arms would have gone through, and then his mother would have regained her right to bear the Arden arms. She, at any rate, was of gentle birth. Why she had ever—— Well, I'll follow these impious meditations no further. But I was obliged to clear from your mind the error that Shakespeare's 'homely ideals', as Sir Sidney calls them, his desire for money, for the coat-of-arms he at last obtained, and for the biggest house in Stratford, derived from a prosaic element in him, unconnected with his imagination. Sir Sidney compares Shakespeare in this matter with Sir Walter Scott, speaking of the sobriety of the personal aims of both, and the sanity of their mental attitude. Scott, it seems, was lame, and thg disability caused him great suffering of mind as a boy, making him value physical strength and agility too highly. His mediæval castle, Abbotsford, was the seat of the robber-baron he desired to be, and, to nourish this dream, he broke down his health by over-work and ruined himself financially. Not much sobriety there.

Shakespeare, too, paid, though in a less material form, for his enslavement to the illusions of his early years."

Cecil opened his mouth. Shakespeare paused courteously; then, as Cecil seemed to have nothing to say, continued:

"The aim of all, Shakespeare writes in *The Rape of Lucrece*, is to nurse life with honour, wealth, and ease in waning age. But a man born to honour, wealth, and ease values them for their present enjoyment, not for the comfort they will afford his decrepitude. Shakespeare is here, after the manner of youthful poets, assigning to all men his particular ambition.

"The way in which, most suitably to his powers, he could realise this ambition was revealed to him by the travelling companies of noblemen's servants, whom the mayor and aldermen welcomed to Stratford with increasing frequency as he grew up. Much as he delighted in strolling players and acrobats and the old-fashioned rustic plays, it was the household servants of the great noblemen, magnificent in their masters' cast-off dresses, who stirred him most; for they showed him that the grandeur denied him by his birth might be enjoyed one day in mimicry though not in fact. Did you say anything?"

"No—no."

"This vision was obscured to him for a time. Life, breathing in his arms, made dim these distant images of a fuller and richer existence.

"When his senses cooled, he realised that at eighteen he was already a married man, and that his wife was eight years his senior. The disparity in age, which had flattered and excited him in the early days of their passion, now repelled him. It was unseemly, her ardour, and the unseemliness thrilled him no longer —I'm afraid your stool is uncomfortable. The first three years of his marriage, before he left Stratford for London, were increasingly wretched for both of them. How these years appeared to him we learn from *The Comedy of Errors*, where the Abbess reproves Adriana for barring the sweet recreation of her husband. The venom clamours of a jealous woman, says the Abbess, whose acceptance of a husband's right to make love to other women the youthful dramatist thinks too natural to require explanation, poison more deadly than a mad dog's tooth."

"May I ask, sir," Cecil enquired, in a cold, hopeless tone, "conceding Shakespeare's unhappiness with Anne, what your grounds are for holding that he left Stratford three years after his marriage? It has been argued—ably, in my view—that he was a schoolmaster in the neighbourhood of Stratford for a considerably longer period than the three years you allot him before his departure for London."

"That is possible. Let him be a schoolmaster, if it means a great deal to you. Nor must you think that Shakespeare was, in my opinion, insensible to Anne's unhappiness and to the love for him beneath her shrewishness. 'My heart prays for him, though my tongue do curse,' Adriana says, in *The Comedy of Errors*. Even in his early years in London, he must often have thought about the failure of his marriage, and his own share of the blame for it; and later, in *Twelfth Night*, his ill conscience appears in the Duke's remark that a man's fancies are more giddy and unfirm than a woman's, so his wife should be younger than himself, 'or thy affection cannot hold the bent.' And in his last play, *The Tempest*, he excuses himself again—not, this time, because Anne was older than he, but because their union had been consummated before marriage; an act inevitably breeding barren hate, sour-ey'd disdain, and discord, he makes Prospero too sweepingly affirm.

"If tenderness as well as passion had entered into his love for Anne, he could not have broken from her so soon. But the marriage was a mistake from every standpoint; and I think he was right to see it so quickly as a failure, nor do I know how he could have managed this failure better than by building on it a comfortable home for his wife and children."

"Always assuming it was a failure," Cecil interjected——

"Always assuming it was a failure," Shakespeare repeated, continuing: "The capacity to recover his balance after abandoning his whole nature to some emotion seems to me the most remarkable of Shakespeare's personal characteristics, and proof of an underlying toughness his critics are silent on. Most of them deny the abandonment. The rest deny the recovery; at least, Frank Harris does, though his thunder is so loud that perhaps I have mistaken his voice for the roar of a multitude."

"You will remember, sir, that I assured you it was entirely unnecessary for you to read Frank Harris. It was only when you insisted that I procured a copy. Dreadful creature!"

"The recovery from his marriage was easy, once he had reached London. His excitement was steadied, though not blunted, by the necessity to provide for his wife and children; and the narrow, wretched life he had escaped from formed a black background against which his new life blazed with intenser brightness.

"But you do not desire rhetoric from me. Your hope is, rather, that I will examine with precision the parts which formed the happy and powerful whole of Shakespeare's existence during his first years in London, whether he arrived there in 1585, or, tired of schoolmastering, in 1588 or 9.

"One of the chief elements in his happiness was satisfaction that he had found a place so quickly in the great world, that he had known how to use the too easy, indulgent, and impressionable nature, which had entangled him in an uncongenial marriage, to his own advantage in the hot competition of the stage. As early as 1592 he was one of the first dramatists of the day, and more securely placed than his master and collaborator, Marlowe.

"When, in this year, Chettle apologised for preparing Greene's attack on Shakespeare for the press, and praised Shakespeare's acting and facetious grace in writing, his civil demeanour and uprightness in dealing, he expressly excluded Marlowe, who had also taken offence at Greene's pamphlet, from this apology. Though Marlowe's genius, supported by the force and daring of his character, had made him the first dramatist of the day, both in merit and popularity, his recklessness was entangling him in difficulties which, but for his violent death in 1593, would soon have ruined him. He had already been thrown out of the Earl of Pembroke's company for atheism, a charge repeated in Greene's pamphlet; and to lose a nobleman's protection was a serious matter, for, as you know, only players under the patronage of a nobleman were exempt from arrest as rogues and vagabonds. The Puritans hated us, and they were very powerful. No plays, since many years, could be acted within the Puritan-ruled city; and though the great nobles were, in a general way, delighted to annoy the City Fathers by encouraging the drama, and fed their own vanity on the adulation of the troupes they supported, they could not challenge public morality by protecting an open atheist, who was also a boy-lover. It's true that Marlowe had for the time being found another patron to shelter him, but how long would Lord Strange have put up with him?"

"Precisely," Cecil interposed. "Shakespeare was a sober, hard-working actor and writer, not an unbalanced adventurer with a streak of amazing genius. Precisely."

"Yes," Shakespeare said uncertainly. He seemed disconcerted. "Yes." He recovered himself. "I did not mean to praise Shakespeare at Marlowe's expense, but to show that he knew how to use to his own advantage his sympathy, his sense of life and knowledge of character, his tact and suppleness; a capacity denied him by some critics, and exaggerated by other critics into his chief characteristic. I wished only to urge that he was not lifted to success by rough men, touched to unwonted charity by his union of spiritual omniscience and practical imbecility. But I had forgotten you would agree with all this. I believe I thought for a moment I had Frank Harris before me, whom, however, I must not mention only in dispraise; he is often very good, and it would have been a pleasure to me to meet him and put him right on the many points where he needs correction. As to your too sharp contrast between Shakespeare and Marlowe, and more especially your assumption that the differences between the two were all in Shakespeare's favour, which do you yourself prefer, Marlowe frightening Lord Pembroke with his loud atheism, or Shakespeare dedicating *The Rape of Lucrece* to the Earl of Southampton— 'What I have done is yours; what I have to do is yours; being part in all I have, devoted yours'?"

"I see no reason, sir, to question the sincerity of Shakespeare's attachment to his patron. The style is, perhaps, a little overcharged by modern standards. . . ."

"Overcharged by any standards. A month or so after this dedication, Shakespeare became one of the chief shareholders in the Lord Chamberlain's company."

"He had his way to make in the world. If Southampton was

privileged to help him with his influence, or, possibly, with a loan, I confess that . . . but, really, sir, . . . I hesitate to . . . but you are perhaps not aware that since your remarks—your, if I may venture to say so, your so admirable remarks on the emotional equipoise of *The Merchant of Venice* and *Much Ado*—you have entirely neglected that side of Shakespeare which, frankly, is the only side . . . at least, to my taste . . . I do not, of course . . . and naturally, in the circumstances. . . ."

"Yes, yes," Shakespeare smiled tolerantly. "How difficult it is," he said after a pause, "to say exactly what one thinks. Half a dozen thoughts, perhaps, on some matter exist side by side in the same mind, but only one can emerge at a time; and the first to get out usually stands at the exit, and hits the others over the head as they try to pass. I have spoken as if Shakespeare flattered South-ampton merely from calculation, though all I have said earlier of his longing for the magnificence of life and discontent with his own obscure rank makes it certain that the notice and friendly attentions of Southampton enchanted and gratified him beyond even his powers of acknowledgment. And I have spoken of Marlowe as if there were not at least as much weakness as strength in his self-assertion—'some fierce thing replete with too much rage, Whose strength's abundance weakens his own heart.' His nature was not open to life, did not welcome it, like Shakespeare's. I must not now go too far in the other direction and altogether excuse Shakespeare's flattery of Southampton, but in those years he flattered everything, saw all things richer and more splendid than they are, and all men as greedy of life and immortality as himself. 'Let fame, that all hunt after in their lives'—as if one man in ten thousand hunts, even in his most sanguine years, after anything except money, position, and women. But it was so that Shakespeare saw the world as it spread around him in the first days of his freedom. His young and tender wit, as he writes in *Two Gentlemen of Verona*, had been turned to folly by love, was losing its verdure even in the prime, and all the fair effects of future hopes. But he had escaped, and what a sense of ease and relief it revealed in the unchecked melody of his early plays!

> I rather would entreat thy company
> To see the wonders of the world abroad
> Than, living dully sluggardised at home,
> Wear out thy youth with shapeless idleness.

Still, among the fair effects of future hopes, which had been imperilled by the folly of love, was love itself. Shakespeare had not fled from Anne to wanton henceforth in unrestrained celibacy. Whom, and how many, did he love in these days of youthful assurance and exuberance?"

"I am afraid, sir, that unless you should yourself furnish the details, this is a question which must remain unanswered, for want of any data of any kind whatsoever."

"You despair too easily. An exact answer is impossible, but one may arrive at a general conclusion."

"Is it really——?"

"Everything that at this time fed his vanity and greed for life forged his later unhappiness, and his greatest work."

Shakespeare's eyes met Cecil's. There was a brief contest.

"Yes, master." Cecil dropped his head.

"Had not Shakespeare, like Richard, been halt and misshapen? A country lout tied to a shrew? And was he not now a rising player, a poet, the companion of noblemen?

> I do mistake my person all this while:
> Upon my life, she finds, although I cannot,
> Myself to be a marvellous proper man.
> I'll be at charges for a looking-glass,
> And entertain a score or two of tailors,
> To study fashions to adorn my body. . . .
> Shine out, fair sun, till I have bought a glass,
> That I may see my shadow as I pass."

"So," Cecil remarked, "Richard III is William Shakespeare with a hump clapped on his back."

"I feel Shakespeare in the exultant energy of Richard's triumph after the long humiliation of his early years. Otherwise there's little in common between them. But, I repeat, there was a day when to Shakespeare, as to Richard, it suddenly occurred that he was a marvellous proper man.

"This discovery I connect, however indirectly, with the original, or the originals, of the long line of gentle and luckless women in the plays: Julia in *Two Gentlemen of Verona*, Helena in *A Midsummer Night's Dream*, Hero in *Much Ado*, Celia in *As You Like It*, and Viola in *Twelfth Night*, and Juliet and Ophelia, Desdemona and Cordelia and Imogen. In the lighter plays this woman is made happy at the close, but the stigma of inferiority, of devotion too carelessly valued by its object, rests on her always. Does not Celia complain to Rosalind, 'I see thou lovest me not with the full weight that I love thee'?"

"But Juliet, sir, and Desdemona. Surely——"

"I shall come to Desdemona later. Juliet, as you rightly feel, is not luckless quite as the others are. Yet is not Romeo more in love with love than Juliet?

> How silver-sweet sound lovers' tongues by night,
> Like softest music to attending ears.

Compare this enjoyment of the situation with Juliet's frightened absorption in her passion. 'O God, I have an ill-divining soul,' she answers to Romeo's

> All these woes shall serve
> For sweet discourses in our time to come."

"Pardon me, master, but does that cry of Juliet's show any greater absorption than Romeo's

> Come what sorrow can,
> It cannot countervail the exchange of joy
> That one short minute gives me in her sight?"

"Yes. These words of Romeo, which are not spoken to Juliet herself, express rather the longing of all passionate and imaginative natures for entire self-abandonment than the instinctive self-surrender revealed in almost every word of Juliet's."

"Is it not possible, sir, if we must look for a common original for such widely different types as, to take three names from your list, Julia, Viola, and Imogen, that Shakespeare had in mind his own wife, since you admit that their marriage was a failure?"

"I think not, or only very faintly. Besides, I did not mean that all these women are copied from one original, or even that each of them had a living model. I meant rather that they all, in however different degrees, arouse the same kind of pity—the pity for those who, like Charmian, are 'more beloving than belov'd.' Later, when it was Shakespeare who loved with inadequate return, the pity he felt for his luckless heroines was mixed with his own self-pity; but at first it reflected only the perhaps rather complacent sympathy stirred in him during his early London years, when we must add to his success as an actor and dramatist the satisfaction to his vanity of being loved by one or several women. I do not say he showed them no tenderness and affection; but vanity, which with him, as with most men, implies sensuality, was the chief spur to his love-making at the time when he wrote:

> That man that hath a tongue, I say, is no man,
> If with his tongue he cannot win a woman."

"His very earliest play! Probably."

"But in the revised version of *Love's Labour's Lost*, some years later, he is still as proud as ever of his tongue, for you will not dispute that he describes himself in Rosaline's description of Berowne:

A merrier man,
Within the limit of becoming mirth,
I never coped an hour's talk withal.
His eye begets occasion for his wit;
For every object that the one doth catch
The other turns to a mirth-moving jest.

'A man replete with mocks,' Rosaline calls him elsewhere in this play.

Full of comparisons and wounding flouts,
Which you on all estates will execute
That lie within the mercy of your wit.

"It was his power over words, whether in talk or writing, which fed his vanity in those years, through the success it gave him in love, friendship, and practical life, a success almost equalling him for the moment, in his own esteem, with the young nobles who were still the chief objects of his admiration, and whose gallantry and wit and magnificent bravado he paints with such overflowing love in Mercutio, and glances at again and again in such phrases as

Rash, inconsiderate, fiery voluntaries,
With ladies' faces and fierce dragons' spleens.

"The excellence of life for him at this time—I see I weary you, but I must make this point, which is the clue to his later development, quite clear—was contained in the glorious existence of noble youth:

There shall he practise tilts and tournaments,
Hold sweet discourse, converse with noblemen,
And be in eye of every exercise
Worthy his youth and nobleness of birth.

"He was himself debarred, by his origin and upbringing, from these aristocratic recreations; and besides, he was somewhat small in person and, though full of energy and passion, neither muscular nor agile. Hence the force of his admiration, though, as we have seen, he found for a time in his gift of speech a certain compensation for all he otherwise lacked.

"It was this exultation in his command of words that entangled him in the morasses of his early humour, and the sounding emptiness of *Venus and Adonis* and *Lucrece*, in which, young and overpowered by the contemporary enthusiasm for Italy and the classic times, he tries in vain to impassion himself by verbal transcriptions of his patron's paintings and tapestries, and by modulations on themes borrowed from Ovid."

"Surely, master, there is exquisite poetry in such lines as 'leading him prisoner in a red-rose chain,' and in 'Or like a nymph with long dishevell'd hair, Dance on the sands and yet no footing seen.' And the lion who, to see Adonis's face, walked behind a hedge, so as not to terrify him—is not that an inimitable fancy?"

"Not half so inimitable as Venus's fancy that the boar who killed Adonis killed him by mistake. It seems the beast merely wished to kiss the boy—

> And, nuzzling in his flank, the loving swine
> Sheath'd unaware the tusk in his soft groin."

Shakespeare threw back his head, and roared with laughter.
"Ha! Quite. Nevertheless . . ."

"But, even in *Venus and Adonis*, his sympathy, unripe and overshadowed by vanity and ambition and the intense excitement of flowering genius, stirs in the picture of the hunted hare, poor Wat, who listens, far off upon a hill, to the loud alarums of his foes; and, as he flees again, 'each envious briar his weary legs doth scratch, Each shadow makes him stop, each murmur stay.'

"In hours or days of exhaustion Shakespeare felt, even in his happiest years, the pain of life, and condemned its prizes; but such condemnation, born of exhaustion not conviction, died as his strength came back. Since this world was his only world, for he had but a faint sense of any other, to the service of which he could have attached his hope and passion, life alone could cure him of life. There was for him nothing beyond life to detach him from its fascination.

"In these years the mood of exhaustion and disgust was itself subject to the universal fascination, for it flowed easily into words, and as it flowed dissolved in delight.

> O God, methinks it were a happy life
> To be no better than a homely swain;
> To sit upon a hill as I do now,
> To carve out dials quaintly, point by point,
> Thereby to see the minutes how they run. . . .
> So minutes, hours, days, months, and years,
> Pass'd over to the end they were created,
> Would bring white hairs unto a quiet grave.

"Tranquillised by the contemplation of eternal repose, he was himself again, and saw the world once more as an endless treasure-house of knowledge and beauty, knowledge in which he would clothe himself with angel-like perfection, beauty recreating itself for ever in new images; now dim, like far-off mountains turned into clouds, now fresh as spring when wheat is green, when haw-thorn-buds appear, or uncertain as the glory of an April day, or calm as the moon, new-bent like a silver bow in heaven."

"The real Shakespeare," Cecil murmured.

"*A Midsummer Night's Dream* marks the end of this period, of his youth. Puck's farewell words, when the other fairies have vanished, 'following darkness like a dream,' are Shakespeare's too.

> If we shadows have offended,
> Think but this, and all is mended:
> That you have but slumber'd here
> While these visions did appear.

"By the end of youth, I mean the end of that period during which a man's sense of what he wishes life to be is stronger than his sense of what it is. Naturally there is no sharp dividing-line between hope and knowledge. The golden mist, however often dissipated, rises from the marsh again, almost to the end of the journey.

"But, for the sake of clearness, I take *Richard II* as marking the first stage of Shakespeare's maturity, although, for various reasons, I think it was written just before *A Midsummer Night's Dream*, the humour in which, though exercised only on clowns, not on kings, looks forward to Falstaff, the fancy back to the nymph dancing on the sands in *Venus and Adonis*.

"In *Richard II* there is no humour. That form of criticism was not yet developed in Shakespeare. But his first strong revulsion against life, against the exhaustion of its struggles, and against its triumphs based on force and cunning, is expressed in the contrast between Bolingbroke and Richard, the triumphant usurper and the ruined king:

> No joyful tongue gave him his welcome home;
> But dust was thrown upon his sacred head.

To take Richard as representing the whole of Shakespeare, at this or any other date, is absurd. . . ."

"I am glad to hear you say that, sir."

"And I rejoice in your gladness. Shakespeare is in Bolingbroke as well as in Richard. Bolingbroke is Shakespeare, the full-sharer in the leading company of the day; Richard is Shakespeare, sick of work and love-making and the methods of success in both, sick of the envy he provoked in others, and the envy he felt himself.

> But, whate'er I be,
> Nor I nor any man that but man is
> With nothing shall be pleased, till he be eas'd
> With being nothing.

"There was another side to this disillusion. In this play, for the first time, his feelings about life seemed nearer to him and of more value than anything he could possess himself of in the outward world.

You may my glories and my state depose,
But not my griefs; still am I king of those."

"Surely, sir, the emphasis here is on '*king*.' Richard's griefs are now his kingdom, and while he lords it over them he feels himself not altogether dispossessed of his state. You do not suggest, do you, sir, that Shakespeare, a prosperous actor, applied this rather far-fetched conceit of a royal weakling to himself?"

"I don't know what else I suggested, nor do I call this natural thought a far-fetched conceit."

"I stand corrected."

"At the same time, Richard is not only a mood of Shakespeare's, but a persistent exemplar, after his fall, of the truth that a king is merely a man, a truth which Shakespeare seems now for the first time to have realised imaginatively.

For you have but mistook me all this while:
I live with bread like you, feel want,
Taste grief, need friends; subjected thus,
How can you say to me I am a king?

"As a closer view of royalty and the aristocracy began to sap Shakespeare's awe and respect, his humour expanded, and in its turn helped on the process of disintegration. The notion that humour is distasteful to power and position had already occurred to him when he was writing *King John*. 'That idiot, laughter,' the king says, 'a passion hateful to my purposes.'

"Laughter is not an aristocratic passion. To most persons, indeed, the use of the word passion in connection with laughter would seem rather exaggerated, but it fell naturally from Shakespeare—

More merry tears
The passion of loud laughter never shed.

Whatever else he admired and imitated in the aristocracy, he never took up the weak, sapless pose of checking his laughter in the supposed interests of good breeding. Of that I am certain."

"I, too, sir."

"You, too?" Shakespeare glanced sharply at Cecil.

"Too rich a nature, master, too puissant."

"Oh, I see. Where was I? The growth of his humour. Yes. In the first stage, as I said, it was exercised on the rustics of *A Midsummer Night's Dream* or, still earlier, on the servants of young noblemen—Launce, for example. In *Romeo and Juliet* it ranges from the nurse to old Capulet, the first of Shakespeare's aristocrats who is also a figure of fun—'We have a trifling foolish banquet towards.'

"A little later, in *The Merchant of Venice*, the conflict between his growing humour and his bondage to worldly values comes out in Gratiano, who tells Antonio he has too much respect for the world—'they lose it that do buy it with much care'; and goes on to ridicule those 'who only are reputed wise for saying nothing. . . .'

> Let me play the fool.
> With mirth and laughter let old wrinkles come."

"If I remember aright, sir, Gratiano is not taken very seriously by the important personages of the play."

"Quite true. 'Gratiano speaks an infinite deal of nothing,' Bassanio says; 'more than any man in all Venice.' I am not arguing that Shakespeare at this time looked at life from Gratiano's standpoint, or at any time looked at life exclusively from this angle. He was beginning, however, to include Gratiano's philosophy in his general view of things; being urged thereto partly by reflection, partly by a growing exasperation with the young noblemen of the day. Friendship with them on equal terms was impossible. He was a mere player, very brilliant and amusing, but, like Gratiano, not taken seriously by important personages; and every aristocrat was, compared with a player, an important personage. Beyond doubt, he often talked too much and too well for their taste, and they eased their self-esteem by treating him as a clown, as Bassanio treats Gratiano. I see Shakespeare and Gratiano's revenge in

Portia's mockery of Falconbridge, her English suitor. 'A proper man's picture, but, alas! who can converse with a dumb-show?' And there are other signs in this play of his ripening irritation against the swagger of his youthful patrons:

> I'll speak of frays
> Like a fine bragging youth, and tell quaint lies,
> How honourable ladies sought my love.

Is it considering the matter too curiously to see another sign in the Neapolitan prince who 'makes it a great appropriation to his own good parts that he can shoe' his horse? Shakespeare, I feel certain, could not have shoed even a rabbit."

"But, sir, really! Shakespeare! Is it possible, do you seriously mean to suggest, that with his divine endowment he could conceivably allow his self-esteem to be ruffled by such immeasurably trivial considerations?"

"It was just what you call his divine endowment, his apprehension of every form of power, that made him sensible to these trivialities. Do you think he could have given so full an image of life if he had not felt life first, felt it, desired it, in all its manifestations, great and small? Is not the freedom he won through his imagination the exact measure of the desire from which his imagination liberated him?"

"Z-z."

"We are agreed, then. Passing from *The Merchant of Venice* to *Much Ado*, we find in Benedick, who, like Berowne, has a great deal of Shakespeare in him, more evidence of the wound to Shakespeare's vanity when his wit and humour were undervalued, treated as the attributes of a clown. Consider these words of Beatrice: 'He'll but break a comparison or two on me; which, peradventure not marked, or not laughed at, strikes him into melancholy'; and Benedick's mortified afterthoughts when Beatrice has called him the prince's jester: 'The prince's fool! Ha! it may be I go under that title because I am merry. Yea, but so I am apt to do myself wrong; I am not so reputed; it is the base though bitter disposition of Beatrice that puts the world into her

F

person, and so gives me out. Well, I'll be revenged as I may.'

"And there's another passage in *Much Ado* to our present purpose:

> What, man! I know them, yea:
> And what they weigh, even to the utmost scruple,
> Scrambling, out-facing, fashion-monging boys
> That lie, and cog, and flout, deprave and slander.

"We—or rather I, for you are a little obstructive at the moment —now arrive at the character in the process of creating whom Shakespeare's humour and social sense came for the first time into desperate conflict, from which his social sense emerged as the nominal victor, but badly wounded, and never to be the same again. I think it's especially true of Falstaff, but in some degree it's true of every imagined person, that as he puts on flesh and blood he surprises his creator. The relation between a poet's experience and emotion and the characters in whom he embodies them never turns out quite as he had foreseen. Some of his characters are richer, more attractive, than his expectation, others meaner.

'Falstaff, to begin with, is the conventional comic butt, the fat lecher, braggart, and coward, against whose real degradation the mock degradation of Prince Hal shows as merely the high spirits of an essentially valiant and high-souled youth.

"Or, rather, this is how Shakespeare saw Falstaff and Prince Hal before he set pen to paper; for Falstaff, as soon as he appears, is already so full of virtue that the set speech of Prince Hal, at the close of this scene, in which the prince excuses his association with Falstaff as a piece of policy, appears as both stilted and irrelevant.

"The virtue of Falstaff is not to be established by explaining away his villainies and weaknesses. He is a lecher and glutton, a swindler and braggart, and genuinely averse from the violence inseparable from a pitched battle. There is the very soul of sincerity in: 'I would it were bed-time, Hal, and all well.' Since, in spite of these frailties, he dwarfs Prince Hal, the old king, and Hotspur, it might be argued that he is, or in the course of the play becomes, even against Shakespeare's conscious intention, a dissolvent of the heroic element in life. But the heroic figures, young Harry with his beaver on, and Hotspur plucking bright honour from the pale-faced moon, and the dying king looking back over his hard ascent to power, are not diminished actually, only relatively, by the presence of Falstaff.

"The qualities admired by society were also admired by Shakespeare, and he never ceased to be concerned with his own social position, which he improved to the furthest extent possible within the limits imposed on him by his profession. But, by the date of Falstaff, much of the poetic illusion in which his desire for social position was rooted had been worn away. The conceit of the aristocracy was beginning to jar not only on his vanity, but on his love of life for its own sake, without reference to personal distinction and advancement. He still retained, and never, except for brief periods in his worst days, lost, his enthusiasm for the heroic element in life. But he wished now, not quite consciously, at any rate at first, to place heroism, which is usually self-centred, and always impoverished of every element in human nature not subservient to its purpose, in its proper perspective. Against the absorption of the hero in his conflict with others he wished to set the enjoyment of life by the senses, and the delight in life of the imagination.

"This enjoyment and delight were his own, but, limited by reality and respect for social obligations, he could no more indulge them to the full than he could emulate Hotspur. Falstaff no less than Hotspur is an ideal figure. His allegiance to life balances Hotspur's allegiance to honour. Hotspur cries:

> Send danger from the east unto the west,
> So honour cross it from the north to south.

The mass of men follow honour with backward glances of regret. Falstaff flatly desires to live—'Give me life; which if I can save, so; if not, honour comes unlooked for, and there's an end.' The ideas of God, patriotism, honour, reputation, which confuse the minds of most men, have no power on Falstaff so soon as they conflict with the imperious obligation of remaining extant. When the prince, before battle, reminds Falstaff that he owes God a death, Falstaff replies, ''Tis not due yet; I would be loath to pay him before his day. What need I be so forward with him that calls not on me?'

"This sincerity is not a criticism of courage, but of the ordinary pretence of courage. Falstaff says what most men think, and this is at the root of our admiration for him; but this admiration is only half realised, since it conflicts with the universal habit of admiring qualities for their social value. If intellectual courage served society, it would be as much admired as physical courage. But it is a virtue of the individual and, unlike physical courage, could not become a virtue of the community without disintegrating the conventions and illusions on which the social order rests.

"On this foundation of a sincerity which he dared not practise himself, Shakespeare erected the superstructure of Falstaff's love of life, an all-inclusive appetite ranging from Dame Quickly's purse and person to honour and piety, two dishes which he would taste more freely but for fear of indigestion. 'I'll purge, and leave sack, and live cleanly, as a nobleman should do,' he says, when the battle is over, and rewards for valour in prospect; and, affronted by the martially innocuous Pistol, he is as impatient to avenge his honour as Hotspur himself.

"Falstaff's love of life is sometimes sensual, sometimes disinterested."

"Disinterested! Falstaff! You do not suggest, sir, that Falstaff is disinterested!"

"How much oftener, Cecil, are you going to tell me I don't suggest what I do suggest?

"Falstaff is both the richness of existence and a spectator of this richness. Although, consistently both with Falstaff's original character and with the character of all who are impassioned for life, Shakespeare roots Falstaff's love of life in sensuality, it rises with its own sap into the region of the imagination.

"Prince Hal, a type of Shakespeare's noble patrons, has no imaginative detachment. His humour, which is never directed against himself, is crude and personal, with Falstaff as its mark. But Falstaff's humour includes the whole spectacle of life, with himself, life's largest object, in the foreground: 'A goodly portly man i' faith, and a corpulent; of a cheerful look, a pleasing eye, and a most noble carriage. . . . If that man should be lewdly given, he deceiveth me; for, Harry, I see virtue in his looks.' When his humour is directed on other persons, it is to enrich his own sense of life, not to wound their vanity, though that is often the result, owing to a failure of the poetic sense in his victims. Compare, for example, Prince Hal's abuse of Falstaff— 'That trunk of humours, that bolting-hutch of beastliness, that swol'n parcel of dropsies, that huge tankard of sack, that stuffed cloak-bag of guts'—with Falstaff's improvisation on the theme of Bardolph's nose: 'When thou rannest up Gadshill in the night to catch my horse, if I did not think thou had'st been an *ignis fatuus* or a ball of wildfire, there's no purchase in money. O! thou art a perpetual triumph, an everlasting bonfire-light.' There is the same contrast between Prince Hal's limited, professional view of Falstaff's ragged regiment—'I did never see such pitiful rascals'—and Falstaff's answer: 'Tush, man, mortal men, mortal men.'

"It is by virtue of this detachment that he disconcerts the Prince and the Lord Chief Justice, the representatives of the social order, above whose attempts to keep the talk to narrow personal issues he floats vastly in the serener air of meditation on many things, from the fall of Adam to the imperfect sympathy between the old and the young.

"From this height, looking down at Prince Hal far below, he says, charitably, 'A good shallow young fellow: a' would have made a good pantler, a' would have chipped bread well.' "

"Falstaff was born from the conflict between Shakespeare's recognition that the social order is a necessity, and his sense of how heavily those who love life pay for the benefits of this order. This sense, deepening as Falstaff took more and more possession of his imagination, made him towards the close of *Henry IV* heighten both Falstaff's lovableness and detachment. When Falstaff is summoned once more to battle—'the undeserver may sleep when the man of action is called upon'—the love of Dame Quickly submerges in the hour of parting the wrongs inflicted on her by the anti-social temperament of the knight. Snatching from the chaos of her mind a horticultural image in which to resume the long history of her intimacy with Falstaff, she sighs: 'Well, fare thee well: I have known thee these twenty-nine years, come peascod-time; but an honester, or truer-hearted man—well, fare thee well'; and even Doll Tearsheet sobs, 'If my heart be not ready to burst.'

"In the Shallow scenes Falstaff, when not engaged in the business of being bribed by the recruits, is—especially in his comments on Shallow's bragging, and as the sympathetic spectator of Master Silence's Bacchic exuberance—Shakespeare himself absorbing the variety of existence. The news of the old king's death sends him back to the character he wore at his first appearance, and it is as youth's misleader that the new head of the social order shatters, wisely from the standpoint of the social order, the vast image of life rejoicing in itself."

CHAPTER THREE

"THE OBVERSE OF Falstaff," Shakespeare continued, after a long pause, as if to allow the huge bulk and burning face of the knight to fade away into the shadows cast by the moon, "the other side of Shakespeare at this time reveals itself in the Sonnets."

"He was now thirty-five; that part of his nature which had conspired with circumstances to give him money and success was no longer in the ascendant, and with its decline his zest in seeing the humorous side of the struggle for position declined, too. In the previous two years he had bought New Place at Stratford, and had at last persuaded the College of Arms to recognise his gentility; but such pleasure as he felt when these ambitions were realised was clouded by the death, shortly before these deals were completed, of his son Hamnet. In him he lost the male heir to the position he had built up, and also a son whom he had seen too rarely, and I think there is some of his own remorse in the cry of Leontes:

> Cease! Thou know'st
> He dies to me again when talk'd of

and in Macduff's lament over the children murdered while he was away:

> I cannot but remember such things were,
> Which were most precious to me.

"The growing melancholy of these years is expressed in the Sonnets. How far they are autobiographical, and, if autobiographical, what exactly is the story they contain, appears to be a problem which no writer on Shakespeare has ever been persuaded to solve except in a way which suits his own preconception of Shakespeare's character; some holding that Shakespeare loved the young man ideally, some that he loved him passionately, some that he played up to him out of snobbish or interested motives, some that he invented him as a peg to hang his poetry on. The other person in the Sonnets has also, I find, been approached from a number of angles, some believing her to be merely the convention of a competent Elizabethan sonneteer, some regarding her as the original of the sensual and faithless women in the later plays, Cressida, Goneril and Cleopatra, some resenting her as a vexatious though trivial interruption of Shakespeare's relations with the young man. To me it seems that the youth and the woman together embody the sum of Shakespeare's desires in the years when vanity and sensuality drove him forward, and an obscure expectation that the ideal could be made real, and perfect love attained in the mutual love of imperfect human beings.

"That the woman in the Sonnets was the chief love of Shakespeare's life I take to be certain, and that she was Mary Fitton, a maid-of-honour at the Court, I shall assume; and that the young man in the Sonnets was of noble birth I take to be certain, and that he was William Herbert, Earl of Pembroke, I shall assume; and about these certainties and assumptions I beg your silence, at whatever cost of inward suffering."

Shakespeare paused while Cecil selected a fresh cigarette, and, after breaking two matches, lit it.

"The Sonnets, most of them at any rate, were, I think, written in the last three or four years of the century, between, roughly, *The Merchant of Venice* and *Twelfth Night*, in each of which plays there is a pair which gives a clue to the relations of Shakespeare and Pembroke. The devotion of Antonio, the merchant, to the young adventurer, Bassanio, is rooted in a strange melancholy, incongruous with the light tone of the play, and the social equality of the two friends. The happiness of Antonio, 'a tainted wether of the flock' as he calls himself, seems to be fed from no other source than the consciousness that he has been, at the cost of his own life, serviceable to his young friend: 'All debts are cleared between you and I, if I might but see you at my death.' Faced by death and mutilation, both incurred to further Bassanio's fortune-hunting projects, he is consoled by the hope, which does not appear to be a certainty, that Bassanio will impress on Portia the fact of Antonio's devotion:

Tell her the process of Antonio's end;
Say how I lov'd you, speak me fair in death;
And, when the tale is told, bid her be judge
Whether Bassanio had not once a love.

"The same entire devotion to a young man is shown by another Antonio, in *Twelfth Night*, who, at the risk of his life, goes ashore in Illyria with Sebastian, and places his purse at the youth's disposal. You will remember that, through a misunderstanding, Antonio believes Sebastian has disowned him, and this gives Shakespeare an opportunity for expressing yet again the bitterness he felt at his own betrayal by Pembroke:

Is't possible that my deserts to you
Can lack persuasion?

"These two examples, combined with our knowledge of Shakespeare's development up to 1597, make clear whatever is obscure in the nature of Shakespeare's devotion to the young man of the Sonnets. The self-confidence and the exuberance engendered by his first successes were over by this date; and the coat-of-arms which transformed him into William Shakespeare of Stratford-on-Avon, gentleman, by placing him as high as it was possible for him to get, made him all the more aware of the altitudes barred for ever to his ambition. His appetite, in brief, had been whetted, but what further means of satisfying it could he hope to find?"

"I thought, sir, that it had been decided in the course of your exposition of the growth of Shakespeare's humour, culminating in Falstaff, that Shakespeare by this date viewed the aristocracy with a certain contempt?"

"But this contempt, when he was not in a Falstaffian or poetic mood, made their contempt the more galling. I need not, I suppose, pause to convince you that the same object may inspire both contempt and adoration. It was Shakespeare's ill-luck, or rather, the logical issue of his development, that his friendship with

Pembroke and, far more profoundly, his love for Mary Fitton were both rooted in this contradiction.

"Pembroke, beautiful, very young, an aristocrat, and un-married, was everything that Shakespeare was not. That he ever cared for Shakespeare seems to me unlikely; but he was probably attracted enough by Shakespeare's wit and humour, and his reputation as the most brilliant dramatist of the day, to meet him for a time on what Shakespeare mistook for the equal terms of a sincere friendship. By virtue of this friendship, Shakespeare managed for a time to persuade himself that he participated in Pembroke's advantages of birth, youth, beauty, and aristocratic accomplishments. This illusion explains the emotion in these Sonnets; a yearning towards Pembroke as the embodiment of what he would have wished himself to be. No doubt he also expected some practical advantages from their friendship; but I do not find any trace of physical desire in his attachment, in spite of what has been urged to the contrary by persons anxious to have their tastes supported by Shakespeare's example, and unable to understand the excesses of the imagination.

"Made lame by fortune's spite, he says, he takes all his comfort from his friend's worth:

> I in thy abundance am suffic'd
> And by a part of all thy glory live;

and elsewhere:

> Thy love is better than high birth to me,
> Richer than wealth, prouder than garments' cost,
> Of more delight than hawks or horses be;
> And having thee of all men's pride I boast.

Against his friend's glory he sets his own outcast state; his player's life—'I have gone here and there, and made myself a motley to the view'—his unending conflict with the degrading circumstances in which he is involved—'almost thence my nature is subdu'd, to what it works in, like the dyer's hand.'

"He sets, too, with an even deeper emotion, his burden of years against his friend's youth and beauty; feeling, though only in the middle thirties, the first cold breath of decline against his cheek. The reverse of Falstaff's overflowing love of life is in these lamentations, echoing from sonnet to sonnet, over the journey of youthful morn to age's steepy night, the pilgrimage of beauty among the wastes of time, the barren rage of death.

> How with this rage shall beauty hold a plea,
> Whose action is no stronger than a flower?

The vain conflict with Time reconciles him at last to death, for 'Death once dead, there's no more dying then.' He speaks of 'my well-contented day, when that churl Death my bones with dust shall cover'; and desires eternal oblivion, to forget and to be forgotten:

> When I perhaps compounded am with clay,
> Do not so much as my poor name rehearse.

"In all these Sonnets I feel Pembroke's indifference to Shakespeare. Pembroke's betrayal of his friend with Mary Fitton does not in itself prove he did not care for Shakespeare. This appears rather from the tone of the Sonnets addressed to him: one has, after a time, the sense of a man addressing someone who is no longer present."

"Or of someone who has forgotten anyone is present to address."

"In the sonnets of pure imagination, you mean? Pembroke as a symbol of youth and beauty. That's true, too. But he loved Pembroke and suffered for a long time from his indifference. You may remember that Henry IV, speaking on his death-bed to Prince Hal, who he believes desires his death, uses almost the words I have just quoted: 'Only compound me with forgotten dust.' It is curious, I think, that Shakespeare should have filled hard crafty old Bolingbroke with such yearning affection towards

Prince Hal. There is something more in it than a successful man's continuance of himself in his eldest son."

"Surely, sir, you do not s——? I beg your pardon."

"*Henry IV* is contemporary with the Sonnets, which seems to me to explain in part the pathos of: 'I stay too long by thee, I weary thee,' and

> Not an eye
> But is aweary of thy common sight
> Save mine, which hath desired to see thee more;
> Which now doth that I would not have it do,
> Make blind itself with foolish tenderness.

"Deeper and richer than any other element in his nature, though obscured during many years by vanity and ambition, was the desire for love expressed in these lines. One gets tired at last of the tumultuous solitude of life. Shakespeare had reached the age when most men begin to wither into barren selfishness, but when those of larger heart seek a more profound consolation than can be found in the outward world. As far as his, or any man's, desire for love can be satisfied, it was ready to be satisfied now, had not the obsession of power and worldly distinction, embodying its fascination in Mary Fitton, intervened, barring him for ever from that approximation to ideal love which life, imperfect though it is, might have afforded him.

"What this witty, lustful, imperious girl really felt about life and about the men—Shakespeare, Pembroke, and the rest—to whom she gave herself as fancy directed, Shakespeare nowhere tells us, and never, I think, fully divined. In the Sonnets he speaks of her mourning eyes, yet never seems to have guessed that her melancholy was the reverse side of her greed for life, and that if he wished to attach her to him he must satisfy her need, not clamour for the satisfaction of his own. The profound discontent of her nature, which he might have appeased, which he had surely enough sympathy and insight to appease, forced her to prefer what was precarious and elusive, the careless love of Pembroke, to the slavish adoration of Shakespeare.

So runn'st thou after that which flies from thee,
Whilst I thy babe chase thee afar behind;
But if thou catch thy hope, turn back to me,
And play the mother's part, kiss me, be kind.

What force did he think such an appeal would have with the
girl whom he sketched as Rosaline, Rosalind, and Beatrice, and
painted in her later years as Cleopatra? The fool!"

Cecil started. Shakespeare was sitting upright.

"But he was a fool from the very start. Using the tongue he
was so proud of to feed her conceit, as if it needed feeding! What
did she, not yet twenty, think of him, the famous playwright,
fifteen years her senior, cudgelling his wits to amuse her when she
strode swaggering into the theatre, the young fools of the Court
at her heels?

How I would make him fawn, and beg, and seek,
And wait the season and observe the times,
And spend his prodigal wits in bootless rimes,
And shape his service wholly to my hests,
And make him proud to make me proud that jests!

Yet she came to love him, in a way; their love, such as it was,
lasted for many years; and I see now that she wished to love him
more than he would ever let her; for she felt something in him
which she needed, but could not find in the others. There was a
flaw in her that nothing could have patched; she was at odds with
life from the beginning, from which sprang, even in her teens, her
rage for men. Lasting happiness with Shakespeare, a married man
and a player, was, in any case, impossible; but he was different
from the rest, if only he had understood his difference! It is so
clear to me now. Why couldn't I see it then? Look at what he
makes Troilus say:

I do not call your faith in question
So mainly as my merit; I cannot sing,
Nor heel the high lavolt, nor sweeten talk,

Nor play at subtle games; fair virtues all,
To which the Grecians are most prompt and pregnant.

As if she wanted him to sing and heel the high lavolt, and sweeten talk after the tedious fashion of her noble lovers! Heel the high lavolt! If she wanted an aristocrat she could find one easily enough without coming to William Shakespeare, of Stratford-on-Avon, gentleman. What was it she wanted from him? I know what he wanted from her. When he took her in his arms, and her mocking mouth warmed against his, and she closed her eyes to veil her passion, he held the vain desire of his life in his arms, had at last subdued nobility to his pleasure. But she was faithless, the bay where all men ride, a common conquest, 'the lees and dregs of a flat tamèd piece.' His desire had escaped him again, and his passion turned to mere revengeful lust—'past reason hunted; and no sooner had, Past reason hated.' So he cheated her of what she desired from him, the tenderness she felt in him, the love which enriched his most casual acquaintance, but was denied to her, who to gain it had given herself to a common player, a man who belonged to some coarse country woman. His lust she punished with faithlessness, and his inflamed unhappy vanity with the disdain of her youth and noble birth. Such was their love, each cheating and cheated."

Shakespeare paused, leant back again, and crossed his legs. The silence oppressed Cecil. "Yes," he at last remarked.

"That she finally became almost as much involved as Shakespeare seems to me probable. At any rate, it may have been so (he glanced sharply at Cecil, whose lips were tight and face inexpressive). But in the first two or three years when, in Jaques's phrase, she was young and fair, and had the gift to know it, she was more flattered by his subjection than conscious of the need which he could have appeased. To this period belong his pictures of her as Rosaline and Beatrice, and, as his subjection deepened and his self-assurance fell from him, Rosalind in *As You Like It*. In Orlando, to whom Rosalind surrenders her heart without a struggle, with his beauty, strength, courage, modesty, and, above all, his laborious insistence on his sonship to Sir Rowland de Boys, Shakespeare assembles all the merits which he lacked, and which he imagined necessary to the conquest of Mary Fitton; and to this model of perfection he attaches, in abject devotion, the faithful retainer, Adam, a part which he himself played, the image of unregarded age in corners thrown.

"All that was most fascinating in Mary Fitton he shows in Rosalind, with no alloy: 'Come, woo me, woo me; for now I am in a holiday humour, and like enough to consent. What would you say to me now, an I were your very Rosalind?' His unhappiness he reveals in the disdainful treatment of the shepherd Silvius by the shepherdess Phebe, and salves his vanity in Rosalind's contempt of Phebe's inky brows, and black silk hair, and bugle eyeballs, and cheek of cream. 'You foolish shepherd, wherefore do you follow her?' Rosalind cries to Silvius. 'You are a thousand times a properer man, Than she a woman.' "

"Sir!"

"Yes?"

"Is that exquisite comedy—that—that—is it—has it no other value than——This mode of approach—it is all so—so *cramping*. That world, that many-hued projection of his incomparable imagination—dissected. And then—what? Débris! *Vie intime du grande poete anglais!* What one sees on Paris bookstalls—is it?—well!"

"The vain faith and service of Silvius's love:

> All made of passion, and all made of wishes;
> All adoration, duty, and observance;
> All humbleness, all patience, and impatience;
> All purity, all trial, all obeisance;

his despairing cry 'O Phebe, Phebe, Phebe!', disturb only for a moment the image of an ideal world to which Shakespeare had fled from the unrest and oppression of desire; a forest where they fleeted the time carelessly in a life more sweet than that of painted pomp—the country of his youth, made pure and fine by distance, where tiny figures walked, he and Anne, in a dream:

It was a lover and his lass,
With a hey, and a ho, and a hey-nonino,
That o'er the green corn-field did pass.
In the spring-time, the only pretty ring-time,
When birds do sing, hey-ding-a-ding-ding,
Sweet lovers love the spring. . . .

Sweet lovers love the spring."

The intense longing in his voice communicated itself to Cecil. Without volition, in unison, they intoned "Sweet lovers love the spring."

"His loss of energy and self-confidence, the humiliation of Mary Fitton's betrayal of him with Pembroke, and his impotent desire to avenge this particular injury and the general slights of life and his trade, are all discernible in his writings towards the close of the century. For a time his contempt, a common phenomenon, directed itself against the victim, against Silvius, against Malvolio—whose last words, when his dream of union with the high-born Olivia is over, are a helpless threat: 'I'll be revenged on the whole pack of you'; and against Pistol, who, as he eats the leek under Fluellen's compulsion, cries: 'By this leek, I will most horribly avenge.' But when he has taken his beating, Pistol's swagger falls from him at last: 'Old do I wax, and from my weary limbs honour is cudgelled.' Dame Quickly, his wife, is dead in hospital of the French malady. Even Falstaff has at last suffered defeat: 'the king hath killed his heart.' "

"Pistol-Shakespeare!"

"More bitter still is the humiliation of Parolles, who, however, for Shakespeare's mood was changing, finds within himself, when all his pretensions have been stripped from him, a kind of desperate support against the world:

Captain I'll be no more;
But I will eat and drink, and sleep as soft
As captain shall: simply the thing I am
Shall make me live.

"The world of his imagination was suffering a corresponding change. Italy, the land of youth and love, was fading—the burning noon of Verona, and the warm nights of *The Merchant* and *Much Ado*. In *As You Like It* he returns to the cool green north, and the sunlight in the Illyria of *Twelfth Night* is subdued.

"Far back, at the grey horizon's bound, lay his past, where he had once stood looking forward, under a bright and endless sky:

> A great while ago the world began,
> With hey, ho, the wind and the rain.

"To the humiliations of his private life were now added other troubles. I need not set forth the evidence which proves that Shakespeare's personal sympathies were closely involved in the fate of Essex, the friend of Southampton, Shakespeare's patron. Even those critics who do not like categorically to admit that Shakespeare ever went outside the discreet routine of breathing, eating, sleeping, and making money, concede that he must have been interested in the execution of Essex and the narrow escape of Southampton from the same fate.

"This tragedy did more than any other single experience to cure Shakespeare of his illusions about royalty, and the great of this world in general, though the cure seems never to have been quite complete and final.

"*Julius Cæsar*, written after Essex's disgrace and before his execution, is the most restrained, the least open and flowing of all Shakespeare's plays. Only in the rhetoric of Antony, and the personal emotion of the quarrel between Brutus and Cassius, and, later, their farewell, is the restraint at all relaxed. The cause of this restraint was the desire Shakespeare felt to express his opinion of the capricious old tyrant who had disgraced Essex in such a form as would not lead to his inclusion among the victims of her fury."

"But, sir, why do you—what necessity is there to identify Elizabeth and Cæsar?"

"I feel Elizabeth in Cæsar's senile conceit and vacillation."

"Shakespeare's material for his picture of Cæsar is lifted, with hardly any modification, from Plutarch."

"The material, yes, but not the tone; and, even if the tone were common to both of them, what would that prove but that Shakespeare found in Plutarch what his feelings at the time demanded?

"The theme he had chosen allowed him to express not only his antipathy to Elizabeth, but his disgust with the populace, whose mad enthusiasm when Essex left for Ireland had already turned to apathy or contempt. From this time onwards his references to the fickleness of the mob are full of bitterness.

"The extraordinary feeling which Shakespeare puts into the love of the impatient, vehement Cassius for his correct and priggish friend——"

"Cassius-Shakespeare now! A composite personality!"

Shakespeare paused. Cecil shifted uneasily. "Your pipe, sir. It is out. May I——?" He struck a match, and applied it to Shakespeare's pipe.

"Meanwhile," said Shakespeare, after puffing at his pipe for some moments in silence, "things were beginning to go badly for Shakespeare in his profession. Two companies of boy-actors, the Children of the Chapel Royal and the Children of St Paul's Cathedral, eclipsed for a time the established companies. The Globe suffered so badly that it shut down for some months, and the company went on tour in the provinces, thus, as Hamlet says, losing both in reputation and profit. Ben Jonson, whom Shakespeare had helped when he was unknown, Chapman, Marston, and other leading playwrights, wrote for the boy-actors, seasoning their work with abuse of the public theatres, 'the common stages.' The ill-feeling thus generated issued in a confused brawl between all the playwrights of the day. There was, in Guildenstern's phrase, 'much throwing-about of brains'; but you are as familiar as I am with the resentment which Shakespeare expressed in *Hamlet* against the 'aery of children, little eyases, that cry out on the top of question, and are most tyrannically clapped for it.' and against the insults they treated the common players to.

"All the complicated bitterness of this period, his rage against

Mary Fitton, his disgust with the Queen and the aristocracy, his contempt for the loud playwrights, his fellows in the trade he was compelled to pursue, and his fears for his own fortunes, poured itself into *Troilus and Cressida*, a play 'never stal'd with the stage, never clapper-claw'd with the palms of the vulgar,' as the publisher discreetly put the fact that it had never been staged. 'This isn't going to help us much,' I imagine Burbage saying to Shakespeare, tapping the MS. 'We can't afford to take risks, with these damned brats at our heels. We'll have to put on one of the old pieces, Falstaff or Romeo. Go into the country. You need a rest—so do I, for that matter, but—[shrugs his shoulders]. And come back with the kind of thing you *can* do when you want to.' Then, in a sudden passion of self-pity, 'Good heavens, man, d'you think *I'm* enjoying myself at the moment?'

"The relation in which *Troilus and Cressida* stands to Shakespeare's private feelings is easy to trace, because his misfortunes had for the time impaired his imaginative force, and power of detachment. His emotions speak through his puppets with hardly any transformation. The extraordinarily witty and penetrating portrait of Ajax 'melancholy without cause, and merry against the hair . . . gouty Briareus, many hands and no use; or purblind Argus, all eyes and no sight' is Ben Jonson to the life; and the long, the disproportionately long, appeal of Ulysses to Achilles to return to the fight reflects Shakespeare's own feeling that he must bestir himself against the boy-actors, and whip up his productivity, now for more than a year gone lame.

> What! am I poor of late? [says Achilles]
> 'Tis certain, greatness, once fall'n out with fortune,
> Must fall out with men too . . .

And Ulysses answers:

> O! let not virtue seek
> Remuneration for the thing it was. . . .
> The present eye praises the present object:
> Then marvel not, thou great and complete man,

That all the Greeks begin to worship Ajax;
 . . . The cry went once on thee,
And still it might, and yet it may again,
If thou would'st not entomb thyself alive,
And case thy reputation in a tent."

"Shakespeare, then," Cecil ventured, "is now Achilles, no longer Pistol, or Silvius, or Malvolio?"

"Yes. His bitterness in this play directs itself outwards. Troilus, himself as lover, is

  as true as truth's simplicity,
And simpler than the infancy of truth.

"Cressida's betrayal of him with Diomedes cannot be excused by anything he has done or omitted to do. He is the image of ingenuous love, and Cressida the image of unrelieved vanity and lust, a sluttish spoil of opportunity and daughter of the game. His longing is purity itself in the cry, 'O Cressida! How often have I wished me thus!' No less pure is the controlled agony in his reassurance to Ulysses, in whose company he overhears the love-scene between Cressida and Diomedes:

You have sworn patience [Ulysses says],

  Fear me not, sweet lord;
I will not be myself, nor have cognition
Of what I feel: I am all patience.

"Against this idealised portrait Shakespeare, to ease his rage against sex, sets the lust of Pandarus, who hops and skips round the young lovers in a senile ecstasy of vicarious satisfaction. 'How now, how now! how go maidenheads?' But the chief vent of Shakespeare's disgust is Thersites.

"Thersites is Falstaff gone rotten. The heroism which Falstaff approved from a reasonable distance, Thersites exposes on the scene of its exploits. Hotspur has become Ajax or Achilles. Both are equally contemptible to Thersites, lumbering bullies—the one 'bought and sold among those of any wit, like a barbarian slave'; the other 'an idol of idiot-worshippers . . . who wears his wit in his belly, and his guts in his head.'

"I do not mean that Shakespeare identifies himself with Thersites. He recognises the envy from which this malevolence derives. 'I have said my prayers, and devil Envy say Amen.' But it calmed him to discharge through Thersites the accumulated resentment of years. 'Speaking is for beggars,' Thersites says of Ajax; 'he wears his tongue in his arms,' an attitude towards those who can use their tongues which Shakespeare had often encountered among the less articulate aristocrats of the day.

"He employs Thersites, too, to degrade sex, so as to ease his own slavery to lust by turning it to ridicule; and for this purpose makes Thersites a fellow-witness with Troilus and Ulysses to Cressida's surrender to Diomedes. 'How the devil Luxury, with his fat rump and potato finger, tickles these two together! Fry, lechery, fry!'

"Tickles them together! Ugh! The filth of it! How could she? The whore!"

Cecil gave a violent start, which he covered by jumping up.

"Cigarettes. Back in a moment."

He glided away, wiping his brow as he went. When he returned, Shakespeare was again composed.

"With Hamlet," Shakespeare continued, "Shakespeare retrieved his and the Globe's fortunes, and took the first step towards that liberation of himself in tragedy which he had already achieved in the humour of Falstaff. But it was only the first step. Hamlet is the most popular theatrical piece in the world, and the most discussed of Shakespeare's plays, neither of which it would be were it a great tragedy.

"Why is it that every actor wishes to play Hamlet? It seems to me that the answer to this question goes at least half-way to resolving the mystery in which this play has been involved.

"So far I have said nothing of Shakespere as an actor, but you cannot understand him completely unless you remember that what first, in his boyhood, attracted him to the stage was the opportunity of aping aristocratic magnificence on the boards. We know that as soon as he had secured his position in the Lord Chamberlain's company, he chose kingly parts for preference——"

"Such as old Adam——"

"Except in his period of self-contempt, when he went to the opposite extreme, and attached himself to youth and noble birth as a senile retainer. The grandiloquence and pomposity of his kings, which reaches its height in the Ghost in *Hamlet*, a part taken by himself, express the weakest element in Shakespeare, which comes out again in the contorted mannerisms frequent in his last plays. This verbal assuagement of his desire for power was a constant temptation; but, considering the circumstances of his life, and the opportunities of his profession, he resisted it stoutly enough, and was never altogether subdued to what he worked in. In *Hamlet*, however, he yielded to the desire to avenge his many mortifications in a figure which passes across the stage of the theatre, as he was passing across the stage of life, misunderstood, betrayed, but, unlike himself, a sinister and baffling mystery to his enemies; a person of reckless courage—'I do not set my life at a pin's fee'—a favourite with the multitude, the object of a beautiful girl's despairing love, a courtier, a soldier, a scholar, a man whose merciless tongue unmasks every attempt to placate his gloomy humour, from the king's to Osric's, and, above all, a man whose destiny is mortal to all who cross his path, the king, the queen, Polonius, Laertes, Ophelia, Rosencrantz, and Guildenstern—a pyramid of victims crowned with the corpse of their satiated destroyer.

"Is it surprising that every actor is anxious to figure in this part? They have more mortifications than most men to avenge.

"Even with Horatio this Hamlet cannot be natural; and Horatio, on his side, falls most obligingly into every booby-trap set for him.

> My father, methinks I see my father.
> O where, my lord?
> In my mind's eye.

and:

> You will reveal it.
> Not I, my lord, by Heaven.
> There's ne'er a villain dwelling in all Denmark,
> But he's an arrant knave.

and:

> These are but wild and whirling words, my lord.
> I am sorry they offend you, heartily.
> Yes, faith, heartily.
> There's no offence, my lord.
> Yes, by Saint Patrick, but there is, Horatio,
> And much offence, too.

"There is the same taint of the stage in his bitter humour with Polonius:

> What do you read, my lord?
> Words, words, words.

and:

> Will you walk out of the air, my lord?
> Into my grave?

"His theatricalism is even more acute with Ophelia:

> He took me by the hand and held me hard,
> Then goes he to the length of all his arm,
> And, with his other hand thus o'er his brow,
> He falls to much perusal of my face
> As he would draw it. Long stay'd he so.

"He then shakes her arm a little, waves his head thrice up and down, raises a piteous and profound sigh, and, with his head over his shoulder turned, walks out of the room. Contrast this scene with any scene in which Falstaff or Lear appears. It is the earth, not the boards of the theatre, which groans under Falstaff's tread, the heavens, not stage-hands with sheets of tin, that crack above Lear's head. But this Hamlet I have described would fall as mute as a tailor's dummy outside the four walls of the theatre.

"There is another Hamlet, not a projection designed to satisfy Shakespeare's impotent cravings, but an embodiment of his rage and weakness, and self-disgust, and, at last, of his resignation. It is this Hamlet which has preserved the other from decomposition, thereby baffling those critics whose sense of something real and profound in the play, combined with their failure to distinguish between the two Hamlets, has diverted so much of their energy to the task of harmonising the man and the puppet.

"This real Hamlet is Hamlet when he is alone, with no one to pose to.

> O God! God!
> How weary, stale, flat, and unprofitable
> Seem to me all the uses of this world.

and:

>   It cannot be,
>   But I am pigeon-liver'd, and lack gall
>   To make oppression bitter . . .

and:

>   This is most brave that I . . .
>   Must, like a whore, unpack my heart with words.

and:

>   To die; to sleep:
>   No more; and, by a sleep to say we end
>   The heart-ache and the thousand natural shocks
>   That flesh is heir to . . .

"At the close of this last soliloquy Ophelia enters, and the puppet at once replaces the man:

>   Soft you now!
>   The fair Ophelia! Nymph, in thy orisons
>   Be all my sins remember'd.

"It is again the man, not the puppet, who rages against his mother's infidelity from an imagination infected by brooding on a woman's surrender of her body to another man.

>   Nay, but to live
>   In the rank sweat of an enseamèd bed,
>   Stew'd in corruption, honeying and making love
>   Over the nasty sty.

The man speaks also in Hamlet's dying request to Horatio to clear his reputation by recording the true story of his vengeance. This absorption of Hamlet's in the fate of his good name rather than in the accomplishment of his task shows, in fact, how little Shakespeare's imagination was engaged by the verbose grievances of 'buried Denmark'. In those years of humiliation he was obsessed by resentment against the malice of the world; a natural emotion, but not sufficiently profound fitly to occupy the whole thought of a dying hero.

"It is the man, too, who embodies Shakespeare's deepening fatalism, his sense that life will have it so, and one must submit, with 'but it is no matter' as one's best consolation; a phrase which I imagine he used increasingly from this time on.

" 'Thou would'st not think how ill all's here about my heart; but it is no matter.'

"And:

> What is the reason that you use me thus?
> I lov'd you ever: but it is no matter.

"But even nearer than these words to his deepest feeling during this period is the prayer of Claudius, the murderer and adulterer:

> Try what repentance can: what can it not?
> Yet what can it when one cannot repent?
> O wretched state! O bosom black as death!
> O limèd soul, that struggling to be free
> Art more engaged.

It was his own soul, limed by the world, which struggled to be free.

"Beneath the fatalism which accepted decay and disillusion as the final goal of strength and desire, a consciousness was stirring in him of something beyond the sensual world. Atheism, as the natural end of sensuality, was the prevailing creed of the cultured Elizabethan, and had been congenial enough to Shakespeare while things went well with him. Now he was beginning to wonder what lay beyond the sensual wall which had girdled him so securely in earlier years, but there was fear not hope in his wonder. In *All's Well* Lafeu says—'We have our philosophical person, to make modern and familiar, things supernatural and causeless. Hence it is that we make trifles of terrors, ensconcing ourselves into seeming knowledge, when we should submit ourselves to an unknown fear.' Hamlet speaks of:

> The dread of something after death,
> The undiscovered country from whose bourn
> No traveller returns

and Claudio, in *Measure for Measure*, cries:

> The weariest and most loath'd worldly life
> That age, ache, penury and imprisonment
> Can lay on nature is a paradise
> To what we fear of death.

"The lament of the king in *Hamlet*, 'My words fly up, my thoughts remain below,' is repeated by Angelo in *Measure for Measure*—

> When I would pray and think, I think and pray
> To several subjects: Heaven hath my empty words,
> Whilst my invention, hearing not my tongue,
> Anchors in Isobel.

In both these prayers I feel that Shakespeare was trying to pierce through to the unknown power, to transform his fear of it into a confidence which would arm him against the world, and that the effort was beyond his strength. If I am right, Isabella is not a mere necessity of the plot, but the factitious and unhelpful form in which Shakespeare's imagination tried to possess itself of the idea of holiness. We are first introduced to Isabella when she is about to join the sisterhood of Saint Clare, and is complaining to the nun who receives her that the sisters are not curtailed of the few privileges they are allowed. You know the play, so I need do no more than remind you of the ferocity with which Isabella turns

on her brother, when he wonders if she will not save him from
death by surrendering herself to Angelo:

> O! you beast!
> O faithless coward! O dishonest wretch!
> . . . I'll pray a thousand prayers for thy death,
> No word to save thee.

"Towards the close of the play, Shakespeare's imagination
declined to grapple further with such alien material, and allowed
Shakespeare the playwright to finish the play as best he could.
The 'ensky'd and sainted' Isabella, leaving the sisterhood of Saint
Clare to wanton in their privileges, marries the Duke, and Angelo
is reinstated in his high office, with expressions of regret from the
Duke for the deception practised on him for the purpose of saving
Claudio's life.

"Returning to his own world from this vain excursion in
search of another, Shakespeare found that for various reasons its
aspect had become much more favourable, under the influence of
which change his imagination began to stir again. Elizabeth was
dead; and the new king whom Shakespeare had welcomed in
Measure for Measure and whose character he had not yet observed
near at hand, had taken Shakespeare's company under his patronage as the King's Men. Shakespeare himself was appointed a
Groom of the Royal Chamber, and was now as close to the centre
of power as he could hope to get. Freed from material anxieties,
the worst days of humiliation in friendship and love over, he
could now rise above the world, and overlook from a height its
pains and his own. In *Othello* he prepared for this ascent, which he
achieved in *Lear*.

"During the composition of *Othello* he was happier, or at least
more tranquil and assured, than he had been for some years, or
was to be again, except when he was writing *Antony and Cleopatra*.
Troilus and Cressida had cleared his mind of much of the venom
and sensual exasperation that was clogging it. He now desired to
isolate and destroy Thersites. In *Troilus and Cressida* Thersites was
permitted to degrade love and heroism, because no one felt

enough conviction about anything to knock him on the head. But now, as Shakespeare's imaginative passion for life rekindled, Thersites turned into Iago, the enemy of an ideal love and beauty in whose existence Shakespeare once more believed.

"*Othello* expresses the struggle between two opposing forces in Shakespeare himself, not, like *Lear*, the conflict between the complete man and the nature of things. Neither of the two principal characters, therefore, is a whole human being. Othello is almost exclusively passion seeking an ideal satisfaction, Iago almost exclusively the intellect disintegrating passion by exposing its roots in sensuality. Neither Othello nor Iago comes out into the open air of the world; they engage each other inside Shakespeare, and are both invisible to him."

"Othello invisible!"

"As a man, not as a magnificent puppet. As for Iago, I cannot see him at all. You will remember that, at the end, Othello looks at Iago's feet to see if he is hoofed like a devil; a touch which, in the equally passionate atmosphere of *Lear*, would seem unnatural if directed against Edmund."

"But Othello—the leader of men? 'Keep up your bright swords, for the dew will rust them.' "

"A good single stroke. But what of:

News, friends; our wars are done, the Turks are drown'd?

No, you must look elsewhere for light on the art of war. The other persons, less important, are more complete, though they lose their reality a little when they are in touch with the two symbolic figures. This is especially true of Desdemona, an exquisite nature, more tenderly drawn than any other woman in the plays, yet not quite in place, not imaginatively related to Othello; too life-like, in fact, to interpret what Shakespeare wished to express, the attempted destruction of the ideal by the intellect, with passion as its instrument. A less human figure was required for the tragic sacrifice. Her murder is, therefore, painful and unnatural. She is a living person strangled by a symbol; and she is also the means by which Shakespeare satisfied the desire to revenge suffering not on the guilty but on the innocent, a common perversion which has its roots in the feeling that to punish the guilty is only to revenge a particular wrong, but to punish the innocent is a revenge on life itself.

"Desdemona was, I believe, drawn from some woman who loved Shakespeare, and whose love he did not fully return. It is not of her that Shakespeare is thinking when Othello greets Desdemona on her disembarkation. She stands there, a lay figure, while Shakespeare expressed the adoration which no man feels more than once in his life, and which Shakespeare assuredly never felt for Desdemona.

> It gives me wonder great as my content
> To see you here before me, O my soul's joy!
>   . . . If it were now to die,
> 'Twere now to be most happy, for I fear
> My soul hath her content so absolute
> That not another comfort like to this
> Succeeds in unknown fate.

How flat, how irrelevant is Desdemona's answer!

>   The heavens forbid
> But that our loves and comforts should increase
> Even as our days do grow.

"For the third time Shakespeare speaks through his tranced mouthpiece of his content:

> I cannot speak enough of this content;
> It stops me here; it is too much of joy."

He repeated the lines in an abstracted voice, and knit his brows as though trying to recall something. " '*Wonder* great as my content,'" he murmured. "Why 'wonder'? . . . The unmixed wonder of ecstasy? Or a memory of some unexpected and unhoped-for meeting?"

"The symbolic value, master, which you attach to Othello and Iago is most illuminating. . . ."

The sentence hung unsupported; Shakespeare, recalled to his surroundings, hastened to prop it up.

"Yes. It saves one from forcing some kind of plausibility into Iago's motives, and into the discrepancy between Othello, the sober, elderly general, and the Othello who strikes Desdemona in front of the Venetian envoy, Lodovico.

"It is the generous, passionate, idealistic side of Shakespeare which is embodied in Othello, whose 'free and open nature' Ben Jonson ascribed also to the creator of Othello: 'he was, indeed, honest and of an open and free nature.' Instinctively Shakespeare placed this embodiment of his re-awakened idealism in the South, in Venice and Cyprus. The sun, faint in *As You Like It* and *Twelfth Night*, eclipsed in *Troilus and Cressida*, in spite of its southern setting, and in the Denmark of *Hamlet*, burns again in *Othello*. Beneath its rays life flowers once more. Noble birth is again the accompaniment of a noble nature: 'I fetch my life and being from men of royal siege'; and war is no longer an occupation suitable only to the idols of idiot-worshippers, but a passion little less exalted than love—'Pride, pomp and circumstance of glorious war!' When love is suspect, war loses its fascination; but when the integrity of love is restored, it blossoms again in Othello's last memories—'I have done the state some service, and they know't.'

"The function of Iago is to force this unqualified idealist to see life from the opposite standpoint, which explains every action in terms of lust or self-interest; and he so far succeeds that, while the agony of Othello is not the mere rage of sensual jealousy, neither is it to be characterised as simply, in Coleridge's phrase, 'the solemn agony' of a disillusioned idealist, but as the medley of both these passions which Shakespeare had himself experienced.

"The torture of the flesh is as extreme in 'Ay, let her rot, and perish, and be damned to-night,' in the gabble of 'Pish! noses, ears, and lips—Is it possible?—Confess! Handkerchief!—O devil!' as the torture of the soul in 'Ah! Desdemona; away, away, away!' and my heart is turned to stone; I strike it and it hurts my hand!'

"The yearning of

> But there where I have garner'd up my heart,
> Where either I must live or bear no life

is no purer than 'Are you not a strumpet. . . . What! not a whore?'
is degraded in its abandonment to the rage of the flesh.

"The tragedy of Othello reflects, then, in a simplified and over-idealised form, the tragedy of Shakespeare himself. Othello's Iago is a liar. The Iago in Shakespeare's mind was not driven to invention; material suitable to his purpose lay ready to his hand.

"None the less, in spite of his experiences with Mary Fitton and with Pembroke, and in spite of the general view of life exposed to his intellect and perceptions, beauty and virtue were for him, at this time, and in some degree till the end, the reality buried beneath the foul surface of things. The verdict of his intellect on love and friendship, however justified by the concrete instances of his own experience, had, therefore, to be reversed in the final court of appeal, his imagination.

"*Othello* is in essence Shakespeare's condemnation of those weaknesses in himself which had, he now believed, misled him in his search for ideal love and ideal friendship. Desdemona is the woman, Cassio the loyal friend, whom he ought to have found. In his despair at having missed them, he threw on his perceptive faculties the blame which should have been divided between his own imperfections and the imperfection of life itself, since life contains only in fragments the unflawed ideal seen by the imagination.

"The power and reality of *Othello* are the intensity of its longing for ideal beauty, and the agony of the failure to attain to it. Its weakness is in the attempt to incarnate this beauty in human beings. With this attempt Shakespeare's sense of reality conflicts throughout the play. Desdemona is too human for her part; and Cassio is at one time quarrelsome in his cups or a little fatuous about Bianca's adoration of him, and at another moment an image of ideal beauty at which materialism, embodied in Iago, gnashes its teeth:

> He hath a daily beauty in his life
> That makes me ugly.

"That neither Thersites nor Iago was the enemy of the ideal, but some defect inherent in life itself, became clearer to Shakespeare after he had revenged himself on Iago and expiated his remorse in Othello."

"Most—most suggestive! Your pipe, master? May I?"

Shakespeare refilled his pipe, and Cecil, with graceful deference, leaned forward and applied a match. Shakespeare, smoking for some time in silence, regarded Cecil with benignant affection.

"I wish," he said, "there was not this opposition between us about the personal relation of a man to his work. You have been so kind, so thoughtful in every way; you stimulate me, too. But —well!" Shakespeare sighed. "It is just this reluctance of other people to think and feel exactly as one does oneself—or, I suppose it would be fairer to say, it is the reluctance or, rather, the inability of any one individual to identify himself with any other individual—which constitutes the true tragedy of life; a tragedy which bears with its full weight only on the few in whom the passing years quicken instead of deadening the feeling of isolation. The tragedy is complicated in these persons by their need of isolation as well as their dread of it. They must renew in solitude the image of love which their desire drives them to search for in the world; the search is fruitless, and they return to their solitude again. Nor is it possible to imagine their search as other than fruitless, for the barrier between human beings is the condition of their humanity. It is our destiny to cling to this barrier even while we desire its destruction."

"Yes." Cecil nodded his head. "But the bearing of these observations, master? I am afraid of losing the thread."

"In the seven or eight years which separate Shakespeare's two greatest creations, Falstaff and Lear, the aspect of existence had altogether changed for him. Into Falstaff he had poured all the appetite for life, sensual and imaginative, of his richest years, and provided for this inexhaustible appetite from the inexhaustible bounty of the world. His own experience of the world's bounty was, necessarily, by comparison with that of his superhuman offspring, pinched, intermittent, and fleeting; but, for a mortal, he had tasted the abundance of the world as fully as man can. I do not

G

mean merely in sensuality, still less in riches and show, but in the absorption of life itself, whether in his fellow creatures, from Rosalind to Dogberry and Aguecheek, or in the beauty of the outward world.

"But even Falstaff put on mortality at last. 'He is very sick and would to bed. Good Bardolph, put thy face between the sheets and do the office of a warming-pan.'

"In Falstaff's sickness and death, after the king's rejection, Shakespeare unconsciously prefigured the time when the outward world became a menace and oppression to his exhausted spirit, and love no longer a passion of the senses or the imagination, but a need of the naked and frightened heart.

"The attempt in *Othello* to isolate and destroy his perception of the evil in which virtue and beauty are entangled on earth, and to re-establish virtue and beauty in unflawed perfection as ideals realisable in this life, derived, as I have said, from a renewal of energy and illusion after James I's accession to the throne.

"After the passionate re-birth of illusion in *Othello*, there would, whatever his circumstances, have been a reaction. It seems to me, however, that the eclipse of the sun of *Othello* in *Lear* and *Macbeth* would have been less complete but for the squalid and contemptible Court, to which, as the chief dramatist of the King's Men, he was now attached. When *Othello* had flamed out, he was altogether alone. From his solitude he looked out on a vaster world than any he had yet seen, and as his passion returned he peopled his solitude from an imagination nourished for the first time by an unconfined vision of existence.

"The question which he confronted in *Lear* was the loneliness of man, the final question, to which the family, the nation, and God are the imperfect answers framed by the mass of men as substitutes for their deepest desire, the perfect love of two individuals. This desire, as unrealisable, most men soon cease to occupy themselves with, though it remains with them as the image of what they aspire to, so that the power behind life is seen by them as a father, and even an alliance between two nations must be figured as the coming together of two strong and tender souls.

"Neither in the family, nor the nation, nor God, nor in any human being had Shakespeare found the answer to this question. His marriage, though now outwardly rebuilt, was a failure, his son was dead many years, and his daughters, whom he loved, were with their mother.

"Still less had he found in patriotism an assuagement of his desire. Patriotism meant to him pride in the triumphs of a monarch and an aristocracy, and he was sick of both.

"Of God in his years of happiness he had felt, with Dame Quickly, that there was no need to trouble himself with any such thoughts yet; and as his happiness vanished he found not God but necessity in the universe: 'It is the stars, the stars above us, govern our conditions.' The champion of free-will in *Lear* is the savage and unscrupulous Edmund, whose dying words bow to necessity. 'The wheel has come full circle; I am here.'

"Finally, partly through his own fault, Shakespeare had failed in his deepest love and friendship.

"His solitude was, therefore, complete; or, rather, was peopled only by the indistinguishable mass of mankind. In his loneliness he looked at them for the first time, and saw their features, and perceived a distorted image of himself in the lowest wreckage, in those who had no longer strength to support the structure that housed the squalid magnificence of the great; beggars, and cripples of the war, madmen, or still more wretched creatures, feigning madness for alms. At night in the London streets, or in the darkening villages as he rode back to Stratford, their faces started out at him, announcing the final ruin of all lives, claiming kinship with his failing strength, and reproaching his past indifference.

> O, I have ta'en
> Too little care of this. Take physic, pomp,
> Expose thyself to feel what wretches feel,
> That thou may'st shake the superflux to them,
> And show the heavens more just.

"It was this sense of how greatly he had himself been at fault in life which prevented him from making Lear a mere victim.

Nevertheless, the central truth and emotion of the play form themselves round the cry: 'I am a man more sinn'd against than sinning.'

"Lear's sin was the selfishness and vanity in which his desire for love had been entangled. The greater sin of his enemies was that they had ceased to feel their isolation in life, or, rather, cherished it, and saw in love a menace to the power based on their isolation.

"The last truth which those who love men learn about their fellow-creatures is the first and only truth which the majority of men trouble to master. What his youthful contemporaries in Stratford already knew before he left them, that self-interest is the directing force of most men, is the truth which Shakespeare fully felt only when he made Lear break his heart against it. Lear's daughters are the custodians of the social system. Their rejection of him is the rejection of passion by organised self-interest. Finally, passion in its most savage form destroys them, too; but in their relation to their father they represent the resistance to a blind need of self-interest, supported by reason. The conflict between Lear and his daughters is summed up in his cry, 'O! reason not the need.'

"After he has ridden out into the storm which engulfs those who have demanded too much from life, Regan gives the moral from the standpoint of society:

> O! sir, to wilful men
> The injuries that they themselves procure
> Must be their schoolmasters.

It is Lear's recognition of this standpoint that sets up the conflict which wears his mind away—his confused realisation that his daughters, in spite of their callousness, are the custodians of the social system, and that since he has handed his power over to them they have reason on their side, though not that deeper right he cannot put into words. Again and again he begs for patience, the mortar of society and of life itself. 'Keep me in temper; I would not be mad!'; 'You heavens, give me that patience, patience, I need!'; 'O me! my heart, my rising heart! but, down!'; 'No, I will be the pattern of all patience'; 'O! that way madness lies; let me shun that.'

"But his desire overpowers his reason, and when he prays on the heath 'that things might change or cease,' he disavows the sanity which recognises that life will neither change nor cease, and that the order of things will always give man desire and deny it satisfaction.

"Throughout this conflict, until his mind gives way, he is attended by his fool, who tries to separate him from his wrongs, so that he may see them from a distance as a fragment in the fantastic chaos of the world.

"The poor trembling fool, himself not too strong in his wits, is the final transmutation of the humour which in Falstaff had lorded it over all the world, in Thersites had raged and jeered, in Hamlet had posed and strutted, and had been silenced in Othello so that the ideal might once more clothe itself in flesh.

"In Lear's last struggle to retain his reason, the fool is for a time alone with him in the storm, labouring 'to out-jest his heart-struck injuries.' But at last the fool can no longer bear the terrors of the night, and begs his master to make peace with his daughters: 'Good nuncle, in, and ask thy daughters' blessing; here's a night pities neither wise man nor fool.'

"The collapse of the fool marks the close of Lear's resistance to madness. As the king's wits begin to unsettle, the fool falls silent, and his last words, in their echo of the king's senseless mutterings, seem to express a half-conscious abdication of his played-out part:

> We'll go to supper i' the morning: so, so, so.
> And I'll go to bed at noon.

Falstaff also was sick and would to bed.

"In the kingdom of madness, which Lear now enters, he is companioned at first by the mock madman Edgar who, like the fool, is half entangled in the horror from which he tries to liberate the king. The fancies of Edgar are those of a child's nightmares, images of the chaos out of which existence evolves, blurred in the noon of maturity, reviving in the twilight of declining strength. His fancies stand in the same relation to beauty as Shakespeare once revealed it, as the humour of the fool to the humour of Falstaff. But in spite of its disorder, Edgar's imagination struggles to compose Lear's passion; and when Lear sees at last even the little dogs barking at him, Edgar converts the image of hatred into a dream image, in which the dogs stream silently in a curving wave out of the distracted mind:

> For, with throwing thus my head,
> Dogs leap the hatch, and all are fled.

"When Lear is separated both from the fool and Edgar, he abandons himself utterly to his ravings against the two enemies of the love he had struggled towards, lust, in which life is rooted, and hypocrisy, with which power veils its own filth in the interests of its security. The sight of the blinded Gloucester, himself seen from the outside, composes his rage for a moment, and he counsels resignation.

> Thou must be patient; we came crying hither:
> Thou know'st the first time that we smell the air
> We wawl and cry.

But his rage flames up again:

> When I have stol'n upon these sons-in-law,
> Then kill, kill, kill, kill, kill, kill.

After this outburst, he is freed from revolt against the cruelty of life: 'the great rage is kill'd in him.' Cordelia appears to him, the image of love, but beyond the reach of his exhausted strength.

> Thou art a soul in bliss; but I am bound
> Upon a wheel of fire, that mine own tears
> Do scald like molten lead.

Since the ideal exists only in his own heart, he cannot be united to it on earth. Cordelia is murdered, but Lear, in whom hope has again revived, bends over her, pushing from him the final realisation. For a moment he forces himself to believe that it is her low voice which deceives him into thinking she is silent, like the dead:

> Cordelia, Cordelia! stay a little. Ha!
> What is't thou sayst? Her voice was ever soft,
> Gentle and low, an excellent thing in woman.

Even when the illusion can no longer be sustained, his despair is not final. After crying,

> Thou'lt come no more,
> Never, never, never, never, never!

illusion returns, he sees her lips moving, and dies on the words:

> Look on her, look, her lips,
> Look there, look there!

"Their creator saved both Lear and Othello from the return to common life. Both die in the vision of an unflawed ideal, born again in their own hearts, after suffering death in the outward world.

"For Shakespeare himself the best wisdom of life, to which he was still bound, now expressed itself in the interchange between blind Gloucester and his son Edgar; passion and reason.

> No further, sir; a man may rot even here.

> What! in ill thoughts again? Men must endure
> Their going hence, even as their coming hither:
> Ripeness is all. Come on.
>   And that's true, too.

"After *Lear*, he was for a time worn out, and fell into the ill thoughts of Gloucester. In *Timon of Athens* he lost all measure, no longer balancing his faults against his love, but seeing himself on one side, as the sole repository of love, and mankind, on the other, given over to lust, and greed, and ingratitude. The cry of Lear for the cessation of all existence: 'No, no, no life!' is the entire theme of *Timon*. There is no Albany or Edgar in the play. Goneril and Regan are in undisturbed supremacy and the one hope is that they will destroy each other. Albany's prophecy is presented as nearing its fulfilment.

> Humanity must perforce prey on itself,
> Like monsters of the deep.

"For many reasons, I believe that Shakespeare pictured his own state when he wrote of Timon: 'his comfortable temper has forsook him; he's much out of health, and keeps his chamber.' The energy and prodigality of nature which had once throbbed in every vein now terrified him. His sick mind recoiled from the horrible shapes in which life clothes itself:

> the black toad and adder blue,
> The gilded newt and eyeless venom'd worm;
> With all the abhorrèd births below crisp Heaven
> Whereon Hyperion's quickening fire doth shine.

In this state he spoke through Timon his own rage as he looked down on London from the hills to the north.

> Let me look back upon thee. O thou wall,
> That girdlest in those wolves, dive in the earth,
> And fence not Athens . . .
> Timon will to the woods; where he shall find
> The unkindest beast more kinder than mankind.

"His disproportioned bitterness was justified to this extent, that his nature had attracted others by its richness, and had lost this attraction when his strength began to ebb. Those who had cared for him were drawn to him by what he could give, not by what they could confer. He had neither the weakness which invites sympathy, nor the self-absorption which exacts it. He had to be always at his best. When he was not at his best, it was he who felt uncomfortable, not those with him—Yes?"

'Do you read this into *Timon*, master? Is it—please excuse the interruption—anywhere implicit or explicit in that play?"

"Explicit, when Alcibiades asks:

How came the noble Timon to this change?

and Timon answers:

As the moon does, by wanting light to give:
But then renew I could not like the moon;
There were no suns to borrow of.

"Yet, beneath the exaggerations of the play, there is an impersonal strain not present in the bitterness of *Troilus and Cressida*. It is life itself he now condemns, even more than his own circumstances.

My long sickness
Of health and living now begins to mend,
And nothing brings me all things.

"In *Lear*, and its overflow in *Timon*, Shakespeare had exhausted the tragedy of love and its inevitable disappointment. After a pause, during which his imagination renewed its strength, he completed his picture of life in *Macbeth*, the tragedy of power as the substitute of love.

"I have already spoken of the large share of Shakespeare's desires absorbed by ambition for material success between the failure of his marriage and the growth of his love for Mary Fitton. At the culmination of this period he gave, in Henry IV's survey of the steps by which he gained the throne, evidence of the insight with which he had studied the conditions of success in practical life.

"In the same play he glanced beneath the methods of success to the reason why desire is diverted into the struggle for power. The function of war, he says, is:

> To diet rank minds sick of happiness
> And purge the obstructions which begin to stop
> Our very veins of life;

a view repeated many years later in *Antony and Cleopatra*.

> And quietness, grown sick of rest, would purge
> By any desperate change.

What is true of war is, though not so obviously, true of less elementary exhibitions of power. If life were adapted to the satisfaction of desire, happiness would be life's natural goal and permanent resting-place. But the happiness attained is so imperfect compared with the image of the happiness desired, that men soon tire of it, or, rather, look for it elsewhere than in the affections.

"As tragedy deals directly with reality, ignoring the modifying and extenuating circumstances which soften reality and make it palatable for daily consumption, Shakespeare embodied the tragedy of power in a man who realised his ambition by treachery and murder. In choosing such a man, Shakespeare was guided by his instinctive and perhaps unconscious sense that unless he took an extreme type he would obscure and complicate his theme, the complete inadequacy of power as a substitute for love. It is a mistake to criticise Macbeth as a study of a criminal, or even to speculate about which events under Elizabeth and James most influenced Shakespeare's view of politics, and so contributed indirectly to the play.

"In *Macbeth* Shakespeare is concerned with a passion which he had both observed in others and experienced in himself, and which his imagination now desired to isolate.

"The physical darkness in which *Macbeth* is shrouded is an image of the night of power preoccupied with itself alone. There is neither love nor lust in the play. The primal need of mankind is in both its forms obliterated by ambition, and with the obliteration of this need the sense of happiness in prospect vanishes; or even in retrospect, for Lady Macbeth is also an incarnation of the desire for power, and the relation between her and her husband is impersonal. She is distinguished from Macbeth only in lacking his imaginative intuition of the unreality of the desire which possesses them both. Lear's desire is not unreal; he struggles towards a mirage which reflects in the outward world the reality in his heart; Macbeth towards a mirage which reflects an illusion, the illusion that power in itself, the control of others simply for the sake of controlling them, resolves desire, as love resolves it, however imperfectly.

"The compulsion to keep on extending his power, which is analogous to the insatiable appetite of lust, so that one may regard power as lust diverted from its natural object, is the trap in which Macbeth finds himself caught.

> I am in blood
> Stepp'd in so far, that, should I wade no more,
> Returning were as tedious as go o'er.

"When, finally, every avenue to power is blocked by his enemies, his passion for power fades out, and nothing is left but a sense of the meaninglessness of life.

> To-morrow, and to-morrow, and to-morrow
> Creeps in this petty pace from day to day
> To the last syllable of recorded time;
> And all our yesterdays have lighted fools
> The way to dusty death.

The false aim of his desire, which had made him see men as puppets to be played with not as the perishable vessels of an immortal essence, is exposed to him in the hour of his ruin; whereas for Lear the final disaster of Cordelia's death leaves his desire for love as the one reality, a desire whose origin and whose end, fruition or annihilation, are hidden in the darkness beyond and around existence."

IT WAS NOW after midnight, and the moon had gone down. From the pig-sty at the farmhouse end of the orchard a rich breathing diffused itself through the warm darkness.

It occurred to Cecil that Shakespeare had now reached the point in his life at which he had been reintegrated. By taking *Macbeth* after *Timon of Athens*, he had placed it at the end of 1606, or the beginning of 1607. There was hardly room for another play before the date of his reintegration. He had, however, been reading his last plays in the past week; and Cecil, in whom the relatively impersonal treatment of the great tragedies had assuaged the pain previously inflicted, felt the importance of having Shakespeare's survey rounded off while he was in the humour for it.

He was preparing a careful sentence when, a little to his annoyance, Shakespeare managed to start again of his own volition.

"There is a sick distaste, unlike anything in *Lear*, in Macbeth's comparison of life to a poor player that struts and frets his hour upon the stage, and then is heard no more. Twenty years of sound and fury lay behind Shakespeare now; writing, rehearsing, acting, cutting out, adding, re-shaping, endless arguments, tumult everywhere, behind the stage, on it, in front of it; and, most exhausting of all to a man of his nature, who valued beyond anything, and had managed to retain, his sense of reality, the perpetual contrast, comic at first but increasingly painful, between the private feuds and jealousies of actors and their public indulgence in all the finer virtues.

"After *Lear* and *Timon* he had realised that there was still something to say, but after *Macbeth* it seemed to him that his last word on life was spoken. I do not think he fell ill, but he was tired out, slept badly, and often cried when he was alone, in unnerved regret for what he had lost, and for what he had never found.

"I am certain that in this situation, his imaginative faculty exhausted, he thought, for ever, he retired to Stratford for a few months, to attend to his properties, which were now considerable, and generally to make the best of what remained to him from life, his position as a country gentleman. If I am right, and this is all pure guess-work, which you may reject without any protests from me, he arrived at New Place in April or May of 1607. At the beginning of June his daughter Susannah was married to John Hall, a physician, who came of a family possessing heraldic honours, a point which the author of *Macbeth* would, in his easier hours, approve. Hall knew the Continent, and was a man of considerable intelligence, the original, beyond question, of the physician, Cerimon, in *Pericles*, who 'held it ever, virtue and cunning were endowments greater than nobleness and riches'; though there is no evidence that the Cerimon of Stratford protested when Shakespeare willed the greater bulk of his fortune to Susannah Hall, for the purpose of founding a landed family.

"Susannah and her husband settled down after their marriage in a house near New Place. In the society of his elder daughter and her husband, and with the hope of a male heir to his estates in near prospect, Shakespeare's spirits revived. The conflict with reality which he had resolved in the great tragedies, to the extent of his powers, was now some distance behind him; and the conflict for material success was also over. A country summer was round him again, and he could at last enjoy it at his ease, drawing new strength from the light and warmth of the long days.

"He began once more, for the first time since Falstaff, to take pleasure in life as a spectacle; the chief item in the spectacle, now, being not the anonymous richness of humanity, but his own experience; I do not mean only what he had himself enjoyed, suffered and achieved, but all the manifestations of energy and passion, all the triumphs and disasters, which had exalted or afflicted him as a spectator in the years between his arrival in London and the fall of Essex.

"But the central emotion of his life remained his love for Mary Fitton, and it was round this that he now grouped the sum of his other experiences. That he was no longer deeply involved in his passion, that it perhaps lay some years behind him, shows in the proportion he has observed between Cleopatra and both the setting and the other characters in *Antony and Cleopatra*. His dominion over her is as absolute as over the clown who brings her the asp.''

Wilkinson at this point records a peculiar snort, the significance of which he does not venture to interpret, and a flash of that grand manner on which he had already commented.

"Not only does he keep Cleopatra in her place, but he looks at Antony and Cæsar from their own level. The old awe of kings was gone; he had seen them at too close quarters, and, besides, he had proved his powers in conditions less impressive to the vulgar but quite as severe as those in which the great operate their policies." Shakespeare paused. "Or perhaps it was simply that he had massacred so many kings on the stage it had gone to his head. Well——" He paused again for a few moments.

"In *Antony and Cleopatra* the sun shines once more, for the first time since *Othello*, but on a far richer and more open landscape. Does Cleopatra love Antony? The question, implicit throughout the play, is never directly answered. At one moment, it seems to Shakespeare that merely to have seen her and felt the force and magic of her nature is enough, without the assurance of her love: 'a wonderful piece of work; which not to have been blessed withal, would have discredited your travel.' In this mood he exults even in Cleopatra's wantonness, her luxurious memories of broad-fronted Cæsar and great Pompey. In another mood he applies balm to his vanity in the recollection of Mary's jealousy of his wife, giving it to Cleopatra:

> What says the married woman? You may go:
> Would she had never given you leave to come!
> Let her not say 'tis I that keep you here;
> I have no power upon you; hers you are.

But this is the jealousy of pride, not of affection; for, as I have said, Shakespeare never attached to himself the affection I now divine in Mary, though even now I don't know if any man could have been patient and self-controlled enough to nurse this affection till it subdued her arrogance and discontent. Shakespeare, at any rate, failed, and so found in the historical Cleopatra a perfect image of Mary as he had known her. Of the ecstasy where desire itself seems suspended, and the vanities of life not even a memory, there is not a trace in the loves of Cleopatra and Antony. All passes on the stage of the lower world, from the first magnificent entry of the lovers, with their trains, eunuchs fanning Cleopatra as she asks, 'If it be love indeed, tell me how much'—to the painless self-murder, which sends her in robe and crown, not disarranged by any pang, to meet Antony in the Elysian fields. She is on every occasion conscious of herself, of what is due from her, whether in rage and self-pity when she hears of Antony's marriage to Octavia, or in exquisite abasement before Antony broken in defeat, or in dismayed incomprehension when he rages at her, or, most characteristically of all, in her substitution, when Antony is dead, of death himself as her lover.

> Let's do it after the high Roman fashion,
> And make death proud to take us,

and again, at the very end,

> The stroke of death is as a lover's pinch
> Which hurts, and is desir'd.

"The absence of any internal conflict in Cleopatra, her entire surrender to lust and vanity, are not quite credible in a woman of her force of character. Shakespeare nowhere suggests the discontent with life which is the obverse of these qualities. He sees Cleopatra exclusively as she showed herself to others. Cleopatra is, therefore, a less complete figure than Antony, who cannot rest in lust and vanity, but feels perpetually that his passion does not correspond to his need, though he is never quite clear what his need is.

> I must from this enchanting queen break off,
> Or lose myself in dotage,

he says, and later, when his marriage with Cæsar's sister is in prospect, he speaks of his love for Cleopatra as a poison which had bound him up from his own knowledge.

"He is divided between love and power, and imperfectly related to both. As soon as he has secured himself by coming to terms with Cæsar, he desires Cleopatra again, but when he returns to her, the power he forfeits becomes once more desirable, and the love he has regained the leavings of a dish first tasted by others:

> I found you as a morsel, cold upon
> Dead Cæsar's trencher; nay, you were a fragment
> Of Cneius Pompey's.

"The final solution of this conflict is death in a double illusion, of love triumphant as he lays the poor last of many thousand kisses on Cleopatra's lips, and of power vindicated even in defeat, 'a Roman by a Roman valiantly vanquish'd'; and though Antony's dying illusions contradict outward fact, outward fact is itself submerged by the sense, under the dominion of which Shakespeare wrote the play, that energy and passion are their own reward, and life a spectacle justified by its own magnificence."

The glow faded from Shakespeare's face, and he sank back in his chair. "But why Antony?" he muttered, half to himself. "Why Antony after Lear? 'A rarer spirit never did steer humanity'— Antony! Was it taking upon me the mystery of things to glorify that brute? How could I look back to Cleopatra, who had looked up to Cordelia from the wheel of fire?"

He was silent for a time, then his eyes brightened and he seemed to Cecil, who did not strain himself to catch the words too precisely, to be murmuring endearments.

"Coleridge, sir," he interposed, "speaks of the 'happy valiancy' which distinguishes Shakespeare's style in *Antony and Cleopatra*." He paused on an interrogation inflection and Shakespeare, squaring his shoulders, resumed—"Much both of the freedom and abundance of *Antony and Cleopatra* derives from the composite origin of Shakespeare's Antony, who is partly Plutarch's Antony, without his savagery, partly Shakespeare as a lover, and partly the generous, reckless, uncalculating Essex. No event in Elizabeth's reign, not even the defeat of the Armada, moved the public, or at least the London public, like Essex's fall. Shakespeare's company, which, as you know, was on the fringe of the revolt, was commanded the evening before Essex's execution to perform before the Queen at Whitehall; her method of revenging herself for the performance of *Richard II*, which the company had been bribed by the rebels to give on the day before Essex tried to raise London.

"The ignominy of this performance, which Shakespeare would feel even against reason, sharpened his hatred of the old tyrant, and deepened his pity and admiration for her victim. But by the time he wrote *Antony and Cleopatra*, his judgment balanced Octavius Cæsar fairly against Antony, Burghley against Essex."

"You imply, master, that in the struggle between Cæsar and Antony, Shakespeare is reproducing the rivalries of Burghley and Essex?"

"It would seem so. Essex and Burghley, as well as Antony and Octavius, are placed before us in less than a dozen words, when Antony calls on Cæsar to revel with the rest:

Be a child o' the time,

and Cæsar replies:

Possess it, I'll make answer.

"All the qualities necessary to a permanent success in practical life, and all those which ruin a man after a decorative string of triumphs, are embodied in these two figures—the balance between whom Shakespeare holds with strict fairness. Cæsar is the less elaborately drawn, because his greatness, though undeniable, is negative and passionless. He is the man described in the Sonnets, 'unmoved, cold, and to temptation slow'; and his chief characteristic is a disapproval of wasted energy. When his sister Octavia laments the division between Cæsar and her husband, Antony, he gives her the comfort of 'Let determined things to destiny hold unbewail'd their way.'

"To correct the greater sympathy he felt for Antony, Shakespeare attached to Antony a mouthpiece of his own judgment on unregulated passion, Enobarbus. As Othello and Iago are the two sides of Shakespeare in his attitude to sex, so Antony and Enobarbus are the two sides of his attitude to worldly success—the former incarnating the ideal Shakespeare dreamt of in his youth, and could realise only in his imagination; the latter embodying the sense of reality which had kept him within the limits of the attainable: a coat-of-arms and New Place.

"But why did Shakespeare fill Enobarbus with passionate remorse after he deserts Antony, and make him expiate his betrayal in suicide? This is quite out of character with Enobarbus's detached weighing of facts. 'I am alone the villain of the earth, and feel I am so most.' Why the last six words? It is almost as if Shakespeare were insisting that this is not the confession of an imaginary person. Was he thinking of some follower of Essex, or is it possible that his acquiescence in the command performance at Whitehall——? There is something in these words. . . . I don't know. . . . Poor Essex! . . . 'O sun! thy uprise shall I see no more.' . . ."

He trailed into silence. "Shakespeare's sun, too," he resumed, "had set, not to rise again in any later play. After *Antony and Cleopatra* his strength was exhausted; and I believe his next play, *Coriolanus*, was followed by a complete breakdown in health. *Coriolanus* itself has every mark of having been written with his last reserves of strength; its violence is of nerves, not of energy, its standpoint that of a country gentleman, familiar with the Court, and disgusted by the growing recalcitrancy of the Commons. It is the one play written throughout by William Shakespeare, gentleman, of Stratford-on-Avon."

"Throughout, sir? But surely Shakespeare holds the balance fairly enough between *Coriolanus* and the populace. You would not say, would you, that Shakespeare identifies himself unreservedly with *Coriolanus*?"

"I suppose not, yet I feel all through the play Shakespeare's accumulated resentment against the common cry of curs, the beast with many heads, to placate whom he had devoted so much of his energy. The affectation of 'speaking is for beggars; he wears his tongue in his arms' is now reproduced as an admirable trait in

Coriolanus, with his 'When blows have made me stay, I fled from words,' and 'I have some wounds upon me, and they smart to hear themselves remembered.' "

"But, sir . . ."

"I know he indicates his disapproval of Coriolanus's conceit and insolence. His intelligence condemned all this braggadocio, but his mood was in sympathy with it. He was exhausted, and bitter in his exhaustion.

> Why should this change of thoughts,
> The sad companion, dull-ey'd melancholy,
> Be my so us'd a guest, as not an hour
> In the day's glorious walk or peaceful night—
> The tomb where grief should sleep—can breed me quiet?

Do you remember this passage in *Pericles*? I think he fell ill after *Coriolanus*, and that these lines give his prevalent mood in the years that followed his partial recovery. His power of unifying life in his mind and feeling had vanished. Beneath his usual temper of passive melancholy stirred a medley of old emotions, no longer subject to his control, so that his last plays are a confused panorama of everything he had thought and suffered. Sometimes he echoes faintly the passion or terror of *Lear* and *Macbeth*, as in

> Yet cease your ire, you angry stars of heaven!

and

> The crickets sing, and man's o'er-labour'd sense
> Repairs itself to rest.

"But the echo is very faint.

"In his weak state the jealousy, hatred, and humiliation of the past revived, with little abatement of their old intensity, and claimed the relief of expression. Too tired to invent a new form, he repeated in *Cymbeline* and *The Winter's Tale* the device of the woman wrongly suspected, by which in *Othello* he had secured a vent both for his lustful rage and for his self-reproach. He had failed, in different ways, both with Anne and with Mary Fitton, and among the other women he had known there was one, at least, whose love he now fancied might have satisfied him, and to whose memory he consecrated the sufferings of Imogen and Hermione.

"In these last plays the verbosity and grandiloquence, to which I have referred as his chief temptations both in his writing and as an actor, often overpower both verisimilitude and emotion. Imogen herself is infected. What could be worse than this address to Cloten?

> Thou wert dignified enough
> Even to the point of envy, if 'twere made
> Comparative for your virtues, to be styl'd
> The under-hangman of his kingdom, and hated
> For being preferr'd so well.

But in her natural moments Imogen embodies perfectly the devotion, tenderness, and loyalty which are the three chief qualities a man wishes in his abstract ideal, and which were also the three qualities Shakespeare could not find in the woman he none the less desired beyond all others. The fascination Mary had exercised on him was hateful to him now. He turned from it to Imogen's longing for Posthumus:

> What shall I do the while? where bide? how live?
> Or in my life what comfort, when I am
> Dead to my husband?

The remorse of Posthumus in his prison cell expresses Shakespeare's repentance for the past, a repentance the object of which he embodied in Imogen, but which extended beyond the individual to life itself, who wore for him in this hour of his broken abasement, out of her innumerable masks, the mask of a victim.

> Is't enough I am sorry?
> So children temporal fathers do appease;
> Gods are more full of mercy. . . .
> For Imogen's dear life take mine; and though
> 'Tis not so dear, yet 'tis a life. . . . O Imogen!
> I'll speak to thee in silence.

"Balancing this regret is the loathing with which he recalls the rage of the flesh. When Iachimo has convinced Posthumus of Imogen's infidelity, and adds 'Will you hear more?' Posthumus exclaims 'Spare your arithmetic; never count the turns; Once, and a million!'; the same word that Othello used:

> Sir, she can turn, and turn, and yet go on,
> And turn again.

The brutality of Posthumus's language measures his disgust at his own enslavement by physical desire:

> O! all the devils!
> This yellow Iachimo, in an hour—was't not?
> Or less—at first?—perchance he spoke not, but
> Like a full-acorn'd boar, a German one,
> Cried "O!" and mounted.

"The jealousy of Leontes is expressed with even less measure, in stammering phrases, with the repetitions of nervous rage, the same words echoing each other, like blows to dull his agony. His images, even when they are not sexual, reveal a mind nauseated by life: 'You smell this business with a sense as cold as is a dead man's nose'; 'I have drunk, and seen the spider.'

"In all this Shakespeare is remembering what he had himself experienced; and the sense of helplessness, which had intensified his suffering, reappears, too.

> Nor night, nor day, no rest; it is but weakness
> To bear the matter thus; mere weakness.

"To allay his remorse, and escape from his rage, he re-entered the kingdom of dreams, which the child leaves for the world of reality and to which the old and exhausted return. Fairy-tales complete existence for the young, and replace it for the old.

"In *Cymbeline* and *The Winter's Tale* the web of life is no longer of a mingled yarn, good and ill together. Innocence is reestablished in unflawed perfection, and even wickedness dissolves before the image of virtue, and is forgiven. 'Pardon's the word to all.' Childhood and youth, in these plays, attract him especially, as the most natural embodiments of fairy-tale innocence and beauty. Guiderius and Arviragus, the princely boys brought up by the exiled Belarius in the mountain solitudes of Wales, have the courage, chivalry, and distinction which, in romances, noble birth confers on its possessors, whatever their circumstances. Polixenes, speaking to Hermione of Leontes and himself as boys, gives them the untroubled innocence which Shakespeare now fancied had sanctified his early years:

> We were, fair queen,
> Two boys that thought there was no more behind
> But such a day to-morrow as to-day,
> And to be boy eternal—

lines which open before the mind an endless sky, filled with a faint light, an old man's vision.

"Above all, his fancy played round a young girl, saved from disaster to live in endless felicity with her lover, and watched over by a father whose only joy is in the contemplation of his daughter's happiness:

> So glad at this as they, I cannot be,
> Who are surpris'd withal; but my rejoicing
> At nothing can be more."

"Forgive me, master, but you are, are you not, speaking only of *The Tempest*? Both in *Pericles* and *The Winter's Tale* the father and the mother, after first being restored to each other, share, and by sharing increase their felicity in the marriage of their daughter."

"Yes, but in *Cymbeline* the wicked mother poisons herself, and in *The Tempest* Prospero is completely alone, both on his island and in his memories of the past; and in *The Tempest* Shakespeare is only half in fairyland. His imagination is, for the last time, working on reality again."

"Yes, master."

"It was probably his unmarried daughter, Judith, in whom during his last years he chiefly sought the satisfaction of his love; but here, too, he seems to have been disappointed. Two months before his death Judith, who was now thirty-two, married Thomas Quiney, a Stratford tradesman, six years her junior. The marriage was hasty and irregular, a circumstance that Shakespeare might have excused, and narrowly escaped being declared invalid. Almost the last act of Shakespeare's life was to alter his will, substituting, in the bequest of his household plate, the name of his granddaughter, Elizabeth Hall, for Judith's. He was clearly very ill when he signed the will a few weeks before his death, but the terms of the will are elaborate, and represent his considered intentions. His chief Stratford friends and his old colleagues at the Globe are remembered, but nowhere in the will is there any touch to suggest the author of *Lear*. Only one charitable bequest, ten pounds to the poor of Stratford—hardly shaking the superflux! And nearly all his estate left to his elder daughter, and entailed on her or her children's male issue. Not a great document, in any sense.

"His granddaughter, Elizabeth, was eight years old when he died; and though she was a girl, not the boy he had hoped Susannah would bear as the heir to his estate, he may perhaps, as a man, if not as a gentleman, have loved her more than a grandson. She is the baby Miranda whose smiles helped Prospero to bear up 'against what should ensue'; the final object of Shakespeare's long-wandering, never-satisfied love, and the least troublesome; for when she howled or was noisy he could at once return her to her mother, or to the grandmother for whom the future held a second-best bed as the last relic of her youthful lover's devotion.

"In the plays of this period, I said, wickedness is forgiven, and this is true of Iachimo and Leontes; but in the last play of all, *The Tempest*, while the aristocratic villains are restored to Prospero's favour, the lesser rogues, Trinculo, the jester, and Stephano, the butler, are, together with Caliban, dismissed from Prospero's presence with summary contempt.

"The Shakespeare who fell silent after *The Tempest*, and made the will I have referred to, was Prospero without Ariel and Caliban; and Prospero isolated, if you look beneath his ancient dignified exterior, incarnates chiefly what was weakest in Shakespeare, that side of him which had retreated before Falstaff, and had vanished in Lear, but which revived in his exhausted and premature old age.

"Prospero's speech, at its most characteristic, is pompous and consequential:

> of temporal royalties
> He thinks me now incapable; confederates—
> So dry he was for sway—wi' the king of Naples . . .

There is much in this style. Caliban, and even Ariel, he bullies and threatens without ceasing, and the harshness with which he treats Ferdinand is not improved by his pretext that he wishes to increase the happiness of Ferdinand and Miranda by making them suffer first.

"He is, in fact, until the quenching of his dryness for sway frees the melancholy beneath, a simple incarnation of avenging power, who cannot rest till he has wiped out all the humiliations of his life in the abject prostration of his enemies. In the curious little scene where Prospero and Ariel set spirits, in the shape of hounds, at Caliban and his associates, the hound that Ariel encourages is called Silver, the three hounds that Prospero urges on are Mountain, Fury and Tyrant; an illuminating distinction."

"Most ingenious, master, I must confess."

"When Prospero's vengeance is nearly completed Shakespeare speaks through him his own longing, no longer passionate as in *Lear* and *Timon*, for the dissolution of all life, the melting into air of the whole framework of the world. Shakespeare's imagination still supports him in this valediction, but at the end, when Ariel has left Prospero, and Caliban has crawled away, and Prospero is alone with his despair, he expresses in his entreaty for the prayers of the audience Shakespeare's own return to his childhood, to the fear of the unknown power which had haunted his early dreams, and faded in the days of his strength, and swelled again as the world grew dark and strange once more.

"In the changeling Ariel, Shakespeare said farewell to the spirit who had beguiled out of the empty air a million bright evanescent shapes to grace his master's rough journey through the world.

"In Caliban he dismissed with the harshness of exhaustion the too faithful companion of his journey, always shuffling and panting at his heels, the body he had once made much of, indulging it till innocence itself was threatened by its lust.

"But Caliban is not always the mere flesh. Sometimes he is half-beast, half-spirit, perplexed and companionless on earth, the sport of apes and hedgehogs and adders, and the slave of an incomprehensible power, whose gift to him of speech he uses to retort with curses his master's cruelty. In his wretchedness he is comforted by the sounds and sweet airs which fill the place of his captivity, and in dreams the skies open and disclose the happiness hidden from his waking search."

From

After Puritanism
1850–1900
(1929)

From Shakespeare to Dean Farrar

POPULAR LITERATURE REVEALS the desires of a nation, and therefore, though the connection is at the time obscure, forecasts its immediate future. From *Amadis de Gaul* and the other chivalric romances which were the rage in Spain during the first half of the sixteenth century, a contemporary might have inferred that in attempting to dominate both Europe and the New World Spain was mistaking dreams for realities and marching to disaster. The extraordinary passion for Sherlock Holmes, the Amadis of Baker Street, especially in Germany, in the decade before the Great War affords an analogous instance of fancy invading real life. In 1908 a Dresden paper published an article on *Das Sherlockismus*, in which the distorting effect on the sense of reality induced by this craze was pointed out; but the article was not read by the Kaiser and his advisers, or its implications were ignored. One may reasonably suppose that Charles V was equally indifferent to the significance of *Amadis de Gaul*; nor was it till 1605, nearly half a century after the chivalric romances had passed out of fashion, that Cervantes in the first part of *Don Quixote* drew the moral of Charles V's attempt at the empire of the world.

In the following pages I shall try to show that the disintegration of Puritanism, nowadays an accepted and perhaps exaggerated fact, was implicit in the writings of Dean Farrar, whose three popular triumphs, *Eric*, the *Life of Christ*, and the sermons on Eternal Hope, express different but related aspects of the mid-Victorian reaction from the Puritan tradition.

Farrar himself was, in the broad sense of the word, a puritan. His opposition to Puritanism remained, therefore, implicit, except in his attack on the doctrine of eternal punishment, where the struggle between his conscious and unconscious feelings involved him from time to time in self-contradictions.

I

Victorian emotionalism over the young, of which *Eric* is perhaps the most luxuriant example, was the fruit of a compromise between Puritanism, decaying but still powerful, and the imaginative faculty, which Puritanism had in the main suppressed between Shakespeare and Wordsworth. Farrar, in *Eric*, Dickens in Little Nell and Paul Dombey, and Tennyson in the May Queen, were reviving, in an exaggerated form, a vein of feeling which is discernible in the enfeebled work of Shakespeare's last period.

Even before his last period, there is in several of Shakespeare's plays, and especially in *As You Like It*, a foreshadowing of sentiments which we are accustomed to regard as dating from the Romantic revival towards the close of the eighteenth century. The exiled Duke and his followers, in the Forest of Arden, "fleeting the time carelessly, as they did in the golden world," prefigure the modern regret for an ideal past; and in the Sonnets Shakespeare expresses this longing directly, in "the holy antique hours," and in "beauty making beautiful old rhyme, in praise of ladies dead and lovely knights."

In the same play, Celia declares that the fool Touchstone will "go along o'er the wide world with me," a phrase which echoes through the lyrics of the German Romantics; and Celia herself, in her modest self-effacing attachment to Rosalind, is the too fruitful mother of a mass of Victorian secondary characters, male and female.

The almost Victorian mood in which Shakespeare wrote *As You Like It* was dissipated in the period of the great tragedies, but reappeared more strongly than before in his last plays.

In the opening act of *The Winter's Tale*, Hermione asks Polixenes what he and her husband, Leontes, were like as boys. Polixenes answers:

> "We were, fair queen,
> Two boys that thought there was no more behind
> But such a day to-morrow as to-day,
> And to be boy eternal."

This expresses an old man's fancy that boyhood is innocent and contented; but Hermione wishes for a little realism, and asks:

"Was not my lord the verier wag o' the two?"

Polixenes, who is actually a young man but is here used by Shakespeare as a mouthpiece of his own emotion, answers in the exalted vein of his first reply:

"We were as twinn'd lambs that did frisk i' the sun,
And bleat the one at the other: what we chang'd
Was innocence for innocence; we knew not
The doctrine of ill-doing, no, nor dream'd
That any did."

By "the doctrine of ill-doing" Polixenes, as he presently explains, means sexual knowledge. To Shakespeare in his premature old age sex was the all-inclusive evil. His imagination, no longer able to create beauty out of the passions of men and women, made for its comfort a sexless paradise of youth. Thus, by a different road, he arrived at the same falsification of reality as the Victorians.

Farrar himself marked the affinity between the enfeebled Shakespeare and the peculiar emotionalism of the Victorian fifties by heading one of the chapters in *Eric* with Polixenes' words: "We were, fair queen." In his university novel, *Julian Home*, he further emphasized this affinity with a chapter heading from *Cymbeline*.

Dr Johnson, who united in himself the Puritanism and the common sense of the eighteenth century, said that criticism of *Cymbeline* would be criticism wasted on "unresisting imbecility." Tennyson died with a volume of Shakespeare open at *Cymbeline*, and Imogen's name on his lips; a situation which, had Boswell presented it to Johnson as a hypothetical possibility, would have drawn from Johnson one of those personal rejoinders which so frequently left Boswell stunned.

The fascination of Imogen for Tennyson, and Farrar's chapter headings from *The Winter's Tale* and *Cymbeline*, were not chance caprices. Puritanism in Shakespeare's maturity had already cast its shadow over the land, and the chill of it is in these last plays, deepening Shakespeare's revulsion from life. The fear of sex present in *The Winter's Tale* reappears in *Cymbeline*. Imogen, her husband Posthumus complains, restrained him of his lawful pleasures, and pray'd him oft forbearance; a trait absent, by implication or direct statement, in Shakespeare's earlier heroines. Shakespeare's imagination, diverted from the substance of life, had turned to fancifulness; with results curiously similar to those produced in the fifties and sixties of the nineteenth century, when the shadow of Puritanism was beginning to lift. Imogen's brothers, Arviragus and Guiderius, are young Victorian heroes, prematurely born. In their mountain home in Wales, they have the wild grace and innocence of animals, tempered by the pride and courage with which they are endowed, though themselves unaware of their exalted origin, by their royal birth. "They are as gentle," Shakespeare calls them, in the quotation borrowed by Farrar:

> "As zephyrs, blowing below the violet,
>   Not wagging his sweet head; and yet as rough,
>   Their royal blood enchafed, as the rud'st wind
>   That by the top doth take the mountain pine,
>   And make him stoop to the vale."

Victorian fiction was congested with boys of this type; while the frisking and bleating of Young Polixenes and Leontes were revived in a more virulent form in Little Nell, the May Queen, and the heroes of Farrar in their earlier years.

The Victorian idealization of the young, the return to Polixenes, as one may call it, was a more extraordinary phenomenon than is generally realized nowadays, when the young, though no longer idealized, are treated with the delicacy and respect due to unsolved psychological problems. This present view of the young, whatever its merits or faults, was made possible by the excesses of the mid-Victorians, in their reaction against the Puritan view of childhood and adolescence.

To frame *Eric* in its proper perspective, it will therefore be

necessary to glance rapidly at the state of the young in the period
between *Cymbeline* and the *May Queen*.

II

The Bible did not affect the English mind deeply before the
rise of the Puritans, which reached its culminating point, politically, in the middle of the seventeenth century. The overthrow of
the Commonwealth, followed by the Restoration, checked the
Puritan movement, driving it underground for a time, where it
gathered new strength from its reverses, and re-emerging in the
Evangelical movement of the eighteenth century gradually permeated the most important part of the nation, leaving comparatively untouched only the highest and lowest classes.

The religion of this period was based on an acceptance of the
Hebrew Scriptures as a literal communication from God to mankind. Life as lived on an evergreen island under mild skies had,
therefore, to be assimilated as far as possible to that of a Semitic
tribe, under a burning sky and surrounded by enemies. To the
Israelites, in their uncomfortable situation, the powers of the
universe embodied themselves in the form of a magnified Hebrew
patriarch, who demanded from his children, in return for the
uncertain protection he afforded them, a somewhat abject sense
of their own entire unworthiness to be the recipients of his favours.

This relationship of mankind to its Creator naturally reproduced itself in the relationship of the children to the head of the
family. A Puritan infant was a double malefactor, a child of
wrath in the eyes of his heavenly and earthly father alike. Jesus as a
human being hardly existed before the nineteenth century for
children. As Son, he was for the Puritans entirely subordinate to
the Father, and owed his importance to the share assigned him by
his Father in the task of saving the elect, and not to his life or
teachings. From the latter the Puritans took only the doctrine of
eternal punishment, a doctrine absent from the Old Testament
but forming an invaluable supplement to the terroristic spirit of
Hebrew morality.

As the eighteenth century advanced, the number of miniature

H

Jehovahs, respectable God-fearing family men, whose only reading was the Bible, increased. The polite classes, the town aristocracy, did not believe in the Bible. The courteous gentleman-to-gentleman tone in which Lord Chesterfield communicated his views on life and love to his illegitimate son was, like the recipient of these views, an implied protest against the current Hebraism of the lower and middle orders. But the Chesterfields were in a relatively small minority. The industrial age had begun; and a life of duty not of happiness, a life, that is, devoted to money-getting, with the family sanctified as the money-getting unit, with Jehovah as the slave-driver, and with everlasting fire for the blackleg, was the form in which the middle classes adapted the Puritanism of the previous century to the requirements of their own age. The evangelization of the lower classes by John Wesley, which saved England in John Morley's opinion from an even wilder outbreak than the French Revolution, imposed, less completely, the same ideal of thrift on the lower classes; though Wesley himself did not care for money, and denounced his followers' money-grubbing.

In the sixties and seventies of the century, the growth of this profit-and-loss morality produced a fashion of moral tales for children. *Tom Thumb* and *Jack the Giant-Killer*, with their improbable incidents and false values, were withdrawn from the nursery, and replaced by *Goody Two Shoes* and *Tommy Prudent*. The change was condemned by Dr Johnson. "Babies," he said, "do not want to hear about babies. They like to be told of giants and castles and of somewhat which can stretch and stimulate their little minds."

Yet Johnson illustrates the growing severity of the age in the bellow with which he lifted up his lion's paw against Hannah More, when she betrayed by a careless allusion that she had read *Tom Jones*. "I am shocked to hear you quote from so vicious a book. I am sorry to hear you have read it: a confession which no modest lady should ever make. I scarcely know a more corrupt work."

Meanwhile the forces of expansion were gathering strength, and presently, in France, exploded in the Revolution. In England the forces of repression were too strong for the revolutionary spirit in politics, diverting it into the more valuable sphere of imaginative work.

New provinces were added to man's consciousness of himself in Blake's child:

> "No, no, let us play, for it is yet day,
>   And we cannot go to sleep;
> Besides, in the sky, the little birds fly,
>   And the hills are all cover'd with sheep."

And in Wordsworth's boy:

> "There was a boy: ye knew him well, ye cliffs
>   And islands of Winander!—many a time,
> At evening, when the earliest stars began
> To move along the edges of the hills,
> Rising or setting, would he stand alone,
> Beneath the trees, or by the glimmering lake. . . ."

But the renaissance of the imagination in Wordsworth and Blake, Coleridge, Keats and Shelley was baffled from the beginning, and at last diverted into Victorian sentimentalism, by the intensified pietism with which the prosperous classes, frightened into their wits by the French Revolution, met the threat of social disruption and anarchy.

The hey-day of what we nowadays call Victorian morality may roughly be placed between 1790 and 1820, the age of the great Evangelicals, the slave-abolitionists and prison reformers, Wilberforce, the Buxtons, Zachary Macaulay, and Elizabeth Fry. It was the diffusion of this Evangelical morality through society as a whole, and in the process its weakening, which distinguishes the Victorian age from the age of the Clapham Sect, as the reforming Evangelicals were called.

The extraordinary change which even by the fifties of the nineteenth century had already disintegrated the Puritan attitude towards the young can be most easily illustrated by setting the doomed angels of Dickens, Tennyson, and Farrar by the side of the Fairchild children of wrath.

It was in 1818 that Mrs Sherwood published the first part of *The History of the Fairchild Family* or *The Child's Manual, being a collection of stories calculated to show the importance and effects of a religious education.*

The Fairchild family were five in number, Mr and Mrs Fairchild, Lucy, Emily, and Henry; Lucy, the eldest, being nine years of age. In the course of the second chapter, which is headed "General Depravity of Mankind in all Countries after the Fall," Lucy asks, "Papa, may we say some about mankind having bad hearts?"

Mr Fairchild is agreeable, and each of the children repeats a verse from the Bible "to prove that the nature of man, after the fall of Adam, is utterly and entirely sinful"; the verse of Henry, aged six, being "I know that in me, that is, in my flesh, dwelleth no good thing."

Another day when the children, who had been quarrelling among themselves that morning, were out walking with Mr Fairchild, they passed a gibbet on which hung the decomposing body of a man in chains. The face of the corpse frightened the children: "O, let us go, papa," they cried, and pulled at his coat.

"Not yet," Mr Fairchild said. "I must tell you the history of that wretched man before we go from this place."

The man, it seemed, had been hanged for murdering his brother, with whom, when they were both children, he had frequently quarrelled in play. The mother, a widow lady, had lost her reason, and was now in a lunatic asylum.

The upper, and unsanctified classes, are represented in *The Fairchild Family,* by Sir Charles and Lady Noble, the chief personages of the neighbourhood, and their daughter, Miss Augusta. Miss Augusta was spoilt and disobedient, but a beautiful dress of hers roused the envy of Emily and Lucy, who were inclined to think her a much luckier person than themselves. They were soon shown their mistake. Disobeying her mother's orders, Miss Augusta went with a lighted candle into an unoccupied room, to look at herself in the mirror. The flame caught her dress, the maid brought to the room by her dreadful screams was too late, and she died in agonies, "a warning to all children how they presume to disobey their parents."

Mr Fairchild's comment was a text from Proverbs: "Withhold not correction from the child; for if thou beatest with the rod, he shall not die."

In opposition to the Noble family, we have John Trueman, a poor working-man, but one of the most faithful servants of God in the district. Trueman's son, Charles, went into a decline after Miss Augusta's death. One day little Henry came upon Charles, reading busily on the trunk of a fallen tree. Henry, who had recently been opposing himself doggedly to Mr Fairchild's attempts to teach him Latin, was feeling very unhappy. "Ah, master Henry," said Charles, after Henry had confided his trouble, "it is because you are under your father's displeasure, and have deserved to be so, that you feel all these fears, and are so miserable. . . . My father has often talked to us children about hell, as we have been sitting round the fire on a Sunday evening, till we have been in a quake. The Bible speaks of it as a lake burning with fire and brimstone: as it is written, 'The Son of man shall send forth his angels, and they shall gather together out of his kingdom all things that offend, and them which do iniquity; and shall cast them into a furnace of fire; there shall be wailing and gnashing of teeth' (Matt. xiii, 41–42)."

In the course of this conversation it came out that Miss Augusta's death had made a profound and terrible impression on Charles, thus indirectly affecting his health. He knew he was shortly to die, but the fate of Miss Augusta had revealed to him his own desperate depravity, he had flown to the dear Saviour, and could now die in the happy consciousness that "Whosoever cometh to Him, He will in no wise cast out."

The unsuitability of the Puritan temper to the inbred good sense and good nature of the English is vividly illustrated by the contrast between the elephantiasis of Hebraism in *The Fairchild Family*, and the charming disposition of its authoress, Mrs Sherwood. The last half of her life was passed at Wick, near

Worcester, with her husband, five children, and three adopted orphans. To support this large family, she took pupils, and worked incessantly on stories to fit the simple pictures with which the children's books of that period were illustrated.

Her writings included "The Governess; or the Little Female Academy"; "The History of Little George and his penny"; "Waste not, want not"; "The Infant's Progress from the Valley of Destruction to everlasting Glory"; "Grandmamma Parker, or the Father's Return"; and "The History of Henry Milner, a little boy, who was not brought up according to the fashions of this world."

These titles express the spirit of the Evangelical movement at its imperious zenith, but in her later years Mrs Sherwood responded to the changing temper of the times. Her relations with her family were genuinely happy, and it was therefore inevitable, with her affectionate nature, that the death of a daughter, in 1832, should lead her to reconsider her views on the future life. "After the death of her daughter, Emily," we are told, "Mrs Sherwood reached in meditation upon the mysteries of life and death the view that 'Salvation was wholly unconditional, a free gift of Divine love, that every creature was safe in the hands of his Creator and Redeemer'."

The Worcester Evangelical party was outraged by this doctrine, and referred to it as "Mrs Sherwood's." "In August, 1835," Mrs Sherwood writes, "I received a letter desiring me to go no more to the Asylum, as one of the reformed penitents who had been set to watch me had brought a charge against me of having asserted that our Lord would in due time save all mankind."

Towards the close of her life, she seems to have quite forgotten the bizarre morality of her Evangelical propaganda in her regret for her dead husband and past happiness. "Oh, my beloved one! not lost but gone before," she wrote in her diary, towards the close of 1850. "I have been parted from you one year, one whole year, and I even miss you more than I ever did. Alas! alas! my heart sinks within me in thinking of the days which are gone." And a little later: "When I began this study, many years ago, I was in a far-off place in India; and now that I have finished it, I could weep very sore at the associations awakened. Ah me! ah me! what is life!"

The last and culminating triumph of Evangelical Puritanism was when Dr Arnold laid his reforming hand on the public-school system; a triumph, as will appear, rapidly modified by currents of feeling outside the control of even the doughtiest Evangelical.

The brutality of the public schools between the Restoration and Dr Arnold's appointment to Rugby is attested by a variety of witnesses, and must be attributed in part to the disappearance of a general standard of culture after the Puritans had split England into two sections, the devout and the indifferent. From Dr Busby to Dr Keate the great schoolmasters regarded boys as young savages to be thrashed into subjection. We learn, on the authority of Dr Johnson, that open warfare between the boys and the masters was, at any rate down to the close of the seventeenth century, part of the routine of the schoolmaster's profession. "The practice of barring-out," Johnson writes in his Life of Addison, "was a savage licence, practised in many schools to the end of the last century, by which the boys, some days before the time of the regular recess, took possession of the school, of which they barred the doors, and bade their masters defiance from the windows. It is not easy to suppose that on such occasions the master would do more than laugh; yet, if tradition be credited, he often struggled to force or surprise the garrison."

Fielding, writing in the first half of the eighteenth century, gives us two views of the public schools. The first is Parson Adams'— "A public school, Joseph, was the cause of all the calamities which he afterwards suffered. Public schools are the nurseries of all vice and immorality. All the wicked fellows whom I remember at the University were bred at them."

This view is somewhat discounted by the fact that Parson Adams was the master of a private school; but that it was in the main Fielding's may be inferred from the champion he puts up on behalf of the public schools, Sir Thomas Booby.

Cowper's condemnation in his *Tirocinium* of the public schools, in the latter half of the century, is far more savage than Fielding's:

> "Would you your son should be a sot or dunce,
> Lascivious, headstrong; or all these at once . . .
> Train him in public with a mob of boys,
> Childish in mischief only and in noise.
> Else of a mannish growth, and five in ten
> In infidelity and lewdness men."

Cowper was timid and physically weak, and had been ill-treated at Westminster. His picture therefore must be accepted with reservation; but even Dr Johnson condemned the public school of his day for boys lacking in self-confidence. Informed that a gentleman with a nervous son proposed to cure him of his nervousness by sending him to a public school, Johnson roared: "Sir, this is a preposterous expedient for removing his infirmity; such a disposition should be cultivated in the shade. Placing him at a public school is forcing an owl upon day."

Dr Johnson was, however, in favour of a public school for a boy of good parts; and Boswell took the same view, placing his eldest son at Eton and his second at Westminster: "In justice to both these noble seminaries, I with high satisfaction declare," he writes, "that my boys have derived from them a great deal of good and no evil," a verdict which he might have modified had he foreseen how his sons would regard his masterpiece, the Life of Johnson.

Finally, there is Lamb's picture of Christ's Hospital. Lamb was at Christ's Hospital, while Cowper was writing *Tirocinium*, and thirty-five years later he wrote of "the severity of the masters, or worse tyranny of the monitors. The oppressions of these young brutes are heart-sickening to call to recollection." There seems to have been no tradition of discipline to support the weaker masters. Under the Reverend Matthew Field, "we lived a life as careless as birds. We talked and did just what we pleased, and nobody molested us. . . . He (the Rev. Field) came among us, now and then, but often staid away whole days from us; and when he came it made no difference. . . . Our mirth and uproar went on."

Boyer, however, was a fierce disciplinarian. "Poor J.B.!" Coleridge exclaimed, when he heard that Boyer was dying. "May all
his faults be forgiven; and may he be wafted to bliss by little
cherub boys, all head and wings, with no bottoms, to reproach his
sublunary infirmities."

The children of the very poor were equally lawless. Crabbe in
The Borough gives us a picture of what he calls a "Day School of
the Lower Kind":

> "Poor Reuben Dixon has the noisiest school
> Of ragged lads who ever bowed to rule;
> Low in his price—the men who heave our coals,
> And clean our causeways, send him boys in shoals."

Such were boys in the eighteenth century. Yet fifty years or so
after the schools of England were a pandemonium of youthful
savages, numbers of mature Victorians so far from recoiling in
outraged incredulity from young saints like Russell in *Eric*, or
Daubeny in *Saint Winifred's* were in imagination kneeling by
their death-beds, in tears.

The first step towards this reorientation of the mature attitude
towards the young was taken when Dr Arnold began to reform
the public-school system. "My view of things," he wrote, when
at the early age of twenty-eight he was appointed headmaster of
Rugby, "certainly becomes daily more reforming. My object will
be, if possible, to form Christian men, for Christian boys I can
scarcely hope to make." His view of boys, this quotation shows,
was essentially un-Victorian. The Busby-Keate philosophy of
education, which consisted in falling on the young savage, as soon
as he arrived, with a big stick, and beating him into a civilized
frame of mind, was by no means discarded by Dr Arnold; but
the stick, whether wielded by himself or by his praeposters, was
only his second string, the first being the sermons he delivered in
the School Chapel.

Yet stick and sermon combined seemed to avail little. Towards
the close of his headmastership, about 1840, he referred despair-
ingly to "the evil of boy-nature, which makes me always unwilling

to undergo the responsibility of advising anyone to send his son to a public school."

The return of Polixenes seemed as far off as ever. What would Dr Arnold, had he been present, have replied to:

> "We were as twinn'd lambs that did frisk i' the sun,
> And bleat the one at the other; what we chang'd
> Was innocence for innocence; we knew not
> The doctrine of ill-doing, no, nor dream'd
> That any did."?

But meanwhile the forces, which in France had exploded in a political convulsion and in England had revealed the child's imaginative sense of reality to Blake and the boy's to Wordsworth, were not exhausted, though driven underground by the dread of revolution. In due course they reappeared, made their peace with the forces of law and order, and in co-operation with these forces produced the Victorian age.

III

The transition from the eighteenth century view of boys to the mid-Victorian is most clearly seen in Thackeray's writings. In the thirties and forties he referred to his school, Charterhouse, as Slaughterhouse, and when he wrote some sketches of school life he gave them the title of *Dr Birch's Academy*. But by the date when he was working on *The Newcomes*, in the early fifties, he had submitted to the changed spirit of the age. Slaughterhouse is transmuted into Grey Friars, and for the bullies, bloods, and sneaks of Dr Birch's Academy we are given "a little red-cheeked, white-headed gown-boy," to whom Colonel Newcome, a dying pensioner of the Grey Friars Hospital, takes a great fancy.

The child prattles by the Colonel's bedside of a cricket match with the boys of St Peter's, exciting the old man with reminiscences of his own cricketing feats in old days; until at last Clive Newcome thinks it advisable to dismiss the child, with a sovereign to buy tarts.

"*I, curre*, little white-haired gown-boy!" Thackeray concludes. "Heaven speed you, little friend!"

This little scene yields to a careful examination the clue to the Victorian idealization of the young, and general cult of innocence. The three personages of the drama, excluding Clive, who is only a super, are the Colonel and gown-boy, symbols of purity, and Thackeray, the remorseful worldling. It is plain from many asides in his novels and essays that Thackeray, as far as his work and responsibilities allowed, lived the ordinary life of a man about town. But the easy attitude towards this life of the eighteenth-century writers, such as Fielding or, more uncompromisingly, Smollett, with their contempt for "enthusiasts", was no longer possible to Thackeray. The accumulated force of the Evangelical revival, from Wesley to Dr Arnold, with the added dread of the impious French Revolution, had imposed piety, or at least a show of piety, on all well-to-do citizens, and on all ill-to-do citizens who could be made to suffer for any breach of their obligation in this matter.

This piety conflicted in the writers of the age with the forces released by the renaissance of the imagination. These forces, it is true, had been suppressed during a long period. Blake had been ignored, Wordsworth and Coleridge had collapsed, Byron and Shelley had gone into exile, and Keats, alternately neglected and insulted, had died young. But, though suppressed, these forces were still unexhausted; and at last, in the late forties of the nineteenth century, came to a working arrangement with their gaoler, morality, by which they were to be allowed out as long as they behaved themselves. If they were harmless, no one would interfere with them; and if they went about saying what a good fellow their gaoler was, they would find they didn't lose by it.

This arrangement, though convenient, was damaging to the self-respect of the writers who conformed with it. In the scene just quoted, Thackeray is clearly suffering from an acute feeling of inferiority, both to the dying soldier with his child's heart and to the red-cheeked, white-haired gown-boy with his innocent delight in tarts and cricket matches. The man is crammed with guilty memories, and all one can say in his behalf is that he is

painfully aware of the distinction between genius and virtue, and
the complete inferiority of the former to the latter.

There is, as we have seen, a faint approximation to this attitude
in Shakespeare's last plays; but on the whole one may say that the
Elizabethans had imagination without an over-developed sense of
guilt; that in the eighteenth century what little imagination there
was functioned apart from the growing sense of guilt; and that in
the Victorians an awakening imagination worked on an exaggerated sense of guilt, producing the cult of innocence, with as
objects of worship those who were immune from sexual temptation: the very old and the very young, and, by an important
convention, all gentlewomen, mothers, wives, sisters and
daughters, unless otherwise specified.

The clash between an awakening imagination and the sense of
guilt is naturally most frequent in adolescence; hence both the
adolescent strain in the Victorian writers of genius, and their
attraction towards that period of life. This attraction is exceptionally strong in Dickens and Tennyson, who, though unlike in all
other respects, envelop their exploits in child-murder in the same
curious atmosphere of ghoulish lacrimosity, and defer the inevitable end with the same lingering relish. The death of the May
Queen covers many months:

"I thought to pass away before, and yet alive I am;
And in the fields all round I hear the bleating of the lamb."

But she continues to talk, indifferent to the reader's growing
passion for what her creator elsewhere calls "the sound of a voice
that is still."

The Puritan notion of youthful depravity still lingers faintly
and unconvincingly in the May Queen's "I have been wild and
wicked, but you'll forgive me now." In the deaths of Paul
Dombey and little Nell, so far as one can speak with certitude
without a special investigation into these enormous transactions,
the desperate depravity to which Charles Trueman confessed has
vanished without leaving any trace. Hell, with the horrors of
which John Trueman used to entertain his family on Sunday

evenings, is not referred to; and Christ is pictured far more emotionally than the Puritan conception of him would have sanctioned. "How green the banks were now," Paul murmurs at the close of his dying soliloquy, "and how bright the flowers growing on them, and how tall the rushes! Now the boat was out at sea, but gliding smoothly on. And now there was a shore before him. Who stood on the bank! But tell them the picture on the stairs is not Divine enough. The light about the head is shining on me as I go!"

The aberrations of these great writers were balanced, when the mature elements of their genius were in the ascendant, by memories of childhood and boyhood inferior only to Blake's and Wordsworth's; the early years of David Copperfield and of Henry Esmond, for example, and, in Tennyson, innumerable "glimpses of forgotten dreams."

IV

After this long parturition, at which most of the great English writers from Shakespeare to Dickens have assisted as midwives, it may appear to the modern reader that in Farrar the mountain has brought forth a mouse. But the mouse was a mammoth in his day. The spasmodic adolescence of his contemporaries was a constant quality in Farrar, and his spontaneous incessant and passionate expression of this quality entitles him still to be regarded as the most complete exponent of mid-Victorian emotionalism in one of its most important branches.

Farrar was born in 1831, the son of a missionary at Bombay. He was sent home at three to live with two maiden aunts at Aylesbury, and at the age of six went to a day-school. "On those benches," he tells us in *Eric*, which is autobiographical in its opening chapters, "gentlemen's sons sat side by side with plebeians, and no harm, but only good, seemed to come from the intercourse. Many a time afterward when Eric, as he passed down the streets, interchanged friendly greetings with some young glazier or tradesman whom he remembered at school, he felt glad that thus early he had learnt to despise the accidental and nominal differences which separate man from man."

This passage illustrates Farrar's sensitive response to the emotional atmosphere of his age, which was trying, among many other things, to feel democratic. Farrar was actually, like the page-boy in one of Mr P. G. Wodehouse's stories, "somewhat acutely alive to the existence of class distinctions." It was a source of great satisfaction to him, whatever it may have been to the ancestor in question, that his family included a bishop who had been burnt by Queen Mary.

Farrar passed from this day-school to King William's College, in the Isle of Man, and from there to Trinity College, Cambridge. Both at school and at Cambridge he supported himself entirely out of exhibitions and scholarships. At Trinity he was a sizar, and, as he discloses in *Julian Home*, was passionately sensitive to the humiliations of that position.

After Cambridge he went to Marlborough as a master for a short time, and then to Harrow for fifteen years. At Harrow, in 1858, when he was twenty-seven, he published "*Eric*, or, *Little by Little. A tale of Roslyn School.*"

On returning to school, after the holidays, Eric pays a brief visit to the headmaster, "who was dignified but not unkindly," and then bounded downstairs to the "boarders' room."

"How many and what varied scenes had not that room beheld!" Farrar writes. "Had those dumb walls any feeling, what worlds of life and experience they would have acquired! If against each boy's name, as it was rudely cut on the oak panels, could have been also cut the fate that had befallen him, the good that he had there learnt, the evil that he there had suffered—what *noble* histories would the records unfold of honour and success, of baffled temptations and hard-won triumphs; what *awful* histories of hopes blighted and habits learned, of wasted talents and ruined lives!"

This rhapsody, which would have astonished Dr Johnson, derives from Dr Arnold's view that boys should be treated as potentially mature moral agents, able, if they exerted themselves, to possess themselves of what he called "moral consciousness."

Dr Arnold, however, was, and expected to be, perpetually dis-appointed by the development of the moral consciousness in his charges. A Christian boy seemed to him almost a contradiction in terms. Farrar in the changed spirit of his epoch, and with his passionately adolescent temperament, saw boys not as potentially but as actually mature. A complete knowledge of the con-sequences, or of what Farrar imagined to be the consequences, of this or that action, is demanded from all his boys, and fright-ful penalties are inflicted upon the careless, the weak, or the intransigent.

The ultimate ruin and early death of Eric, for example, are traced to his desire for popularity, which prevented him from speaking out when, in dormitory No. 7, he for the first time heard indecent words.

"Now, Eric, now or never! Life and death, ruin and salvation, corruption and purity are in the balance together, and the scale of your destiny may hang on a single word of yours. Speak out, boy! Tell these fellows that unseemly words wound your con-science; tell them that they are ruinous, sinful, damnable. . . . Lose your purity of heart, Eric, and you have lost a jewel which the whole world, if it were 'one entire and perfect chrysolite' cannot replace."

But Eric remained silent, after a half-hour of agonizing self-conflict, during which the speaker, a certain Ball, no doubt fell asleep.

Ball, "who had tasted more deeply of the tree of the knowledge of good and evil than any other boy," is expelled; but his place is taken by Brigson, "a fore-front fighter in the Devil's battles, who did much to ruin many an immortal soul. . . . Never did some of the Roslyn boys, to their dying day, forget the deep, intolerable, unfathomable flood of moral turpitude and iniquity which he bore with him."

Association with Brigson, and a younger boy, Wildney, "a jolly fearless-looking little fellow, with great black eyes," involves Eric in drink. Drink leads to a temptation to theft. Theft is com-mitted, and the suspicion that attaches, though falsely, to Eric drives him to sea, where brutal treatment on a small trading schooner, bound for Corunna to take in a cargo of cattle, added to mental anguish, fatally impairs his health. He gets back home, but only to die. His mother, heart-broken at his misconduct, had predeceased him, as had his younger brother Vernon, who had fallen from a cliff in the course of the story.

Eric, as exhibited in this brief analysis, is the kind of book which Dr Arnold might have written had he taken to drink. Farrar, and the other mid-Victorian emotionalists, were, in fact, Puritans intoxicated by the Romantic movement. Ball and Brigson are by-products of the clash between the imaginative renaissance and the theory of human nature handed down through three centuries by the Puritans. This clash produced not only juvenile devils, but also young angels, the cult of depravity and the cult of innocence having become interdependent. "Farrar seemed always to have before him," Dr Butler, the headmaster of Harrow, wrote, "two haunting visions, the one of boyish innocence and the other of boyish wickedness."

Against evil, embodied in a Ball or a Brigson, Farrar set the figure of Russell, who represents the angelic principle contesting for Eric's soul against the powers of darkness.

Here is a vignette of Russell and Eric, in the first stage of Eric's degeneration. Mr Gordon, a master, had just smiled at Russell but hardly noticed Eric.

> " 'What a surly devil that is,' said Eric. 'Did you see how he purposely cut me?'
>
> 'A surly ——? Oh, Eric, that's the first time I ever heard you swear.'
>
> Eric blushed. He hadn't meant the word to slip out in Russell's hearing, though similar and worse expressions were common enough in his talk with other boys."

The symbols of innocence in Victorian literature inevitably die young, owing to the metaphysical connection between innocence and undeveloped sex.

Russell, therefore, is mortally injured in jumping from a rock which had been cut off by the advancing tide.

"One day Eric brought him a little bunch of primroses and violets. 'Eric,' said Russell sadly, 'these dear flowers are the last spring blossoms that I shall see—*here* at least. . . . There stop, dear fellow, don't cry,' said he, raising his hands quietly to Eric's face; 'isn't it better for me so? I own it seemed sad at first to leave this bright world and the sea—yes, even that cruel sea,' he continued smiling; 'and to leave Roslyn, and Upton, and Monty, and, above all, to leave *you*, Eric, whom I love best in all the world. . . . Oh, Eric, Eric, I am young, but I am dying, dying, Eric, my brother—let me call you brother—I have no near relations, you know, to fill up the love in my yearning heart, but I *do* love you. I wish you were my brother,' he said, as Eric took his hand between his own. 'There, that comforts me; I feel as if I *were* a child again, and had a brother; and I *shall* be a child again soon, Eric, in the courts of a Father's house.' . . . The child-like, holy, reverent voice ceased, and Eric rose. One long brotherly kiss he printed on Eric's forehead, and full of sorrowful foreboding, bade him good night."

Eric, Farrar wrote to a friend from Harrow, had received "the warm encomiums of the boys and masters here"; and he adds that he does not trouble himself about "The Saturday Wasp."

The Saturday Wasp was *The Saturday Review*, which had recently been founded to express a body of opinion equally opposed to Evangelican puritanism and to the imaginative renaissance, though to some extent influenced, unconsciously, by both. One of the strands in the complicated texture of the Victorian spirit was a counter movement, derived from the common-sense tradition of the eighteenth century, against the emotionalism of the age. This movement had for its chief dogma the belief that the Englishman was a hard-headed fellow, who left music, poetry and love to foreigners, and especially to the French. Paganism, with a sufficient infusion of Christianity to make it respectable, was what the adherents of this movement worked for, though they did not formulate their ideal quite so baldly.

The forces which were modifying, on one of its sides, the spirit introduced into the public-school system by Dr Arnold are plainly visible in *The Saturday Review's* criticism of *Eric*. "In former times," the reviewer writes, "the escapades of schoolboys used to be looked upon and referred to principally as matter of joke. . . . To Dr Arnold, and those who derived their views from him, such notions were a sort of abomination of desolation. It was one of his most favourite maxims that boys were moral agents as well as men, that they were as capable as men both of crimes and of sins, and that to speak or think lightly of their offences was to sap the very foundation of morality. *Eric* is written entirely on this principle. . . . The boys are always getting worse or better, they never seem to enjoy themselves quietly for a moment."

The reviewer continues with a criticism of "the system of praepostors which was so much approved by Dr Arnold. He (Farrar) thinks that it improves the discipline of the school, and makes the head boys manly by investing them with authority."

In the reviewer's opinion, "nothing can possibly be more unwise than to insist, to the boys who occupy such positions, on their importance and responsibility"; and he goes on to speak of "Jacks in office . . . Pharisaical self-importance and self-complacency."

Here the reviewer is casting back to the good sense of the eighteenth century, not foreshadowing the future; for the practice of deliberating the problems of discipline on equal terms with young persons just emerging from puberty has not yet been discarded by public-schoolmasters.

In his attack on the sentimentality in *Eric*, however, the reviewer was in touch with the change to which Victorian emotionalism submitted itself from the sixties onwards.

"To say nothing of three more or less violent deaths," he growls, "two of which involve angelic death-beds, everything is served up with tear sauce. The boys quote hymns, and, to the infinite indignation of all English readers, occasionally kiss each other (principally, however, when they are *in articulo mortis*), exchanging, moreover, such endearments as 'dear fellow' and the like."

That "infinite indignation of all English readers" is a false touch, and might, in base minds, give rise to injurious suspicions of the reviewer himself. The emotionalism in *Eric* has a certain foothold in reality. In the years before and merging into adolescence boys indulge secretly many brief but intense adorations; and a death or an accident produces among the young a mass emotion of the same order. An instance of each occurred at the writer's preparatory school; and still more extraordinary was the leave-taking of a popular master, who shook hands with the assembled boys in rotation, and embraced two. Many of the boys wept without restraint.

The peculiarity of *Eric* is that this emotion fills the book to the exclusion of more prosaic matter. Farrar's adolescent temperament, which would have had to limit its display in any other age, was stimulated, in the Victorian fifties, to an astonishing exuberance. His death-bed pathos is not in itself unnatural or artificial. It is only its expression by a mature writer which is startling. Imaginary death-beds are a favourite diversion of the young, who use them to express emotions which they are ashamed to disclose in real life. They serve also to soothe the sense of neglect, always strong in the adolescent. The dying are inevitably in the centre of the stage; and in his dying boys Farrar, whose feeling of neglect was acute and continuous, saw not only those whom he had loved but also himself.

v

Eric, we have seen, received the warm encomiums of the boys and masters at Harrow. Even after allowing for the possibility that if any boys and masters did not care for *Eric* they would not tell Farrar so, the date of *Eric*, 1858, was just early enough to allow public-school boys to enjoy it, if they were so minded, without embarrassment.

But in the sixties the genius who presided over Victorian sentiment turned his hand to a less luxuriant and more sophisticated form of emotionalism, the cult of games and the team-spirit. Farrar himself remained immune, though *St Winifred's*, which appeared in 1865, witnessed to the change in the atmosphere by its comparative restraint. It contains only one death-bed scene, Daubeny's, the Martyr-Student, killed by overwork, and the only recorded kiss is exchanged between Daubeny and his mother. In the epilogue, Charlie Evson, the hero's brother, is killed by savages; but perfunctorily, as a matter of form. He had gone to the South Seas as a missionary; and this, in Victorian fiction, is the usual capital sentence passed on characters who, while not important enough to die at home, are felt to have deserved some kind of premature end.

It is difficult to mark the precise date at which games began to be invested with religious importance. There is a good deal of football and some cricket in *Tom Brown's Schooldays*, but the book is not dominated by them. In *Eric* and *St Winifred's* games are played, in the intervals between drinking bouts and violent deaths; there is no prejudice against them, and the virtuous and industrious take part in them without any fuss. We find no hint of the youthful intellectual who does not shine on the football field. The first sketch of that tragic figure, whose importance was fully recognized in the first two decades of twentieth century fiction, may perhaps be found in *Gerald Eversley's Friendship*, a school story, published in 1895, by the Reverend J. E. C. Welldon, then headmaster of Eton, and now Dean of Durham. The two chief personages of the book, which though nearly forty years later than *Eric* is curiously like *Eric* in tone, are Gerald Eversley, a scholarly bespectacled plebeian, and Harry Venniker, the blue-eyed curly-haired son of a peer. The period is the sixties, and games are already important.

"You've not got to earn your living, you know," are Lord Venniker's parting words to Harry, "so you need not work your eyes out; I'd much rather you got into the eleven."

"Work hard then," are the last words of the Reverend Eversley to Gerald. "Remember that Satan finds some mischief for idle hands. You have been brought up in the faith of Christ as your Redeemer and your Master. . . ."

The main theme of the book is the adoration felt by the pious and scholarly Gerald for the athletic and essentially pagan Harry. "There had arisen in Gerald's mind a passionate admiration, a sentiment akin to hero-worship, for the boy, his inferior in

intellect, but so brilliant, so prominent in the common ways of
school life. . . . He looked up to him as to a being of higher order.
. . . To Gerald Eversley Harry Venniker was all in all."

The relationship of these two exactly symbolizes the subjection, during the latter part of the century, of the Dr Arnold
theory of education to the theory of games and the team spirit.

In its origin the cult of games was an expression of the pagan
spirit, which was beginning to revive throughout England, and
which embodied itself most naturally in athletic prowess with the
conservative type that read *The Saturday Review*. The cult was
supported also by full-blooded Broad Churchmen, like Charles
Kingsley, who felt that to move rapidly about in the open air was
the best safeguard, for man or boy, whether against Popery or the
Fine Arts, lust or infidelity.

So games began to be encouraged, with the aim of lowering
the emotional temperature all round. But the genius of Victorian
sentiment handled the situation with easy mastery. Had Moloch
himself landed on our shores during the Victorian age, he would
presently have been found in a meadow, weaving daisy chains for
his little friends, while the happy tears rolled down his cheeks.

The most important name in the games movement is Bowen, a
colleague of Farrar and Welldon at Harrow. Bowen's songs, some
of which, and notably *Forty Years On*, spread throughout the
public schools, invested games with the emotions of patriotism
and even of religion.

> "Four sad years of a long defeat
>   Over and gone to-day;
> Flash the news till the gladness greet
>   Continents far away;
> Say how, honour and fame at stake,
> Somebody play'd for the old School's sake."

It might be supposed that in these and similar verses he is
writing down to his youthful audience, were it not that the same
solemn view of athletics is expressed in his prose: "The common
English games," he wrote in 1884, in a paper on games, "are of

indescribable value. Without any exaggeration, I declare that in our whole system there is nothing which, in my opinion, approaches them in value . . . there lives more soul in honest play, believe me, than in half the hymn-books."

The result of this conviction was that Bowen's school songs took on the character of a hymnal, with games as the Deity's instrument of salvation.

"God give us bases to guard and beleaguer,
Games to play out, whether earnest or fun;
Fights for the fearless and goals for the eager,
Twenty and thirty and forty years on!"

Instead of returning boys to the obscurity befitting embryos, the Bowen reaction, as it may be called, against Dr Arnold, and less directly against Farrar, very much increased the self-importance of the schoolboy. By giving the team-spirit, playing for one's side, the same weight as Dr Arnold had formerly given to the pursuit of individual virtue, Bowen and his fellow-religionists hoped to wipe out the overstrained morality of Arnold and the unhealthy sentiment of Farrar. The fallacy that collective emotionalism purifies the individual was once again demonstrated. By the first decade of the twentieth century, a master who, without any business excuse, managed to engage a member of the school cricket or football team in small talk knew that he was making a success of his life's work.

Bowen did not venture to attack Arnold directly, but in one of his essays he constructed a lay figure, Arnoldides Chiffers, in whom he assailed the Arnoldian inquisition into the state of a boy's moral health. The sanctuary of a boy's soul was to Bowen a sacred place which a master should enter very rarely, and in a mood of proper reverence. The ordinary relation of a master to the boys in his charge, Bowen implies, should be that of the chairman of a company with a casting vote, which he trusts the spirit of friendly co-operation among his fellow-directors will make it unnecessary for him to use.

Yet the curt colloquial tone in the following passage from his paper on games very imperfectly conceals the sophisticated emotionalism of the games cult, an emotionalism in no way calculated to lessen the "Pharisaical self-importance and self-complacency" of the "Jacks in office" attacked by the Saturday Reviewer.

"The day I began to write this essay, a captain of a house football eleven asked me to go down to his house game that day. There was a small local trouble; two important boys had a quarrel on, and it was very awkward, and, in short, he wanted to be advised. I played, and everything went on as usual. After it was over, I asked about the quarrel. It had vanished into the delight of exercise and the glory of play."

The Bowen who existed beneath this bluff of manliness was moved by the distant Hampstead lights, visible from the windows of his house as he went his nightly rounds, to a lyric which brings the ageing bachelor rather pathetically before our eyes, with his sentiment for his boys; a sentiment the subdued expression of which shows that the curve of Victorian emotionalism had, after all, descended, by the eighties, a considerable distance from *Eric*.

"Good night! Sleep, and so may ever
Lights half seen across a murky lea,
Child of hope, and courage, and endeavour,
Gleam a voiceless benison on thee!
Youth be bearer
Soon of hardihood;
Life be fairer,
Loyaller to good;
Till the far lamps vanish into light,
Rest in the dream-time. Good night!"

VI

That Farrar observed the growth of the games cult with uneasiness may be inferred from a sentence of his, aimed at one of his Harrow pupils—"the most case-hardened victim of Circe that ever conceived the world to be formed in the humble imitation of a cricket ball."

But in no circumstances would he have been happy as a school-master. The contrast between fact and fancy was too glaring.

When he went to Harrow from Marlborough, he seems to have been ragged at first. This, at any rate, may be inferred from a letter he wrote to a Marlborough master; but the quivering passion of the letter, involving an imperfect control of grammar, suggests that the alarm inspired by his rage must soon have out-weighed the pleasure of arousing it.

"MY DEAR BEESLY:

I am perpetually annoyed by letters from the boys at M—— speaking as if I had been subjected to personal violence (!) by the boys here, and to-day I was informed that I had been tied by a great-coat, and pelted with cinders!! I can't tell you the ineffable disgust which these preposterous reports give me; and as they are as grotesquely and groundlessly and absolutely false, and as diametrically the reverse of anything possible as they can be, I do wish, once for all that they could be authoritatively contradicted. Whence such absurdly and gratuitously non-sensical tittle-tattle can have originated I cannot even dream, unless some Harrovian has been humbugging one of the M—— fellows.

The idea! I wonder whether you all think me made of straw! Likely that I should be roughly handled, everyone and all of whom instantly obey my slightest order, and who are in as complete a state of subjection *now* as any form in Marlboro'."

With his adolescent temperament, to which this kind of intensity belongs, went a self-pity which his varied triumphs were unable to assuage. He could never free himself from the illusion that the world was behaving unfairly by him. On his appointment as Archdeacon of Westminster, he wrote to a friend: "How odd is one's destiny. Here I am stranded—like a desolate wreck on the lonely shore!" When he became Dean of Canterbury, Canon

Page Roberts noticed that "it was as though a load of suspicion and depreciation had been removed from his shoulders, as though his deserts, so long disregarded, had at length been acknowledged." Yet at that date he had long been the most popular preacher in the Church of England. The same sense of ill-usage preyed on him at Harrow. He would have been happier breaking stones, he told a pupil one day, when they were out on a walk. This was not a momentary feeling. Mr Lawley, the master of the day-school in *Eric*, used the same image: "Often did he tell the boys 'that it was an easier life by far to break stones by the road-side than to teach them'; and at last his eccentricities became too obvious to be overlooked. The dénouement was a tragic one . . . the handsome proud scholar became an inmate of the Brerely Lunatic Asylum."

It is possible that some of Farrar's unhappiness may have been due to his popularity, gratifying though it was. Both as a writer and a preacher his chief appeal was to an audience which was neither socially nor intellectually all he could have wished in those moments when he forgot that the differences which separate man from man are accidental and nominal.

The tributes he received most frequently were of the kind represented by the following letter, written from Norwich, sixteen years after *Eric* appeared, and fifteen years after *Julian Home*:

"Reverend Sir,
    As Secretary of a very influential Literary Class, and that moreover in connection with a Churchman's Club, it may perhaps give you some amount of pleasure to hear that a great many members of the class have derived a very great and lasting benefit from those eloquent and beautiful books, *Julian Home* and *Eric, or Little by Little*. I myself have to thank you most sincerely for writing them. . . . They give tone, health, and vigour to the spiritual frame, and feed the lamp of Shekinah with oil pure as crystal."

The transmutation of the Puritan view that everyone is wicked into the mid-Victorian vision of two extremes, one devilish, the other angelic, has been illustrated with examples from *Eric*. In *Julian Home*, Farrar reveals another aspect of this vision. Gentlewomen, in the Victorian age, were automatically excluded from the law of original sin; and women generally were not regarded as responsible moral agents, a view which led eventually to the woman's movement, and other expressions of a revolt against a doctrine more flattering in essence to the male sex than to the female.

Superficially, however, men got very much the worst of it, as is shown by this passage from *Julian Home*, where the hero addresses as follows a Cambridge undergraduate who had taken first to drink and then to women:

> "If you are dead and indifferent to your own miserable soul, think that in this sin you cannot sin alone; think that you are dragging down to the nethermost abyss others beside yourself. Remember the wretched victims of your infamous passions, and tremble while you desecrate and deface for ever God's image stamped on a fair human soul. Think of those whom your vileness dooms to a life of loathliness, a death of shame and anguish, perhaps an eternity of horrible despair. Learn something of the days they are forced to spend that they may pander to the worst instincts of your degraded nature; days of squalor and drunkenness, disease and dirt; gin at morning, noon, and night; eating infection, horrible madness, and sudden death at the end. . . . Is it not a reminiscence sufficient to kill any man's hope that, but for his own brutality, some who are now perhaps rotting in the lazar-house or raving in the asylum, might have been clasping their own children to their happy breasts, and wearing in unpolluted innocence the rose of matronly honour?"

The theory that prostitutes were the victims of male lust was an unavoidable corollary of the convention that women of gentle birth were free from original sin. The same freedom had, logically, to be conceded to women of the lower orders, with male depravity, and especially aristocratic male depravity, to account for the numerous exceptions that seemed to contradict this theory. A prostitute was "unfortunate", in the same sense that someone stunned by a falling tile, or knocked over by a runaway horse, was unfortunate.

This attitude had not even the advantage of alleviating the unhappiness of a prostitute's life. To the girl it was oppressive to feel that a sinful woman was a *lusus naturae*; and the man, submitting to the power of suggestion, was apt to behave more brutally than he would have behaved in a natural atmosphere.

With what extreme reluctance the Victorian mind relinquished this victim theory is shown in a pamphlet to which Farrar contributed a preface in 1890. The pamphlet is entitled, "Work among the Fallen as seen in the Prison Cells," by the Rev. G. P. Merrick, Chaplain of H. M. Prison, Millbank. "When several years ago," the Rev. G. P. Merrick writes, "I commenced my work within the prison walls, I was of the opinion, as many people are, that the career of every 'woman of the streets', could be written and summed up within a few words—seduced, deserted, cast off by relations. I thought that every poor outcast was the victim of some man's brutal lust and heartless abandonment. But, much to my astonishment, and it saddened me to learn it, I soon found, on the authority of the erring women themselves, that the common impression and my own were altogether wrong. . . . The record of some three thousand cases made several years ago corrected my old and more chivalrous ideas on the subject, and that which after a further observation of many years I now mention only confirm what my former figures testified."

In the course of this enquiry, Mr Merrick interviewed 16,022 women. Of these 11,232 owed their ruin to the exercise of their own free will. They were tempted by inducements which Mr Merrick tabulates as follows:

"Your own mistress."
"Nothing to do."
"Plenty of money."
"Being a lady."
"Perfect liberty."

In only a very few instances, Mr Merrick says, were grosser tastes confessed to. The remaining 4,790 owed their ruin to men. Yet, even of these, 1,954 owed their ruin to men only in the sense that they had quarrelled with their husbands or lovers, a certain proportion of whom, it is fair to assume, were less at fault than the women.

Thus, out of the original total of 16,022, only 2,836 were directly betrayed by men. But even here disillusionment awaited the Reverend G. P. Merrick, who deserves high praise for the intellectual honesty with which he faced conclusions so repugnant to his sense of what should have been.

He had had, he says, "a notion that seduction was an art practised somewhat exclusively by members of the so-called higher classes." Yet of these 2,836 women, 2,179 had been betrayed by men of their own rank; so that out of 16,022 women, only 657, about four per cent. of the total number, had been betrayed by gentlemen.

No one could have reproached the Reverend G. P. Merrick had he stayed his investigations at this point. But the devoted man pressed forward.

The word "gentleman," he ascertained, "was used in a very large sense." There were "gentlemen" and "real gentlemen"; and the former category included "clerks, commercial travellers, and shop assistants." One cannot but feel curious as to how many real gentlemen, as distinguished from gentlemen, figured in these 657 instances. On this point, however—and who can blame him?—the Reverend G. P. Merrick is silent.

VII

The angel-devil antithesis, to the disintegration of which towards the close of the century Mr Merrick's pamphlet testifies, was, as has been shown, the creation of an awakened imagination working on the sense of guilt inherited from the Puritans.

But the mind of even the most emotional Victorian, even Farrar's mind, could not repose on this antithesis for ever. A time came when the assumptions of Puritan theology, and particularly the doctrine of eternal punishment, became too painful to be sublimated any longer by the imagination.

As early as 1835, Mrs Sherwood, as we have seen, turned from

the terroristic Puritanism of her youth to a belief in the unconditional salvation of all mankind. The new forces released at
the opening of the nineteenth century had touched her imagination, and the doctrine of hell-fire ceased to be a truism. It had
become either a truth or a lie, and, faced by these alternatives, she
instinctively rejected it as a lie.

The resentment of the Worcester Evangelical party against
Mrs Sherwood has been referred to. This was in 1835; yet even
in 1877 when Farrar preached his sermons on Eternal Hope in
Westminster Abbey he was, in his own words, "savagely and
generally anathematized." But these anathemas came from a
losing side. Within a few years the idea of Hell, sustained and
elaborated through so many centuries, had almost entirely passed
out of the popular consciousness.

Like many forms of mania, it reached its most extravagant
stage shortly before its collapse. Although Hell was incorporated
in Christianity on the authority of words attributed to Christ
Himself, and although its terrors were from the Fathers onwards
threatened against sinners, and in the Middle Ages stimulated
poets and painters to finer achievements than the relatively vague
felicities of Heaven, the cult of Hell reached its fullest expression
only under the careful tendance of the followers of Calvin and
Knox in England, and more especially in Scotland and America.
Calvin himself, and the Calvinists generally of the sixteenth
century, were less extreme about Hell than their disciples in the
two succeeding centuries; though it was Calvin who was responsible for giving a new lease of life to Saint Augustine's doctrine
that far the greatest part of mankind is predestined, before birth,
to everlasting torment.

One would expect Hell to be an Old Testament invention. But
the authority actually appealed to by the Puritans while elaborat-
ing their instrument of terrorism was not any Old Testament text,
but a few sayings of Christ, the most explicit of which was: "The
Son of Man shall send forth his angels, and they shall gather out
of his kingdom all things that offend, and them which do iniquity;
and they shall cast them into a furnace of fire; there shall be
wailing and gnashing of teeth."

The idea of Hell would, however, seem, in effect, to be derived from the Old Testament. In the Old Testament the unit is the Jewish nation, not the individual Jew. A nation, practically considered, is immortal. The pains it suffers at the hands of an angry God can be indefinitely protracted in this world. The Old Testament equivalent of Hell is, therefore, the future threatened to Israel throughout the major and minor prophets, unless it mends its ways. Had it been possible to Jeremiah and Ezekiel to imagine Israel dying a collective death, and coming collectively to life in another existence, they would have needed no other materials than those they had already used in forecasting Israel's future to construct a hell that would command even Jonathan Edwards' approval.

When the individual Jew replaced his nation as the unit of religious consciousness, a development which reached its highest point in Christ, the Hebrew habit of rewards and penalties rejected personal extinction at death; and communicating itself to the early exponents of Christianity created Heaven and Hell.

The idea of Hell, though in contradiction to Christ's teaching, having apparently received Christ's sanction, logic unchecked by reality and malice unchecked by fear were free to elaborate its torments to the furthest limits of human ingenuity.

At first, among the Fathers of the Church, Hell seems to have been chiefly valued for its disciplinary uses. Some of the Fathers, practising what was called the doctrine of "accommodation", withheld from the masses their own disbelief in eternal punishment. "The many," said Origen, "need no further teaching than the punishment of sinners. For it is not expedient to go any further on account of those who scarcely through the fear of eternal punishment restrain the outpouring into any amount of recklessness." Saint Augustine, however, believed in Hell without any mental reserve, and consigned unbaptized infants to its flames in an entirely unaccommodating spirit.

By the thirteenth and fourteenth centuries, the pains of Hell had been classified with a minuteness not exceeded by any Puritan; nor did any Puritan surpass Saint Thomas of Aquinas's remark that "the bliss of the saved would be all the more keen because they are permitted to gaze on the punishment of the wicked."

But mediæval Christendom was too easy-going, and too scattered, to be terrorized by theologians. The fear of Hell, as a general sentiment, was far stronger in Puritan England than in the Europe of the Middle Ages, and reached its zenith in the isolated New England of the eighteenth century.

"The world," said Jonathan Edwards, a famous New England divine, "will probably be converted into a great lake or liquid globe of fire, in which the wicked shall be overwhelmed, which shall always be in tempest, in which they shall be tossed to and fro, having no rest day or night, vast waves and billows of fire continually rolling over their heads, of which they shall ever be full of a quick sense, within and without; their heads, their eyes, their tongues, their hands, their feet, their loins and their vitals shall for ever be full of a glaring, melting fire, enough to melt the very rocks and elements. Also they shall be full of the most quick and lively sense to feel the torments, not for ten millions of ages, but for ever and ever, without any end at all."

Elsewhere Jonathan Edwards tells his congregation that "the God that holds you over the pit of hell, much in the same way as one holds a spider or some loathsome insect over the fire, abhors you and is dreadfully provoked." It would be natural to infer from this that it was Jonathan Edwards' practice to pick up a spider or cockroach with the sugar-tongs, and fry it over the parlour fire. But such a relatively human and genial occupation lay outside the range of the Calvinist divine. The suppression of all natural emotion confined him to his own imagination, whose horrors he could not ease in action but only in communicating them to the imaginations of others. The effect produced by the Calvinist divines on their congregations is conveyed in an incident narrated by Farrar. "When Dr Nathanael Emmons was once depicting the state of the lost souls, a woman rose up in the congregation, and shrieked, 'Oh, Dr Emmons, Dr Emmons, has God no mercy at all?'"

Christ existed for the Puritans only as the founder of their Hell, and as an indispensable part of the mechanism by which the elect were saved. But when the Puritan system began to disintegrate, men turned to Christ for support against Calvin, a movement already visible in the hymns of Charles Wesley, whose Arminian Methodism represented a characteristically English modification of Calvin's inhuman theology. Yet even in the middle of the nineteenth century, a cool agnostic like John Stuart Mill could not distinguish between Calvinism and Christianity. Compared with the doctrine of endless torments, he said, "every other objection to Christianity sinks into insignificance."

The angel-devil antithesis of the fifties marked the first stage of the Victorian revolt against hell, for though the devil still bulked large, the angel promised redemption. As the century advanced, the growing disbelief in the supernatural element of Christianity so far affected the orthodox as to make them transfer the emphasis of their worship of Christ more and more from his function as a magician to his character as a man, until he finally became what Charles Wesley had in effect already called him, a symbol of love. "Thy nature and thy name is love." The immense popularity of Farrar's *Life of Christ*, which appeared in 1874, was due to its expression of this rejection of Calvin in favour of Christ; a rejection only half-conscious in Farrar, as in many of his readers. In his sense of depravity Farrar was essentially Calvinist; and this sense is still present in *The Life of Christ*, between which and *Eric* there is a curious parallelism. Russell reappears in Saint John. "The rare combination of contemplativeness and passion, of strength and sweetness in the same soul—the perfect faith which inspired his devotion, and the perfect love which precluded fear —these were the gifts and graces which rendered him worthy of leaning his young head on the bosom of his Lord." Peter is a second Eric, poised between virtue and vice. "At this period of his life his easy impressionable nature was ever liable to be moulded by the influence of the moment, and he passed readily into passionate extremes." Judas is another Ball or Brigson; and even Calvin could not have troubled himself less than Farrar to find any mitigating circumstances in Judas's conduct. "Judas, the false smile of hypocrisy on his face, but rage, and shame, and greed, and anguish, and treachery in his heart." Accounts differ, Farrar says, "as to the wretch's death." He may have hanged himself. Or he may have perished in a hideous attack of elephantiasis. Or he may have been crushed by a passing wagon.

In his *Life of Christ*, Farrar restored to general consciousness the hope which the mass of Christians would naturally derive from the life and teachings of Christ when presented to them in a popular form and undistorted by Puritan terrorism. But Puritan terrorism had not yet been directly attacked. The most famous Nonconformist preacher of the seventies and eighties, Spurgeon, equally immune from the reaction towards Christ and from the queries as to the exact location of hell raised with increasing insistence by students of geology and other exact sciences, was engaged during this period in restoring to his vast congregations their waning interest in the fate that probably awaited them. "Thou shalt look up there on the throne of God, and it shall be written 'For ever!' When the damned jingle the burning irons of their torment they shall say, 'For ever!' When they howl, Echo cries 'For ever!' "

The interest of Farrar's sermons nowadays is that, living at a time when Spurgeons were still at large, he felt compelled to qualify his disbelief in hell.

He was attacked on all sides for having denied the existence of hell, and denounced the doctrine of eternal punishment. To these attacks he replied that what he had denied was:

1. The physical torments, the material agonies, the *sapiens ignis* of eternal punishment.
2. Endless duration for all who incur Hell.
3. That it is incurred by the vast mass of mankind.
4. That it is a doom passed irreversibly at the moment of death in all who die in sin.

The Reverend C. F. Childe, Rector of Holbrook, in Suffolk, replied to Farrar in a lengthy pamphlet, entitled "The Unsafe Anchor or 'Eternal Hope' a False Hope."

Even Gentile writers, Mr Childe points out, speak of the punishment of the wicked as:

I

1. Judicially inflicted.
2. Agonizing.
3. Eternal.

And "the greatest of uninspired poets," Shakespeare, "bears witness to the restraining power of hell—'the dread of something after death'."

Turning from the relatively unimportant corroboration supplied by pagan mythology and uninspired poets, Mr Childe sets forth the numerous passages in the Bible which establish the vindictiveness of God, and the material and permanent nature of his punishment.

Having settled the fact of eternal punishment, Mr Childe concludes by disposing decisively of any false hopes as to its nature.

"It is said, 'After all, the "fiery indignation" is not actual, but only metaphorical fire—not real, scorching, burning flame, but only wrath and displeasure.' I answer, it is infinitely worse than material fire, infinitely more real."

A more important answer, based on exhaustive erudition, came from Dr Pusey, a very gentle and courteous champion of Hell.

Dr Pusey admitted that while the Church had laid down eternity of punishment to be matter of faith, it had not laid down the material character of the punishment; though he himself believed in a literal fire, as did, with very few exceptions, all those who had expressed an opinion on this question.

Farrar's belief, Dr Pusey continues, is better than his book. Although in his book he had stated that he did not believe in the final salvation of all men, he unhappily did not observe that all his arguments were Universalist, "extending even to the restoration of Satan."

A correspondence was entered into between Farrar and Pusey, in the course of which Pusey wrote: "You seem to me to deny nothing which I believe. You do not deny the eternal punishment of 'souls obstinately hard and finally impenitent.' I believe in the eternal punishment of no other."

But at bottom, inconsistent though he is on this point, Farrar was too sensitive to contemplate a permanent Hell, even for a Ball, a Brigson, or a Judas.

"I believe in the restitution of all things," he writes in *Mercy and Judgment*, his final summary of his opinions on eternal punishment; "and I believe in the coming of that time, when, though in what sense I cannot pretend to explain or to fathom, God will be all in all."

In the same book he writes "there may be for some souls an endless hell"; but a few sentences of this kind passed unnoticed, except by Dr Pusey.

To his congregation in Westminster Abbey, hundreds of whom could not find sitting room, and to the thousands throughout England who read him in book form, he was the master of moving speech, who sanctioned with the combined authority of learning and saintliness their own inarticulate revolt against the devil-worship of their fathers.

From

The Progress of a Biographer
(1949)

Bernard Shaw

IN HIS PREFACE to *Immaturity*, and elsewhere, Bernard Shaw has dramatized his childhood so as to take the sting out of it. But to become even relatively invulnerable is a long business; it was not until his middle teens that Shaw began to form a protective covering for himself, and many hours of his childhood, he told his biographer Hesketh Pearson, were spent in tears. Both his parents were Anglo-Irish and well connected, but his father, a kindly, humorous man, was shiftless, took to drink, and was ostracized by his own as well as by his wife's relations. A shabby-genteel existence, slowly deteriorating towards real poverty, was Shaw's first experience of the world; and the fear and hatred of poverty which it created in his mind were intensified by frequent visits to the Dublin slums, where his nurse had her relatives and friends. Meanwhile life at home was, in his own phrase, anarchical. The third and last child of his parents, Shaw was born when his mother was already completely disillusioned with her husband, and was turning for consolation not to her children but to music. 'It never occurred to her,' Shaw says, 'that other people, especially children, needed guidance or training, or that it mattered in the least what they ate or drank or what they did so long as they were not actively mischievous.' The estrangement between the parents reproduced itself in the children; Shaw and his two sisters lived their own lives, and in this household of five there was no intimacy between any of its members.

Mrs Shaw went to a music-master called Lee to have her voice trained, and after a time Lee invited the family to share his house with him. For Shaw, as for his mother, music proved an escape from the dreariness of everyday life. In Lee's home he absorbed and could sing and whistle from end to end leading works by

Handel, Mozart, Beethoven, and the other great composers. His sisters were musical, too, and the whole family, the father excepted, used to join together in song, and so for the time being forget themselves and one another.

When Shaw was fifteen the home broke up. Lee went to London, presently followed by Mrs Shaw, who had decided to teach singing. Her elder daughter accompanied her, her younger was in delicate health and was sent to a sanatorium, where she died. The father, driven to total abstinence by all these events, remained in Ireland, and Shaw became a junior clerk in an estate agent's office in Dublin. It was about this time that he saw and was profoundly impressed by Mephistopheles in Gounod's *Faust*. Lee had bought a cottage for Mrs Shaw on Dalkey Hill, overlooking Dublin Bay. Wandering on the hills above the bay or bathing in the sea was, with music, Shaw's chief happiness during these years. After seeing *Faust* he decorated his room in the cottage with drawings of Mephistopheles, and began to model himself on that detached and invulnerable spectator of the human scene. But he had his witty, sceptical, broken-down father before him as an object-lesson in how not to detach oneself from life. The cynicism of failure disgusted him, and in *John Bull's Other Island* he describes it, through his mouthpiece Larry Doyle, as a peculiarly Irish characteristic—'And all the time you laugh, laugh, laugh! eternal derision, eternal envy, eternal folly, eternal fouling and staining and degrading. . . .' The detachment of Mephistopheles was combined with energy, with an active manipulation of men and events, and it was this kind of detachment that Shaw aimed at and achieved.

When he was twenty he left Ireland and joined his mother in London. Ireland represented to him his dreams and his affections— the world which he had entered through music and looked down upon from Dalkey Hill, the emotions which had been wounded in his early years and which he was resolved not to expose to further hurt. England represented all the possibilities, including money and fame, realizable through energy and will. The two aspects of his nature symbolized by Ireland and England respectively seemed to him irreconcilable. He had felt in Ireland, he would act in England. In *John Bull's Other Island* he has revealed the internal conflict of this period through Larry Doyle, a civil engineer whose partner is a jovial, eupeptic Englishman, Thomas Broadbent. Attempting to explain Ireland and himself to the thick-witted Broadbent, he cries: 'You've no such colours in the sky, no such lure in the distances, no such sadness in the evenings. Oh, the dreaming! the dreaming! the torturing, heart-scalding, never satisfying dreaming! dreaming, dreaming, dreaming! . . . An Irishman's imagination never lets him alone, never convinces him, never satisfies him; but it makes him that he can't face reality nor deal with it nor handle it nor conquer it.' It is, he continues, by living with Broadbent and working with him in double harness that he has learnt to live in a real world and not in an imaginary one. 'You will admit,' he says, 'that all my friends are either Englishmen or men of the big world that belongs to the big Powers.'

By splitting life up into the external world, which was real, and the internal world, which was unreal, Shaw committed himself from the beginning of his career to looking for the kingdom of heaven outside himself. The passion with which he applied himself to social problems was the measure of his misery as a child. If his mother had looked after him he would have been happy—this was his unconscious thought—and if the state looked after its members they would be happy, for suffering came from without, not from within, was the product of poverty and insecurity and would cease when they were abolished. Meanwhile, pending the establishment of a Socialist Utopia—and this was a refrain which ran through all his work and no doubt helped many to bear with complacency his invective against existing conditions—only the rich could lead lives worth living. Undershaft, the armaments manufacturer in *Major Barbara*, tells his daughter, who has been working among the poor, that he has saved her soul by providing her with a private income. Poverty, he says, is the worst of crimes, and the seven deadly sins are food, clothing, firing, rent, taxes, respectability, and children—'Nothing can lift those seven millstones from Man's neck but money; and the spirit cannot soar until the millstones are lifted.' *Pygmalion* enforces the same moral.

In the old legend a statue is transformed into a living woman. In Shaw's play a flower-girl is transformed into a lady; and in a postscript Shaw adduces Nell Gwynne as proof that such a trans-figuration, as he calls it, is possible, but does not take into account that its drawbacks might overbalance its advantages, or indeed that it could have any drawbacks at all. The spell of money on his imagination is still more strikingly revealed in *The Doctor's Dilemma*. Here are assembled a number of Harley Street specialists, none of them, according to Shaw, worth more than £250 a year at the outside and none of them receiving less than five thousand from a gullible public. Over against them stands Louis Dubedat, a painter, according to Shaw, of genius, who by various devices squeezes enough cash out of the world to produce a number of masterpieces before he gives up the struggle and expires in the penultimate act. Yet, poverty being the greatest of crimes and wealth, consequently, the greatest of virtues, the villain of the piece is Dubedat, mean, callous, and treacherous; the heroes are the doctors, whose faults are of the head not of the heart, and whose prosperity seems therefore to proceed from God's kindness to innocence, not from man's susceptibility to bluff.

Louis Dubedat is Shaw's conception of what Larry Doyle would have been if he had remained with his dreams in Ireland instead of joining up with Broadbent in the real world. But was it, after all, the real world? That is the question-mark dotted all over the world of Broadbent by Shaw's irrepressible and enchant-ing humour, the faculty through which his soul continued to breathe. Having split himself into two and labelled one half real, the other half unreal, he could never free himself from the impulse to change the labels over. Louis Dubedat dies proclaiming the unreality of the world in which he had lied and swindled and his faith in the redemption of things by Beauty everlasting. This was effective theatrically, for it confirmed the Broadbents in the stalls in the belief that, not being artistic, they must be honest, and filled them at the same time with a magnanimous tolerance for the misconduct necessarily attached to the practice of art. But it was also a sincere expression of Shaw's intermittent revulsion against reality as understood by Broadbent, or even by Sidney Webb.

The goal which Shaw reached as a result of suppressing his feelings, of treating the imagination as an escape from reality not as a means of apprehending it, and of looking for the kingdom of heaven anywhere except within himself, is revealed in *Back to Methuselah*. Men must live longer, is his final conclusion. At fifty or sixty a man does not know enough to organize life properly. If he could get to three or four hundred he would be reasonably well equipped for the job. Perhaps, if he was Bernard Shaw. If he was Hitler, the longer and more elaborate his training the worse for the world. The last part of the play is called 'As Far as Thought can Reach'. It is not very far; for thought is merely the formulation of feeling, and where feeling has been stifled thought has little to work on. 'The day will come when there will be no people, only thought,' mumbles the Struldbrug in whom Shaw has embodied his conception of what man will eventually be. This is the forlorn gospel of a soul languishing in time, as 'Blessed are the pure in heart, for they shall see God' is the revelation of a spirit living in eternity.

Tennyson and W. H. Auden

REPRESENTATIVE WRITERS, those who mirror the mood of an age, must necessarily be mediums for what is temporal, limited, and egotistic in human nature rather than for what aspires towards the universal life which underlies the discord of time. Writers are idolized not because they love their fellow men, which is never a recommendation and in extreme instances leads to crucifixion, but because their self-love is in tune with current fears and desires, and in giving it expression they are speaking for an inarticulate multitude. Hence the fact, curious only on the surface, that literary idols, as is shown in the four great English examples of the last century—Byron, Tennyson, Dickens, and Kipling—are self-absorbed much beyond the average, are prone to self-pity in their youth and to misanthropy in their later years, and die ringed round with glory but lonely and comfortless within.

In the introduction to his selection from Tennyson's poems W. H. Auden writes: 'There was little about melancholia that he didn't know; there was little else that he did.' This is carelessly put, for if Tennyson was as thoroughly versed in melancholia as Auden affirms he must have experienced it, and life through it, in many forms. What these forms were Auden would no doubt have learnt from a more careful examination of Tennyson's work than he seems to have made. Tennyson's melancholia had its roots in his sense of isolation in an alien universe. His sensibility was out of all proportion greater than his love; his awareness of life unwarmed by any feeling that he belonged to it or it to him. A phenomenon outside himself, it appalled him under three aspects: first, as an immense void in which millions of stars circled indifferently for ever, 'innumerable, pitiless, passionless eyes', while he, a speck of dust on a minute planet, moved wretchedly through

> A life of nothings, nothing-worth,
> From that first nothing ere his birth
> To that last nothing under earth!

In its second aspect, when he looked around instead of up, he saw Nature 'red in tooth and claw', careless not only of the single life but of its types:

> She cries, 'A thousand types are gone:
> I care for nothing, all shall go.'

And when he turned from Nature to Man, men seemed to him

> The flies of latter spring,
> That lay their eggs, and sting and sing
> And weave their petty cells and die.

To distract himself from this threefold oppression he wove, like the Lady of Shalott, a magic web out of the pictures reflected in his mirror from the world passing by outside; but like her he soon began to sicken of shadows:

> Out flew the web and floated wide;
> The mirror cracked from side to side;
> 'The curse is come upon me,' cried
> The Lady of Shalott.

Beneath the exquisite slow music of his dreams drummed the horror of his isolation, which he both hated and clung to, a division of feeling apparent in all his work, but most fully expressed in an early poem, *The Palace of Art*. It opens with a picture of the lordly pleasure-house he had built for his soul, full of long-sounding corridors and great rooms hung with tapestries and the silver music of bells swinging in the towers. His soul prospers there for three years, and then

Deep dread and loathing of her solitude
Fell on her. . . .
And death and life she hated equally,
And nothing saw, for her despair,
But dreadful time, dreadful eternity,
No comfort anywhere.

In the last stanza but one his soul prays to God to make her a
cottage in the vale, where she may mourn and pray. In the last
stanza she qualifies this petition:

Yet pull not down my palace towers, that are
So lightly, beautifully built;
Perchance I may return with others there
When I have purged my guilt.

Desiring to keep his palace as well as to save his soul, Tennyson
damaged the one without affecting the salvation of the other, for
the compromise which in due course he adopted was to add to his
palace a new and unsightly wing reserved for the celebration of
private and public virtue, and terminating in a chapel where
doubtful honesty knelt in the garb of honest doubt. Yet the old
music still sounded from the main building. In the epilogue to the
Idylls of the King Tennyson might assure Queen Victoria that
King Arthur was really the Prince Consort, and that our 'crown'd
Republic's crowning common-sense' would save her from fierce
or careless looseners of the faith, from softness breeding scorn of
simple life, and cowardice, the child of lust for gold, and Labour
with a groan and not a voice, and Art with poisonous honey
stolen from France. But in the poem itself King Arthur is his ideal
self whom he had loved and lost in Arthur Hallam:

He is not here; but far away
The noise of life begins again,

the vanished saviour whom he would rejoin in the island-valley
of Avilion, the king deserted and defeated in this life, erect and
triumphant in another:

Then from the dawn it seem'd there came, but faint
As from beyond the limit of the world,
Like the last echo born of a great cry,
Sounds, as if some fair city were one voice
Around a king returning from his wars.

War, imaginatively considered, had a spasmodic fascination for Tennyson as providing through collective violence an antidote to solitary languor. In *Maud*, for example, the woeful hero ('nameless and poor' he calls himself, and confesses that he keeps only two domestics, a man and a maid) hails the solution to his private troubles provided by the Crimean War in terms familiar enough to modern ears:

And myself have awaked, as it seems, to the better mind;
. . . I have felt with my native land, I am one with my kind,
I embrace the purpose of God, and the doom assigned.

But this was only a passing mood. The blessings of war, the blessings of peace—in the end they were all equally meaningless to Tennyson, for whom the reality underlying both the dreams of his haunted solitude and the factitious enthusiasms of his incursions into ordinary existence was fear, and the anger bred by fear. Fear sees clearly what is within its range, and *Locksley Hall: Sixty Years After*, spiritually as immature as the poetry of his youth, is more detailed and concrete in its trembling perception of the menace and horror ranging the external world:

Envy wears the mask of Love, and, laughing sober fact to scorn,
Cries to Weakest as to Strongest, 'Ye are equals, equal-born.'

Equal-born? O yes, if yonder hill be level with the flat.
Charm us, Orator, till the Lion look no larger than the Cat,

Till the Cat thro' that mirage of overheated language loom
Larger than the Lion,—Demos end in working his own doom.

That was how the dawning Century of the Common Man looked to Tennyson in his old age, and it must be admitted that he saw it clearly from his own standpoint, however paltry and limited that standpoint may seem in one to whom the world had given all that the world can give.

Neither Auden's selection, though it contains some of Tennyson's most beautiful verses and some of his most characteristic, nor his rather perfunctory and offhand introduction, suggests that he has formed a comprehensive view of the poet. It may raise Tennyson in his esteem, unless it lowers him in his own, if I summarize how much he and Tennyson have in common. Each began as the central figure of a coterie, and was early recognized as a poet representative of current thought and feeling. Each absorbed and was profoundly affected by the scientific and philosophical ideas of his time. Each sympathized with a Spanish revolution, though only Tennyson got as far as Spain ('In the summer of 1830', Auden writes, 'he made a curious journey with Hallam to the Pyrenees to take money from English sympathizers to a Spanish revolutionary general, his first and last excursion into practical politics'). Each preferred violence to remain on the far side of the Pyrenees, as is evident in Tennyson's references to revolutions nearer home and in Auden's

> The evil and armed draw near;
> The weather smells of their hate
> And the houses smell of our fear.

Each treated art as a means of evading experience, not of realizing it; the Lady of Shalott's mirror reappearing in Auden as Prospero's, and Prospero, when he parts from Ariel, constraining himself for the first time to confront reality:

> And now, in my old age, I wake, and this journey really exists,
> And I have actually to take it, inch by inch,
> Alone and on foot, without a cent in my pocket.

But Tennyson's dissatisfaction embraced himself. He chafed against his eternal adolescence instead of resting complacently in it, and in spite of everything a shadowy majesty invests his great and desolate figure.

Meetings with W. B. Yeats

A FEW MONTHS before the war, walking through Cork one morning, I saw a poster with these words on it: 'Hitler mentions Eire twice.' I had just been thinking of the effect England must have had on the Irish consciousness from Henry II down to Lloyd George, a brutal, powerful land just beyond the horizon always about to disgorge ships and troops upon its weak, poor neighbour. The poster showed me the other side of the Irish situation, how galling it was to Ireland to be ignored when it was not being laid waste, and what pleasure the nearest modern equivalent to Cromwell could give by casting a casual glance in the direction of Drogheda.

This Cork poster came back to me a few days ago when I was reading the letters exchanged between Yeats and Lady Gerald Wellesley. Anglo-Irish writers have always drawn even more attention to themselves than to their books. With Swift one thinks first not of *Gulliver's Travels* but of the tortured soul no longer lacerated by savage indignation, and so with the others, Goldsmith the wise zany, Sheridan witty even in the gutter, Wilde witty even in the dock, Shaw on a tub in Hyde Park, George Moore and shaded lamps, Yeats and Celtic Twilight. With Yeats, however, this urge towards self-dramatization was more embarrassed than with the others, both because he was more of a poet and because he had a less clear idea of the self he wished to dramatize. His effect on those who met him began by being mysterious but ended by being only mystifying.

The first time I met him was in the autumn of 1912, when I was supposed to be helping Frank Harris to edit a ladies' paper called *Hearth and Home*. As Harris took no interest in anything but the salary he drew and the expenses he managed to extract from his unfortunate fellow-directors, I was free to write what I liked, and hearing that Yeats was living behind St Pancras Church, hardly a hundred yards from where I was, it seemed to me that I could fill a page of *Hearth and Home* with very little trouble if Yeats would give me an interview. At this time he was in his later forties, and apart from his convenient situation I was anxious to see one of the most famous writers of the day. Getting no reply to my letter, I went round one morning after breakfast, rang the bell and waited in some nervousness for the door to open. The house was one of a row in a thoroughfare for pedestrians but not for traffic, an isthmus connecting two streets, a faded unpushful backwater with two or three small shops, and perhaps a shoemaker who subsisted on resoling shoes and a tailor who did not aspire beyond turning old suits. Presently the door opened, and there unmistakably was Yeats, in a dressing-gown, a narrow dark passage behind him. Some moments having passed during which I had a feeling as if his body were being slowly reanimated by its soul, returned for that purpose from some far region, Tibet perhaps, I explained who I was. Yeats, pushing his straggling hair back from his forehead, murmured, 'Yes, yes, I remember. . . . Will you come upstairs?'

Seating himself in an upright arm-chair between the fire and a table on which a large volume rested, he said, in answer to a question put by me from the far side of the table, 'I do not read my contemporaries. I cannot see their faults: for I share them, and so I read only in men who have been dead two or three hundred years. In them I am able to distinguish what is of permanent value from what is trivial, what is temporal.' He opened the volume on the table. 'This morning I have been reading in Donne, though indeed Donne has no faults.' He smiled in a wan, abstracted way, as though the faultlessness of Donne were a mystery he had lost all hope of communicating to others. A little later, having mentioned Baudelaire, he paused to spell the name. I told him I knew it, and he explained that a journalist in New York had made him speak of 'Bandolier'. Taking advantage of a slight relaxation in his attitude, I asked if he thought Oscar Wilde a snob, a crudely framed question, but I had just been reading Harris's *Life of Wilde*, a work devoid of nuances. 'Wilde was not a snob,' Yeats answered. 'He was an Irishman; and England to an Irishman is a far, strange land. To Wilde the aristocrats of England were as the nobles of Baghdad.' Frank Harris, I said, held that it was a nervous collapse not courage which prevented Wilde from fleeing the country before his trial. Did he agree with that view? 'Wilde,' Yeats replied, 'was an Irish gentleman. It was with him a point of honour to face the trial. It could not have occurred to him to act otherwise.'

My next meeting with Yeats was in the summer of 1924, at Maloja, in the Engadine. He was sitting outside the Palace Hotel with Lennox Robinson whose lively friendliness was in strong contrast with Yeats's gloom. Introducing myself, I mentioned the interview of twelve years earlier, and he said he remembered it, and that it was the best interview he had had, his sombre expression leaving me to infer what the other interviews were like.

He was spending two or three days at Maloja as the guest of my father, the head of a tourist firm, and Yeats's part in the arrangement was to deliver a lecture to the visitors at the Palace Hotel. Shortly before his lecture the headmistress of a fashionable girls' school came up to me and said: 'I saw you this morning sitting on a sofa with Mr Lennox Robinson. You were talking with him for half an hour. Didn't you feel proud?' This amiable lady was not below the general level of Yeats's audience, which, when Yeats recited 'Innisfree' with an air of suppressed loathing, beamed ardently at him, as though ready at a word to fall in behind him and surge towards the bee-loud glade.

Yeats had changed a good deal since 1912. He was stouter, and carefully as well as picturesquely dressed. An aristocrat had been superimposed on the poet, and his small black eyes, hard as marbles, looked out upon the world with a mixture of contempt and mistrust. One evening when I was sitting with him and Lennox Robinson we were joined by H. A. L. Fisher, whose very proper eagerness to hear what Yeats thought of various famous writers brought out no responsive geniality in Yeats, his tired disdainful air quickening only at the name of Balzac, whose romanticization of any and every form of power seemed to move him deeply. 'All Nietzsche is in Balzac,' he intoned, and on my expressing some surprise at this opinion, in view of Nietzsche's contempt for Balzac as a vulgarian obsessed with money, Yeats gave me an angry look and withdrew into himself for a minute or two. Mr Fisher, who was my tutor at Oxford, where I failed in my Finals, clearly being no more anxious than Yeats to hear further from me, I did not intervene again.

On another occasion a story I told brought out a certain humour which I had not suspected Yeats of possessing. 'That is bizarre,' he said. 'I like what is bizarre in life. A short while ago I was asked by John Harris to give a lecture in Cambridge. The father of John Harris is a surgeon in Harley Street, and when I went into a barber's shop the barber was speaking of the father of John Harris, who, he said, was in reality the only surgeon in London, the others being merely his agents. A patient, the barber said, would call upon one of these men, who would be reputed to be skilful in some branch of surgery, and an operation would be arranged. But when the patient was under chloroform, the father of John Harris would come up through a trap door, perform the operation, and vanish before the patient was again conscious.' Yeats laughed, there was a cunning gleam in his eye, and he looked very Irish.

Lady Gerald Wellesley compares Yeats with Coleridge. Each was a teacher as well as a poet, and neither achieved anything approaching what was expected of him. But whereas the genius of Coleridge is like a sunken treasure ship, and Coleridge a diver too timid and lazy to bring its riches to the surface, the genius of Yeats is like a rare plant, and Yeats a skilful, pertinacious gardener wrestling vainly with the weeds and sterile soil of Protestant Ireland.

Humour

As I was too late in applying for a review copy of Harold Nicolson's essay on *The English Sense of Humour*, Mr Edward Shanks was so very kind as to comply with my suggestion that I should call at 32, Great Ormond Street, and examine one of the three copies still at the Dropmore Press. Bound in full buckram with a gold band on the inside of the cover, set in 16-point Bembo and printed by hand on hand-made paper, it was a noble volume which Mr Shanks's secretary, Mrs Santhouse, laid before me; but it had the drawback, from my standpoint, of being unopened, as bibliophiles express it, or uncut, in the loose terminology of the man in the street. Even so, half the book was accessible to me, and there were in addition many pages of which, as they were unopened only at the top, I managed to get the gist, though perhaps at some risk of contracting a permanent squint. So I have some ground for hoping that I have missed nothing essential to Harold Nicolson's argument; and, to obviate the prolixity of diffidence and the circumlocutions of doubt, I shall treat this hope as a certainty.

Mr Nicolson quotes with approval Dr Sully's view that the sense of humour is found only in races of Teutonic stock. The extreme temperamental lucidity and the habit of precise and rapid thought found in the Latin races create, Mr Nicolson says, a climate less favourable to the growth of a sense of humour than the misty imprecisions of the Teutonic lands. His remarks on English humour may therefore be taken as applying to humour in general, the English disposition providing in his belief a more fruitful soil for humour than that of any other people.

Humour to Mr Nicolson is essentially a method of self-defence, a device for taking the sting out of life. Contrasting it with wit, he says that wit has an object, is critical and aggressive, and requires an audience; humour has no object, is a shield not a sword, economizes instead of entailing intellectual and psychic effort, is private, contemplative, ruminating, and conciliatory. Contrasting it with irony and satire, he prefers their 'nobler and more didactic purpose', for humour, he says, is indulgent to frailty and cannot be troubled to correct it. Kindly to weakness, humour is hostile to all superiorities, whether good or evil, and tries to reduce their stature by ridicule, converting Hitler, for example, into a talkative little man with an absurd moustache, and disparaging culture and intellect in such catchwords as 'high-brow' and 'the Oxford accent'. Neither this world nor the next owes anything to the humorist, for while the mystic concentrates on the infinite, and the realist on the finite, the humorist is amiably tolerant of both and sees absurdity everywhere. 'One cannot have a sense of humour unless one be without conscience or respon-sibility,' Mr Nicolson quotes from Goethe, adding, however, that the examples of Lincoln and Winston Churchill show that humour does not always have a debilitating effect upon character. Yet (he concludes), though humour may be a rather childish, self-protective, and indolent quality, it is assuredly benevolent, con-ciliatory, kind, a lubricant in our anxious lives, an unguent for our wounds.

Within its limits this diagnosis is sound, but the limits are narrow. There are, broadly speaking, three levels at which humour operates. I once asked a Russian, who had worked for some years with Stalin, whether Stalin had a sense of humour, and, if so, what it was like. After reflecting for quite a time, his sombre expression relaxed a little, a glint came into his eyes, and he replied, 'If you were leaving this room, and absent-mindedly walked into that door, striking it with your nose, then Stalin would laugh.' This is humour as Hobbes understood it when he wrote that 'the passion of laughter is nothing else but a sudden glory, arising from some sudden conception of some eminency in ourselves by comparison with the infirmity of others, and with our own formerly'. On the next level, the one to which Mr Nicolson confines himself, it is the victim who laughs, not the spectator; the motive behind his laughter being twofold, to anticipate and therefore neutralize the derision of the bystanders and to minimize to himself the shock he has sustained. Now to deal with a single mischance in this way is well enough; but Mr Nicolson's case against the humorist is that he is a feeble though astute fellow who, temperamentally disposed to bump his nose on doors, gives this tendency full rein, so as to flatter the bystanders with their superior adjustment to reality, and conciliate them with his whimsically rueful acceptance of his own imbecility.

This personal self-conscious use of humour is discernible in *As You Like It*, which Shakespeare wrote in a mood of self-pity, and appears, fully developed, in Laurence Sterne, the first writer to smile of set purpose through his tears. During the opening decades of the nineteenth century the 'laughing tear', as Sterne's German pupil Heine called it, flowed freely throughout Europe, and though, as the century advanced, the emotional climate became less moist, humorists, especially in England, continued to dramatize themselves as ingenuous, unworldly creatures, babes in a wood which turns out to be not half so bad as some people pretend; for this kind of humorist is, as Mr Nicolson points out, an optimist, desiring mental and emotional ease for himself and ready to purvey it to others.

That humour, like any other faculty, can be exploited for personal ends is no reflection on it. It is not humour which has a debilitating effect upon character (Lincoln's and Churchill's excepted), but lack of character which has a debilitating effect upon humour. As a diagnosis of the abuse of humour in the last one hundred and fifty years, Mr Nicolson's essay is excellent. There is hardly an intellectual or emotional flaw from Sterne to Mark Twain, from Heine to J. M. Barrie and J. K. Jerome, on which it does not touch. But of humour on the level where it is impersonal and disinterested, an illumination of reality not a refuge from it, Mr Nicolson has nothing to say. On this level the humorist is not a Neapolitan beggar displaying his sores for alms, or a tearful zany the misty imprecisions of whose mind are reflected in his quavering picture of the external world. He is Cervantes (a Latin) in the prison of Seville dispassionately projecting the lifelong conflict between his illusions and his belated common sense in the persons of Don Quixote and Sancho Panza; Molière (another Latin) holding the balance evenly between the egotisms of solitude and society; Shakespeare showing in Falstaff that no wit or humour, however rich, can triumph in the end against the nature of things; Fielding as detached in his description of the watermen who jeered at his wasted and horrifying appearance when he was carried aboard for the voyage to Lisbon as in his portrait of Jonathan Wild the Great.

It is natural that those who are interested in preserving or intensifying the illusions which justify human egotism to itself and consecrate the vanities and follies that lay life waste should be hostile to humour. King John's

> That idiot laughter,
> A passion hateful to my purposes,

is echoed in the remark Mr Nicolson quotes from Goethe, a marvellous poet in his inspired hours but in his uninspired a worshipper of Napoleon; in Nietzsche's imprecation on *Don Quixote*, which the dreamer of the Superman condemned for its derision of all noble effort; and to descend to lesser and later persons, in the efforts of George Moore and his disciples to make the English novel safe for the kind of distinguished worldling they hope themselves to be. To these names the author of *Some People* must now, provisionally but not, one hopes, permanently, be added; for he has certainly in this essay diminished humour to a point at which even King John would have passed it as completely innocuous to his purposes.

Lloyd George

THERE IS A well-known story of a Hollywood magnate who, when his staff brought him a scenario of H. G. Wells's *Outline of History*, asked them if they couldn't work in a love interest. Much ridicule has been levelled at this excellent man. What! The ages of stone and iron and bronze, the migrations of primeval man, the first empires and their fall, the clash of contending creeds, the great trade routes, the conquest of nature, the miracles of applied science—and it misgives this cretin that the public will yawn unless he throws in a pair of lovers gazing into one another's eyes! None the less, the magnate's instinct was sound. He was on the right track, even if he had not gone very far along it. Had he developed his thought more fully he might have expressed it in some such terms as these, with what effect on his standing in Hollywood I cannot say offhand: 'Gentlemen, humanity, under which heading I include you no less than myself, is looking for something, and all this turmoil of empires and creeds and trade routes and misapplied science springs from its failure to find it. You have brought me an outline of history. But I do not want a panorama, I want a revelation. I do not want a mob, I want a man. Infinity is not in the world about us; it is in our hearts, the meeting-place and battleground of eternity and time. That is the only real conflict, and through the individual alone can its varying fortunes be expressed. Would Homer have been remembered if his theme had been the trade routes of the Eastern Mediterranean? Does David still live for us because his reign marked a certain stage in the political development of a Semitic people? Is *King Lear* a supreme masterpiece because it suggests the uneasy internal state of Britain before the Romans arrived? Or *Macbeth* because it foreshadows the increasingly important role played by England in the affairs of her northern neighbour? No, only what takes place in the heart of man, at the intersection of time and eternity, is of enduring interest. Only the experience of the individual is truth. The rest is information. We remember Homer, because we also, like the old men who wondered at the surpassing loveliness of Helen, have been lifted by the vision of beauty out of time and pain. Each of us, like David, has loved himself when he supposed he loved another, and was wept for Absalom too late. Like Lear, we have all desired power and love simultaneously, and some, like him, have turned to Cordelia in the end; others, like Macbeth, have followed their dead souls into the darkness.

'So, gentlemen, I should be grateful if you would take this scenario away, and bring me back something relatively human, if it be but the story of a simpleton who makes good after being sacked for not knowing his job.'

This enlightened magnate would unquestionably have found in Mr A. J. Sylvester's recollections of Lloyd George[1] the raw material of the kind of scenario he was looking for. Mr Sylvester was Lloyd George's private secretary from 1923 till his death, and for five or six years after 1917 was in close contact with him in London and in the post-war conferences at Paris, Cannes, and Genoa. He therefore knew Lloyd George thoroughly as a human being, and it is as such that he pictures him, honestly and at the same time humbly, for his adoration of Lloyd George is clear on every page. He was hurt by Lloyd George as a Hindu is hurt when the Juggernaut car grinds over his prostrate body, but his sufferings have not bred resentment. Lloyd George was Lloyd George, just as life was life. One groaned and bowed the head.

Mr Sylvester's first close view of Lloyd George was in December 1915, when he attended a Cabinet meeting as a shorthand writer and caught snatches of a conversation between Lloyd George and the Prime Minister; Asquith quoting experts to support his objection to increased expenditure on munitions, Lloyd George vehement, contemptuous, and overwhelming: 'You sent me to France to see what was wanted. I have seen for

[1] *The Real Lloyd George.* By A. J. Sylvester.

myself what the troops need. I've promised them they shall have what they need. More and better guns, more and better shells than the Germans, and I'm going to keep my promise to them, experts or not.' He had reached the Promised Land at last, and only Asquith stood between him and his heritage. A year later he became Prime Minister.

As a general rule men with an inordinate appetite for power have been both spoilt and humiliated in their early years, the spoiling accustoming them to expect attention, and the humiliation hardening their resolve to get it. Two obvious examples are Frederick the Great and Hitler, each of whom was indulged by his mother and bullied by his father; and Hitler had also his obscure birth to resent and the fact that he was a native of a ramshackle, declining country which bordered a great and expanding empire. Unlike Hitler, Lloyd George was happy as a child, for he was pampered by his uncle and his mother and his grandmother; but as he grew older he began to realize that he was a privileged person only in his own home. A poor Welshman, he stood in much the same relation to England as the Austrian Hitler to Prussia. What affection and poetry were in his nature had their roots in Wales. England magnetized his ambition; it was a challenge to his audacity and resource, the theatre of his star performances as social reformer, pacifist and war minister. But it touched nothing in him deeper than his vanity. The scene of his power was not the scene of his affections, and so he was cut off from the secret influence which has preserved men as greedy as himself for the world's applause from degenerating into mere adventurers.

Politics to Lloyd George was a conflict of wits and wills, and he had every weapon at his disposal; an unsurpassed faculty for absorbing the relevant details, perfect self-command at the critical moment, an infallible instinct for cajoling or threatening, according to the immediate need, and, when violence was required, neither scruples nor compunctions. For many years his career was a succession of personal triumphs, but in the end he was ruined by his own virtuosity. Some kind of coherence is required in a politician, some kind of pattern must be discernible in his achievement. As a Radical, Lloyd George had championed the

masses and small nations rightly struggling to be free. As something not easily distinguishable from a Tory, he had knocked
Asquith and Germany out, nearly hanged the Kaiser, and flayed
the hide off a small country wrongly struggling to be free. So far,
so good or so bad, according to the point of view. There were
numerous precedents for this kind of political development or
retrogression. But when he invited the Irish gunmen to Downing
Street, and a few months later was figuring at Genoa as a kind of
St Francis radiating love in a jungle of wolves and boars, the
Tories had had enough; and as the Liberals had already had far too
much and Labour was not having anything at all, there was nothing for it except retirement into the leisure and well-appointed
comfort of what politicians call the wilderness. In 1922 Lloyd
George ceased to be Prime Minister, and, although he lived
another twenty-three years, never held office again.

   In the year after his retirement he went on a triumphal tour
through the States and Canada, accompanied by Mr Sylvester,
who, now that Lloyd George was no longer in public life, bore
the full weight of his appetite for power, in sudden changes of
plan, peremptory and impossible demands, silence when Mr
Sylvester wanted to ascertain his wishes, rage when his wishes
had not been divined. Yet Mr Sylvester continued to love and
adore his tyrant. 'I could not help feeling tremendously proud of
my chief that night,' he writes of a speech Lloyd George delivered
in New York. 'Despite the stress and strain of the last month, the
number of times he had spoken, and the difficult and delicate
topics with which he had dealt, not once had he made a *faux pas*.
That night as he addressed the great audience he looked the
picture of health.' In Toronto, as Lloyd George was walking from
his car through a cheering crowd, an old woman ran forward and
caught hold of his coat. Lloyd George stopped, stared at her for a
moment, and held out his hand. 'Oh, sir,' she gasped, 'I only
wanted to touch the hem of your coat.' He was deeply stirred,
perhaps for a moment realizing the infinite irony in this confusion
of himself, the medium and manipulator of mass emotion, with
Christ. In general, his sense of any but mundane realities was weak
even for a politician. There was nothing of the mystic in him. He

once said to Mr Sylvester: 'I feel I have no contact. I do not know which way to look to get hold of Him. I am more of a pagan. . . . Beaverbrook, on the contrary, is very religious.' What, one wonders, did he mean by pagan? What by religious? Was he classifying himself with Plato and Marcus Aurelius, and Lord Beaverbrook with St John of the Cross and Father Damien? Or was his meaning simply that while he did not know which way to look to get hold of God, Lord Beaverbrook was strongly under the impression that God knew which way to look to get hold of him?

The last act of the drama opened in 1936 when Lloyd George paid a visit to Hitler. During his long exile from office he had been sustained by the thought that he had brought the greatest war in history to a victorious conclusion, and Churchill's increasing insistence in Parliament that another, and perhaps still greater, war was in the offing disturbed and exasperated him. To Ribbentrop he spoke of Churchill as a brilliant writer, but lacking in judgment, and on his return he described Hitler as the George Washington of Germany, a country now purged of its old imperialistic temper, and with no desire to invade any other land. The war came; he tried at first to believe that peace could be restored without much difficulty, but slowly was forced to realize that England, though without the allies who had helped her to win the first world war, was determined not to treat with Hitler. When Churchill took over from Neville Chamberlain, Lloyd George's entrance into the Cabinet would have impressed Hitler as a sign that England's position was less desperate than it seemed, for to embark on a sinking ship was not in Lloyd George's character as Hitler conceived it. But Lloyd George would not yield to Churchill's urgings, or to the entreaties of Lord Beaverbrook, Lady Astor, and many others. He had never loved England, was much less interested in her future than in Churchill's, and used Churchill's refusal to drop Neville Chamberlain as an excuse for declining office; though he seems also to have been genuinely irritated by it, perhaps regarding Churchill's treatment of Chamberlain as an oblique reflection on his own treatment of Asquith, or else, a still more provoking thought, as evidence that

Churchill was resolved not to alienate the Tories as he himself had alienated the Liberals. 'I am not going in with this gang,' he said, '. . . . Winston is no leader, of course he is not. It is true he is an excellent speaker, but that is not everything. Look at the Dardanelles.' Yet Churchill and England worried through, and the moment never came for Lloyd George to step forward and charm Hitler into granting generous terms to a country that had once been great and greatly led.

In January 1941, Lloyd George set out from Churt, his Surrey farm, for Criccieth, where his wife was dying. His car was twice buried in snowdrifts from which it had to be dug out, he could not reach her in time, and was told of her death over the telephone by Mr Sylvester, who heard him sobbing, 'She was a great old pal.' He was now in his eightieth year, but his immense vitality ebbed slowly, and it was not till the autumn of 1944 that he felt the time had come to return to Wales. When the car was all packed up ready to leave Churt, Mr Sylvester narrates, Lloyd George suddenly got out and went slowly back to his library for a last look at the Freedoms in their valuable caskets, the open fireplace by which he had written much of his memoirs, and the lakes and orchards and woodlands beyond the huge plate-glass window, the idea of which had been suggested to him by the window in Hitler's villa at Berchtesgaden. In his last months he spent many hours sitting in a bay window through which Criccieth was visible and the sea and the Merionethshire hills beyond. The greater war and the greater glory were distant rumours there, and once when Mr Sylvester hurried in to him, brimming over with the latest news, he threw his arms about and ejaculated, 'I don't want to hear *anything* about *anything*.'

What are Politics?

Times have changed since I edited the literary supplement of the *English Review* in 1935. Ten years ago people assumed that a literary supplement was a literary supplement—that is, a collection of reviews, written by individuals each with his own standpoint. Nowadays, if I may generalize from my experience since the spring of this year, a large number of persons approach a literary supplement with the assumption that it is a co-ordinated series of reviews planned to reinforce such political opinions as are expressed in the main body of the paper. On this kind of reader the mere contents of a literary supplement produce no impression at all, to judge from an article by George Orwell which I have just read in *Polemic*, a magazine whose policy, according to an editorial introduction, 'is prejudiced in the direction of encouraging discussions about those trends in contemporary thought which we think are most significant'.

Orwell's article is entitled 'Notes on Nationalism', and is concerned with nationalism 'as it occurs among the English intelligentsia'.

By nationalism, Orwell explains, he means, first of all, 'the habit of assuming that human beings can be classified like insects and that whole blocks of millions or tens of millions of people can be confidently labelled "good" or "bad" '; and, secondly, 'the habit of identifying oneself with a single nation or other unit, placing it beyond good or evil, and recognizing no other duty than that of advancing its interests'. Among the eleven varieties of nationalism noted by Orwell in the English intelligentsia of to-day there is one which he calls Neo-Toryism. The unit with which the Neo-Tory identifies himself, placing it beyond good and evil, is Britain; and the two chief blocks of alien millions whom he confidently labels 'bad' are Russia and America. His organs of opinion are the literature of the Tory Reform Committee, the *New English Review* and the *Nineteenth Century and After*; typical Neo-Tories are Lord Elton, A. P. Herbert, G. M. Young, and Professor Pickthorn; and among the writers who illustrate the tendency of Neo-Toryism or are psychologically affiliated to it are F. A. Voigt, Malcolm Muggeridge, Evelyn Waugh, Hugh Kingsmill, T. S. Eliot, and Wyndham Lewis.

Animal Farm, a fable of the Russian Revolution, revealed the poetry, humour and tenderness in Orwell; but it seems to be only when he thinks of men as animals that he can see them as human beings and feel at one with them. In his direct relations with them he is always the party man, disgusted with all existing parties by repeated disillusionments, but still involved in the collective mania of the age, and determined to implicate everyone else in his own predicament. I understand this desire of his, but I see no reason why I should indulge it, though it is certainly harder to reply to a nonsensical charge than to one with some substance in it. Othello, firm and lucid in his statements after marrying and after murder-ing Desdemona, might have fumbled his opening sentences had an albino charged him with being an albino.

As I have never belonged to any party, I have no authority to speak for others, and shall therefore confine my remarks on Orwell's account of Neo-Toryism to its relevance to myself as a writer and as the editor of this supplement. The first thing which struck me about his list of Neo-Tories was the very faint con-nexion existing between myself and eight of the other nine. Malcolm Muggeridge and I are old friends, but I doubt if even Orwell could see in Muggeridge and myself the cell of a reaction-ary underground movement. Lord Elton I do not know; A. P. Herbert, except for a distant glimpse at the Savage, I have not seen since we were at Blandford twenty-nine years ago; from G. M. Young I have had two letters on non-political matters; I am indebted to Orwell for my introduction to the name of Professor Pickthorn; F. A. Voigt once wrote asking me to con-tribute a literary article to the *Nineteenth Century*, I replied that I should be delighted to, and, after two years of silence at the other end, wrote again in the same sense and with the same result; Evelyn Waugh I last saw when he was living in Golders Green; T. S. Eliot I have met three times, Wyndham Lewis once.

These social jottings define the position I occupy in the Neo-Tory conspiracy to aggrandize Britain at the expense of Russia and America, though it is, of course, open to Orwell to reply that I am a pawn in the hands of the key-men, and that, when the hour is ripe, I shall receive my instructions from Professor Pickthorn.

I now come to Orwell's suggestion that, as a Neo-Tory, I am one of those who divide mankind into blocks of millions or tens of millions of people, label some blocks 'good' and others 'bad', and recognize no other duty than that of advancing the interests of the unit with which they have identified themselves.

In the introduction to *The Poisoned Crown*, which appeared in the spring of 1944 and which Orwell reviewed in the *Observer*, I wrote: 'Many remedies for a shattered world are now being offered to mankind, but they are all collective remedies, and collective remedies do not heal the ills produced by collective action. . . . What is divine in man is elusive and impalpable, and he is easily tempted to embody it in a concrete form—a church, a country, a social system, a leader—so that he may realize it with less effort and serve it with more profit. Yet, as even Lincoln proved, the attempt to externalize the kingdom of heaven in a temporal shape must end in disaster. It cannot be created by charters or constitutions nor established by arms. Those who set out for it alone will reach it together, and those who seek it in company will perish by themselves.'

Twenty years before *The Poisoned Crown* I expressed a similar thought in *The Dawn's Delay*, through a character who defines history as the record of the convulsions caused by the grown man's efforts to find in company with others what he has failed to find alone as child and boy and youth. From the war of 1914 and the opening years of the Russian Revolution I had learnt what the last fifteen years have illustrated on a still larger scale, that revolutions and wars are always in their essence, whatever their secondary causes, an attempt to carry Eden by weight of numbers, and effect by the pooling of millions of egotisms what can be effected

K

only by the single individual through the transformation of his own nature; a transformation which I do not believe can be completed in this life, for it seems to me self-evident that even the purest and highest souls cannot achieve perfection within the limitations of time. If, then, even Jesus and Buddha did not realize heaven in this life, if to Beethoven and Wordsworth it was visible only in moments and expressible only in snatches, if all the active goodness of Johnson could not dissipate the melancholia which veiled it from his sight, what meaning is to be attached to the large offers of secular paradises made to mankind by political leaders from Moses to Lenin and Hitler, from Mohammed to Cecil Rhodes and the author of the Four Freedoms and the last Minister who has spoken of 'winning the peace' as though it were an analogous operation to winning a war? What, in short, are politics, and why too often do they cause men to gibber? In theory they are the method by which the administration of the community is directed and supervised; and here and there, for example in Switzerland, whose size and position make it unsuitable for the purposes of a Napoleon, politics do really confine themselves within these salutary limits. Hence the obscurity in which Swiss politicians pass their lives, and the contempt for Switzerland felt by Lenin and Trotsky and Mussolini and the other revolutionaries who used that stable republic as a base from which to launch an ordered life upon their fellow-countrymen. In less stable countries politics are proportionately less rational, and in extreme cases (the Puritan Revolution, the Napoleonic Empire, the totalitarian states of to-day) all the hopes and dreams of men are absorbed into politics, which become for the few the technique of self-aggrandisement, for the many the key to paradise, and to all a collective hallucination which at last collapses in despair.

Such is my view of what Orwell calls nationalism; and he will find nothing inconsistent with it in any of my books or in my contributions to this paper. Nevertheless, I do not wish to pretend that I am editing a literary supplement in a Tory review by pure chance, or that my sympathies are equally divided between the Right and the Left. On the Right there is room for those who believe that the individual is the only absolute unit, and that all larger units are temporal and transient groupings; and a Tory paper could include without incongruity a literary supplement which, though it might not mean much to Disraeli or even to Burke, would be approved by Johnson, who was sentimental neither about the future nor the past, who lived, far more consistently than Milton, as ever in his great Taskmaster's eye, and who did not shift the responsibility for man's fate on to the institutions created by men.

> How small, of all that human hearts endure,
> That part which laws or kings can cause or cure.

Uncollected Essays from

The New English Review Magazine

(1948-9)

G. K. Chesterton

ROUND ABOUT 1930 G. K. Chesterton was the chief catholic apologist writing in English. Nowadays, Mr Herbert McLuhan says in his introduction to Mr Hugh Kenner's revaluation of Chesterton,[1] books by Chesterton are seldom included in the reading lists of catholic students. Chesterton, says Mr McLuhan, had "an unwavering and metaphysical intuition of being . . . a kind of connaturality with every kind of reasonableness;" but this element in his work has been swamped by the extravagances of "the Toby-jug Chesterton of a particular literary epoch." From Stevenson, Mr McLuhan continues, Chesterton borrowed a desperate jauntiness and pseudo-energy; from Henley, a note of professional heartiness which he employed to debunk the pessimism of the 'eighties and 'nineties; from William Morris, dramaturgic gestures, medieval trappings, ballad themes and banal rythms; from Rossetti, the pale, auburn-haired beauties who haunt his stories; from Swinburne, a tiresome trick of alliteration; from Edward Lear, the vein of anarchic nursery wisdom which helped the Victorians to keep sane. The influence of Whitman and Browning on Chesterton seems to Mr McLuhan too obvious to need any more than a mention, and he does not even refer to the still greater influence of Dickens, about whom Mr Kenner also maintains an unbroken silence.

Having claimed that Chesterton had an unwavering insight into being, and then presented him as swayed by every passing fashion in thought and expression, however shoddy, Mr McLuhan concludes abruptly, "It is time to see him freed from the accidental accretions of ephemeral literary mannerisms," and hands on his smoky torch to Mr Kenner, who snatching it blithely from him speeds buoyantly on his way. Chesterton, Mr Kenner says, was not so much great because of his published

[1] *Paradox in Chesterton*, by Hugh Kenner.

achievement as great because he was right. He scarcely left a page
that is not in some way blotched and disfigured; his perceptions
are metaphysical rather than æsthetic; he never achieves a great
poem, for his poems are compilations of statements not intensely
felt but only intensely meant and have a philosophical not a
poetic meaning. Celebrations of cosmic fact, they are a noisy
rather than a perceptive celebration. The conflicts they deal with
are not in Chesterton's mind but out in front of him, in the things;
he does not feel involved in them; they are in an odd way painless, for he never experienced the self-distrust mirrored in some of
Gerard Hopkins's verse, "There is a sense in which it is to his
praise that he could not be a poet."

It would be useless to enquire how a man can be right whose
work is blotched and disfigured on nearly every page; how he
can mean intensely without feeling intensely; how though noisy
rather than perceptive, he can yet be philosophically sound; or
how he can resolve mental conflicts which take place outside his
mind, and bring great truths painlessly to birth in a kind of
twilight sleep. Mr Kenner is, what Chesterton became, a
Thomist. Thomas Aquinas, the most gifted of mediaeval dialec-
ticians, has been revived of late years in order to supply sceptics
anxious for a faith with a complete set of answers to persons
willing to engage with them in arguing about what can neither
be established nor disproved by mental processes. The Thomist
seeks refuge from the complexity of things in the more manage-
able complexity of words. With the inexhaustable verbal arsenal
of Aquinas to draw upon, he is able at the same time to preserve
the Christian virtue of humility by affirming nothing of himself,
and to claim that he is always right because Aquinas is never
wrong. To this type the free exercise of the imagination is a pre-
sumptuous attempt to by-pass the theological route to truth, and
careless or tawdry writing such as Mr McLuhan and Mr Kenner
note in much of Chesterton's work, a pleasing sign of indifference
to the artist's ideal of perfection. From Mr Kenner's standpoint
the trouble with the Toby-jug Chesterton is not that he is unreal,
exaggerated, rhetorical, but merely that he obscures the later
Chesterton, the master of analogy and paradox whose course even

from the earliest years, was set towards the haven of Aquinas. In rescuing Chesterton from Dickens and Browning and Stevenson and aligning him with such verbal artificers or contortionists as Gerard Hopkins and T. S. Eliot, James Joyce and Gertrude Stein, Mr Kenner may well have made him more palatable to catholic students, grateful for an up-to-date flavouring in their theological dish. But his Chesterton is no more authentic and much less amusing than the mythical figure of twenty years ago, the roaring, beer-swilling swashbuckler at whose name capitalists and cocoa-drinkers turned pale. His book, however, contains many illuminating quotations which could give some idea of Chesterton to a careful and reflective reader.

In his autobiography Chesterton narrates that in his late teens he passed through a phase of mental disease bordering on madness. He had horrible fancies which he used to put into drawings. They were not, he says, of a homosexual nature, but he tells us nothing else about them, though from the prevalence in his stories and poems of blood and slicing swords, one may surmise that they expressed the craving for violence which permeated his otherwise kindly and pacific nature. In a poem to his schoolboy friend E. C. Bentley, he speaks of "the sick cloud upon the soul when we were boys together," and defines it as an exhalation from the decadent 'eighties and 'nineties, when "science announced nonentity and art admired decay," the age of Wilde and Whistler and Haeckel. He and his friend were upheld in their despair by Stevenson and Whitman; Whitman sent "far out of fish-shaped Paumanok some cry of cleaner things," and "Truth of Tusitala spoke." Then "God and the good Republic came riding back in arms," and they "found common things at last, and marriage and a creed."

The sick cloud was not an exhalation from the age, it was within Chesterton himself. Whitman was hardly a sure prophylactic against Wilde, nor the author of *Dr Jekyll and Mr Hyde*, with his cry "Shall we never shed blood?" a breath of fresh air after the far less subterranean Whistler. But Stevenson and Whitman inevitably attracted Chesterton, who like them longed for health, and like them hoped to achieve it not only by facing his nature but by externalising it in the outer world as a conflict between health and disease, with himself as the protagonist of health. It is in his imaginative work that one most easily perceives how little of daylight and freshness he had by nature. Much of his poetry and more of his fiction are overshadowed by the evil twilight of a child's nightmares, swelling to a horror which only some sudden act of violence can dissipate. This internal tension he resolved, both in his critical and imaginative work, by simplifying every situation into a conflict between an evil oppression and a liberating champion. His Dickens is the English embodiment of the French Revolution, a man who "panted upwards on weary wings to reach the heaven of the poor." His Browning is a plain man who made poems out of the simple things of life, shaming the æsthetes at their dubious diversions in velvet-curtained rooms. His King Alfred is Free Will and Christian Hope wiping the floor with the pagan Guthrum and his determinist Danes. And so on. He applied the same simplifying process to countries. In *An Alliance*, written, as will easily be credited, before he knew Hilaire Belloc, good embodied itself in "the Saxon lands", England and America, evil in Spain, who had recently been defeated by the United States—"Four centuries doom of torture, choked in the throat of Spain" is Chesterton's way of putting it. Later, Spain was replaced by Germany ("O thousand folk and frozen folk") by the Orient ("land of purple and passion and glamour"), and finally by all non-Catholic countries, including England, of whom, a few years before she was left as the sole defender of all he valued, Chesterton wrote: "This noble and generous nation which lost its religion in the seventeenth century has lost its morals in the twentieth."

Chesterton was at his best in the first decade of this century, when his conversion to Roman Catholicism lay many years ahead. Work and success had lifted the cloud of his adolescence; his wit was keen, his fancy wonderfully fertile, his sense of reality intermittently active, and his quibbling and rhetoric with which in his last years he tried to dispel his fretful uneasy gloom still far from being in complete control of his mind. The progressives, led by Wells, and the æsthetes, from Pater to George Moore, were his chief targets. Wells's happiness in the thought that just as the motor-car was quicker than the coach, so something would be quicker than the motor-car, Chesterton echoed and amplified in a Dr Quilp, who foretells a machine on which a man could circle the earth so quickly that he could keep up a talk in some old world village by saying a word of a sentence each time he came round. George Moore, served Chesterton as a type of self-conscious artist who values everything only as a setting for himself—*The Grand Canal with a distant view of George Moore, Effect of George Moore seen through a Scotch mist, Ruins of George Moore by moonlight*. Religion in those years still meant more to Chesterton than creeds and institutions; and to measure the change between what he then was and what he later became, one need merely place side by side his criticism of Pater's view that we must enjoy the passing moment for its own sake and his defence of the wealth and pomp of Rome. Moments of love or of any other great emotion, he says, in reply to Pater, are filled with eternity: "These moments are joyful because they do not seem momentary. Man cannot love mortal things. He can only love immortal things for an instant." Visiting Rome after his conversion he concedes that the Catholic faith "might have scored in some ways if it had remained absolutely austere and unworldly; as poor as the birth in the stable; as naked as the Victim on the cross." But, he continues, unless it could have been kept at the last extremity of severity, it was right to rush to the last extremes of splendour: "The Pope is the Vicar of Christ, and when he goes splendid in white and silver and gold, with the ostrich plumes and the peacock fans borne before him, he is only making the approximate attempt that every picture makes, to symbolise a sort of vision. Rome had to decide whether it would express the simplicity of Christ in simplicity or the glory of God in glory."

It would not have taken the early Chesterton long to reply that the glory of God is in the simplicity of Christ not in the magnificence of Caesar.

Hilaire Belloc

AMONG THE FIFTY-FOUR essays collected[1] by J. B. Morton, the most devoted and richly gifted of Hilaire Belloc's disciples, there are two, on *King Lear* and on Milton, which anyone trying to bring some order into his thoughts about Mr Belloc should find particularly helpful.

Roman Catholic propaganda has been Hilaire Belloc's chief occupation in his later years, and it is from the standpoint of its possible use to Roman Catholicism that Belloc considers *King Lear*. His argument is as follows. Christendom, broken into pieces by the Reformation, must be put together again, and to effect this it is necessary to explain one national soul to another. By constantly reading Racine, and by associating with those who understand what Racine is, an Englishman will at last see into the soul of Gaul. Conversely, to present England to the French intelligence, one may choose *King Lear*, which is thoroughly English in its formlessness, in its immense vitality, its half-knowledge of unknowable things, its rush of air, as of a storm in an English upland, and its sudden silence at the end.

Propaganda written by a poet must be fantastic, for a poet cannot keep reality out, and the reality he admits will clash with the unreality he is trying to impose on the reader. In this essay Belloc, the poet, feels and communicates the storm in Shakespeare's soul imaged in the storm on the heath and in the conflicting passions of the characters in the play. But Belloc, the institutionalist, is not concerned with the storm in Shakespeare's soul, with the heaven and hell which each man bears within himself. He is concerned with the welfare of the church to whose authority he bows in accordance with his view that "all the wisest men have accepted a received answer from authority external to themselves." To an instutionalist nations are much more important than individuals, and so Belloc excogitates this scheme of steeping Frenchmen in Shakespeare and Englishmen in Racine as a pre-

[1] *Selected Essays of Hilaire Belloc.* Edited with an Introduction by J. B. Morton.

liminary step to bringing England and France back within the Roman fold. Urged in his firm and weighty style, the scheme has an air of meaning something; but it will not bear much analysis. It is improbable that, whatever mingled finesse and energy were employed, even as many as five thousand Englishmen would be worked up into a passionate love of, say, *Phèdre*, or the same number of Frenchmen be kindled with fiery enthusiasm for *King Lear*. Let us however, suppose these two tasks accomplished. What then? Is there anything either in *King Lear* or in *Phèdre* to propel its readers along the path to Rome? And if there were, is there any reason to believe that a group of Phedrists in England and a Learist group in France would in any measurable degree help to bring their respective countries once more beneath the triple tiara?

Perhaps because of its shortness, there is no trace in this essay of the cynicism with which Belloc so often makes nonsense of his argument, the poet in him suddenly interupting the propagandist with an almost audible—"What rubbish this is! I'll say so." In illustrating this trait I shall confine myself, for the sake of brevity, to his monograph on William the Conqueror. Part of Belloc's case for Latin Christendom is that its statesmen and soldiers are free from the cunning and ambition which characterise great men of action born beyond the Mediterranean periphery. The talents of intrigue, Belloc writes, were not present in Napoleon; and Mussolini, with whom he once had a talk, impressed him as interested in his job, not his name. Treating the Normans as honorary Latins, he contrasts William the Conqueror, who had no conception of right based upon force, with Godwin and his sons, who, tainted by Scandinavian influences, were utterly without scruple, piratical and evil. William the Latin Christian, who does not "conqueror" England in the modern sense, but, finding himself there, is "blessed in the ordeal of battle", and Harold the Nordic crook, who sickens Christendom by seizing the English throne which William was expecting to mount with Harold's loyal help—that is Belloc's argument; and he does not help it by the merry suggestion that one of Godwin's evil Scandinavian connections was—"reputed (I think falsely) to be descended from a bear," or by giving as the impulse behind the Norman conquest of "petty loot and spoil for the lesser men, rewards in land for their leaders, increase in wealth for all."

It is in Belloc's treatment of Milton that his divided nature, due perhaps to racial admixture, is most evident. In order to dispose of Milton as a great Protestant figure Belloc wrote a book some years ago presenting Milton as an undersexed moneylender who used his financial stranglehold on a Cavalier family to procure himself, in spite of his dismal unattractiveness, a pretty bride. The Milton of his essay is, except in one particular, an idealised picture of himself, his humour, of course, omitted. He praises above all Milton's landscape, but also approves him for disdaining intensity of grief, and for standing somewhat apart from other men, "as though he desired but little friendship and was not broken by one broken love and contemplated God and the fate of his own soul in a lonely manner." In all this Belloc is delineating his own nature and destiny, and separates himself from Milton only at the close —"of all the things he drew the thing he could never draw was a collectivity." It is true that Milton never accepted his religious beliefs from an external authority, and was to that extent an anti-collectivist, but he became a savage partisan of the Puritan revolutionaries. The Commonwealth was to him what Rome has been to Belloc, and in its service he wasted his genius, fed his hatreds and embittered his personal life. Too great for cynicism, he was not too great for revenge, and the pure dawn of L'Allegro led on to the bloody sunset of Samson's holocaust.

The broken love in Belloc's life is glanced at several times in his work and is narrated in The Four Men through one of his mouth-pieces, Grizzlebeard. In his youth (Grizzlebeard says) he loved a woman older than himself, a wealthy orphan with a title and an ancient country seat. Returning from his service in a foreign army, he learnt that she had recently married—"A veil was torn right off the face of the world and my own spirit, and I saw reality all bare, original, evil and instinct with death. . . . I had fallen in those moments from an immeasurable height." Calling on her the next day, he noted certain defects he had previously overlooked—"Her skin . . . was mottled with patches of dead-white. Her teeth were various; I am no judge whether they were true or false . . . . her gestures were sometimes vulgar; her conversation was inane;" and, on the whole, he preferred her husband, a manufacturer of rectified lard.

The blow, it seems clear, was rather to Belloc's self-confidence than to his heart. She had embodied his mundane desires, and his failure with her prefigured and perhaps helped to bring about his later failure to make a great career in the political world. It affected him also as a writer. A natural solitary, he became after this disillusionment increasingly shut off from the others. He has praised "laughter and the love of friends"; he has celebrated beer and good company; he has championed a faith which, if one goes back far enough, is found to be based on love and compassion. Yet even in his best work, poetic or humorous, he is in spirit if not literally, always alone; no companion being present to the reader's mind even in such an uproarious outburst of inspired nonsense as the song in which he complains that all the animals, from the dog and the cat to the "lion of Africa, verily he," have hides all covered with hair.

His source of inspiration has been the beauty of the visible world, image of a divine reality which receded with the years— "In very early youth the soul can still remember its immortal habitation, and clouds and the edges of hills are of another kind from ours, and every scent and colour has a savour of Paradise." As he grew older he turned to the sea for consolation—"The sea has taken me to itself whenever I sought it and given me relief from men. It has rendered remote the cares and wastes of the land." But the sense of loss and emptiness remained, and in an unfinished poem he speaks of "that outer place forlorn Which, like an infinite grey sea, surrounds With everlasting calm the land of human souls." The night approaches, "and the stars are put out and the trees fail", but he prays that in the hour of dissolution he may recover the beauty of the world, "and fade In dreaming once again the dream of all things made."

Oscar Wilde's Fairy Godmother

LAST SEPTEMBER (1947), Hesketh Pearson and I visiting Oxford for the day, entered Brasenose College, and stopping an alert and genial-looking young man, who seemed to be in his late twenties, asked him if he knew whereabouts in the college Walter Pater had lived. "I don't belong here," he said, "but my friend may be able to tell you." He indicated a youth who was walking along the far side of the quadrangle, and raising his voice shouted, "I say, where did Walter Pater have his rooms? You know—Oscar Wilde's fairy godmother." Curtly, in rather exasperated tones, the other shouted back that he didn't know. Apologising to our would-be helper for having raised an uncongenial topic, and he having depreciated our regrets with undiminished amiability, we went on our way, grateful for a most felicitious and illuminating phrase, though a little stunned at the thought of Walter Pater's feelings could he have foreseen that on a quiet afternoon in autumn, towards the middle of the twentieth century, such an epitome of his days and works, so lacking in fine gradations, so imperfectly adjusted to its pretended subject, would be bellowed across the quadrangle of his own college.

The ordinary human god-parent is among the least helpful of mankind. To turn to a godfather or a godmother when in trouble is one of the last things a man does before hitching a rope to a convenient hook. Yet it is better not to be helped at all than to be helped ostensibly for one's own sake but really to fulfil one's benefactor's desires. Does anyone suppose that Cinderella's fairy godmother, if she could have got the prince for herself, would have exhausted the resources of her occult equipment to get him for Cinderella? Cut off from human intercourse, but a prey to human cravings, she could gratify her social and sexual appetites only by proxy. Cinderella was the agent through whom the old fairy enjoyed a handsome and royal youth, vanishing when the first raptures were over, and leaving Cinderella to decline through disillusion and disenchantment into the long misery of a loveless union with (if I have my facts correct) the most brutal and profligate of husbands.

There is an obvious analogy between fairy tales and false philosophies, for every false philosophy is an imagination of a world propitious to irrational demands and unregulated desires. The false philosopher's dream infects someone in closer touch than himself with everyday experience, this agent of his desire seeks to translate the dream into reality, and disaster follows. It is the Cinderella story in actual life. Rousseau was Robespierre's fairy godmother, Karl Marx was Lenin's, Nietzsche was Hitler's and Walter Pater, as the quadrangle of Brasenose is now aware, was Oscar Wilde's.

In the introduction to his ample and skilful selection from Walter Pater's writings[1] Mr Richard Aldington refers rather sourly to Wilde as Pater's "most notorious disciple." But, after all, it was Wilde not Pater who did two years hard, and if the Old Bailey in 1895 was foreshadowed in the aesthetic doctrines, promulgated by Pater in 1873, sympathisers with Wilde would seem quite as entitled to a sense of grievance as admirers of Walter Pater.

Aestheticism is materialism in its most rarefied form. The aesthete, no less than the seeker after power or wealth, has to be nourished by external things, to be stimulated by sensations pursued in the outside world not by feelings rising spontaneously within. Poets are not aesthetes. An object is beautiful to them if it answers to an inner feeling; otherwise it does not exist. In their surroundings what they value most is enough comfort to enable them to forget where they are. Very little comfort will achieve this end for some poets. A visitor to Blake and his wife wrote: "I had the felicity of seeing this happy pair in their one apartment in South Moulton Street. The bed on one side and a picture of Alfred and the Danes on the wall." Beethoven was even less superfine than Blake, it being his habit when heated by composition to pour a jug of water over his head, and to be both surprised and indignant when the landlord rushed up from below to demand that the cascade under which he was sitting should be dammed at its source. Wordsworth, if he was reading a book at tea, would cut

[1] *Walter Pater: Selected Works.* Edited by Richard Aldington.

the leaves with a knife he had just used for buttering the toast. I do not applaud these practices. I merely adduce them in order to make clear that poet and aesthete are not synonymous terms.

The aesthete is all circumference and no centre. Maimed at the heart of his being, he conceives a universe as sick as himself; unable to divine order, he denies that order exists. All that is left to him is the titillation of his sensibilities, which he claims to be the sole rational employment in an otherwise meaningless exist-ence. In the conclusion to *The Renaissance*, which appeared in 1873 and became the bible of the aesthetic movement, Walter Pater approved what he called the growing tendency of modern thought to regard all things and principles of things as inconsistent modes of fashions. Life was merely a stream of impressions, and "every one of these impressions is the impression of the individual in his isolation, each mind keeping as a solitary prisoner its own dream of a world. . . . While all melts under our feet, we may well catch at any exquisite passion, or any contribution to knowledge that seems, by a lifted horizon, to set the spirit free for a moment, or any stirring of the senses, strange dyes, strange flowers, and curious odours, or work of the artist's hands, or the face of one's friend." The symbol Pater chose to enforce his view that there are no absolute values, and that all kinds of experience can flourish freely side by side, was Leonardo da Vinci's Mona Lisa, in whose face he reads a message, undecipherable to anyone else, the purport of which was that she had supped the essence of ten thousand experiences, had suckled Helen of Troy and the Mother of the Virgin Mary, had sampled the animalism of Greece and the lust of Rome, the mysticism of the Middle Ages and the sins of the Borgias; and all this had been to her but as the sound of lyres and flutes, though to a close scrutiny she might seem rather fatigued, for "the eyelids are a little weary".

Aestheticism inevitably gravitates towards tyranny. Exhausted by empty dreams, sick of self-love where the parched self becomes with each year more arid and tasteless, the aesthete in the end turns to the outside world not for fresh sensations but for the order he cannot find within himself. The former anarchist calls for an overriding authority, the denier of order in the Universe demands the strictest order on earth. He may desire to wield authority himself, like Stefan George with his circle of youthful narcissists, who in due course became Nazis. He may, like W. B. Yeats, be in such a state of confusion between unsatisfied lust and unsatisfied rage as to see in authority nothing but a shower of blows on bloody heads. Or, like Pater, mild and remote to the close, he may turn from Athens to Lacedaemon, that antique model of a totalitarian state, whose citizens, Pater notes, were not allowed to visit other lands—"No! Lacedaemon was in truth before all things an organised place of discipline, an organised opportunity also, for youth, for the sort of youth that knew how to command by serving—a constant exhibition of youthful courage, youthful self-respect, yet above all of true youthful docility; youth thus committing itself absolutely soul and body, to a corporate sentiment in its very sports."

The difference between Oscar Wilde and Walter Pater is suggested in Blake's saying—"If a fool would persist in his folly he would become wise." To suppose that a grand marriage will bring happiness is foolish, but it is better to marry a prince and weep like Cinderella, than to dream about marrying a prince, and have no tears to shed, like the fairy godmother. Wilde was a poet entangled with an aesthete by some inner malformation. The rich, vigorous nature which should have fed his genius was diverted into the service of the aesthete, and the sensations which Pater pursued in fancy Wilde tried to realise in fact. The sins of the Borgias as detailed at the Old Bailey had little indeed in common with the sins of the Borgias as delicately participated in by Mona Lisa to the sound of lyres and flutes. Yet because Wilde persisted in his folly, he enjoyed hours of freedom from his servitude, such as Pater, in his weary coma, never knew. In these hours he was a wonderful being, kindly and magnanimous, healing and quickening, as high above the common level of men as in his other aspect he was below it. Wilde, the aesthete, was a medley of other people's unsifted and unassimilated tastes. Wilde, the poet, expressed himself through a humour which was at the same time sharpened by a clairvoyant insight into the incongruities of life and warmed and irradiated by an irresistibly happy and buoyant disposition.

Winston Churchill's War Memoirs

IN A REPUBLIC of letters, as in other republics, highly placed persons are treated with much more sensitive regard for their feelings than the obscure. Had George Canning or Lord Castlereagh published a book in 1818, it may be taken for granted that no one would have referred to its "calm, settled, imperturbable drivelling idiocy"—the welcome that Lockhart in this year gave to Keats's first volume of poetry. From his early thirties Winston Churchill has been politically as well as socially in the foreground of English life, and has received correspondingly delicate and deferential treatment as a writer, some of his eulogists not caring to exercise their critical faculty upon him, and others having no critical faculty to exercise—for example, the biographer who said that Churchill's life of his father must rank with Morley's *Gladstone* and Boswell's *Johnson*, which is like trying to give an idea of a horse by saying that it is fit only for the knacker's and a certain Derby winner. Churchill's status as a writer was also helped by his disappointments as a politician. The feeling grew that something ought to be done to make up to him for Gallipoli and the extreme unlikelihood that he would ever become Prime Minister. "He will be remembered for his writings," Lloyd George once said, conscious, no doubt, that he himself formed a trinity with Chatham and the younger Pitt, and happy to allow Churchill a place with Gibbon and Macaulay.

The correct procedure when someone who has been awarded a consolation prize suddenly shoots to the head has yet to be decided. Certainly, Churchill's literary reputation so far from declining during the Second World War became more and more magnified. The bulldog who has brought the armed burglar crashing to the ground was seen through a transfiguring haze which gave to the valiant animal wings to outsoar the eagle and horns to outruminate the cow. That vision is now a little faded, yet anyone who abides by the facts of natural history will probably be regarded as rather a churl.

The first volume of Winston Churchill's war memoirs covers the period from 1919 to Hitler's attack on Holland and Belgium in May, 1940. In his preface Churchill suggests that the Second World War should be called "The Unnecessary War".[1] After the end of the first World War, he writes in the opening paragraph of his book, there was an almost universal hope that peace would reign in the world, a hope that "could easily have been gained by steadfastness in righteous convictions, and by a reasonable common sense and prudence". In the second paragraph of his book he writes that the war had been one not of governments but of peoples, that the whole life-energy of the greatest nations had been poured out in wrath and slaughter, and that the war leaders in Paris had been borne thither upon the strongest and most furious tides that have ever flared in human history. Was this a propitious setting for the practice of reasonable common sense and prudence? Does wrath generate righteous convictions and slaughter make them steadfast? The world of 1919 longed for peace as a man after an attack of delirium tremens longs for a draught of running water, but sickly cravings do not restore health to a ravaged world or uncorrupted tastes to an exhausted dipsomaniac.

As soon as the nations began to recover their vigour after the First World War, they fell inevitably into two groups, those who were satisfied with the status quo and those who were not. If at this moment a supernatural being, with unlimited power to raise men to his own level had appeared and told the unsatisfied nations to lay aside envy and hatred and cruelty, and the satisfied nations to lay aside inertia and greed and cowardice, there would unquestionably have been no Second World War. In Churchill's opinion the same result could have been attained if the victors at Versailles had stuck together and treated Germany with a judicious mixture of severity and kindness, or, failing that, if England had listened to his warnings in time and formed a grand military alliance nourished by the League of Nations. The greatest convulsion that has ever racked humanity, the supreme expression in the

[1] *The Second World War* by Winston S. Churchill. Vol. 1. *The Gathering Storm.* Cassell 25s.

outward world of the torment in the soul of man, need not have been, if the House of Commons had listened to Churchill instead of to Baldwin and Neville Chamberlain.

Let us suppose, however, that the war was unnecessary for everyone else. It was still very necessary for Churchill. It is in human nature to want it both ways, but we must firmly decline to be moved by Churchill's lament that his strivings as a pacifist proved fruitless. On this point we feel as Andromeda would have felt if, as with swelling heart she rode away with Perseus from the slaughtered dragon, he had grumbled that all this fuss could have been avoided had his prescription for vermicide been applied in time by the competent authorities.

Churchill's praise of peace does not spring from the heart. The phrases fall listlessly—"Five years ago all were looking forward to peace, to a period in which all would rejoice in the treasures which science can spread to all classes." This is rhetoric—words strung together to produce a certain effect on a particular audience. As a politician Churchill is habituated to weigh what impression his words will make, a bad training for a writer, who is, or ought to be, solely concerned with getting his meaning clear. A speech can be entirely sincere, like the great speeches in which Churchill exposed the growing danger from Hitler. Here the impression he made exactly corresponded with the impression he had himself received. But the rhetoric which, lightened from time to time with flashes of rich sardonic humour, permeates his writings is not controlled by the sense of imminent menace. It is the sportive wallowing of a whale who has sunk his hunters without trace. The penalty of not taking the living Hitler seriously was clear to Churchill, but he perceives no reason why he should not romanticize Hitler dead.

A realist under pressure, a romantic by natural inclination, Churchill loves war, not as a means to tyranny or a vent for hatred, but ardently and generously, as a tourney in which valiant knights put forth all their strength, and the victors and the vanquished embrace when the fight is over. Hitler, the chief character in this volume after Churchill himself, is a very unembraceable object, but Churchill comes as near as possible to embracing him. Mindful, perhaps, that the fiercer the dragon the greater its destroyer's glory, he introduces Hitler as "a maniac of ferocious genius, the repository and expression of the most virulent hatreds that have ever corroded the human breast." But in most of his later references he tones down the maniac and touches up whatever traits are in any degree susceptible of romantic treatment. He praises Hitler for nursing a fervent and mystical admiration for Germany in his miserable youth, instead of allowing his poverty to drive him into the Communist ranks; he is careful not to suggest that Hitler arranged the burning of the Reichstag; he gives no hint of Hitler's guttersnipe malignity when Schuschnigg went to Berchtesgaden; and he pictures Hitler entering the desperado Roehm's bedroom "alone and unarmed", a detail for which our only authority is Hitler, who presumably had his bodyguard within call and was besides fully aware that Roehm's personal habits were such as to render a surprise visit to him in the early hours of the morning what most insurance offices would accept as a reasonable risk, provided, of course, that the visit was not a friendly one.

The comparative tenderness with which Churchill treats Hitler springs also from his inbred veneration for high office, by whatever means achieved. Even as a boy his dreams were of political eminence, the passion to rise in public life shaped all his thoughts and actions, and his instinctive feeling, though doubtless not his considered judgment, would probably favour a gorilla at the top of a tree in preference to Plato meditating at its foot. Baldwin and Neville Chamberlain were Prime Ministers, and accordingly he lets them off lightly; to some extent, it may be, because they were his immediate predecessors at the head of the Conservative party, but chiefly because he does not deem it fitting to take the many into his confidence about their superiors. This is not the temperament, nor are these the circumstances, which help a man to picture life as it is.

While I was discussing some of these points with a distinguished journalist, he remarked sharply—"Churchill does not require to be a great writer." With this I very cordially agreed, adding my regret that more persons were not of his opinion. There is a page in this volume which reveals Churchill's real greatness, the underlying sincerity, simplicity and honest human feeling which, joined with his courage and genius for leadership in war, qualified him for his great task. He is describing Molotov, of whom he saw a good deal during the war, and after saying how Molotov had survived the fearful hazards to which all the Bolshevik leaders were exposed, and had thrived in a society where ever-varying intrigue was accompanied by the constant menace of personal liquidation, he concludes—"How glad I am at the end of my life not to have had to endure the stresses which he had suffered; better never be born." This is the candour of a naturally heroic man, who has no need to buckram himself with fanaticism and no desire to transform the world into an inferno which can be traversed only by those who have robotized themselves into a sub-human insensibility.

From

The Dawn's Delay
(1924)

"W. J."

CHAPTER ONE

So EASILY DISSATISFIED with achieved results are some persons that a journalist, writing in 1975, referred to the war of 1966-1972 as "a mere pothouse brawl compared with the interplanetary struggle which, if the science of levitation progresses at its present rate, must inevitably, and far sooner than most people imagine, . . ." etc., etc.

Still, for a mundane tussle, this clash between the white and yellow races was sufficiently devastating. If we examine the casualties of the black races we find that these alone equalled the total casualties in the war of 1914–1918; yet the blacks entered late into the fight, taking up a reasonable share of the white man's burden only under pressure, and with a very real reluctance.

The fecundity of the African, and simple mode of living, enabled him to recover far more quickly than his white brother, whether in Europe or in America. Neither of these continents, indeed, regained till the decade preceding the war of 2021–2026 anything like the prosperity which had been its portion during the decade preceding the war of 1966–1972.

For various reasons, too tedious to claim inclusion in this narrative, the purchasing power of the pound sterling in the critical decade after the war of 1966–1972 diminished far less than the purchasing power of the mark, the lira, the French franc, and, of course, the dollar. As, however, it diminished sufficiently to make life in England unsatisfactory to persons of limited means, many citizens of that country repaired to the Continent, preferring comfort in exile to a straitened existence at home.

One such exile was Miss Elizabeth Taylor, who, on a Thursday afternoon early in the May of 1975, might have been observed in the station at Munich, nay! actually was observed by a porter, unobtrusively seeking the platform for Andernach.

The porter swiftly balanced probabilities. An elderly spinster, and so likely to be mean; but from England, that was clear, and amiable in appearance. He hastened towards her and addressed her in English.

She laughed nervously, and confided that her luggage was in the cloak-room. She had arrived by air from London that morning, and was going on to Andernach by the 4.53.

"What a polite obliging man!" thought Miss Taylor, as she leaned out of the window to tip him. "A corner seat and a carriage all to myself!"

She handed him his tip. He surveyed it with sour disillusionment.

"Oh, I'm sure it isn't enough," she quavered under her breath. "Mr——!" she called after him.

He turned back.

"A mistake. . . . I meant to . . . Please!"

She pressed a bundle of small paper money into his hand. He smiled; she sighed with relief, and sank back into her corner seat.

For some time she looked out of the window, gasping in delight at the steep-roofed farmhouses, with their overhanging eaves. Yes! This was Dürer's country, indeed! How rich, those farms, how secure! . . . full of earthly poetry . . . monuments of ancient well-being . . . symbols of Teuton strength and geniality . . . yet touched with the pathos of time . . . last strongholds of antique simplicity in an age of change, conflict and confusion. . . .

"Last strongholds of antique simplicity. . . ." Miss Taylor repeated this and the preceding phrases several times to fix them for use either in a letter home or in that book—novel or travel sketches—which was to be the fruit and justification of this adventurous journey.

But now her mood changed. The enthralment of the Düreresque landscape faded. She felt lonely and frightened, like a child. Oh, dear, dear Golders Green! How infinitely remote it was! Why, why had she ever left it for these wild outlandish regions?

There is a school of thought which traces all human actions to economic causes. The disciples of this school prefer the freedom of poverty to well-paid jobs, and allow no economic considerations to interfere with the duty of preaching that man is actuated by economic considerations alone. In conformity with the teaching of these devoted men, I have implied that Miss Taylor left England in search of cheap living, but I am now compelled to adulterate the pure doctrine of economic determinism with foreign matter.

Miss Taylor supplemented a small private income by writing. Her second novel, "Mary. The Story of a Plain Woman," had quite a success, and a number of women all over England added her name to the list of authors whose latest book their libraries were required to supply. Now a novel, now a record of rambles in Old London, now a collection of essays on the quieter aspects of England in war-time appeared at regular intervals, keeping up the mild demand for her work. But since the conclusion of the war the cost of living had mounted rapidly, her last book, though it had sold well, dissatisfied her, and she began to feel the need at once of economy and of something fresh to write about.

Her thoughts turned to the Continent, but none of her friends was free to leave England for longer than a month at a time, and how could she go alone?

Then one day that circular arrived. "*That* circular," so in retrospect she now termed it, filled with sickly amaze at the enthusiasm it had roused in her three weeks ago, as she sat at breakfast in her Golders Green flat.

"Continental Comfort, Limited"—"Limited"! The suggestiveness of the word! Yet at the time she had missed it.

She pulled the circular out of her handbag and, though she knew it by heart, read it through again.

"The general impoverishment of the country due to the War," so ran the circular, "has resulted in a decrease of the purchasing power of the paper pound.

"People living comfortably enough in 1966 on definitely settled revenues now find themselves with less than half their effective pre-war income. Their ranks have been added to by numbers of disabled officers and their dependants.

" 'Continental Comfort, Limited' has been formed to enable

people of limited means once more to lead a life worth living and well within their income.

"A representative of the Company has just returned from a lengthy tour of exploration in France, Germany, and Italy. Owing to a variety of factors, living in certain districts of these countries was found to cost less than at home.

1. Foodstuffs are home-grown, NOT imported.
2. Producers sell direct to the consumer, thus eliminating middlemen's profits.
3. The lower rate of exchange counteracts the increased cost of living, in effect bringing it down for Englishmen to the 1966 standard.

"It may be stated definitely that, *provided one knows where to go*, life at the rate of £150 per annum is possible, on a scale of comfort and food totally out of proportion to what the same thing would cost at home."

Arrangements, the circular continued, had been made with Country Houses, Châteaux and Private Residences, in Northern Italy, Touraine (France) and Southern Germany, to receive clients of the Company as paying guests: the total cost of lodging, service and food ranging from £150 per annum, Class A (*pro rata* for shorter periods. Minimum stay, One Month), to £275 per annum, Class D.

Solicitors' and Bankers' references were required from each client.

Miss Taylor replaced the circular in her bag. She felt slightly reassured: there was, after all, an air about it. Too much air, perhaps? "Hot air" as her Army uncle used to say?

Her visits to the offices of "Continental Comfort" had left in her mind an almost unconscious misgiving, and this misgiving now began to swell and torment her. The offices themselves were situated in the very respectable quarter of Leicester Square. A lover of the past, Miss Taylor regretted the Empire and the Alhambra, which, with many other notable landmarks of prewar London, such as the Crystal Palace and the Y.M.C.A. headquarters in Tottenham Court Road, had been blown to pieces by Japanese airmen in the famous Fourth Bombardment.

It hurt her that the statue of Shakespeare, which once had gazed with thoughtful approval at the blazing lights of the Empire, should be compelled to bestow the same tolerant benediction now touched with fatuity, on the premises of Bastard's Non-Alcoholic Intoxicants.

Still, she could not criticise the offices of "Continental Comfort" on the score of style or of situation. What she had felt on the occasion of her first visit, helplessly, and now felt resentfully, was the way in which Mr Theodore Melmoth, the managing director, had—well! submerged her.

A curiously intense man, with those large horn-rimmed spectacles, through which he projected so mesmeric a glare.

He had come round the table at which he was sitting, bowed with severe dignity, and waved her into a chair—"Please! Please!"

Her submission to this entreaty to seat herself seemed to reassure him. Clasping his hands and resting them on the table he gazed at her with the air of a man who had got a difficult situation well in hand.

"I have come about this circular," she murmured. "I wondered if..."

"Precisely. ..." A monologue began, lasting about fifteen minutes, at the end of which he decided that she had decided in favour of Southern Germany against Northern Italy or Touraine, and in favour of Schloss Bardenstein, near Andernach, against the other castles and private residences controlled by "Continental Comfort" in that quarter of the world.

"You are quite sure the people you have already sent there are ..." she hesitated, searching for a tactful epithet.

"Quite exceptionally charming and congenial people, Miss ...?"

"Taylor."

"—Miss Taylor. I have interviewed them all personally."

"Oh," weakly, "you have interviewed them all personally."

"Personally," in a firm voice. "And you understand, of course, that in each case references were submitted. This is not a mere form. All references are taken up, and if they fail to satisfy our

Committee, the persons in question are notified that we cannot accommodate them. You will realise that we owe this precaution to the various proprietors who have placed their residences at our disposal. And in pursuance of precisely the same policy of complete candour we submit to the client detailed information about whatever house he proposes to visit.

"In regard to your own references, my dear lady, I have no doubt at all ..." He lifted and dropped his clasped hands; a sudden smile gleamed at her. "But we cannot waive this condition in any particular instance. You will understand."

"Oh, of course ... most essential ... naturally."

The telephone rang. He snatched up the receiver. "Mr Melmoth speaking ... Helen? ... yes, simply swamped ... pouring in all day ... ring me up again twelve-thirty, meanwhile I place myself at your feet ... all my homages."

He put back the receiver. "Ah, I had forgotten. A very important stipulation, to which, Miss Taylor, I have not yet drawn your attention, is contained in Clause 12 of our contract. It bears most vitally on this question of the society in which you will find yourself."

Mr Melmoth laid a contract form on the table, opened it, smoothed it, handed another form to Miss Taylor, indicated Clause 12, and leaning well forward made a due pause. Then slowly and with careful articulation, he read out:

"The proprietor agrees, under penalty of a fine of five pounds sterling for each several breach of the stipulation contained in this clause, not to receive into his house as guest, or paying guest, or member of indoor staff or outdoor staff, or otherwise any citizen or naturalised citizen of any of the following countries: namely, Japan, China, the United States of Arabia, the United States of India excluding Ceylon, Siam, the Confederation of Peru, the Persian Empire, the Turkish Empire, Bulgaria, the Revillagigedo Islands, and the Siberian Republic."

He leant back and regarded Miss Taylor, who murmured inarticulate admiration.

"Tolerably comprehensive, I think," he said. "There was some question, Miss Taylor, as to whether we should insist on the exclusion of Euro-Russians. But I felt strongly, and the rest of our Committee eventually came round to my view, that it would be both unwise and ungenerous (Miss Taylor lowered her eyes, unable to sustain the intensity of his gaze)—both unwise and ungenerous to include the Euro-Russian in the catalogue of our ex-enemies. The Russian Revolution was pro-Ally in senti-ment. Petrograd changed its name to St Petersburg two weeks before our armies reached it, and the Kingdom of Euro-Russia has chosen a German prince for its first Monarch.[1]

"Do you quarrel with my position?"

"Oh dear, no!"

But in her present mood the grandiose irrelevance of Clause 12 seemed to Miss Taylor symptomatic of an unreality in the whole business. This castle in the Bavarian Highlands, this Baron Adalbert von Niederhofen ("You will find him a most charming host. He is, of course, very much 'born,' one of the oldest families in Bavaria. He impressed me most favourably"), this selected group of charming and congenial fellow-countrymen —did they exist, were they at this very moment actually there?

Miss Taylor looked out of the window . . . a fat priest strolling across a field, pear and cherry trees in blossom, the long shadows of late afternoon, and many miles away a glowing, snow-covered range of mountains . . . her face relaxed, the lines of worry and suspicion vanished, and her brown eyes filled with tears. She gazed out in a rapture too intense for phrase-making. Never had she seen anything so beautiful.

[1] The Poet Laureate celebrated this event in *The Times*, November 16, 1917. The verses, unsatisfying as poetry, have a certain historical interest, and are perhaps worth quoting.

"*To a Teuton Prince*"
"Even as a careful painter doth o'erpaint
    A tint that's faulty or a line that's bad,
So Teuton wit expels the Mongol taint
    St Petersburg erases Petrograd.

"Oh, fair and true and tender is the North!
    And yellow, fierce and fickle is the East!
Go forth, O noble Teuton Prince, go forth!
    Essay and subjugate the Mongol Beast!"

CHAPTER TWO

"WHAT A DEAR he is!" cried Frau Dernberger.

Cyril Smith heard the exclamation as he walked away from the little group down the avenue. He knew they were looking after him, and a curious stiffness pervaded his limbs and body. It was painful, the distinctness with which he visualised them, Frau Dernberger rocking her baby, pretty Marie, her sister, a hand on her slender hip, and old Frau Schreiner, grandmother and great-grandmother. The girl and the young woman were standing, the old woman was sitting on the bench, smiling vaguely, her wrinkled hands crossed on her lap.

This stiff awkward feeling! How idiotic to be so self-conscious! He walked jerkily, on his heels, like an old man whose limbs are no longer in perfect communication with the brain. To dispel his stiffness he whistled, but the stiffness was not dispelled. Stooping he picked up a stone, aimed carefully at a beech tree, and missed it, Still this stiffness! He kicked at a twig and all but fell over his feet. "Damn!" The dryness of his lips interfered with his whistling. He tried to hum and blushed at the croaking noise.

A bend in the avenue hid him from the castle, and the stiffness vanished, yielding to an exquisite sense of light and supple ease. An unmusical but cheerful noise welled from his throat. He bounded forward and ran till his breath was spent.

Presently he sobered down and began to think of Marie. He was glad that Frau Dernberger had called him "a dear" in front of Marie. Frau Dernberger was grateful to him, of course, for offering to meet Miss Taylor at the station; and, apart from this, as the ingenuous youth well knew, he was useful in a hundred ways to the much-tried housekeeper at Schloss Bardenstein. Knowing no English, Frau Dernberger was always employing him as her intermediary with the Waldens, and Victor Bull and Mr Fleet, and even with "W.J."; for though "W.J." knew German, Frau Dernberger disliked and was rather afraid of him, and avoided him as much as possible. What he needed, she often said, was a wife with a will of her own to keep him in order.

But it was not of his usefulness to Frau Dernberger that young Smith was now thinking. Before setting out for the station, a few minutes previously, he had taken the infant Dernberger from his mother and rocked him gently.

The mother had exclaimed with delight, Marie said nothing but gazed at him as she had often done of late, and old Frau Schreiner suddenly began to smile. Words were rare from her. She was eighty-four years old, and had outlived her own three children. Her two grandsons had been killed in the war, and her granddaughter's husband, Herr Dernberger, had died since. So far as she lived at all, it was in memories of the war of 1914, and of her youth beyond that war, and a little in her great-grandchild.

"Ah, how gently he would hold a young girl!" she murmured suddenly. "I know these young Englishmen."

Marie crimsoned, and swayed involuntarily towards him; Smith, too, blushed, handed the baby back to Frau Dernberger, and made off.

Eighteen miles to the south, as he walked towards Andernach, stretched the Karwendel range, on whose summits the winter snow had not yet melted, and beyond was Tyrol, and beyond Tyrol, Italy. To his right, two hundred feet below, lay the lake of Andernach, a little over two miles long, bordered on the opposite shore by low hills. The road he was following diverged slightly to the left, down to the village, thirty-five minutes walk from Schloss Bardenstein.

"Oh, the world, the world!" cried Smith, gazing at the mountains, brown and warm in the setting sun. The words of the old woman seemed to him an omen, a blessing, a promise of infinite happiness. Marie swaying . . . and the sun and the lake and the mountains, and rushing streams, and other lands . . . other lands! Faces, wistful with long waiting, pale and exquisite! He flung out his arms towards the world.

A peasant approaching regarded Smith with dull misgiving. Smith feigned trouble with a too tightly fitting coat and continued to exercise his arms, not very convincingly.

The train from Munich, now visible in the distance, provided an excuse for flight, and he tore down the road, arriving at the station hot and dishevelled.

Three or four villagers were getting out. It was easy to distinguish Miss Taylor among them. He advanced, breathing hard and embarrassed.

"Excuse me! Are you Miss Taylor? My name is Cyril Smith. I've come to meet you. I'm stopping at the Schloss."

"How very kind! Really most kind!" Miss Taylor was confused with gratitude.

The business of collecting her luggage and transferring it to the decrepit Schloss car put them both more at their ease. Smith suggested that they should walk instead of driving, and soon they were talking quite easily.

"Are you the author, I mean authoress, of 'Mary. The Story of . . .'" Smith hesitated and blushed. "'The Story of a Plain Woman'?"

"Do you mean to say you have read it? How nice of you!"

"I thought it might be you. It's very true to . . . it's very sincere, I mean . . . I liked it very much."

"How nice of you!"

There was an uneasy silence. Miss Taylor knew that at a first meeting she was disappointing both in her looks and her talk. She wished she could accept praise of her work more easily and gracefully.

Smith had guessed she would be plain. But she was much plainer than he had expected, small and thin, a reddish nose, mouse-coloured straight hair. A fascinating ugliness, he had hoped for, a voluptuous irregularity of feature, set off by a supple figure.

Miss Taylor, however, thought him the most charming boy in the world, so tall, such a nice complexion, and blue eyes and thick brown hair: hands and feet rather large—he hadn't grown into them yet: still a little clumsy, but a dear!

Presently she broke the silence. "What is the Baron at the Schloss like Mr Smith?"

"Oh, he's all right, but he's not here now, of course—went to Capri three weeks ago, just after the Tecklenborgs arrived, two girls and a mother. He can't stand women, told me so himself, and, besides, I don't think he liked seeing his house turned into a sort of hotel, though Madame Tecklenborg says he's not much to boast of, bought his title during the war, and then lost most of his money speculating.

"Anyway, it certainly didn't suit him here. I turned up on the 3rd of April, and the Waldens, Bull, Fleet and 'W.J.' at intervals in the next few days, and the Baron chucked up the sponge on the 14th. Pretty quick work!"

Miss Taylor, a practised listener, kept spurring Smith on by a series of nods, and curious little sounds, denoting interest, amusement or concern. Smith began to warm to it.

"Still, he really wasn't a bad sort. He was always very decent to me, but he seemed to lose his temper rather easily. He had a row with 'W.J.', who cursed him for overcharging for baths, but then anyone might have a row with 'W.J.' And he had a row with Major Walden, but then Major Walden was crabbing the German Air Force. And, of course, he had a fearful row with Victor Bull, but it was enough to annoy anyone, bellowing up and down the corridors at one in the morning! Of course, Bull was very tight, had drunk a lot, you know, but that's not exactly an excuse.

"Oh, and there was some unpleasantness between the Baron and Mr Fleet. The Baron said all journalists were born liars, and improved with practice. He speaks English perfectly. Of course, he didn't know Mr Fleet was a journalist, but that led to rather an awkward scene. Mr Fleet can be extremely cutting in a quiet way."

"Well, really! I think it's just as well the Baron's left. But the managing director in London, Mr Melmoth, you know, told me . . ."

"Oh, Crumpet!"

"Crumpet?"

"Yes, that's what we call him—a sort of abbreviation of Continental Comfort. I must say I rather liked him myself, though he talks a lot of rot, theosophy and that sort of thing; says everyone's got an 'aura,' a halo, you know, which shows their real character. We had lunch together the day I called for my tickets, and he'd left all his money in his overcoat in the office, so I paid.

"But the other people here are awfully sick with him. They say he's misrepresented everything, and yesterday Fleet, Walden and Bull began a joint letter which is going to take the skin off his back, according to Bull. Crumpet told Bull there was fly-fishing here, and all kinds of shooting, especially chamois. Of course, there isn't any fly-fishing, and as for the chamois, they're about twenty miles away and thousands of feet up. Walden, Fleet and Bull did get up a party about a fortnight ago, and took a guide, but they never got near a chamois, and Bull was so fed up he shot a goat on the way home. There was a dickens of a row, and Bull had to pay compensation, and a huge fine. And when they got back that evening, Fleet and 'W.J.' nearly came to blows. Fleet's awfully good at pulling people's legs—he does it so ser-iously—and he described to 'W.J.' how they'd shot a boar that was suck ... that was nursing its young, and how the young boars howled and whimpered round their dead dam, and 'W.J.' swore at him and said no wonder the world was in a mess when so-called civilised men did that sort of thing. Leagues of Nations, he yelled, what was the use of Leagues of Nations? The new one would peter out just as the old one did. Men were brutes and would never be anything else. Of course, when he found out his leg was being pulled he got sicker than ever, and there was a general bust-up.

"Since then he sits alone at lunch and dinner, and the Waldens, Bull and Mr Fleet have a table to themselves. We used all to sit at the long table, which is now used only for breakfast. I think the present arrangement is really more satisfactory, and I wanted to ask if you'd sit with us, Madame Tecklenborg, her two daughters, and me. Er—Madame Tecklenborg asked me to suggest it."

"Really, Mr Smith, it's too kind of you. Of course, I shall be delighted. Are you staying long?"

"Till the end of June. That makes three months. I'm up at Oxford, and people who read modern languages get off a term in their first year, so that they can spend six months in Germany and France, or wherever the countries are. I'm going to France in

July. It's a sound scheme. They introduced it after the war, but they're thinking of dropping it next year. Hullo! There *is* 'W.J.' That's his sunset seat."

Smith pointed to a bench a hundred yards ahead of them, which commanded a view of the lake, and, through a depression in the hills opposite, of the undulating westward-stretching country beyond. A man was sitting on the bench with crossed legs and folded arms.

"But who *is* 'W.J.'?" murmured Miss Taylor.

"I'll tell you in a minute," Smith whispered.

The enforced silence as they drew nearer invested the seated figure with a kind of mystery. Miss Taylor noted with awe the high projecting forehead, the bushy eyebrows, the large mouth, clean-shaven, and turned down at the corners. A very small man, hardly over five feet, as far as Miss Taylor could judge.

He seemed as though sunk in a final abstraction, beyond hope and beyond despair; but as they came up to him he started violently, and glared at them for an instant, fear and suspicion in his large hazel-coloured eyes.

"Good evening, Mr Gleg," quavered Smith.

Gleg shook his head impatiently, as though a fly had settled on his nose. Smith and Miss Taylor passed by in trepidation.

"Not over-courteous, is he?" questioned Smith, bitterly.

"Poor man!" Miss Taylor sighed. "He looks so unhappy. But do tell me about him, Mr Smith, and why do you call him 'W.J.'?"

"Oh, that's short for the Wandering Jew. One night, before we sat at separate tables, he came into dinner rather drunk. I must say it was the only time I've seen him like that. Until that night I thought he was a total abstainer. Anyway, instead of sitting glum as he generally does, he started telling us all that he was a genius and that he was writing a masterpiece called 'The Wandering Jew,' which would beat anything that had ever been written, and contained the last word on morals and religion, and war, women, politics, and so forth.

"Well, no one knew how to take this for about half a minute, and then Bull started puffing at him, in a funny sort of mock-pompous mock-heroic way he has—' 'Pon my soul, Mr Gleg, these are brave words! Pouf——pouf——Whoever heard the like?' and Mrs Walden tried to say something cutting, but Fleet just said 'Who's the lucky publisher?' and that started Mr Gleg off in the most extraordinary way. He said the whole world was against him. He was hated and persecuted by everyone, and he was short and ugly and a laughing-stock.

" 'D'you know my Christian names?' he cried. 'Douglas Ferdinand! Ha, ha! Born on Armistice Day, November 11th, 1918, and called after those mighty heroes, Haig and Foch! Good God, even my names are ludicrous!' and then his tone altered, and he swore he'd win a mightier victory than any uniformed nincompoop sending vermin to destruction, and that drew Major Walden. He wanted to know what the devil Gleg meant by calling better men than himself vermin, and they yelled at each other, and suddenly Gleg burst into tears and rushed out of the room.

"It was very awkward at meals the next day or two, and then came the row between Fleet and 'W.J.', which led to us splitting up and sitting at different tables, and a good job, too!

"I dare say he's quite a decent sort really, and perhaps it's rather caddish calling him 'W.J.', but the name's stuck. I'd like to talk to him, but I funk trying. He's so jumpy."

They were approaching Schloss Bardenstein, a rambling three-storeyed building, deprived by frequent alterations of whatever formidable appearance it might once have possessed. It looked to Miss Taylor very charming and peaceful in the setting sun.

"I'll find Frau Dernberger and introduce her to you," said Smith. "She's the housekeeper, and a very good sort."

"Really, Mr Smith, you are *too* kind. I don't know what would have happened to me without you."

"Oh, not at all!" Smith blushed, yet was secretly aware that Miss Taylor had cause to be grateful.

Virtue and self-importance inflated him: he walked rather heavily.

A stoutish man, of twenty-nine or thirty, with a toothbrush moustache, full lips, and a hearty truculent manner strolled out of the Schloss, smoking a cigarette.

"Ha! The studious Smith!" he growled. "Composing an ode to the setting sun, perchance?"

"Perchance not," muttered Smith, sulkily.

"Perchance not! A pretty answer! Perchance not!"

He caught sight of Miss Taylor behind Smith, removed his cigarette from his lips, and drew himself up stiffly.

"An introduction, Smith!" he whispered.

"Oh, Miss Taylor, this is Mr Bull."

"Charmed!" said Bull. "Charmed!" and bowed low.

Miss Taylor was very nervous as she came down to dinner; wondering if Madame Tecklenborg and the daughters would resent her intrusion. It was clearly Mr Smith who had suggested inviting her to their table.

The dining-room, a long room with two bay windows, was empty. Miss Taylor hurried across and took refuge within one of the window recesses. The lake, smooth in the evening light, and the warm pines on the encircling slopes soothed her.

She was roused by a clear voice.

"May I introduce myself, Miss Taylor? Mr Smith has told me you are giving us the pleasure of your society. I am Louise Tecklenborg, Shall we sit down? This is our table, and that table by the other window belongs to Major Walden and his party. Do please sit down, Miss Taylor! You will be very much tired after your journey."

"How beautifully you speak English!" Miss Taylor exclaimed.

"Well, mother, Hilda and I were in England for three years during the war. Ah, here is my mother and Hilda."

The introductions completed, and her poise regained, Miss Taylor began to take stock of the Tecklenborgs. She noticed a certain resemblance between the mother and her two daughters. All three were sallow-complexioned, with dark hair and eyes. But the differences were equally marked. Madame Tecklenborg was stout and rather stupid-looking, amiable in a tired fashion. Hilda, a girl of eighteen, was very thin and restless—"sly," Miss Taylor thought. Louise was immediately her favourite—"Distinguished and certainly good-looking," Miss Taylor mused, "not merely pretty; pale really, not sallow, and what lovely silky hair, not like her sister's. I'm sure she came down early to make me feel more at home. Mr Smith must have asked her. She did it to please him. Yes."

Everything, against likelihood, had gone so well with Miss Taylor till now that she expected dinner, too, to be a success. She doubted not that there existed between Cyril and Louise, those two young people already so dear to her, a love, not yet perhaps quite conscious, whose blossoming she might watch, and, even, tend.

Smith, however, had lost his talkativeness, and the conversation was kept up almost entirely by Louise, who said how anxious she was to read Miss Taylor's books, and showed herself remarkably well acquainted with English literature. Her knowledge was, perhaps, too much of a text-book kind; yet it was just matter for wonder to Miss Taylor that a young foreign girl should be familiar, not only with the great names, Shakespeare, Words-worth, Dickens, Hardy, but also with such little-read though meritorious writers as Tobias Smollett, H. G. Wells, Rudyard Kipling, and the Reverend George Crabbe.

Miss Taylor expressed her admiration to Madame Tecklenborg.

"Ah, Louise is so clever," her mother remarked, complacently, in broken English. "What you even speak of, she knows."

"Mechanical subjects, too," Hilda interjected, with a malicious smile. Her mother frowned at her; Smith and Louise tried to look unconcerned.

The talk dwindled. Smith seemed ill at ease, and in his curt replies to friendly remarks from Louise almost sulky. Miss Taylor became morbidly conscious of her hands, of her knife and fork, of the process of mastication, and above all of Hilda, bored and hostile, sending occasional smiles of self-pity to the Waldens' table. Beyond the long breakfast table, at the far end of the room by the door, "W.J." sat alone. A bottle of whisky, to which he referred from time to time, suggested that he was once again arranging a gap between two periods of total abstinence. Twice Miss Taylor found his eyes fixed on her, and throughout the dinner she was uncomfortably conscious that he had both tables under observation.

Smith, meanwhile, was ignobly preoccupied by the impression made on the Waldens and Bull by Miss Taylor. Fleet, he noted with relief, was absent; staying over-night in Munich, he remembered.

A whispering just after they had sat down, Mrs Walden's lifted eyebrows, the Major's sneer, Bull's puffy, sardonic gaze, a high-pitched laugh from Mrs Walden, commiserating glances between Mrs Walden and Hilda, and "Well! Well! Well!" loudly from Bull, a sigh of robust resignation to an increasingly grotesque environment—none of these indications was lost upon Smith.

"Vulgar cads!" he growled, yet the consciousness of their vulgarity was not strong enough to lift him into the comfortable region of dispassionate disdain. He was nineteen, and felt that he was involved in the ridicule directed against Miss Taylor; and it is a serious thing to be ridiculed at nineteen, or at twenty-nine, or thirty-nine, or ninety.

Loathing of Mrs Walden submerged him. He imagined scenes exquisitely hurtful to her vanity; he placed her in situations where no woman's wit could avail her, where the brassiest insolence must falter, fail, dissolve.

The subject of these day-dreams belonged to a type which, having no especial reason to be pleased with itself, nourishes its self-esteem by despising others. Her person, actually, was not repellent; she was a wiry-brunette, with a loud voice and weather-beaten complexion; and her address was considerable. Schloss Bardenstein affected her nerves painfully, but she meant to endure it till the middle of September. Her and her husband's way of life in London required money, and here she could save; and even in Schloss Bardenstein there was some scope for her skill in intrigue and division. The isolation of "W.J." would doubtless have occurred without any manœuvring on her part. But the further sub-division into two groups, the relegating of her young compatriot, Smith, to the German group, the attachment of Hilda Tecklenborg to herself, and the intensifying of that attachment by the pathos of meal-time separation, for Hilda could not have left her family unless urgently solicited, and no such solicitation was made—all this was in the main Mrs Walden's work. Particularly to her credit was the enslavement of Hilda. Hilda hungered for a love affair, but Smith disliked her and Bull found women of his own class more bother than they were worth, and Fleet was elderly and remote. Major Walden remained: glances were exchanged between the major and Hilda, and an interesting situation was ready to be developed when Mrs Walden, who had observed the glances, intervened.

Hilda was flattered by the overtures of the smart English-woman, whom she had previously disliked only because she felt herself too young and inexperienced to be regarded with anything but indifference by the older woman. Gratified vanity flowered into adoration. Major Walden receded into the background, and Mrs Walden's domestic felicity remained unimpaired.

Mrs Walden had a private sorrow. She was childless and must remain so. Her husband, she told Hilda, could not face the risk of losing her.

Major Walden almost deserved not to lose his wife. His thin lips and vague blue eyes expressed conceit and a stupid shrewdness. If any particular vice is denoted by large and projecting ears, Major Walden was entitled to the enjoyment of it.

Dinner was over, and the Tecklenborgs were about to rise, when Bull came bustling over to enquire if Miss Taylor would make a fourth at bridge. Miss Taylor, flustered and apologetic, confessed that she did not play.

Bull blew hard, fixed a recriminating eye on Smith, and bustled back to Mrs Walden, who wore the tired smile of a person waiting for a foregone conclusion to accomplish itself.

Miss Taylor went up to her room directly after dinner. It was a tiny room (Class A), but it looked southwards over the lake and towards the Karwendel mountains. She finished her unpacking, and ranged her books on a little table against the wall. The sight and touch of them cheered her—Jane Eyre, David Copperfield, the Letters of Mademoiselle Despard, the Oxford Book of English Verse, the Oxford Book of German Verse, and half a dozen others. Ah, what friends they were to her, would always be!

Miss Taylor drew a chair to the window and gazed up at the night sky, watching its blue dissolving into the light cast up from behind a distant mountain by the still hidden moon.

At fifty sensitiveness to beauty was keener than ever. The force of her emotions had not been worn away in the vicissitudes of passion, and the long pain of blotting out all hope of the satisfaction of her own desires had faded, leaving no other traces than a nervousness among strangers and a shrinking from the cruel and ugly side of life. She found her happiness and the satisfaction of her egotism in sympathising with those who were willing to be sympathised with, and in contemplating and reproducing in words whatever her fancy could invest with a gentle and soothing beauty. She had freed herself from the unrest of youth, and still retained its illusions.

Her thoughts turned to "W. J." The mistrustful, frightened look, as she and Smith passed him, had moved her profoundly. What was the secret of this unhappy man? She saw again the huge forehead, the large angry eyes, the loose trembling lip. She thought of his boasting under the influence of drink ... this book of his, a life s labour ... a masterpiece ... and he, friendless and despised.

Her eyes filled with tears. The Karwendel range, shimmering faintly, unsubstantial ... genius insulted and ignored ... the lake and the still trees ... herself here! ... how sad, how exquisite, how fascinating life was!

After dinner, Walden and Bull wandered into the smoking-room, drank cocktails, watched "W.J." sipping whisky in a corner, cursed the Schloss, and invented fresh insults for the letter to Crumpet.

"The fellow," muttered Walden, "can't even send out some-one able to make up a fourth at bridge. I don't blame a person for not being a beauty ..."

"I should bloody well think you didn't," Bull guffawed.

"That's damned offensive, Bull ...'

The door opened and Mrs Walden, putting her head in, asked with a constrained smile if she was going to be left to die of boredom.

Bull followed the Waldens to the salon, but as he entered it a misty sense of estrangement from Walden propelled him across the room towards Smith, who was sitting in a corner with a book. Bull's mood demanded a companion, and in his more exalted moments he was drawn to Smith, a wise young man who read deeply and pondered the mystery of things. Usually, he suspected Smith of intellectual pride, and delighted to abash him with broad raillery.

"Got a good book, Smith?" he asked, seating himself and laying a hand on Smith's knee.

"Heine," said Smith, awkwardly. He could never feel at ease with Bull, though there was a gross humanity in the man which appealed to him.

Bull took the volume from Smith, gazed at it long and shrewdly, and handed it back.

"Poetry?" he queried. "No use for poetry. I'll tell you a book I like—Kenilworth. Grande!" (There are subtleties which the French tongue alone can express, and Bull, whose historical periods were mixed, saw in confused vision Versailles and Kenilworth, ruffling Elizabethan gallants and proud beauties with powdered hair.)

"Grande?" queried Smith.

"Grande! Grande!"

"Oh, 'grand'!"

Bull bowed and made a sweeping circular motion with his hands ... "Courts ... homage," he explained, "festal magnificence."

"Fancy you liking Kenilworth!" exclaimed Smith.

"What the hell d'you mean? 'Fancy me liking Kenilworth!' "

"Sh—sh—sh," from Mrs Walden.

Hilda, at Mrs Walden's request, had gone to the piano. She played really well. The yearnings of her maiden spirit, questionably expressed in ordinary life, expressed themselves in unalloyed beauty at the piano.

Bull's eyes reddened, he groaned and clenched his fists.

"By God, Smith, she plays wonderfully," he growled. "By God, she does! I want to smash things, I want to burn down houses and tear up trees." His right hand closed over the clenched fist of his left and squeezed it with a force that spread his mouth in a grin. His pose and expression were such as Jordaens, but not Fra Angelico, would have approved for a Saint Anthony in the most poignant moment of his temptation.

Major Walden, who was turning over the music for Hilda, seemed to Mrs Walden to be inspecting the contour of Hilda's neck and shoulders rather too closely.

"Thank you so much, Hilda," she said. "You mustn't tire yourself. Fred, sing."

The major, collecting his faculties, sat down and began to reel off his repertory of music-hall songs.

Presently the door opened, and "W.J." entered, uncertainly. At a frown from Mrs Walden, he closed the door and stood gazing at the major, who was playing the opening air of a song.

"Ah!" sighed "W.J."

The major began to sing:

> Dolly went paddlin',
>   Dolly and a pal,
> I caught a sight o' Dolly's knee.
>   Oh, what a lovely gal!

> The sun was shinin',
>   And birds on every tree.
> It's queer how I remember
>   That sight o' Dolly's knee.

"Oh, great, great!" cried "W. J." For a moment the major, his face illumined by the lights at the piano, a certain gusto in his voice, and in the swaying of his head and body, seemed to "W.J.'s" inflamed vision invested with a grotesque beauty: and the song itself touched a nerve in "W.J.'s" soul to a pang of ecstasy.

"Oh, great!" he cried again.

The major stopped playing and gazed blankly at "W.J.", who crooned:

> The sun was shinin',
>   And birds on every tree—
> It's queer how I remember
>   That sight o' Dolly's knee.

Uneasy and amazed, the room stared at "W.J." Their faces vexed him.

"Good God!" he cried. "Can't you see it? Can't you feel it?

It's queer how I remember
That sight o' Dolly's knee.

All the longing of life there, light of the sun and singing birds, and the glimpse of unattainable beauty, and the long regret of memory. Miserable creatures, can't you see it? Don't you know that the half's greater than the whole, a snow-peak seen beyond a pine-wood clearing lovelier than all the ranges of the world? Why, why, why? You fools, because the half suggests infinity, the whole obscures it, the poor, limited, earthly whole.

It's queer how I remember
That sight o' Dolly's knee.

Oh, God, God, God!"

"You'd better get out of here," said the major, advancing on "W.J."

"But why . . .? What have I . . .?"

"Bull, take his other arm."

"A pretty exhibition," Bull boomed. "Insulting ladies!"

"Please!" exclaimed Louise, rising. "Mr Gleg meant no disrespect. Mamma, let us go."

"No, Mademoiselle," Bull replied, majestically. "The man is d—drunk. Pray leave him to Major Walden and myself. There is no necessity for you to move." He turned to "W.J." "Out with you, sir! Out with you, I say! 'Fools, miserable creatures'! Pretty language! I say, out with you!"

"Damn it, Bull," cried Smith. "Don't talk like that to an old man!"

"Who the devil asked you to interfere, you young puppy?" snarled the major, releasing his grip on "W.J." and turning on Smith.

"I may be young, and I may be a puppy, but I'm not a c-cad," stammered Smith.

"What you want's a damned good hiding!"

"Give it me, then!"

"Fred!" exclaimed Mrs Walden, sharply. "Don't be ridiculous! Quarrelling with babies!"

Just indignation and the desire to avenge innumerable slights to his vanity seethed within Smith.

"Cads and humbugs!" he cried.

Victor Bull and Walden, deaf to his wife's protests, began to converge on Smith, when "W.J.", who had not stirred since the major released his grip, stepped forward and took Smith by the arm.

"Come along, Smith," he said, quietly.

Smith, his protest lodged, was glad of a chance to retreat with dignity. Slowly, and regarding the enemy with just so much disdain as not to provoke them to the frenzies of action, he accompanied "W.J." from the salon.

"W.J.", followed by Smith, immediately left the house. Plunging down a narrow track, the two of them came out on a level path which skirted the shore of the lake for over a mile. The night was warm and full of a faint light.

"To forgive a beaten foe," said "W.J.", "that is easy and human. But when your enemies are blatant and triumphing, and it's you who are beaten and humiliated, and their evil, shining faces frighten and nauseate you, and your soul faints, and your body is racked with pain, then to get outside yourself and pity the poor wretches—that is superhuman.

"Oh! the vile beasts!"

"But I kept calm, Smith, at least I kept calm!"

Smith muttered a sulky assent to "W.J.'s" boast. He was already regretting an explosion which had outlawed him from respectable society, and associated him with this truculent eccentric.

They walked on in silence, broken at last by "W.J.", who spoke in an embarrassed tone.

"You showed pluck and generosity, Smith. You surprised me. I've watched you. I knew you were intelligent and sensitive, but I didn't expect..."

Smith blushed with pleasure. "They behaved like cads, sir," he mumbled. "They don't understand you."

"W.J." was silent, reflecting. "I have the same effect on everyone," he remarked, at last. "Other men can drink too much, can get excited and noisy, without forfeiting sympathy, and provoking loathing."

"Oh, not loathing, sir," protested Smith.

"I say 'loathing.' Do you know, Smith, I haven't walked with anyone as I'm walking now with you, in sympathy, talking freely, for twenty years or more. Genius—oh, yes, I have that. But there's something wrong with me, a poison that taints me through and through."

Smith made a husky, deprecating sound.

"Oh, Smith, the lake, the mountains! That beauty and," beating his breast, "this hell!"

Embarrassment and curiosity contended together in Smith. He was half repelled, half touched by "W.J.'s" sudden friendliness and cries of self-pity. But this was a real experience; he must see it through. Not caring to put himself forward nakedly as the confidant of a soul in distress, he made a circuitous approach.

"What is this book, sir, of yours—'The Wandering Jew'? I'm fond of reading, and I should like very much . . . it would be very interesting . . . if you would care to . . . it might be a relief . . . not that I'm capable of understanding, but . . ."

"A poison in me?" "W.J." soliloquised, disregarding Smith's experiments in tact. "But why throw all the blame on myself? If I came to terms with life, like Shakespeare buying gentility and a nice property in his native town, or like Goethe, courtier and laureate of the daily toil, they wouldn't hate me. They've made their peace with life, caved in, grovelled, and they loathe the man who won't grovel, won't feign contentment. Why, even Schopenhauer sheltered himself from rage behind his work, pretended that the philosopher is no longer the slave of desire and slaked his egotism in the savage analysis of the egotism of others. Envy disguised as contempt. But I'll have none of these lies. How tall are you?"

"What? Me? Oh, five eleven and a half."

"You don't look it. I should have said five ten. However, five foot ten or six foot, you're tall enough. Look at me! Barely five foot four ("Barely five foot two," thought Smith). From fifteen to twenty-three or so I suffered hideously, looking at myself in every shop window and trying, by an erect carriage and fierce eye, to supply my lack of inches. In society I was reserved and morose, like Keats. Keats was five foot. Did you know that? No, of course you didn't. The important things are never mentioned. Fine tall men filled me with anguish. I worshipped and hated tall women. In a word, I sounded envy to the bottom, and, taught by my own feelings, discerned its universal operation. In me it raged more wildly, perhaps, than in most, but I found it everywhere.

"You ask about my book. It's a vast unco-ordinated miscellany.

I have anatomised envy, vanity, lust, through hundreds of pages and shown their relation to what is called history. Wars, revolutions! Cure man of envy and desire, and the reign of universal peace will begin."

"But," asked Smith, interrupting a tirade against political panaceas, "why, sir, do you call your book 'The Wandering Jew'?"

"Why, indeed?" snarled "W.J." "You were there the other day when Fleet taunted me with 'Who's the lucky publisher?' I was unmanned, I disgraced myself. But, Smith, I've worked on this book for over thirty years, written and rewritten it, given it every form, epic, dramatic, narrative, essay; and all that's left me is a vast rubble-heap, with here and there a fragment, perfectly conceived and executed, embodying some thought or emotion. Analysis does not satisfy me. I wish to present the whole of life in one dramatic whole, a feat never attempted before. The material is there, but I cannot fuse it.

"I grow old. Men unborn when I was already a man are famous, and I am obscure still, and the butt of envious knaves. Fleet feels the genius in me, and like all the merely clever loathes me. At nineteen or twenty, your age, such men are on the side of genius, still hoping they possess it. At thirty they hate all greatness. I know those men. They bow, sick at heart, before acknowledged genius, but against genius without proofs let loose their spite, feigning incredulity and disappointment. 'Why doesn't he produce?' I know their cry—only too willing to acknowledge a man's genius if only, if only, he will produce. To hell with them, the rancorous hypocrites!

"But I grow old, and my heart fails me often, and I ask myself if I am one of those who cannot bring their genius to birth. Hundreds such have lived and died in unrecorded agony. In every age, says Goethe, there are men who while achieving nothing give an impression of greater genius than the acknowledged masters of the day. Am I such a man? Shakespeare, too, writes:

So, oft it chances in particular men,
That, for some vicious mole of nature in them,
As, in their birth (wherein they are not guilty,

Since nature cannot choose his origin),
By the o'ergrowth of some complexion,
Oft breaking down the pales and forts of reason . . .

You know the lines. Of course, in the third and fourth lines
Shakespeare is thinking of his own low birth, which plagued
him all his life. Shakespeare, too . . ."

"Yes, sir, but what about 'The Wandering Jew'?" asked
Smith, dazed but persevering.

"Yes, I must limit myself, curb this passionate confusion. You
see how I talk. I cannot constrain myself. But I will, I will!"

He swallowed several times and resumed more calmly.

"I'm fifty-six, Smith. Surely the worst rages must be over.
Lusts and envy are weakening. The time for the final rewriting
is at hand. I begin to see my way. Everything has gone wrong
with me in life. I've known neither love nor friendship nor power,
and I have longed and still long for all three. Oh, their disillusionments! I divine those clearly enough, but I won't turn my eyes
from life and repose in a vision of perfect felicity beyond this
torturing world. Why was I given these desires and denied their
fulfilment? I rebel against this iniquity, I say I rebel!" His voice
rose to a scream.

"And to embody this thirst for life, Smith, and this rage against
it, I choose this figure, 'The Wandering Jew.' Why was he, not
Judas or Pontius Pilate or Herod or Caiaphas, singled out for the
punishment of unending life on earth? I see him as the antitype of
Christ; and it is as this I drew him once in a half-finished play,
with three characters: Christ, who has transcended and sub-
jugated life; Mary Magdalene, the symbol of life; the Jew, the
slave of life, abject before the woman. But the play turned to
sentimentality, and I tore it up. Maudlin sensualists enough have
bepawed Mary Magdalene. I'll not add myself to the number.

"I shall not touch her again, but Christ I must draw, though
words, in reference to him, have almost lost their meaning.
Everything has been said about him, and for the most part said
badly, and said a million times. Still, draw him I must.

"If I were a painter, I should give three portraits. In the first portrait he is coming from the wilderness towards a village. His eyes see nothing in the external world, men nor women, beauty nor barrenness. The struggle is over, he has put away the dream of earthly dominion and the dream of earthly pleasures; and in his shining eyes you see reflected the serenity of the Heaven to which he will lead men from the dark world.

"In the second portrait he sits alone on the slope of a hill above the unheeding villages of Galilee. The light has faded from his eyes, and his face is set with anger and resolution.

"In the third portrait he is on the cross. The light of Heaven is obscured in his eyes, but the love which sent him out into the world conquers the pain and the darkness. In his own defeat he understands and forgives the defeat of others, and in the moment when he rises highest above humanity, he is most at one with it."

"W.J." paused and looked at Smith. Smith was bewildered by the alternations of arrogance, wounded vanity, and simple deeply felt emotion. His mood a few minutes earlier had been hostile, and he had meditated an ironic interruption, but faced by the childlike appeal of "W.J.'s" look he now murmured admiration and understanding.

"I'm glad you see it, however dimly," said "W.J."

Smith started. "Gratitude!" he thought, but said nothing.

"You understand, of course," "W.J." resumed, "that my treatment throughout is imaginative. I shall write neither history nor theology. I shall write a poem. No erudition, no local colour. I know neither Hebrew nor Palestine. But I know myself, and the Wandering Jew, restless, embittered, longing, is myself. Is there a connection between my endless beginnings again and the endless wanderings of the legendary Jew, a fatal likeness between the subject and the writer? Well, be that as it may! These two figures, Christ and the Jew—that is my task: to oppose them to each other; a theme requiring the highest imagination, tempered by many years of pain."

For a long time he did not speak. At last, in a remote meditative tone, he resumed:

'I must trace unrest from the first years of life. A field or a wood, in a child's imagination, a blue hill beyond the bounds of its little walk, a hollow tree hiding in its recesses an entrance into another world, are all promises of a heaven near by which the chance of a moment may reveal. The common things, too, of the nursery and the street, a coal-scuttle, perhaps, or a pillar-box, become at times obscurely significant, as though inarticulate with the mystery. Even their games, which children are supposed to enjoy so whole-heartedly, are never quite satisfying: beyond them lies still the thing which is always sought and never found. I remember once, as I walked by a wooden fence behind which workmen were laying the foundations of a public building, a small boy crossed over from the opposite pavement and peeped through a chink, then turned wistfully away. The pain of these ever-recurring disappointments grows slowly in a child's heart, till it vents itself in an outburst of agony, some trivial check or failure leaving behind a sense of irretrievable loss which lingers through the years, becoming at last an anticipatory symbol of life itself.

"A child's nightmares, the familiar face suddenly twisted with laughing madness, a horror without shape or sound, crouching to leap out, the roar of waves in black night sweeping from all sides to overwhelm the dreamer, are all confused images of desire baffled at every turn.

"In the beauty of a dream hill, a lake, a face, more poignant than any waking beauty, the child sees his desire for a moment, then awakes."

"Yes, yes!" exclaimed Smith, once again charmed. "It's all true! I remember a very vivid dream . . ."

"I want in some such brief outline as this to express the imaginative relation of a child to life. Perhaps it would be best to embody these reflections in the Jew's story of his own life. All general reflections are exposed to assault from insensate creatures who 'cannot remember ever to have felt anything of the kind, and greatly doubt if that is at all a usual experience.' Fools!

"Yes, the Jew must tell his story from childhood up." "W.J.'s" head drooped on his chest; he began to mutter to himself, and to clench and unclench his hands. "Yes!" he exclaimed, "my childhood and my youth," and was silent.

"As child," he continued presently, "I shall show him seeking in everything, however beautiful or however common, the solution of his unrest. At last he acquiesces in the uselessness of the search. For a few years, from eight till twelve or so, he busies himself with his own affairs as seriously as a grown man. Then mystery returns, and in confused reveries of sense and spirit, embarrassed and allured by the outward world, he stumbles on first love.

"Oh, boy, that hour, those days!" He clutched Smith's arm, and the moon showed the convulsion of his harsh lined face. "The white dress hiding her sacred loveliness . . . her room, the sanctuary of life not yet possessed, inviolate and waiting . . . all beauty an image of her beauty . . . her voice, her movements, her silence, the sound and motion and tranquillity of life itself."

His hand fell from Smith's arm.

"The fear of death rouses at the vision of life. But her, at any rate, corruption can never touch, and in the assurance of her immortality the hope of his own is confirmed.

"Why did I outlive that time? How have I struggled through the foul marsh of life who once stood on that mountain?

"But the long story of lust and hatred and envy must be told. I want to show a man whom some malign and intractable element in his nature debars even from the imperfect satisfactions of life, and who, because he is so debarred, thirsts the more savagely for happiness.

"In obscure and contemptible employment he looks at power and pleasure from a distance. A girl dancing, a man riding, lovers pressed against one another as they walk, the pomp of processions, friends laughing at table, every manifestation of life and energy menaces and insults his quivering nerves.

"Then one day he sees Christ, hears him preaching to a crowd, and feels at once the tranquillising power of a man not involved in life, a voice speaking from another world not subject to dominion with its laws and armies, its ceremonies and palaces, its masters, its pleasures, and its slaves. In the crowd he sees men like himself, the refuse of the earth, gaping at new perspectives— 'Blessed are the meek, for they shall inherit the earth.'

"He is fascinated and repelled. Often he yearns to withdraw his soiled and thwarted desires from the world, and, filled with an undefined but passionate hope, give them into the keeping of Christ.

"But his vanity is affronted by the outcasts who clutch like himself at this rope to drag them from the waters of humiliation. Christ, he thinks, appeals only to the failures, and, in his campaign against life, regards the respected and successful man as his enemy, and the publican and harlot, those whom life despises, as his allies. The one lost sheep is more prized than the ninety-nine who do not feel the need of Christ.

"Power and glory—the Jew sickens for them with that thirst which presently corrupted Judas and a few years later created in the New Jerusalem of Revelation a replica, more gorgeous than the original, of Imperial Rome.

"A purer feeling than vanity is unsatisfied. His sense of the infinite suggestion, beyond analysis, in everything, in a casual gesture or attitude, light falling on a wall, a sudden sound or scent, branches swaying, is thwarted when the lilies of the field, a man sowing, a bowed woman with loosened hair are constrained to enforce a defined truth. He contrasts the inspiration of the poet, varying and receptive, with this fixed inspiration, owing nothing to the movement of life. One day he is present when the wit of a woman surprises Christ—'Even the dogs eat of the crumbs which fall from their master's table.' For a moment Christ looks round him in a world where the differences of human beings, some dull, some witty, are felt. The moment passes, and Christ withdraws again into a soul nourished from a remote and unknown source.

"Another day he listens to the terrible anger of the man, whom love had sent into the world, against the blind villagers of Capernaum and Chorazin and Bethsaida. Yet each man has but his own eyes. Who made the blind blind?

"No, he cannot see with Christ's eyes, nor follow him into the unknown. Though life tortures him, he will not turn from its promise of happiness, for ever unfulfilled; sweeter and nearer to him than any unimaginable heaven are those rare moments when rage is stilled, and he looks at life far off, enchanting as a village among meadows, seen from a high hill.

"On the day when Christ climbs slowly up to Calvary, the Jew stands by the roadside. The faces of the disciples, seen here and there in the surging mob, are white with agony. Life, the monster which breathes confusedly through earth's millions, has mastered their champion. Who can save them now?

"The Jew weeps bitterly as he looks into the eyes of Christ, no longer angry or remote, but filled with a sublime compassion, for all men as for himself. In the moment of life's victory, the Jew kneels before Christ for the first time. But the figure recedes in the distance, the ecstasy of abasement and renunciation fades, he turns and goes down into Jerusalem."

"Oh, great!" cried Smith, but "W.J." said nothing. His eyes were wide and fixed, and he was silent for a long time.

"W.J.", when he began to speak again, passed by obscure transitions to an analysis of war. "Three years ago," he said, "everyone affirmed that there could never be another war. Mankind had suffered too much. Mankind had learnt its lesson. But they said just the same in 1918, and they will say just the same in another fifty years when the next great war is over. Life is not adapted to the satisfaction of desire, and what are wars but the explosions of unsatisfied desire?"

"Yes," said Smith, a little doubtfully.

"History, Smith, is simply a record of the convulsions caused by the grown man's efforts to find in company with others what he has failed to find alone, as child and boy and youth."

He murmured this aphorism over to himself, very happy at having outlined in so lucid a form a thought which had long haunted him. As Smith appeared to have not quite grasped it, he repeated it again, twice, with slow emphasis . . . "History, my dear Smith, is simply the record . . ." and "I say, Smith, that history is no more than the record . . ."

At the third repetition Smith made a mistake. "Yes," he said, "that sounds pretty obvious."

"Obvious!" snorted "W.J." "Obvious!" He was terribly put out. He had felt on the verge of seeing how to work these general considerations on war into the framework of the Jew's story. Now this young fool had upset him. It was time to go to bed.

They climbed in silence up to the Schloss, and parted coldly. A great evening suddenly gone flat.

The next morning, Smith awoke with a feeling of apprehension which presently defined itself as uneasiness about the Waldens and Bull.

Walden and the Tecklenborgs were at breakfast when Smith came down. Smith looked at Walden nervously, and Walden ignored him.

The easy, charming life at Schloss Bardenstein, which he was enjoying so much, suddenly became overcast. He began to wonder if he had not made an ass of himself the previous evening. After all, "W.J." had been drunk and offensive. Women had been present. "W.J." had insulted everyone: he was an intractable, overbearing crank. Oh, clever enough, more than clever—he had said some wonderful things, but, damn it, the usual run of mankind couldn't be expected to see beneath the surface. They had a right to demand ordinary manners even from a genius. And he, Smith, had butted in, and yelled at them, and called them "cads and humbugs."

Ought he to apologise? No, damn it, that would be too much. After all, "W.J." was an old man, and, if it came to that, Bull wasn't any too sober himself. A couple of infernal bullies, treating an old man like that, in front of women. A genius, too, poor devil! Rather a trying old card, of course, but genius had a right, damn it, to be trying. Who the hell were Walden and Bull? Apologise! He'd see himself damned first.

Smith, preoccupied by this alternation of hot and cold fits, ate little. After breakfast, instead of working in his room as usual, he retired to the salon with a novel.

Louise had noticed his worried look, and presently joined him in the salon. He received her glumly. Here was another complication!

Louise had been engaged, a year and a half previously, to an engineer, and was to have followed him to Brazil, but two months after his arrival in that country, he ceased to answer her letters. A year passed, and one day Louise received a newspaper cutting which announced her lover's marriage. The strain of waiting, thus sharply ended, affected her health, and it was not till she came to Schloss Bardenstein that she began to recover hope and vitality. She had told her story to Smith, and Smith was moved and indignant, in the incoherent fashion of youth.

His sympathy, however, had recently been modified by other emotions. On the previous Sunday Madame Tecklenborg had manœuvred him into an intimate talk. She praised Louise in the warmest terms, telling how passionately she had immersed herself in the study of engineering, so as to fit herself to assist her future husband in his profession, and then that scoundrel—but of him Madame Tecklenborg could not trust herself to speak. Ah, how different was Tsireel! (as she called Cyril)—so good, so gentle, so true! She could not say anything—here she smiled and allowed a mild confusion to appear—Louise would be very angry with her, for having said even what she had. She would not for anything that Louise should know. Indeed, Tsireel must not suppose that her remarks had any particular significance. Ah, poor Louise! It was good to see her looking so happy again.

Smith, although affronted by this view of him as a true and gentle young man, did not blame Louise for her mother's disgusting misconception of his character; nor did he flatter himself that Louise was in love with him. He felt, however, that she might, young though he was, look upon him as likely to prove a good and considerate husband to a girl disillusioned with love. The notion appalled him. He was not that kind of man, and it was horrible that any girl should think of him in that kind of way. He began, unobtrusively, to see as little of her as was consistent with politeness and their former friendly relations.

And now here he was, cornered by her! The salon was empty, and no one ever came into it during the morning.

Louise seated herself beside him on the sofa.

"You are worried, Cyril," she said gently. "Is it because of last night? You were very brave. It was right that someone should speak in defence of poor Mr Gleg."

"I'm so glad you think so . . . you're a jolly good sort, Louise." After all, what fine eyes she had! There was something so cool and steady and reassuring and encouraging about her.

"You *are* a good sort," he blurted, and seized her hand. He had one friend, anyway, in this confounded hole.

He was squeezing her hand more fiercely than he realised.

"Oh, Cyril!" she cried.

"Have I hurt you, Louise?"

"No, no, oh, no!"

"I have! I have! Darling!"

"Cyril!"

"Darling!"

He flung his arms round her, roughly and clumsily, and the unhappiness of Louise, a long and wearing pain, and the unhappiness of Smith, a discomfort of a few hours, sought euthanasia in a kiss.

A sound between a grunt and a snarl shook them out of their embrace. Jerking round, they saw "W.J." regarding them balefully from the doorway.

"S—sorry," gasped Smith.

A sneer contorted "W.J.'s" face. He bowed and retreated.

Louise rose, and, taking Smith's hand in both hers, looked at him long and searchingly.

"Awkward about 'W.J.'," he muttered, feeling the need to say something. His brief frenzy had subsided, her gaze embarrassed him, and he wondered uneasily what on earth would come of this outburst.

"I think we had better not tell mother yet," Louise said, at last, and released his hand. She paused, but Smith, paralysed by the implication of this remark, was beyond speech.

"Well, Cyril, I must leave you now."

"Good-bye, Louise."

He tried to add a loving phrase, but his tongue refused its office. Not to pick up his novel until she had left the room was the only sign of passion to which his disordered faculties were at the moment equal.

"W.J." meanwhile was walking off his chagrin. The comfort of Smith's society had not been fully realised by him on the previous evening. "Quite an intelligent young fellow, but too fond of the sound of his own voice," was his verdict, as he undressed for bed. But the absence of Smith revealed the advantage of his presence, as a man often becomes conscious of a sound only in the moment when it dies away.

As soon as he had breakfasted he set out in search of Smith. And he had found him! Oh, yes, he had found him all right!

That his only disciple should be enjoying himself in the embraces of a girl, while his master wandered forlorn and unloved, impressed him like an act of treachery or a deliberate expression of contempt.

Exercise and reflection calmed "W.J." "I am balanced and reasonable at bottom," he mused, "but on the surface hasty, without judgment, irritable. . . ."

In the course of his life, "W.J." had been a schoolmaster, tutor, lecturer, private secretary, and finally, during the war, a hack-writer in the Ministry of Information. Everywhere he had illustrated the truth of the latter part of the verdict he had just passed on himself, alienating his colleagues and superiors by irritability and truculence. In his latest job, being commissioned to write a eulogy of the Allied cause from the stand-point of a sensitive, cultured and, naturally, disinterested Laplander (Lapland did not abandon its neutrality till the last year of the war), he had unpent himself in a sketch, "England at War," to such effect that his immediate resignation was demanded. Having sunk his savings in an annuity of £200, he was now trying to put by enough money to defray the publishing expenses of "The Wandering Jew," when completed.

While "W.J." was recovering his poise, Smith was plunging more and more deeply into gloom and apprehension. The need for moral support against the Waldens and Bull had betrayed him into making a fool of himself with Louise, and Heaven alone knew what would come of that! Engaged! At nineteen! Could such things be? He tried to warm his imagination with pictures of Louise as a bride, and a false glow cheered him for a space. But no! But no! He could not approximate her to the ideal he dreamed of, white-skinned, supple, warm dark hair (*not* silky), swift, yielding, not calm, measured. Why, Marie was a thousand times nearer the love of his dreams, and even Marie . . . but what a darling she was! He would, he must, make an opportunity to see her alone. . . . Damn everyone else! The Waldens, Louise, what did they matter, if only . . .

Too restless to read, he got up and strode out into the hall. The post had just arrived, and Marie was assuring Walden and Bull, in simple German, that no tobacco had arrived for either of them.

"But it's two days overdue!" they expostulated in chorus.

"Oh, Mr Smith!" she cried. "Please tell these gentlemen there is no parcel, but no parcel! arrived."

How charming she looked! Light brown hair, eyebrows much darker than her hair, large grey eyes, shining with impatience, a foot tapping the ground.

"Fräulein Schreiner says no parcel has arrived by this post," Smith explained, adding stiffly, after a pause—"I've got a tin upstairs, the same kind as you smoke, if you'd care to . . ."

"I prefer to wait," said the major.

"Oh, very well!" Smith walked off and out of the house. He had not gone above a hundred yards, when he heard Bull calling after him . . . the sound of a man running . . . no doubt Bull . . . well, let him run.

"Smith!" Bull, puffing loudly, was now too close to be ignored.

"Yes?" said Smith, pausing.

Bull, coming up with him, took his arm and began to march him along. Bull's manner, at once confidential and assured, accorded well with his character of a plenipotentiary sent by Walden to treat with Smith.

"Look here, Smith," he began, as soon as he had recovered his breath. "Walden's a regular, been in the Army twenty years. He's a married man, too. You were damned offensive last night. That doesn't worry me, but Walden's not accustomed to backchat from lads of your tender years. It's up to you to put things right. You needn't run to a formal apology."

"I should damn well think I needn't! What about Major Walden starting off the apologies with one to Mr Gleg?"

"If you're going to take that line, Smith, it'll be the worse for you. You won't get off so easily next time. Here's Walden without any tobacco. You've got your chance, and you carry on with your damned sauce. By God, Smith, your asking for trouble, you are, by God!"

"Well, I offered him my tobacco, didn't I?"

"Offer it again, Smith!" Bull squeezed Smith's arm. "Offer it again! Take a straight tip!"

Bull wheeled Smith round, and began to walk him back towards the Schloss.

M

"How do I know he won't turn me down again?" Smith protested.

Bull gave a reassuring wink. "You'll find him in the smoking-room," he said.

"He'll have to drop his damned airs, if he wants my tobacco," Smith muttered as he went upstairs; ignoring a feeling of relief at this solution of an awkward situation.

The major was reclining in an easy chair when Smith entered the smoking-room. Bull was sitting on a table, swinging his legs. Smith placed his tobacco tin on the table.

"Now look here, Smith," said the major. "You're very young. If you were five or six years older I should be compelled to take a very different line. As it is, I'm not going to say anything about last night. I appreciate this offer of yours, and I'm perfectly willing to cry quits."

Bull plunged his hand into the tin and began to transfer a large portion of its contents to his pouch.

"But take a tip from a much older man than yourself, Smith. Don't get mixed up with that fellow Gleg. He's a bad hat." The major reached over and possessed himself of the tin. "He's 'bunda.'[1] Of course, you're literary, aren't you? That's perfectly all right. But there are certain things that stamp a man. A fellow can drink as much as he likes in the Army, but he's got to carry it like a gentleman. And you'll find it's more or less the same everywhere. This fellow Gleg appeals to you because he writes or says he does. Well and good. But there are writers and writers. The man's a damned pro-Jap—you heard him insulting our Army the other evening. He's a bad egg, he's bogus. Drop him. Thanks." The major handed the depleted tin back to Smith.

"He's not half as bad as he seems," Smith protested. "He really isn't. He's had rotten luck."

"Yes, yes." The major, filling his pipe, smiled tolerantly. "But take my tip, Smith. Don't get mixed up with him."

"He's got genius. He has!"

"Well, it's your own funeral. I've told you how he strikes me,

[1] "Bunda." An East-African term, signifying "worthless, dishonest, a ne'er-do-well." Introduced into Army English during the Kenya War—1953-54.

and I've knocked about a bit. How about a stroll, Bull? This infernal hole plays the devil with my liver."

Linking arms, Walden and Bull strolled off, puffing out great clouds of smoke. As they rounded a sharp bend about a hundred yards down the avenue, they came upon "W.J." He, like them, was in the centre of the road, striding with bent head.

"He'll butt into us," said Walden.

"Let him!" said Bull. "He'll get the worst of it."

"W.J." looked up. Their smiling faces enraged him. He saw that they meant him to give way. The memory of the previous night's outrage went to his head.

"Dogs!" he cried, and raised his stick.

Bull released Walden's arm and stepped back. "Ha!" shouted "W.J.", and pushed his way between them.

Walden gazed after him, too taken aback to speak.

"You damned old rip!" he at last ejaculated, but "W.J." was now out of hearing.

CHAPTER SIX

Sмɪтʜ ᴄᴀᴍᴇ ɪɴᴛᴏ lunch looking constrained. Uneasiness, about Louise had succeeded to uneasiness about Walden and Bull. Before he was seated he was already talking hurriedly to Miss Taylor. How had she slept? What had she been doing all the morning? What did she think of the place? What was her room like?

Adequate answers were furnished; a lull threatened, and Smith plunged into a paraphrase of "W.J.'s" talk the previous evening.

Hilda presently interposed with a malicious account of the scene in the drawing-room, but Louise defended "W.J." warmly.

"It's a pity he doesn't carry his wine better," said Smith. "Still, the man has genius." He began to feel easier about Louise. She understands, he thought, she's going to ignore the whole incident. A real sportsman!

His spirits rose. "I'll introduce you to 'W.J.' after lunch, Miss Taylor," he cried.

"Oh, but do you think . . . are you sure . . . hadn't you better wait a little?"

"No! No! 'W.J.'s' perfectly all right, if you know how to handle him."

Miss Taylor protested a little longer, but when lunch was over she allowed Smith to lead her in search of "W.J."

"W.J." was sitting on the bench where Miss Taylor had seen him for the first time, on the previous evening. His face lit up as Smith came into view, but at the sight of Miss Taylor he frowned.

"May I introduce Miss Taylor, Mr Gleg? Miss Taylor has just arrived. She writes, too. She is very much interested . . . I told her about your book . . . if you would care to . . . she would be very glad . . ."

Miss Taylor bobbed and murmured. Smith, alarmed by "W.J.'s" glare, turned and retreated towards the Schloss.

The substitution of an elderly spinster for a good-looking young man exasperated the master. It was not this kind of disciple that could soothe his vanity, outraged by the indifference of the world. "Smith prefers that girl to me," he thought. "This woman,

whom nobody else wants, is good enough for me. Is she?" He
glared at Miss Taylor.

"So you write, do you?" he barked. "And, pray, what do you
write? Love-stories?"

"Sometimes."

"What do you know about it?"

Miss Taylor flushed and turned away.

"Good God!" "W.J." raised his voice and Miss Taylor, to his
satisfaction, halted. "Good God, madam, is there no other theme?
Look!" he waved his hand to the plains and mountains. "Can't
you see them, bending at their desks, the world over, at this
moment, as I speak, thousands of fools spilling ink on the same
stale theme? And while they scribble, millions, I say millions,
now, now, this minute, north there!" he jumped up and stabbed
his finger at the north, then whirled round, "south, there! east,
there! west, there! millions, I say, sighing, groaning, clutching
each other, or restless with expectation, or dulled by satiety. And
still the fools scribble."

Miss Taylor flushed yet more deeply, and was silent. An obstinate look came into her eyes.

"Well," snapped "W.J." "What have you to say?"

"I don't believe you feel like that," she said, haltingly. "I
don't believe you can look at life in that way. One can't think
of human beings in millions. How can the rest of the world
dwarf a man and woman when they love each other? The whole
world is in their hearts then." Her voice shook, but he had
wounded both her pride and her faith too deeply for her to be
silent. "You may despise me for thinking and writing about
love, but one needn't have been loved to understand it. One
need only have loved. There is love everywhere. I see it everywhere. Yesterday, when the snow on those mountains turned to
rose-colour, kissed by the setting sun . . . and that lake, look how it
takes the sky to its heart!" Her voice broke, and a tear rolled down
her cheek.

"W.J." was abashed. "Pooh! Don't cry!" he exclaimed, and
looked searchingly at her. It amazed him that one so little
indebted to life should speak of it so lovingly.

Vexed with himself, he wished to be rid of the feeling and jumped up.

"Come, let's stretch our legs," he said.

They climbed down the rough track to the lake, and skirting its northern end, followed a path which wound up to the summit of a hill. It was a warm afternoon: they seated themselves on a dry grassy hummock and looked down the slopes of the hill, waving with meadow-grass, and over the rolling country and at the distant mountains.

"God knows I don't want to be bitter and offensive," "W.J." said at last. "You, Miss Taylor, look at this world and are happy looking. But merely to look exasperates instead of satisfying me. To be what I look at—that is what I thirst for. Do you understand? You know, when one's young one expects, without analysing the hope, to identify oneself presently with the thing looked at. That train down there, tiny, a toy, moving over the plain as though conscious of a delightful goal, yet in no hurry; or that cow lying in the shadow of the tree, a patch of sunlight on its flank; or those clouds, warm and white and unmoving—if I were a boy again, the longing awakened by these sights would be stilled by the hope of merging myself in them. Of course, this aspiration is ludicrous to the commonsense of later years. A man can't merge himself, with any profit, in a train, a cow, or a cloud.

"That cow is a dull mass of flesh and blood and bone. That train is a contrivance of wood and steel, freighted with melancholy fools. That cloud is a damp mist.

"Yet that cow is also an image of calm encircled by beauty; that train expresses movement without unrest; those clouds are the happiness promised to my soul.

"They are one thing in themselves, another thing in my imagination. Why?" He jumped to his feet. "I say, why? How can other men live at ease, blind to the mockery of sight and scent and sound? How can they? Well!" he unclenched his hands and sat down again.

"Perhaps, after all," he said, "there is a heaven where each desire infuses itself into the thing desired, so that they are no longer two but one, and there I shall be myself and yet a cloud and yet the curve of a girl's neck and a wave beyond the Hebrides and a hill bright at dawn, the smell of a primrose, the sound of a horn far off. I want no other heaven. I want no undistinguishable bliss."

He got up, paced to and fro several times, then, sitting down, rested his chin on his hands.

"Yes, yes, I understand," cried Miss Taylor, suddenly, "and, you know, it isn't only life that tantalises one like that. Books, too—it's hard to explain, but while you were talking, so wonderfully, just now, I tried to conjure up *my* heaven, the things *I* wanted to be, to be in your sense, you know, and all kinds of longings have been sweeping over me which I had never clearly realised as longings before, and I would wish to be the seashore where David Copperfield played with Emily, and the trees and crows of Castlewood on a summer evening, and little Harry Esmond walking there, and Ruth's watermill 'by spouts and fountains wild,' and the misty mountain-tops when Romeo kissed Juliet good-bye, and a street in mediaeval Paris, snow glistening on the steep-roofed houses, warmth within and outside the creaking lamps and the distant howling of wolves—oh, and a thousand thousand other things, back, back through my life, back to Little Boy Blue and the sheep and the sky of nursery rhymes, so far away, so free from pain!"

She twisted her hands convulsively, and, abashed by her outbreak, glanced sideways at "W.J."

He was pleased with her quick understanding, and with the excitement he had stirred in her, but thought it salutary to mark a distinction between her sensibility and his own.

"Very nice, Miss Taylor, very nice!" He smiled at her sardonic yet affable. "Very nice, and very literary."

The deadly epithet found its mark. Miss Taylor shrivelled into herself. "I suppose books do mean too much to me," she quavered. "I have always been a great reader. I suppose if someone ... if I had been different ... you see, no one ..."

"What a brute I am!" thought "W.J." "The poor little woman was so eager, and she feels subtly and beautifully. I must gloze it over."

"Please," he said, aloud, "don't see a sneer in the word 'literary.' It can convey a very high compliment."

She turned grateful brown eyes towards him, and he smiled reassuringly. They rose and continued their walk, and "W.J.", his conscience placated, began to talk about himself. Time passed, they had tea in an inn at the southern end of the lake, and then turned homewards, joining the road from Andernach to the Schloss at about half-past five.

Never had "W. J." had such a listener, nor Miss Taylor heard such talk. She saw his egotism; he could not get outside himself and walk about disinterestedly in the world of common life, but sometimes he could rise above the earth in sudden flights and look down upon it with eyes tranquillised by distance. She cried as he told the story of the Jew, amplified and brought nearer to perfection since its recital to Smith. "W.J." marked her tears, and his stride lengthened and his heart expanded.

"Let's get off this road," he cried. "It's cooler in the wood, and easy walking."

Smith passed the earlier hours of the afternoon on his bed, smoking, reading, dozing; lazy in mind and body, restless in fancy and desire. He roused himself shortly before five, and went downstairs; and, to avoid Louise, about whom, however, his mind was now fairly easy, ordered tea in the smoking-room.

He was obsessed by the picture of Marie colouring and swaying towards him. Where was she? With her sister and grandmother, no doubt, or helping in the housework. He opened the door so as to command the passage. Steps in the hall . . . he jumped up. Mrs Walden!

"Have you seen Major Walden?"

"No. He hasn't been here. Perhaps . . ."

"Thank you."

Smith sank back. What an infernally offensive woman! Didn't she realise that he was practically keeping her husband in tobacco? As he glowered over her lack of breeding, Marie came through the hall and glanced quickly at him as she passed. There was a question in her look.

When he reached the entrance of the Schloss, he saw her walking slowly down the avenue. She was hatless; not going to Andernach, therefore, and she almost certainly knew that he was having tea in the smoking-room. His heart beat thickly. He glanced about—no one in sight. Bracing his shoulders, he strode down the avenue.

As he drew near she turned her head, and looked at him, but without a smile.

"Good afternoon, Fräulein Schreiner."

"Good afternoon, Mr Smith."

They walked side by side in silence. A track diverged from the road into a pine wood.

"This way!" he muttered, and clutched her hand.

It was cooler in the wood. The sunlight quivered on the ground in patches, and on her hair, her cheek, her neck. She gave a little cry and turned into his arms.

They kissed and kissed, she with sudden sobs, he between long breaths, and pressing his hands down her slender inwardcurving back.

The sound of steps drew near through the wood. Abruptly Miss Taylor and "W.J." came upon them.

"Oh!" cried Miss Taylor, and shook from head to foot. "Their passion! and oh, how beautiful they were, and the sun through the trees!"

"Good God!" screamed "W.J." "Again! And another girl!"

Smith released Marie, and turning saw "W.J." glaring, and by his side Miss Taylor, crimson with confusion.

"W.J." spun on his heel and plunged through the wood. Reaching the road he waited for Miss Taylor, and as soon as she appeared shouted at her.

"That young blackguard was kissing Louise Tecklenborg this morning. Good subject-matter for your next book. Gr—r—r!"

He paced furiously up the road.

"Oh dear, oh dear!" murmured Miss Taylor. "I'm very sorry to hear that. He really shouldn't. But oh, how sweet they looked!"

Her eyes followed "W.J." "Oh, poor Mr Gleg!" she cried.

"Why is he like that, why? . . . If he had a wife who understood him."

"W.J." went up to his room, rang the bell for hot water, pulled off his boots, and, huddled in a chair, sat glaring at the floor, sick with rancour and loathing. Miss Taylor! He grinned savagely—a proper companion for a contemptible old outcast. That infernal young coxcomb . . . life clasped in his arms—oh, the lines of her girl body! And the sun playing on them, and the air murmuring round them, and the scent of pines in their nostrils.

A groan twisted itself out of him.

The door opened, and the chambermaid, Martha, robust, ruddy, steeped in a slow but prodigious vitality, entered with the hot water.

"W.J." stared at her and began to breathe quickly.

"Martha!" he gasped.

She turned, in mild surprise, and saw him advancing on her with outstretched shaking hands.

"Na, na!" she said. "Don't be stupid, now!"

"I must! I must!" he cried. He tried to put his arms round her, but she shook him off with a vigorous wrench of her body.

To clasp her, to feel the warm life pulsing through her, to be sheltered from himself, for one moment, in her arms—that was all he desired. It must be, she must, she must grant him this. He tore a handful of notes out of his pocket-book.

"Take them! Take them!" he cried.

"Pfui!" she exclaimed. "You ought to be ashamed of yourself, you wicked old man!"

"I will not let you go!" He rushed at her, but she was strong and, in her resentment, active. Pushing his hands away she smacked his cheek smartly. He stepped back and she darted from the room.

CHAPTER SEVEN

THE HEAT OF the day discharged itself in a thunderstorm during dinner.

Mrs Walden, looking out of the window, perceived "W.J." pacing up and down.

"What on earth is the man doing?" she exclaimed, addressing Fleet, who had returned from Munich during the afternoon. "It's raining cats and dogs!"

"Perhaps our friend is fond of animals," suggested Fleet. He spoke habitually in a low, mournful tone, which contrasted effectively with the satirical tone of his remarks.

"Ha! Good!" cried the major. Bull guffawed. Mrs Walden gave a sharp laugh.

The Waldens and Bull were sufficiently intimidated by Fleet's brains to treat him with respect. He wrote, they had gathered, for the heavier monthlies—yet did not seem to live in a more rarefied atmosphere than themselves. This was gratifying, and as a return they affected a rather exaggerated relish for his wit; while Fleet accommodated his sarcasm to their understanding, and over-emphasised for their benefit the dislike which he felt for "W.J." and his pretensions to genius.

"W.J." came in when dinner was nearly over; wet through and hair disordered, but calmer after his violent exertion than might have been deduced from his appearance.

A bout with a chambermaid! Hardly a matter to take tragically. He had behaved very absurdly and frightened the poor fool. If she complained to the housekeeper a few words would put everything right—"A touch of the sun, Frau Dernberger . . . thunder in the air . . . I regret exceedingly . . . might I suggest a little *douceur* to the girl?"

After dinner "W.J." went straight to his room. The last twenty-four hours had been too full: he felt exhausted. Wet through, too. A hot bath was just the thing . . . hm, hm . . . simply ring the bell and order one. . . . No!

He washed in cold water, undressed, and got into bed.

Meanwhile, the Goddess Rumour was handling the history of the elderly libertine and the virtuous chambermaid with her usual command over publicity, and skill in amplification.

Before dinner Martha, smiling complacently, had put Frau Dernberger in possession of the actual facts which, as they did her credit in every particular, needed from her standpoint no elaboration. After dinner Rumour instructed Frau Dernberger to waylay Madame Tecklenborg with a foolish query about the number of blouses sent to the wash on the previous Monday by the Tecklenborg family. The query answered, Frau Dernberger disburdened herself of her news. "A fat lump like Martha, too!" she added, a stroke omitted by Martha, but dramatically right, as deepening the degradation of the villain.

Madame Tecklenborg hastened to the salon, and panted out the tale to a group made up of her two daughters, Smith and Miss Taylor. The effect of her version, which differed from Frau Dernberger's in laying emphasis on the victim's distress, was heightened by the reticence due, in the presence of strangers, to the innocence of her daughters. Before the imagination of her listeners there rose up the unequivocal outline of a satyr.

Smith and Miss Taylor, who had a clue to the cause of "W.J.'s" outbreak, avoided each other's eyes and looked embarrassed.

"Such a creature needs a wife to keep him in order," moralised Madame Tecklenborg.

"He lacks character," said Louise. "It seems a common fault in those who read much and have few responsibilities. In such cases it is best to say nothing and choose other friends." She looked calmly at Smith, who felt the force of her words and blushed. The cold firm sentences filled him with respect for the redoubtable girl who uttered them, quenching at the same time any lingering tenderness.

Hilda made no comment on her mother's story, but her eyes gleamed, and she looked across the salon at the others who were playing bridge. She determined to wait up. It would be worth it.

Play ceased shortly after eleven, and Hilda hurried over to Mrs Walden, whom she drew aside. She had not over-estimated the interest of her news.

"The disgusting creature!" cried Mrs Walden. "Fred, Mr Fleet, Victor, do listen! That nasty old thing 'W.J.' . . ."

"Infernal blackguard!" exclaimed the major, as Mrs Walden concluded with "the poor girl has had fit after fit of hysterics. The doctor has been with her the whole evening."

Bull had blown hard throughout the narrative, "Good God!" he now ejaculated. "Martha!" . . . "Martha!" . . . puff, puff . . . "Good God!"

His reaction to the outrage clearly differed from that or the others; but they were too much engrossed to bother about Bull's reactions; and he, on his side, did not care to obtrude a purely personal view of the situation.

"Something's got to be done about this," said Walden. "We've stood Gleg long enough. The fellow's impossible, utterly 'bunda.' Drunk and damnably insulting last night, barges people about on the public thoroughfares, damn him, and now this! What are we going to do about it?"

"Perhaps Martha might be induced to make an honest man of him," suggested Fleet, but the remark fell flat. It was out of place. In the nerve-wearing boredom of Schloss Bardenstein, the tonic of moral indignation was exquisitely acceptable. The Waldens, Hilda, and Bull, too, were determined to savour each drop of it to the full.

At last, after the incident had been traversed a score of times, and every penalty from a prosecution in the courts to an immersion in the lake suggested and examined, they separated, still glowing, for the night. Fleet alone had not caught the infection; but not caring to spoil sport he kept quiet, going up to bed filled with distaste for himself and everyone else.

One of the minor tribulations of Schloss Bardenstein, and the subject of many of the messages conveyed by Smith to Frau Dernberger, was the rat-a-tat-tat with which Martha roused the Schloss inmates each morning. The Waldens and Fleet were especially bitter on this point, and Bull had at first shared their resentment; but of late Martha had accorded him preferential treatment, tweaking his nose gently, or in some other playful fashion wooing him to wakefulness; an informal private arrangement which Bull had not communicated to Fleet or the Waldens.

Martha's devil's tattoo on the following morning, a crude but searching comment on their sympathetic distress of the night before, galled the Waldens to speechless frenzy. Mrs. Walden sat up in bed and opened her mouth, but whatever she said could not but dissipate beyond recovery the emotional atmosphere of the previous evening. She sank back.

Fleet, another victim, finding Walden at breakfast, was less reticent.

"Singular powers of recuperation our Martha possesses," he murmured. "A very formidable Lucrece for a Tarquin of 'W.J.'s' unimpressive physique to trifle with. By the way, has anyone seen 'W.J.'? Is he still extant?"

"I neither know nor care where Gleg is," snapped Major Walden. "Martha's recuperative powers, as you call them, don't alter the fact that the fellow's a criminal blackguard."

"Possibly not. But they may have some bearing on the extent of his criminality."

The rest of the meal passed in silence, and the major left the table in a bad humour. Fleet was devilish witty, no doubt, but there were times when wit was in infernal bad taste.

Bull was not yet down. Mrs Walden always breakfasted in bed. The major seemed to himself bereft of all support in the vendetta against "W.J.", inaugurated so enthusiastically the night before.

Hilda, sitting at the other end of the table, noted the effect of Fleet's levity on the major. Last night's excitement had been to her taste, and she was no less annoyed than the major with Fleet.

Could she not have a talk with the major? Smoothing back her hair with her lean brown fingers, and wiping her face with a pocket handkerchief, she stepped across the hall to the smoking-room, opened the door and looked in.

"Oh, Mr Smith is not here!" she exclaimed.

The major jumped up, and they stood looking at each other for a few moments.

"I thought Mr Smith was here." She turned to go. The major felt a dryness in his throat.

"I say . . . er, Hilda!"

"Yes, Major Walden."

Mrs Walden called her Hilda, but the major rarely and with difficulty and hitherto only in his wife's presence.

"Won't I do as well as Smith, Hilda?" This time he lingered over her name, and smiled ingratiatingly.

She returned his smile, but said nothing.

"What about a cigarette, Hilda?" He held out his case.

"I do not think I ought to stay. Ladies must not come into a smoking-room." She smiled.

"Nonsense, nonsense! Your mother won't smack you, will she? Too old to be smacked!"

His eye held hers. They both coloured.

"If she threatens, I'll offer to smack you for her. Eh, Hilda? I wouldn't hurt. Smack you nice and gently!"

They had moved within reach of each other. He clasped her wrist and patted her back. "Smack you like that, what!"

She tried to disengage her wrist. His grasp tightened and he leaned towards her.

"No! No!" she strained from him, and averted her face. "Please!"

His arms were round her waist, and he buried his face in her hair.

"No! No! Your wife, Major Walden!"

Placing a hand on her cheek, he forced her face round, and pressed his mouth to hers. Her struggles relaxed, ceased. She flung her arms round his neck.

Her ardour withered his. His heart sank at the fury of her response. "Better be careful," he murmured, and backing out of her embrace, seated himself on the edge of a table. Her narrowed eyes, the long breaths she drew, her hands hanging limply by her sides, frightened the major.

He lit a cigarette, and laughed nervously.

"Pull yourself together, Hilda! Fleet may come in at any moment!"

She started, and began to smooth her hair and dress.

The major looked at her coldly. She was no beauty, by God! It was the difficulty, he realised, not the girl that had attracted him. "We'd better forget all about this," he said, curtly. Hilda was silent.

"You're a sportsman, Hilda," he said, softening his voice. "You understand."

"I understand that you despise me."

"Despise you! Good God, my dear girl, have I behaved as if I despised you?"

"Yes!"

The major was desperate. This was not an occasion for half-hearted rhetoric.

"Hilda, it's just because you're so infernally attractive that we've got to drop it. Won't you help me?"

She looked searchingly at him. His genuine alarm furnished forth a convincing enough expression of anguish.

"I understand," she said, and gave him her hand, which he raised gently to his lips. They were silent for a time.

"It's rather funny after Mr Gleg last night," she said.

"Dash it, Hilda!" expostulated the major, but with a smile. The danger had passed, and in his relief he was willing to prolong the situation a little. Hilda smiled back.

"The comparison is not quite fair, is it?" she said.

"I should say not!"

"A chambermaid, who was not even willing!"

"Yes, by God. I don't pretend to be a saint, but there are some things I draw the line at."

"Oh, you men are all alike. You think no one can resist your beautiful eyes. I am sure if I looked twice at Mr Gleg he would think I loved him."

"Good God, what an idea! Really, my dear girl!"

"It would be quite amusing, would it not? A punishment for him. He would be so angry when I laughed at him!"

"You mean, make him think you were really bitten by him? But the fellow's so revolting. Besides, you don't know what you might let yourself in for."

"Oh, I can manage him! A few sighs, a little pity for his genius, like Miss Taylor and Cyril Smith. Or impertinence—they like it at that age. Believe me, it would not be difficult. There would be a grand scene. He would fall on his knees, and declare his love. A fine comedy!" Her eyes gleamed and she writhed her body.

"I believe you've devil enough to do it, by God! And it would serve the blighter right—seems to think he's bought the place—gets drunk and rows us all like a bargee one day, and makes violent love to a chambermaid the next. And we sit down under it. The blighter needs touching up. It's a warm scheme. I like it. But where do I come in?"

"Let me think a minute." Hilda went to the window and looked out.

"Yes," she said at last. "Be near the music-room at half-past six this evening—perhaps you might bring Mr Bull, too? The others will be dressing then. Do not speak to me, or even recognise me if we meet in the hall. But as soon as you hear me playing you can come along, and open the door a little." She laughed. "Good morning, Major Walden!" She made a low curtsy and swept out of the room, already the fascinating temptress. Nature, she was angrily aware, had not designed her for this part, nor could she have sustained it once in a thousand times. But this was the thousandth time. "W.J." was an easy victim, and her faculties were screwed to the highest pitch by the desire to astonish the major with the power, brilliance and seduction of her acting. Her malice against "W.J.", the object of Smith's and Miss Taylor's tedious admiration, was sharpened by the consciousness that the major's coldness was not merely the effect of prudence. The humiliation of "W.J." would be a double triumph.

"Weird girl!" reflected the major, as the door closed. "Damned clever ... rather startling ... Well, that's that!" He rang the bell and ordered a whisky.

"W.J." was sitting by the lake. Neither Miss Taylor nor Smith had been near him during the day, and it was now after six. He supposed that they had heard about his stupidity with Martha. Depression and a feeling of uneasiness weighed on him. He shrank from getting up and going back to the Schloss for dinner. They would look at him and sneer and whisper. They were all against him. They hated and despised him. He must leave, go to France, Italy, anywhere, it didn't much matter where.

"Well, Mr Gleg?"

"W.J." looked up with a start. Hilda was standing on the path, facing him with a quizzical glance.

"What do you want?" snapped "W.J."

He did not like and never had liked the look of the girl.

"What do I want? Why, politeness, Mr Gleg!"

"The devil you do! And d'you expect to get it from me?"

"In time, Mr Gleg."

"Oh!" "W.J." was taken aback. He looked more closely at Hilda. The girl had vitality and assurance. What did she want with him?

"Oh, I'm tired of them all up there," she burst out. "Fools and hypocrites! They speak of nothing but you and Martha. But you, too, are stupid, Mr Gleg. Oh, I know of your writings! I hear of them at every meal. But can you find no better confidants than a silly boy and an old maid? And must you turn for affection to a fat chambermaid? You geniuses! Have you no eyes?"

"W.J." stared at her, amazed. She spoke with passionate resentment, and resentment was the emotion he felt and sympathised with most easily. So she was angry at being overlooked? He interested her, did he?

"But I am a fool to talk like this." She turned on her heel.

"Don't go!" exclaimed "W.J."

"I have my music to practise—half an hour before I dress for dinner."

"I am going back, too."

Hilda said nothing. They climbed in single file up to the Schloss. At the top of the track Hilda turned to "W.J."

"Please forget what I have said, Mr Gleg," she said, gently.

She looked at him for a moment with a deep tenderness in her regard.

"Where do you practise?" he asked, huskily.

"In the music-room."

"May I sit there? You play beautifully. It will soothe me. I am tired."

"But certainly!" she smiled, and it seemed to him that his previous opinion of her looks had been quite superficial and obtuse.

They passed Walden in the hall, and went straight to the music-room, which was at the end of a passage on the ground floor of the eastern wing of the Schloss.

A few minutes later Walden, Bull and Fleet approached the music-room. Walden had dug the other two out of the smoking-room to come along and see "W.J.'s" leg properly pulled, and Bull with enthusiasm, Fleet reluctantly, were following him, all three treading cautiously.

As they went down the passage, a languorous air was being played. Walden grasped the door handle and opened the door a few inches with extreme care. "W.J." was turning over the music for Hilda. His fingers were trembling, his lips moving. Hilda raised her face towards him from time to time, and gazed at him with troubled eyes.

"By God, she does it well!" thought the major. Bull, looking over the major's shoulder, strangled a guffaw. Fleet leaned against the wall of the passage and yawned, displeased at being there, yet unable to go away.

"Hilda!" cried "W.J.", and putting his arm round her shoulders bent down to kiss her. She shook him off and jumped up.

"Come in, Major," she cried. "Come in!" and broke into peals of laughter.

Major Walden threw the door open and burst in, followed by Bull and Fleet. Hilda, her arms akimbo, surveyed "W.J." with a malice half histrionic, half real. A sense of kinship in unattractiveness worked in her, and the malice swelled to rage and broke in vituperation.

"Oh, you funny, funny little man!" she cried. "You thought I was conquered by your beautiful eyes, did you? How dare you try your tricks on a girl like me? Keep them for your chambermaids, if any chambermaid will look at you."

She advanced on him and raised her hands as if to strike.

"You would try to kiss me! You horrible old man!" Her hands fell. "Bah! I cannot touch you!"

"W.J." was very pale and beads of sweat gathered on his forehead. With bent arm shielding his face he backed away from her. Fleet ran forward, took his other arm, and led him out of the room.

"Feeling all right?" he asked.

"Thanks, thanks! Let me go, please!"

Fleet released his grip, and "W.J." shambled down the passage and disappeared. Returning to the room, Fleet looked at Hilda in silence. Bull, embarrassed, was puffing gently. Walden wore a foolish grin. Hilda, spent and frightened, leant against the piano, trying to outstare Fleet.

"You . . ." Fleet's lips seemed to be essaying the second letter of the alphabet. Finally, he shrugged his shoulders, and turning left the room.

CHAPTER EIGHT

THE NEXT MORNING, while Smith was dressing, Fleet came in and asked him to accompany him to Frau Dernberger. He was tired of Schloss Bardenstein, he said, and proposed to leave the next morning. Smith expressing surprise, Fleet related with plain vigour the scene in the music-room, discarding his usual mannerisms for the moment. The Schloss, he went on, resuming his plaintive style of talk, had gone bad. He, Fleet, objected to the sex-motif in fiction, and liked it still less in life, and it seemed to have become dominant at the Schloss.

"You, Smith," he said, "have been under my observation of late in this matter, and I am not, speaking as a consultant, quite satisfied with you; and there are other cases of a graver nature. Walden's relations with that poisonous young creature are suspect. Mrs Walden was not amused by yesterday's incident. She was curious about the origin of the plot, and Walden's replies were irrelevant and obscure. Then there is Bull. I am not very easy about his occasional trips to Munich. Bull, I fancy, might cry with Tennyson's Galahad:

> I never felt the kiss of love,
> Nor maiden's hand in mine.

And last of all we have our erratic, impolitic, uncalculating 'W.J.'"

"Poor old chap!" cried Smith. "And he really has genius!"

Fleet shrugged his shoulders. "I shall believe in his genius when he produces something with genius in it," he said shortly.

They went along to Frau Dernberger, who was distressed by Fleet's decision. "The second in one morning!" she cried, and explained that Mr Gleg was leaving for Munich by the 11.20. She had already packed for him. "It is strictly forbidden to me by Herr Melmoth," she went on, "to return any of this month's payment. Mr Gleg was very nice about it. He was so gentle, he made no talk about it at all."

Smith translated Frau Dernberger.

"Yes, it would be strictly forbidden," said Fleet. "Well, I shall have a chat with Crumpet on my return. Don't bother the poor woman. It's not her fault."

Smith and Miss Taylor were alone at breakfast. He told her about the practical joke and that "W.J." was leaving by the 11.20. Miss Taylor was too much distressed to say anything, and soon left the table.

After breakfast, Smith went in search of "W.J." He was very sorry that "W.J." was leaving, and vaguely remorseful. Poor old buffer, he thought, what a dickens of a time he's had!

"W.J." was not at his usual seat, but Smith found him at last by the lake.

The expression on "W.J.'s" face, as he turned at Smith's approach, surprised the youth by its serenity. But "W.J." looked old; for the first time, Smith realised. The angry vitality which had informed every word and movement was gone.

"I'm awfully sorry you're leaving, Mr Gleg," blurted Smith.

"W.J." nodded.

The tears and rage and convulsions of the night hours had worn him out, leaving him in a happy lassitude; his mood still coloured by the fading beauty of a moment at daybreak.

He had woken up with a start, and stumbled half asleep to the window. To his senses, refined by exhaustion, the dawn landscape revealed itself as the world which he had always divined behind the heat and confusion of the common hours, and desired so terribly. Fearing the spell might break if he looked too long, he crept back to bed filled with the assurance of an immortality awaiting him among the hills and waters of that bright and silent land, lying out there, beyond the darkness of his room.

"You're going by the 11.20, aren't you, sir?" said Smith.

"W.J." roused himself. "Yes," he said. "I had better be getting along. They are sending the luggage down."

"May I come with you?"

"Certainly, certainly."

At this moment Miss Taylor emerged from the track that connected Schloss Bardenstein with the lake, and came running along the path. She was carrying an envelope which she thrust into "W .J.'s" hand.

"Good-bye," she gasped. "A pleasure and a privilege!—to help in publication. Good-bye!"

Before "W.J." could say anything she turned and disappeared up the track.

The envelope contained a cheque for £25.

"W.J." took out his pocket-book, folded the cheque, and put it carefully in.

"I have been watching the reflection of that poplar in the lake," he said, as he and Smith set off—"It is very beautiful." After a short silence he added—"A small dog passed me just now. Large ears. It sneezed—utchoo!—very quaint and charming." Nothing further was said during the walk. On arriving at the station, Smith secured a corner seat for "W.J." and saw to the registration of his luggage.

"Good-bye, Smith," said "W.J." leaning out of the window. The look of age and exhaustion was already passing. 'Tell Miss Taylor it's all over, rage, unrest, division within, everything. I'll send her my book, quite soon, it won't take me long now. Thank her and bless her from me, Smith." The train began to move. "I won't write now, tell her to wait for the book, I can always find her through her publishers. Good-bye, Smith, good-bye."

"Good-bye, Mr Gleg."

The train moved on. "W.J." leant from the window and waved his hand. Tears came into Smith's eyes. Poor old "W.J."—how happy he looked at last.

Four days later a telegram arrived for Smith. It ran—"Delighted if you would meet the 6.15 from Munich am arriving on tour of inspection tell no one—Melmoth Managing Director Continental Comfort."

Smith and Miss Taylor walked down to Andernach together. It was agreed, as the telegram was theoretically private, that Miss Taylor should leave Smith at the station.

"Just a week to-day since I arrived and you met me," said Miss

Taylor, as they approached the little wood-built station. "What years it seems!" She sighed. The memory of "W.J." was always with her. Where was he now, she wondered; had he settled down comfortably, was he working well and easily?

"Perhaps Mr Melmoth has news of Mr Gleg," she murmured. "Will you ask him, please? I'd better leave you now."

"Well, walk back slowly," Smith suggested. "Crumpet and I'll catch you up. There's the train!"

Melmoth was out of the train before it had come to a stand-still. He wore a pearl-grey suit of woollen whipcord, a light overcoat to match, and straw hat. A neat bow-tie completed the effect of a trim and business-like personage; while the large horn spectacles lifted the total impression above the merely humdrum.

"Ah! God is good to me once more," he cried, catching sight of Smith. Dropping a heavy portmanteau, he advanced and clasped Smith's hand. "All well?" he asked. "Everyone in the arbour happy?"

"I wouldn't go as far as that," said Smith, smiling.

"Not? What's happened? Tell me!"

"Oh, nothing terrible. No murders yet."

Melmoth laughed. "I praise God daily for my sense of humour," he said. "You have it, too. Take everything else from me, but leave me my sense of humour. The car is here, I suppose?"

"No, it isn't. Your telegram said 'tell no one.' We can take a carriage up, or send down for your bag."

"Let me think! There is a train to Munich at seven-twelve." He clasped his head with both hands; then shot into the waiting-room, and presently emerged without his portmanteau.

"The stationmaster is sitting on it," he explained. "I have refreshed his spirit mightily with certain indications about the future of Continental Comfort in this quarter of the globe. But let us walk towards Schloss Bardenstein and explore the situation."

They set off, and Melmoth continued—"The position is this. I have not a moment to spare—an urgent appointment in Munich to-night. On the other hand it might be well and wise to come back with you for the purpose of registering mutual goodwill and sympathy all round. Tell me: what am I to do? I place myself in your hands. Your 'aura' pleases me. You may remember I told you so in London."

"Well, if you've such an important engagement, I don't see that there's much point in wasting a night at the Schloss. As to registering goodwill, I don't think you'll get much assistance from Walden, at any rate."

"Walden! I remember him. A nasty bit of work. His 'aura' filled me with dismay. Light green with pink spots."

"Why, damn it, you told me in London that I would find him a charming fellow; the best Army type, you said."

"No, Smith, I couldn't have said that, because my impression of him was the exact opposite. But what of the Baron?"

"Oh, he left ages ago! Surely you knew that!"

"He hasn't returned then?"

"No."

"Strange! He wrote me he was returning this week."

"You're pretty quick," said Smith, and Melmoth, after a moment's indecision, laughed.

"I suppose you know Fleet's cleared out," said Smith.

"Fleet! Cleared out! How God makes me suffer! But I distrusted Fleet. A badly introverted 'aura.' All fishhooks. No possibilities of expansion."

"Gleg's cleared out, too."

"Gleg? Of course—that's the fellow's name. I saw him last night in Munich. An awkward piece of work, cramp in the pit of his spiritual stomach. But I thought he was just up for the night. Cleared out, too! How God persecutes me!"

"You saw Gleg, did you? One moment, Miss Taylor!"

Miss Taylor, who was a little distance ahead, turned round and waited till they came up.

Melmoth took Miss Taylor's hand and scrutinised her piercingly. "This air has worked wonders with you," he said, at last.

"Mr Melmoth," Smith interrupted, "saw Mr Gleg last night in Munich. Tell us about him, Melmoth. How was he looking?"

Melmoth halted. "Is he a particular friend of either of you?" he asked, impressively.

Miss Taylor gave a frightened gasp, but Smith answered

lightly—"Oh, no! but we're interested in him. Quite a character."

"Good!" said Melmoth. "Miss Taylor, you are a woman of the world. The story is a simple one, and can be simply told. I saw Gleg last night in a Munich café. I recognised him, but couldn't for my life put a name to him, and I doubt if he could have put a name to himself. Tight as a Tonga boy.[1] He was flanked by a brace of venal hags who were absorbing champagne at maximum velocity. A third speedily blew along and, after some sultry back-chat with her colleagues, staked out a claim and ordered up what was left of the cellar.

"The old ruin made a stout attempt at festive expansion, bit one of 'em in the arm, tried a song, and handed out wads of notes all round. After which he collapsed, and when they woke him up to pay the bill, went right off the deep end, registering loathing of them and much private remorse. Then *they* hit the ceiling, and, having gutted him completely, urged the waiter to quod the old boy for ordering stuff without cash to back his requisitions. At which stage I got busy, put the waiter wise, and organised a forced levy. When it was all over, bar the shouting which is probably still going strong, I offered to escort our friend to his bower; whereupon he woke up for the second time, damned me heartily, and staggered off."

"Oh, Lord!" cried Smith. "Poor old chap! And I thought he was really going to turn over a new leaf. What an awful pity! And the worst of it is he really has got genius."

The word "genius" recalled Melmoth to himself. Business, he told Smith, was not his real line. Of course, he had a *flair* for it. His trouble was that there didn't seem to be anything he hadn't got a *flair* for. But Nature had intended him, primarily, for a singer. Smith was inattentive, and at last Melmoth broke off.

"Well!" he said. "I'll leave you. You are right. It would be a waste of time to spend a night here."

"You're sure there's a train back at seven-twelve?" Smith queried.

"If my feelings do not betray me."

[1] The Black Boys of Tonga were noted for their sustained intemperance in the line, and their spasmodic ferocity behind it.

He shook hands with Miss Taylor and Smith, expressed himself at ease about the general situation, hoped he would hear
from them repeatedly, and recommending Touraine, when if
ever they should weary of Bavaria, turned and left them, carolling
as he strode down the road:

> Wenn ich früh im Garten geh'
> In meinem grünen Hut,
> Dann ist mein erster Gedanke
> Was wohl der Liebste tut.

"Awfully amusing fellow, and really not a bad sort," said
Smith, glancing at Miss Taylor furtively.

Miss Taylor was very pale. "The swine!" thought Smith.
"To spend her money like that! Genius or no genius." But
he did not care to say anything. She looked too cut up; and besides
she would probably stick up for Gleg.

As they drew near the castle, Smith saw old Frau Schreiner
enjoying the warm evening on her bench by the main entrance.

Smith thought of them all: "W.J." and Miss Taylor, Louise,
Hilda, the Waldens, Fleet, even Bull, and looked again at the
old woman, wrinkled and placid.

"She's well out of it!" he muttered.

Marie came out to warn her grandmother that it was time to
go in—the sun had nearly set. Miss Taylor hurried past them into
the castle.

"By the lake at nine?" whispered Smith. Marie nodded, giving
her arm to the old woman, who leaned heavily on it.

Smith, drawing back to let them pass in, was moved by the
contrast of age and youth.

"Poor old thing!" thought Smith.

Two Poems

After A. E. Housman

1

WHAT, still alive at twenty-two,
A clean, upstanding chap like you?
Sure, if your throat 'tis hard to slit,
Slit your girl's, and swing for it.

Like enough, you won't be glad,
When they come to hang you, lad:
But bacon's not the only thing
That's cured by hanging from a string.

So, when the spilt ink of the night
Spreads o'er the blotting-pad of light,
Lads whose job is still to do
Shall whet their knives, and think of you.

2

'Tis Summer Time on Bredon,
   And now the farmers swear:
The cattle rise and listen
   In valleys far and near,
And blush at what they hear.

But when the mists in autumn
   On Bredon top are thick,
And happy hymns of farmers
   Go up from fold and rick,
The cattle then are sick.

In a Charabanc

(Robert Browning's version of A. E. Housman's
"Bredon Hill.")

A FINE hill that, sir! Roomy spot
   To fodder sheep, you say?
That's how it strikes you? Well, why not?
   You see it first to-day.

But I . . . your pardon whilst I blow.
   Spring brings the old catarrh.
My snuffling discommodes you? No?
   Thank you—how kind you are!

That hill, sir, has a boldish bluff.
   You'd hardly think the crest
Affords a level couch enough
   For panting folk to rest.

Our Sunday couch one spring. Church bells
   Pealed useless from the plain,
And steeples, jumped from hidden dells,
   Solicited in vain.

They buried her that winter. Springs
   Hurt since. There's no excuse
Pestering strangers with such things.
   May I? Catarrh's the deuce.

From

The Table of Truth
(1933)

Clubs are Trumps

(A Sequel to "The Purity of the Turf.")

After P. G. Wodehouse[1]

[NOTE.—In "The Purity of the Turf," Bertie Wooster tells how Steggles, who is at Twing Vicarage as a member of the Reverend Heppenstall's reading-party, makes a book on the Twing village sports. Guided by Jeeves, Bertie's famous valet, Bertie and his friend, Bingo Little, both of whom are staying with Lord Wickhammersley at Twing Hall, place various bets with Steggles. There is foul play by Steggles, and a countermove from Jeeves, which leaves Steggles heavily in debt over Prudence Baxter, the unexpected winner of the Girls' Egg and Spoon Race.]

YOU'D HAVE THOUGHT that when, thanks to Jeeves's ready resource, that blighter Steggles came unstuck over the book he'd made on the Twing village sports, he'd have paid over to our little syndicate without a murmur. And been bally well grateful for the lesson, too. I mean to say, if ever Providence gave a young fellow in the morning of his life the straight tip that crime doesn't pay, Steggles got it when he stubbed his toe on a long-priced outsider like Prudence Baxter, after nobbling a couple of fliers like Harold, the page-boy, and Mrs Penworthy, the sack race speed fiend. And yet, by Jove, instead of weeping in pure thankfulness that he wasn't chipping flints on Dartmoor, the low hound—but there, what's the use of hotting one-self up over the frightful depths to which human nature sinks when it gets itself tied up inside a Steggles. I mean to say, punishment enough without other people rubbing it in. What I mean is, fancy always going about with a chap like Steggles, which is what a chap would bally well *have* to do if he was Steggles . . . where was I? Oh, yes

[1] For the theme of this story the author wishes to acknowledge a certain indebtedness to Shakespeare's *Othello*.

... I was saying you'd have thought Steggles would have paid over without a murmur; and that's what Bingo Little and I were thinking, too, when we bumped into the blighter the morning after the sports.

We were passing the Twing Arms when we met him, being engaged in shaking up the jolly old gastric juices before lunch with a smartish to-and-fro between the Hall and the village. And poor old Bingo was just beginning again on his scenario of what he proposed to do with his share of the winnings. I think I mentioned, didn't I, that he was tutoring old Wickhammersley's male heir at the moment, and the first item on his programme was to push that somewhat scaly infant into the ancestral pond, and then beat it due east for the metrop., complete with sack of gold.

So you can understand how it took him when he saw Steggles's face. He just stood there giving out a low whuffling noise, like a hedgehog at bay. Like one of those stories where the chappie in the dock looks at the foreman of the jury, and reads his doom slap off. I mean to say, no words needed. And I don't mind telling you I was shaken myself. But we Woosters are chilled steel in a crisis, and I handed the man Steggles a cheery "Hallo-allo-allo," which held him for a moment. Nonchalant bonhomie, if you know what I mean. Party of the first part standing by with easy grace while the party of the second part unbelts with a smile. Gentlemen all, in a word. And I daresay it might have worked, too, if that poor fish Bingo hadn't cracked under the strain, and wanted to know what the devil Steggles thought he was looking at.

"I'm memorizing the pair of you," said Steggles, with a slow, nasty smile. "Not that I like the job, but duty before pleasure, and when Scotland Yard wants your descriptions I'll be able to supply them."

At which Bingo unleashed a scream like a hyena having a tooth stopped. "So that's your game, is it?" he yelled. "You bally bilking bookie! I'll hound you off the Turf! I will, by Gad! I'll show you up at every race-meeting in the country. I'll——"

Altogether a painful scene, and, if you don't mind, I'll skip the details, never having been one of those chappies who get much juice out of the fouler aspects of human nature. The fact is, we weren't in a frightfully strong position when it came to menacing Steggles with a showup. To start with, we couldn't prove that it was Steggles who had jammed old Heppenstall's sermon amidships by dropping a beetle down young blighted Harold's back during evensong. And, anyway, as Steggles pointed out what action could Heppenstall take except hoofing him out of his reading party? And we didn't need Steggles's word for it that the old top was coaching him for cash and not for love. I mean to say, coaching Steggles for love!

So what with one thing and what with another our parley began to look as if it had blown a fuse out, and I was about to signal Bingo that the hour had struck to beetle off in silent scorn, when Steggles had the infernal crust to come back with a show-up of his own. Said that he proposed, in the interests of clean sport at Twing, to lay the facts about Jeeves's action in connection with the Girls' Egg and Spoon race before Lord Wickhammersley. Now the wheeze by which Jeeves had lifted Prudence Baxter into the proud position of Twing's leading egg-and-spooner undoubtedly displayed intelligence of a very ripe order. But, if looked at from the wrong angle, it might show a crack or two, and something seemed to tell me that if Steggles moved further in the matter old Wickhammersley would be handing me my hat right speedily, not to say eftsoons, and Bingo would be legging it due east with the imprint of the baronial boot on the seat of his pants.

You know those stories where a fiend in human shape keeps on worrying a blameless chappie who's got a foul deed in his past, and then one day something goes crack in the blameless chappie's bean, and he reaches for the meat-axe and soaks the fiend good and proper. Well, read Steggles for the fiend in human shape, and Bertie Wooster for the blameless chappie, and you've got the posish when Steggles stopped talking measured to a hair. Except that there wasn't a meat-axe handy. So there was nothing to do but stand there emitting lofty scorn, while privately wishing that the good old Wooster pride would let up for a moment so that I could ask the blighter to call the dog off.

And then Steggles raised his hat. Funny the bally rot that zips through under the hair when something unexpected happens. I mean to say, I actually thought it was remorse. Uncovering in shame, and all that sort of thing. Then I heard a fizzing noise on my right. Somehow I knew what it was without looking, and, good enough, when I turned round there was Bingo, the human celluloid, in flames again.

The couple to whom Steggles, imitating the procedure customary among gentlemen, had just raised his hat, were rather out of the ordinary for Twing. The man especially. One of those swarthy sheik-like chappies, you know. Untamed, if you get me. A word and a blow, on off days. Otherwise just a blow. Altogether a bit under measure as a boon companion, though doubtless a dashed useful fellow to keep in front of one in a mix-up with Fuzzy-Wuzzies. As for the girl with him, I'm bound to admit that this time there really was some excuse for Bingo. Rippling gold hair, you know, and large blue eyes with a sort of soft appealing look as if she was flashing a chappie a message, and hoped he'd understand. Nice figure, too, willowy, and all that. And hands a fellow wouldn't mind stroking.

Well, they passed on, faded down the village street, and I was looking after them with a kind of empty feeling when I heard Steggles saying: "I don't know which of you it was. But one of you has made a hit. I wonder she had the nerve to give a glad eye like that. Lucky her husband didn't see it."

"That's a bally rotten remark," I cried with some heat. "She just gave me a friendly smile, and only a bally pot of poison like you would——"

A nasty tearing sound on my right cut me short. It was Bingo, trying out a scornful laugh. "Gave *you* a friendly smile!" the poor prune croaked. "That's ripe. *You!* My hat!" and he turned to Steggles, fawning loathsomely. "I say, Steggles," he babbled, "who is she, Steggles? What's her name, Steggles? Did you say that chap was her husband? Where are they staying, Steggles? Who is he?"

I had a dashed good mind to walk straight off. A dashed good mind, by Jove!

"It's General Raikes," said Steggles. "Heppenstall's cousin. The old boy's putting Raikes and his wife up at the Vicarage for a week or so."

"Heppenstall's cousin? Why, the fellow's a Dago. A bally Dago!"

"A touch of the tar-brush. Grandfather married a Creole. But I don't advise you to remind him of it. He's a fizzer."

"Is she——Steggles, old son, is she h-happy with him?"

I didn't wait for any more. Heel and toe at five m.p.h. to the Hall, and the deaf ear for Bingo babbling by my side. Outraged, by Jove! And then some.

Jeeves received the news about Steggles with his usual calm. "I had anticipated something of the kind, sir," was all he said.

"But, dash it," I cried, "it's a heavy loss!"

"Not a loss, if you will pardon the correction, sir. As I read the situation, no money is passing in either direction between you and Mr Steggles."

"In other words, a bally wash-out all round."

Jeeves inclined his head.

"But if the blighter stirs things up with Lord Wickhammersley? What-ho for the young master then, eh, Jeeves?"

"I should be disposed to regard such an eventuality as a very remote one, sir."

"Bluff, eh?"

"An ebullition of chagrin, sir. Understandable in the circumstances."

"Well, I hope you're right. Jeeves?"

"Yes, sir."

"Know anything about General Raikes?"

"May I enquire, sir, if you are referring to the Reverend Heppenstall's cousin?"

"That's the chappie."

"I understand, sir, from such information about the gentleman as has come my way, that his career in the army has given uniform satisfaction."

"Happen to know his wife's name?"

"Yes, sir."

"Well, what is it?"

"Mrs Raikes, sir."

I looked the fellow square in the centre of the eyeball. A single flicker and I'd have been through him like tissue paper. Not a hope, of course. But I wasn't jolly well going to leave it at that, so, bracing myself a bit, I put it to him straight.

"Jeeves, what's her Christian name?"

"Mrs Raikes's full name is Mrs Violet Raikes. Would you require anything further at the moment, sir?"

"No, I bally well wouldn't."

"Very good, sir."

Bingo and I didn't see much of each other for the next few days. Tension and all that. So I used to swing a solitary shoe Twing-wards, feeling somewhat mouldy, and rather hoping I'd get a sight of Mrs Raikes. Not that I had designs, or any bally rot of that sort. I've never been one of those chappies who spend their days doing a bit of no good to the sacred bond and what-not. As a matter of fact, even if I wanted to, I wouldn't be much of a hit as a snake in the matrimonial grass. Women rather frighten me, especially pretty ones. I sort of go unstitched when they smile at me. The jolly old legs try to take cover behind each other, if you know what I mean. And I make roopy noises with the throat, not unlike the sea lions at the Zoo when they go whooshing round as sick as dammit to think what they're missing at the North Pole. You may say it was funny I should want to see Mrs Raikes again, if it was going to take me like that. If so, it only shows what a bally lot you've got to learn about human nature.

Well, one afternoon I was hoofing it past the Vicarage, thinking how jolly it would be if Mrs Raikes suddenly popped out. It was one of those hot summer days when there's a sort of humming all round one, as if about a million bees and things were sleeping it off after a heavy lunch. Soothing, you know. I slowed down a bit as I passed the Vicarage gate, and peered up the gravel drive, thinking how bally all right it would be if Mrs Raikes should happen to come round the bend. Which made it all the more of a jar when Bingo suddenly curved into view, came down the straight in half a dozen bounds, did a handspring over the gate, and shot up the road towards the Hall. Before I could begin to wonder what it all meant, General Raikes had taken the straight in one bound under Bingo's, and vanished in a cloud of dust. And at the end of the procession came Steggles, moving with comparative languor. As soon as he saw me, he slowed down to a walk. "Anyone passed this way?" he asked with a foul leer.

"Yes, there bally well has," I yelled, "and you bally well know it! I don't know what's up, but whatever it is, you're in it, you low wart!"

White-hot, by Jove! But wasted, of course. The blighter just leaned on the gate, and looked thoughtfully up the road.

"They ought to have reached the Hall by now," he said. "I'll bet Bingo's been running straight for once. Pity there aren't any gentlemen in these parts. It might have been rather interesting to make a book on the result. But, of course, with all these crooks about——"

"You'll hear from me later," I shouted, and legged it up the road. Chump or not, Bingo was my pal.

The Hall looked devilish peaceful and deserted as I charged up the avenue. A general absence of retainers and what not, due no doubt to old Wickhammersley being in the next county for the day, at one of those Boy Scout jamborees. Not a soul about as I sped upstairs. For a moment I was afraid that I'd been wrong to bank on Bingo's homing instinct. The next moment a frightful hammering sound, fighting for first place with a maddened roar, told me I needn't worry.

Bingo had been parked in a somewhat distant wing, and as I drew near I let out a yell. More by way of introducing myself than in any unfriendly spirit. The hammering stopped dead, likewise the roar, and when I rounded the last corner there was the General, a whacking big club at the ready, crouching for a spring.

"Hullo-ullo-ullo! What! What! What!" I babbled. Matey, you know.

The General gave a low growl. You know, they say a chappie's

whole life whizzes past him in a flash when he's drowning. Well,
it wasn't quite as bad as that with me, but as the club went back
I distinctly remembered a hymn I used to prattle at nurse's knee,
beginning "Now I lay me down to sleep."

While I was waiting for the end, eyes closed and general
attitude one of prayerful meditation, I heard a sort of a snort.
Hitching the left eyelid up a peg, I peeped out and there was the
General goofing at something behind me. "Jeeves!" he murmured. "Good old Jeeves, by Gad!"

"Thank you, sir. I trust you are in good health, sir." A flicker,
a kind of faint stir in the air, and Jeeves was by the General's side.

"If you will pardon the liberty, sir." Jeeves's hand floated over
the General's hair, collecting a twig, a couple of leaves and a
large spider, which was looking pretty peaceful. I remember
wondering if it was dead or just stunned.

"Thanks, Jeeves. Efficient as ever. We must have a pow-wow.
But," and the General began to blow out again, "I've got a job of
work to do first." And up went the club.

"Stop him, Jeeves!" Bingo yelled from the other side of the
door. "It's all a bally mistake, Jeeves! It's that hound Steggles!
Call him off, Jeeves! I can explain. I swear I can explain."

"If you have no objection, sir," murmured Jeeves, resting the
club against the wall.

"But, Jeeves! Damn it, man! Look at that!"

The General opened his left fist, uncovering a bit of paper.
"Take it! Look at it! Dropped outside my room! Is it that young
blackguard's writing, or is it not? Show it to that blithering
waster behind you, and tell him to deny his friend's writing if he
dares!"

Jeeves smoothed the paper out. Feeling it was more or less
expected of me, I slithered forward and bent over the document
with an air of zeal.

"Read it out, Jeeves! Dammit, read it out, man!" the General
bawled.

"Very good, sir. The contents are as follows: 'Don't worry,
Vi. I'll settle with Steggles. Toujours Bingo.'"

"Toujours Bingo! Jeeves, I knew her a year before I called her by her Christian name, and this post-war pup——! What does it mean, Jeeves? What does it mean? Youth to youth, eh? eh? But I'm not old, Jeeves! Jeeves, I'm not old! No, by Gad, she took me with her eyes open, and, by Gad——"

"Thank you, sir." And Jeeves rested the club against the wall again. "There can be no question, sir," he rippled on, "that this document is a forgery. Mr Little does not form his B's in this manner. And the downward stroke in the capital V is too heavy. There are other indications with which, suggestive though they are, I need not trouble you at the moment."

"Then who the——"

"If you would be so very obliging, sir, as to afford Mr Little an opportunity of laying such facts as are within his knowledge before us, I have no doubt that we shall quickly arrive at the solution of the mystery."

"Have it as you like, man! Have it as you like!"

It took some doing, but at long last Bingo unbolted the door, nipping to the far side of the bed as the committee filed in. Proceedings were held up for a moment while Jeeves shimmered back into the corridor, bearing the club with him. Then Bingo began.

Boiled down, what it amounted to was that Steggles had lured Bingo into the Vicarage to play contract with Mrs Raikes. The poor egg had been there about five times. "Mrs Raikes and I always played together, Bertie, old man," he bleated. "Steggles said it ruined contract to swop partners, and Baynes, the other chap, agreed. A low hound Baynes, Bertie, old man. Another bally Steggles."

"Do you suggest, sir," barked the General, "that Mr Steggles and Mr Baynes are card-sharpers?"

"I don't bally well suggest anything else!"

Jeeves gave a faint cough. "I have heard, sir, from various sources that Mr Steggles is uniformly successful with the cards."

"Very well! Very well! But, sir," turning on Bingo, "the letter! Why did you run, sir, if it wasn't yours? Dammit, answer me that!"

"And why did you come at me with that bally club? I thought it better to explain later."

"Might I put a question to Mr Little, sir?" Jeeves bowed courteously to the General.

"Wk!"

"I thank you, sir. Mr Little, may I enquire if anything passed in writing between you and Mr Steggles?"

"Er—what do you mean? Er—one or two I.O.U.'s, of course. Which reminds me, by Jove, that's where that bally list of French words must have gone. It was on the back of one of them. For dictation to Wickhammersley's young hopeful, dash him! And I spent an hour sorting them out, too!"

"By Gad, Jeeves!" I burst forth. "I see it. That's how the low hound got Bingo's fist. Jeeves, you stand alone. I've said it before, and I say it again. Jeeves stands alone. Jeeves stands——"

"Will you stop, sir?"

"——alone." Dogged, by Gad!

The General threw me a "Pah!" and turned to Jeeves. "All highly ingenious, Jeeves, but——"

"Might I ask you to excuse me for a few minutes, sir? An idea has just occurred to me, which I confidently believe will convert supposition into certainty."

"Jeeves! I say, Jeeves!" Bingo yelped, but Jeeves had already faded from the room.

There was a kind of a heavy silence after he'd left us. Brooding, you know. Being more or less out of the ring myself, I thought it might be a good wheeze to help things along with a bit of patter. So I turned to the General, beaming somewhat. "Dashed odd, sir," I said, "old Jeeves having been with you. One of those what-do-you-call-its. The long arm and all that sort of rot."

"Hold your tongue, sir!"

Well, I mean to say, what!

After which, there was silence till Jeeves returned.

Jeeves opened out at once. "I have just been on the telephone, sir, to Brookfield, who, as you are doubtless aware, is the butler at the Vicarage. My surmise, I am happy to say, has proved correct. A rapid examination of the contents of Mr Steggles's waste-paper basket has revealed a number of trial attempts at Mr Little's Christian name, and at other words figuring in the document under consideration. The contents of the waste-paper basket have been impounded by Brookfield, and await your detailed examination, sir."

"Thanks, Jeeves, thanks!" The General looked across at Bingo. Conflict of emotion and all that. "Forget anything I may have said," he growled, and stamped out of the room, followed by Jeeves.

Jeeves's voice came rippling back to us, blending with the crisp sound of crackling paper.

"Thank you, sir. I am very much obliged. One moment, sir, I think you will be requiring this."

"The club! I will, by Gad!"

"You hold a strong hand, sir, if I may be permitted the pleasantry."

"Poor old Steggles!" murmured Bingo.

Bingo always was so dashed weak, you know.

Bibliography

THE WILL TO LOVE (1919). Novel. Chapman & Hall. Written under the name of Hugh Lunn.

THE DAWN'S DELAY (1924). Short novels. Elkin Mathews. Contains: *The End of the World*; *Disintegration of a Politician* and *W.J.* New edn. Duckworth 1928. New edn. Eyre & Spottiswoode 1948.

BLONDEL (1927). Novel. Ernest Benn.

MATTHEW ARNOLD (1928). Biography and Literary Criticism. Duckworth.

THE RETURN OF WILLIAM SHAKESPEARE (1929). Fiction & Literary Criticism. Duckworth. Revised ed. published in 1948 with short novels under the general title of *The Dawn's Delay*. Eyre & Spottiswoode.

AFTER PURITANISM (1929). Biography and Literary Criticism. Duckworth. Contains studies of Dean Farrar, Samuel Butler, Frank Harris and W. T. Stead.

INVECTIVE AND ABUSE (1929). Anthology. Eyre & Spottiswoode. Cheap edn. 1933.

MORE INVECTIVE (1930). Anthology. Cheap edn. 1933. Eyre & Spottiswoode. Incorporated in a revised edition of "Invective and Abuse" in 1944. Eyre & Spottiswoode. New edn. 1949.

BEHIND BOTH LINES (1930). War Memoirs. Morley & Mitchell Kennerley Jr.

THE WORST OF LOVE (1931). Anthology. Eyre & Spottiswoode.

FRANK HARRIS (1932). Biography. Jonathan Cape. Revised edition printed in 1949 in the Holiday Library by John Lehmann.

THE TABLE OF TRUTH (1933). Parodies. Jarrolds.

SAMUEL JOHNSON (1933). Biography and Literary Criticism. Arthur Barker.

THE CASANOVA FABLE (1934). Biography in collaboration with William Gerhardie. Jarrolds. New edn. 1949. Jarrolds.

THE SENTIMENTAL JOURNEY (1934). Biography and Literary Criticism. Wishart. A Life of Charles Dickens.

WHAT THEY SAID AT THE TIME (1935). Anthology. Wishart.

PARENTS AND CHILDREN (1936). Anthology. Cresset Press.

BRAVE OLD WORLD (1936). Newspaper Parodies in collaboration with Malcolm Muggeridge. Eyre & Spottiswoode.

SKYE HIGH (1937). Talk and Travel in collaboration with Hesketh Pearson. Hamish Hamilton.

MADE ON EARTH (1937). Anthology. Hamish Hamilton.

D. H. LAWRENCE (1938). Biography and Literary Criticism. Methuen.

NEXT YEAR'S NEWS (1938). Newspaper Parodies in collaboration with Malcolm Muggeridge. Eyre & Spottiswoode.

THE ENGLISH GENIUS (1939). Anthology. The Right Book Club. Eyre & Spottiswoode.

COURAGE (1939). Anthology. Geoffrey Bles.

THE FALL (1940). Novel. Methuen.

JOHNSON WITHOUT BOSWELL (1940). Anthology. Methuen.

THIS BLESSED PLOT (1942). Talk and Travel in collaboration with Hesketh Pearson. Methuen.

THE POISONED CROWN (1944). Biography. Eyre & Spottiswoode. Contains studies of Elizabeth, Cromwell, Napoleon and Lincoln. Reprinted 1946 as Guild Book No. S196. Services edition.

TALKING OF DICK WHITTINGTON (1947). Talk and Travel in collaboration with Hesketh Pearson. Eyre & Spottiswoode.

THE PROGRESS OF A BIOGRAPHER (1949). Literary Criticism. Methuen.

THE HIGH HILL OF THE MUSES (1955). Anthology. Eyre & Spottiswoode. Published posthumously and containing a note on the Kingsmill anthologies by Hesketh Pearson.

Some Critical and Biographical Studies.

ABOUT KINGSMILL (1951). An exchange of letters by two of Kingsmill's friends, Hesketh Pearson and Malcolm Muggeridge. Methuen.

HUGH KINGSMILL. A CRITICAL BIOGRAPHY. (1964). By Michael Holroyd. John Baker. Rev. edn. 1967.

PENDING HEAVEN (1930). Novel by William Gerhardie written round the character of Kingsmill under the name of Max Fisher. Rev. edn. 1948. Macdonald.

MEMOIRS OF A POLYGLOT (1930). Autobiography of William Gerhardie. Duckworth.

THE EYE OF THE BEHOLDER (1956). Reminiscences of Lance Sieveking. Hulton Press.

COME WHAT MAY (1940).
MEMORY TO MEMORY (1956).
UNKILLED FOR SO LONG (1968).
} Autobiographical volumes by Sir Arnold Lunn.

SWITCHBACK (1948). Autobiography of Brian Lunn. Eyre & Spottiswoode.

AN AUTOBIOGRAPHY (1954). By Edwin Muir. The Hogarth Press.

MY BROTHER EVELYN AND OTHER PORTRAITS (1967). By Alec Waugh. Cassell.